Judged by Love

Judged By Love

A Biography of
William X. Kienzle

Javan Kienzle

**Andrews McMeel
Publishing**

Kansas City

04 05 06 07 08 FFG 10 9 8 7 6 5 4 3 2 1

Library of Congress Cataloging-in-Publication Data

Kienzle, Javan.
   Judged by Love : a biography of William X. Kienzle / Javan Kienzle.
       p.cm.
   ISBN 0-7407-4191-8
   1. Kienzle, William X. 2. Kienzle, William X.—Marriage. 3. Novelists, American—20th century—Biography. 4. Catholic priests—United States-Biography. 5. Catholics—United States—Biography. I. Title.

   PS3561.I35Z75 2004
   813'.54—dc22
   [B]

                                              2004044861

Book design by Pete Lippincott

For Bill

and for all those who have loved him

Who shall ascend into the hill of the Lord? Or who shall stand in his holy place?

He that hath clean hands and a pure heart, who hath not lifted up his soul unto vanity, nor sworn deceitfully.

He shall receive the blessing from the Lord, and righteousness from the God of his salvation.

—PSALM 24:3–5

Contents

Acknowledgments

ANNE MORROW LINDBERGH said that one can never pay in gratitude; one can only pay "in kind" somewhere else in life.

Had I all the riches in the world, there are so many people whom I could never fully repay. In addition to those mentioned in this book, to whom I owe so much, there are many others to whom I am grateful beyond words. I must mention a few.

Glen and Claudia Papke Estrin, whose contributions made this book possible.

Elena Fallon, former vice president of Andrews McMeel, whose timely no-nonsense support kept me upright when I might otherwise have fallen.

Sister Susanne Hofweber, OP; Sister Carolyn Nelson, OP; and the St. Owen kaffeeklatschers, who exemplify the words of the old hymn, "They will know we are Christians by our love."

Anthony Michaels, DO, who took care of "Bill's girl."

Catharine Rambeau, who was a bulwark of solace and sanity during a summer of sorrow.

Robert F. Ricci, CPA, who for a quarter of a century shepherded Bill and me through a financial maze that boggled our brains.

And first and last, John Keyes Byrne—who first suggested, then urged, and finally insisted: "Write that book!"

Introduction

I WAS PRIVILEGED TO KNOW FATHER KIENZLE for fifteen of his twenty years as a priest. After that, I was blessed to be Bill Kienzle's wife for twenty-seven years.

In the film version of the life of Robert Schumann and Clara Wieck Schumann, as a wedding gift Clara gave her new husband her diary. She thus made a present to him of the life she had lived before she met him.

Bill Kienzle liked stories. He liked to listen to them and to tell them. Over the years, he made a present to me of the life he had lived before he met me. He told me stories of his family, his childhood, and his seminary days. And from his accounts of his life as a priest, I grew to know his love for the priesthood and his fellow priests.

During the twelve years that Bill was editor of the *Michigan Catholic*, he wrote weekly editorials. In his two and a half years as editor of *Mpls.* magazine, he wrote a monthly column. For several years, he was a contributor to *Sound of a Sermon*, a monthly newsletter for clergymen. His writings expressed his view of life— what the Germans call *Weltanschauung*. In the twenty-five years that Bill was writing the Father Koesler mysteries, he spoke to countless individuals, as well as groups, both in person and on radio and television. Over these years, he also wrote many articles and was interviewed by many publications.

After having heard his stories for the umpteenth time, I did come to wonder whether some of them might be hyperbole. However, corroboration came when I met Bill's friends, including active and inactive priests, as well as former seminary schoolmates. I discovered that many told the same stories that Bill had told, often in exactly the same words and phrases.

One ex-priest compared Bill to Inspector Luger on the old *Barney Miller* TV sitcom; they both had a soft spot in their hearts for the Good Old Days—the days that no longer existed except in memory.

It is because of the gift that Bill gave me in telling me of his family, his childhood, his years in the seminary and the priesthood, as well as having been present during his speeches and interviews, and having read and edited his many writings over the years, that I am able to recount, in most cases in his own words, the story of his most unusual life.

—JAVAN KIENZLE
Detroit, Michigan

PART

1

In the beginning . . .

I DUCKED AS THE TOASTER FLEW across the kitchen. Our baby son
started to cry. Rick, scowling, stormed out of the room, slamming
the door behind him. I comforted Mike, telling him that everything would be all right. When he stopped crying, I picked up the
phone and dialed the parish rectory.

Rick's parents had lost everything in the depression when his
father injured his back and was unable to work. By the time he was
able to return to work, the family, which now included two young
boys, was on welfare. Memories of their former standard of living—a
beautiful home, a grand piano, an upscale neighborhood—mocked
their current misery. In addition, Rick's parents had not been able
to marry in the Church because his father was divorced. Although
Rick's mother went to daily Mass and remained a fervent Catholic,
she could not receive Communion. Nonetheless, both the boys
were baptized and raised Catholic.

It was all too much for Rick's dad, an Irish orphan who had
been adopted by a Scottish family. He began to drink. Each payday,
Rick's mother would phone the parish rectory, and the Italian pastor would head for the neighborhood bar, where he would collar
and shame the errant one and send him home while there was still

some money left in his pocket. Eventually, Rick's dad, worn down by his wife's prayers and the pastor's perseverance, said farewell to the demon of drink, making it possible for his sons to have an occasional pair of new shoes, and his wife to send a few saved coins to Maryknoll.

This was the Good Old Days when the parish priest had the ultimate answer to everything. Father had straightened out Rick's dad's drinking problems; now he could straighten out Rick's marital problems.

❧❀❧

A male voice answered. "Patronage of St. Joseph."

"Father Pomponi?"

"No. He's not in right now. May I help you?"

"Are you a priest?"

"Yes. Is someone dying?"

"No . . . not yet."

"What's the problem?"

"It's family troubles. We need help. Can you come?"

"Well, I have devotions in a few minutes. But I can come over after that."

❧❀❧

I was not happy. I had hoped for Father Pomponi's experienced hand. Instead, I was getting a young assistant. What could he know of such family problems?

At the appointed time, a knock came at the door. I opened it to find a tall, cassock-clad man filling the doorway. I invited him in.

Rick, having been informed that the priest was on his way, had calmed down. He gestured toward an armchair. The priest sat down, took out a pack of cigarettes, tapped one out, turned to Rick, and said, "Do you have an ashtray or have you smashed them all?"

Thus did Father Kienzle enter my life.

Be traditional without being dogmatic.

—Bryn Terfel

My family were atheists—secular humanists. Mother's people were Southern Protestants. Her father's ancestors were Prussian Junkers; her mother's family traced their ancestry back through British monarchs to William the Conqueror. Dad's parents were Orthodox Jews. His father's family had come from Lithuania, his mother came from Ukraine.

Rick and I met in an Army hospital in New Jersey. I was visiting a friend in the next bed. Rick's family was horrified at the thought of his marrying a non-Catholic; my family was horrified at the thought of my marrying a Catholic. We were under twenty-one. The chaplain refused to marry us without our parents' signed consent. We eloped, and were married by a justice of the peace.

Father Kienzle was a traditional priest. To him, it was quite obvious that the solution to our marital problems was for Rick and me to have our marriage "regularized," i.e., for us to be married in the Church.

Rick, like so many people who find an excuse to not do what they don't want to do, had refused to go to Mass since the chaplain had refused to witness our marriage. He was further alienated when the pastor of our parish church refused to baptize our son because we hadn't been married in the Church. Mike was finally baptized by an elderly Italian priest at a parish on the wrong side of the tracks. But Rick never forgave the Catholic Church.

The bottom line was that Rick wasn't having any of this Church stuff. So Father Kienzle—going by the book—did the next best thing: He suggested that I, who had been raised an unbaptized pagan, become a Catholic. I was amenable to anything that might keep this marriage together. So I began to take instructions in the Catholic faith.

One evening a week on the way home from work I would stop in at the rectory, where Father Kienzle would lead me along the path to Catholicism. This continued for some months. One night, as I was leaving the rectory, I realized that Father looked exhausted. I felt guilty. "You look so tired. I know you're busy. If it's a problem to meet after work, I can come on Saturdays—"

He smiled. "Gladly would I spend myself for thee." I thought that sounded very biblical.

Something seemed to be helping. Rick and I were getting along better. We went house hunting and bought a small home just down the block from a grade school. I could stand on the front porch and watch until Mike was safely inside the school yard.

We now lived outside Father Kienzle's parish. So his rule of never going to dinner at a parishioner's home no longer applied to us. He came to dinner. He and Rick and I went to the theater, to ball games, to movies. Rick was pleased; here he was a renegade Catholic and yet he could boast of having a priest as a friend.

Mike hero-worshiped Father Kienzle. Rick and I asked Father if he would accept the responsibility of being Mike's guardian should Mike be left parentless. He agreed and it was so entered in Rick's and my will.

❧

One night, after nine months, as our evening session came to a close, Father Kienzle leaned back in his chair behind his desk and said, "I think that's the end of our instructions. I've taught you everything you need." I was startled. I felt as if the ground were being pulled out from under my feet.

"Now, is there anything else you'd like to know? Any question you have?"

There *was* one thing that I was curious about. I knew how difficult it was for me to button up my blouses in the back; I frequently asked Rick to help me. "Well, yes, Father . . . uh, would you tell me: Who buttons up your shirt in the back?"

He looked bemused. Then, with a grin, he slipped the white plastic insert out of the collar of his clerical vest and waved it at me.

He shook his head. "Here I've just spent nine months teaching you everything I know . . . and the only question you have is, Who buttons my collar?"

There is in unhappy marriages a power of misery which surpasses all the other sorrows of the world.

—BENJAMIN DISRAELI

TIME MARCHED ON. Despite Father Kienzle's best efforts, my marriage went from bad to worse to impossible.

I pleaded with Rick to try professional marriage counseling. His response, which I later discovered is a typical male reaction, was, "I've got no complaint; if you have problems, *you* go to a marriage counselor."

Things went from impossible to incredible. Photos of me taken during this period show a young woman so gaunt she looks like she barely survived Auschwitz. I was barely surviving this marriage. I filed for divorce.

The Friend of the Court, whose job it was to care about what happens to the children when a marriage breaks up, did his best. Rick and I reconciled. I took Mike to Mass on Sundays. But it was just a question of time.

Now, with my health at risk, Rick and I semi-separated. I got my own apartment, and spent half the week there and half the week at the house. Eventually, I no longer came to the house. Exhausted, I slept for twelve hours straight after work during the week, even longer on weekends. Mike, now a teenager attending a Catholic prep school, stayed with his dad.

Father Kienzle remained friends with both Rick and me. There must have been many times when he wondered where he had gone wrong, what he had left undone, what he had overlooked. After all, those textbooks that he had studied in twelve years in the seminary held the Answer to Everything. Why hadn't he found the answer to this?

I have no clear memory of when they first took me to Mass. But I am aware that I never made them regret it. I took to church and Mass as a squirrel to a tree. Whenever I was in a church, it felt natural. I loved it, every minute of it.

—WILLIAM X. KIENZLE
Why I Am Still a Catholic

LITTLE BILLY KIENZLE was being taken for a walk by his sister. A priest stopped to say hello. "What a nice litle boy," he said. "What's he going to be when he grows up?" "He says he's going to be a priest," said his sister.

At that point, little Billy was barely even vocal. Certainly he had never expressed such a wish. That his sister would state this as an expressed desire shows how his future was taken for granted. If the family could have arranged to have the boy ordained at five, they undoubtedly would have done so.

Mary Louise Boyle was the baby of an Irish–French Canadian family. Legend had it that one of her maternal ancestors had accompanied Cadillac on his founding voyage to Detroit. Legend further said that one of the settlement strips along the Detroit River had been owned by the family. Louise was originally slated to enter religious life. One day she met a tall, attractive young man of German-American parentage. He fell like the proverbial ton of bricks. Louise took that as an omen. But he was Lutheran. Louise let him know that was a problem.

Without saying a word to Louise, Alphonse Kienzle went to visit the parish priest. He asked to be shown around the church and the rectory. Somewhat mystified, the priest complied. Alphonse was ushered all through the church, the nave, the apse, the sanctuary, the choir loft, the sacristy, the confessionals. Then to the rectory, where they went upstairs and downstairs, in and out of bedrooms, up to the attic and down to the basement, with

Alphonse opening doors and peering into closets. Finally, the priest asked, "What exactly are you looking for?" Alphonse replied, "The guns . . . you know, all the weapons you keep for when you Catholics take over the country."

Alphonse kept his secret well. One day at Mass, without a word of warning, Alphonse accompanied Mary Louise up to take Communion. And in time they walked up the aisle again.

First came a son—who died at age three of pneumonia. Then came Pauline. Then, some eight years later, along came Bill. His birth was not propitious. No sooner was he born than he was baptized. The priest told his mother, "This baby will be with the angels before morning."*

It wouldn't be the first time a priest had not been infallible. The baby did not die that night. He didn't even cry, merely lay in his crib, silently surveying his new world. He was, his mother was to say, saving it up: Once at home, he cried unceasingly. At that time, postpartum depression was not a familiar term; his mother later said that one day she almost threw him in the furnace.

What with the new baby taking up Louise's time, Pauline was left to her own devices. Her parents decided that she needed someone to keep her company. Enter Anne.

Anne's parents were dead. An aunt had taken her in and maltreated her to a Dickensian childhood. Someone took pity and little Anne was sent to a Catholic institution for girls. After spending time in a series of miserable foster homes, she was rescued by the Kienzles. Naturally, she came to be known as Little Orphan Annie.

Anne was two years older than Pauline. But the two did not become bosom pals. Instead, Anne took to little Billy like a mother

---

* The rush to baptism caused some confusion later in Bill's life. His baptismal record read William Xavier Kienzle. Years after, when he applied for a passport, he discovered that the hospital birth certificate read William Joseph Kienzle. So he was William Xavier in everything but his passport, which was issued under the name William Joseph.

cat to a stray kitten. Bill was never quite sure who had the larger hand in taking care of him as a young child, Anne or his mother.

Whichever, he grew up secure in the love of all around him, although Pauline, as is the wont of many older sisters, more often than not looked upon him as a pest. Once, when his mother went to meet his sister downtown, she took young Bill along. As they approached Pauline, Bill hid behind his mother and then peeked out at the last minute. "Did you have to bring *him*?" a miffed Pauline asked.

❧❀❧

It was an ideal childhood. His sisters helped his mother cook and clean and do the dishes. Bill played baseball or rode his bike with neighborhood pals till bedtime. He accompanied his family to church and took to it, as he said, like a squirrel to a tree. He sat quietly, looking around, enjoying the music, and drinking in the mystery of the Latin Mass. When he was old enough, he became an altar boy.

Annie had been prescient in stating, "He says he's going to be a priest."

Louise had a natural talent for art and music. At one time she had played the organ, accompanying the silent films at a downtown theater. When she met Alphonse, she was playing the piano at a store where customers came to hear new sheet music played. Louise could barely read notes; she played by ear. Thus, when someone handed her some new sheet music and asked, "What does this sound like?" Louise would play whatever fanciful tune came into her head. Later she would laboriously work out every-good-boy-does-fine on the score until she could play the actual melody.

Pauline took piano lessons, but it was Bill who sat and listened, then crept onto the piano bench and played. Later he also became proficient at the organ, and pretty good on the drums.

His mother's large extended family—aunts, uncles, and cousins— enjoyed getting together for music and talk—what the Irish call *craic*. Little Bill loved to sit in a corner and watch and listen to the goings-on. His mother, seated at the piano, was always the life of the party.

"Louise, play this; Louise, play that." Louise would play, and the others would join in the singing, everything from George M. Cohan to Gilbert and Sullivan operettas. And the boy would take it all in— the music, the singing, the stories, the jokes, the banter. He was quite content to be an onlooker. Nonetheless, at an early age—so early that he was as yet unable to correctly pronounce his last name—he proved that he had a very definite sense of himself as a person.

It was at a large family gathering. Several relatives had journeyed some distance to attend. Lacking identification tags, each of the far-flung relations stood and introduced himself or herself. However, no one took any particular notice of the wide-eyed lad on a stool in the corner. This oversight would be rectified. With the introductions seemingly concluded, little Billy stood up on the stool and announced in a firm voice, "And dis is me—Kuna."

Lovely Lady, dressed in blue/Teach me how to pray.
God was once your little boy/And you know the Way.

—CHILDHOOD PRAYER

IT'S NOT UNUSUAL for independent-minded children to run away from home. Few announce it in advance. After being punished for some childish infraction, little Billy made such an announcement.

His mother calmly packed a small suitcase and handed it to him, leaving him no alternative but to head out. He didn't realize that Annie had been deputized to follow him at a distance to assure that no harm came to him.

Soon tiring of trudging along with the suitcase banging against his legs, he plopped down on a curbstone to ponder his options. He didn't have to ponder long. His softhearted sister, who couldn't bear to see the little boy suffer, rescued him from his lonely perch and returned him to the bosom of the family.

He had learned his first major lesson: Life calls your bluff.

At the appropriate age, young Billy was sent to kindergarten. He spent less than one day there. After lunch, the children were supposed to stretch out and take a nap. Billy did not want to take a nap. He got up and went home. His mother did not send him back.

As a lad, he joined the Boy Scouts. At their first get-together, the group was told to line up and do what amounted to drill steps. Bill didn't like this regimentation. He never went back.

How would this nonconformist fit into the ultimate regimentation of the seminary? Could such independence be curbed or channeled? Not from without as much as from within.

He attended grade school at Holy Redeemer, where the boys and girls were separated. When Bill graduated from eighth grade, he knew exactly one Holy Redeemer girl—his cousin, Mary Anne.

The nuns teaching at Holy Redeemer ran a tight ship. Yet Bill must surely have tried their patience. Years later, he recalled a nun saying to him, "Mr. Kienzle, you would have Job chewing carpets!"

In September 1942, on the eve of his fourteenth birthday, Bill Kienzle put aside the things of a child, and entered ninth grade at Sacred Heart Seminary.

After only a few days, the boys, from different backgrounds, different sections of the city, different grade schools, melded. Whether they would eventually be ordained, or leave before—or after—ordination these young men would be friends for life. They lived, ate, slept, studied, prayed, played, and misbehaved together. During the rare times at home, they met at each other's houses, attended movies together, went to ball games together, hung around together. They were as close as or closer than brothers. As Bill Kienzle later wrote, it was as if, literally, they could not get enough of each other.

At the end of each school year, many of them worked as counselors at Catholic summer camps. But first they had to be certified as lifeguards. Before they could accept any job offer, it had to be cleared with their spiritual director. When teenage seminarian

Kienzle sought permission to be a lifeguard at a public beach he was informed that was not allowed. He could lifeguard at a boys' camp, but not at a public beach. What did one find at a public beach that one would not find at a boys' camp? The lesson was clear: One could save girls' souls, but not their bodies.

Bill Kienzle spent nine full summers as a counselor at Camp Ozanam, a camp for inner-city boys, on the shores of Lake Huron. He and eleven classmate-counselors were known as the Twelve Apostles. The events of his twelve years as a seminarian, including his nine summers as a counselor, later found their way into many of his books.

Tradition called for counselors who were soon to be ordained to be thrown into Lake Huron by the other counselors. The lower classmen had their hands full in Bill's last year. The Twelve Apostles were pretty formidable, and they did not look kindly on such immersion. It took some doing by combined forces, but finally, the foul deed was accomplished. Larry Conley, one of the lower classmen, recalls that on the day they "got" Bill, "I took a lot of elbows in the ribs."

Homesickness was endemic at Camp Ozanam. Children—many of them actually too young to be campers—spent two weeks in cabins whose mattresses reeked of years of enuresis, with counselors who treated them with roughly the same gentleness as a Marine drill instructor. They downed food that was less than tasty, suffered poison ivy, the frigid waters of Lake Huron, and the bullying of bigger bunk mates. No wonder they wanted to go home.

Occasionally, one would try. He would pack up his meager belongings and take off down the road. But in all those years, not one miscreant made it. Frequent buddy checks were held, and the minute a boy was missing, the camp car, Old Betsy, would be saddled up and would overtake the runaway, who was trying to thumb a ride home—or at least away from what he considered purgatory. He would be swooped up and carried back to finish out his two-week sentence.

One youngster, however, set a memorable record for creativity in trying to escape.

Camp Ozanam had a grotto. It was created out of the side of a small hill. Rocks were piled around it, and it boasted a statue of the

Blessed Mother. Of course, as years went on, she began to be missing parts—a finger here, a toe there; the tip of her nose. Still, it was the Blessed Mother, and the camp periodically gathered to pray at what was left of her feet.

One day, a serious-faced inmate came into Bosco Hall, where the counselors were gathered. He went up to his counselor, Dick Ward, and, with much gravity, tugged at his sleeve. Dick got up and went outside with the boy. "What's the problem?"

"Well," said the lad, "I went to see the Blessed Mother."

"Yes?" Dick prodded.

"She told me to go home," said the boy solemnly.

"Really?"

"Yes." He nodded firmly, almost triumphantly.

"Let's go see," said Dick. He took the lad's arm, and off they went to the grotto.

They stood there in silence for some time, the counselor looking at the Blessed Mother, and the boy looking at the counselor.

Finally, Dick spoke. "Yes. I see," he said.

"What? What?" asked the boy.

Dick turned to the boy. "The Blessed Mother . . . she says you've got to stay."

The counselors had little sympathy for the campers. The counselors felt that Ozanam would've been great if it weren't for all those rotten kids.

Learn from others what to pursue and what to avoid, and let your teachers be the lives of others.

—Dionysius Cato

ONCE, DRIVING PAST THE SEMINARY where his son was studying, Alphonse Kienzle was asked by his traveling companion what that huge building was. "It's a seminary . . . where they train guys to be priests. My son's there," he added.

"Well, I guess that's as good a racket as any," his passenger commented.

The seminary of that era comprised twelve years of study, or, some might say, indoctrination. Four years of high school, four of college, and four of theology. The first eight years constituted minor seminary, the last four major seminary.

In time-tested fashion, the Church knew what it was doing—and what it wanted to turn out. Mostly, it wanted—not unlike the military—strong, disciplined men, aware of rank, able and ready to take orders and carry them out. Unlike the military, however, these men were to be men of prayer, and asexual. Masculinity without sexuality was the byword. No easy task, but one that, at least in the first half of the twentieth century, not only succeeded but overachieved.

Early in the seminarians' first year, they were assembled in the somber presence of the seminary's spiritual director and given a one-class indoctrination on S-E-X. It would set the tone for all future approaches toward sexuality—one of ignorant embarrassment.

The essence of that lecture was that somebody—it either had to be a man or a woman—had a penis, and that whoever had it should keep it clean at all times.

The rector—who would later become a bishop—before turning the young seminarians loose on vacation, did give them some added advice.

"Boys, don't think that you have to 'try' girls to know that you like them. Just presume that you'd like them. It's not for you, boys. It's one of the things—family, hearth, home, children—that you'll be giving up for the glory of the priesthood. Time to start now, boys. If you can give it up now, boys, you can give it up then."

For some strange reason, it seemed to make sense at the time.

In later seminary days, the students learned another rule of thumb: Between every "good" boy and every "good" girl there should be a six-foot-thick brick wall.

On the other hand, one of the seminary profs, in an attempt to keep things in perspective, cautioned his earnest charges to beware of excessive scrupulosity. Take St. Alphonsus Liguori, for instance: "Listen to him long enough, boys, and you'll be putting on your pants with a shoehorn."

Then there was the matter of "particular friendship," a euphemism for homosexuality—which was one of those words not heard among the saints, covered by the umbrella of embarrassment.

Particular friendships were so far out they were punishable by dismissal. Thus, visiting another student in his room, *solus cum solo*, was grounds for dismissal. Masturbation of course was one of those sins that had "no parvity of matter," i.e., was no small thing; it was always mortal, and always meant hellfire.

In textbooks on the Commandments translated into English, two chapters—on the Sixth and Ninth Commandments—were *not* translated, but remained in Latin. The seminarians concluded that sex was dull in Latin—especially in Moral Theology textbooks.

The total lack of social intercourse with anything remotely resembling a female led to an intensification of the "boys will be boys" syndrome. This was before the time when odor became a major marketing factor on the American scene. That, added to the absence of an opposite gender who would be offended by unpleasant odor, led to a distinctly gamy smell throughout the seminary. Especially in the locker room.

If odor was relatively unimportant in the arenas of study, prayer, and social lives, it lost all relevance on the field of combat. Each seminarian had, for instance, one basketball "uniform," consisting of a pair of sweat socks, tennis shoes, athletic supporter, one pair of old trousers, and a T-shirt. One wore this very same uniform, without benefit of wash, throughout the season. By April, one's socks had a tendency to walk out by themselves whenever the locker door was opened.

The sisters who staffed the minor seminary were Sisters of St. Joseph, of Nazareth, Michigan, a far more humble and serving group than their Dominican sisters in the major seminary. Hardly a student of those days could in later years look back at the vague presence of the St. Joseph nuns without gratitude.

The students were supposed to send their clothing down the chute for laundering by a bevy of elderly nuns, whose recreation consisted of washing, ironing, and mending the seminarians' clothes—repairing rips and replacing buttons as needed. The good sisters would sew patches on patches, thus prolonging the life of the clothing. This was a genuine boon, as many of the students came from families that could ill afford an abundance of replacement clothing.

But there was a sense of thoroughness to the sisters' work: no loose ends allowed. Thus, if a button was missing and no similar button was available, the mending sister would sew shut the buttonhole. At one point, one of seminarian Kienzle's more venerable shirts eventually lost not only all its buttons, but all its buttonholes.

The one item that was not to be included in the laundry was the athletic supporter. This was to be washed by its wearer. Such an expectation on the part of the seminary administration was totally unrealistic. Jock itch ran rampant.

On one occasion, a student, either thinking to test the waters, or having forgotten the order, put his athletic supporter down the chute with the other soiled clothes. Eventually, it was returned to its owner. It had been washed, starched, and ironed. A note was pinned to the supporter. Written in the nun's neat, spidery hand was the following: "These undershorts are beyond repair."

Only then did the students begin to suspect why it was they were not to consign athletic supporters to the laundry. Not only did the nuns not know what they were, nobody wanted them to find out what they were.

Thus, in sacred ignorance, did the seminarians and the nuns cohabitate.

As far as the students were concerned, there seemed no particular reason to subject a washcloth or towel to the laundry. After all, the washcloth experienced soap at each shower, and the towel was used only to dry a freshly washed body. However, after months of use and being stored in its fetid locker, each towel took on a marked rigidity, leading to the probability that an army of towels could have stood upright without support.

Man doth not live by bread only.

—DEUTERONOMY 8:3

DINING, ESPECIALLY AT THE MINOR SEMINARY LEVEL, was definitely a matter of survival. There simply was not enough food provided for active growing boys. Caesar would have been concerned: Nearly all the boys had a lean and hungry look.

Each dining table seated six young men, who would be served no more than six thin slices of near-to-burned beef, or six small portions of greasy fish—or whatever the pièce de résistance of the day happened to be. If there were, say, cherries for dessert, they were meticulously counted so that each diner received an equal share. Should there be an extra cherry, it was subjected to a lottery.

One commodity—bread—was in ample supply. And the students were allowed to bring peanut butter from home. If not for bread and peanut butter, many felt, they would have perished.

In photos of the young Bill Kienzle and most of his fellow students of that era, the boys are almost literally indistinguishable from scarecrows as far as comparative gauntness is concerned.

Each table was supervised by an appointed "table captain," whose position was roughly comparable to that of a prison warden. The troops were frequently fractious. Once, as table captain, Bill Kienzle looked on in astonishment as one of "his" boys, dissatisfied with the breakfast cereal, dumped it on the tablecloth, another poured milk over it, and a third sprinkled sugar on the mess.

On another occasion, one lad asked for milk. His table companion, who had prepared for the request by filling a water pistol, gave him three shots of milk in the face.

In the midst of this chaos, carts filled with "real" food—steaks, chops, succulent goodies—were wheeled past hungry eyes, destined for the "Priests' Table," where the faculty ate. This experience taught valuable lessons: Rank hath its privileges, separate seldom is equal, and—a maxim that would recur frequently in the priesthood—Nothing is too good for Father.

What all minor seminarians yearned for and few achieved was to become a "Priest Waiter." These lucky students handled the carts filled with excellent priest food, served the priests, and—the point of it all—ate the leftovers. And to hell with bread and peanut butter.

To add insult to indigestion and insufficiency, seminary dinners were topped off by a reading of *The Roman Martyrology*, a listing of each of the martyrs who had been done in on that particular date in history. As St. Whoever's final agonies were described in nauseatingly juicy detail, one could relate her amputated breasts to the fatty lumps of pork one had just barely ingested.

Matters improved somewhat in the major seminary, where the *Martyrology* was read in Latin. Members of the captive crew could distract themselves by refusing to translate, pleading ignorance, or critiquing the reader's pronunciation.

If a student fell ill enough to require relief beyond a burp or a belch, there was always the infirmary. It was difficult to get in, but once in, even more difficult to get out.

The infirmarian was Sister Sabina, known irreverently as "The Sabine Woman." Sister Sabina was probably the oldest nun of all, judging from the generous spread of wrinkles on her face and hands, which was all the skin anyone could see on nuns of those days. Sister Sabina had a practiced eye for the malingering seminarian. Students who merely wished a modicum of rest and relaxation from the seminary's tedium never got past the infirmary's portals. But if one was genuinely ill, he damn well stayed in till he was more than well.

Sister Sabina was direct. A future priest once suffered from major constipation. As the days of nonmovement multiplied, The Sabine Woman tried one laxative after another. Finally, administering what she obviously considered the *ne plus ultra*, she commented, "Mr. Murphy, if this doesn't work, we'll try a stick of dynamite." She probably would've too.

The nuns who staffed the major seminary belonged to the Order of St. Dominic—Dominicans. Definitely high class, principally educators, and as unlikely to be found performing menial tasks in a seminary as Ian Paisley cleaning toilets at a Papist convention.

But there they were, bound by their vow of obedience, preparing food, dusting, and cleaning. Clothed from head to toe in Dominican white, with black veils, these women did not get too close to real dirt, i.e., they did not clean the students' rooms. As a result, those rooms—each of which was supposed to be cleaned by its occupant—were not, generally, notably clean.

Actually, the cleanliness of the students' rooms in the major seminary depended on which faculty member lived on which floor. Each floor in the residence halls was blessed with the presence of one faculty member, whose responsibility it was to check the rooms once each week. Some did and some didn't.

The faculty member on one fairly immaculate floor was a former Navy chaplain. He gave each room the white glove treatment. One student on his floor, after a cleaning day, found an admonitory note that read: "Toilet, bed, floor, ETC." It was the "ETC" that threw the student. Not only did he redo the toilet, bed, and floor, but everything else in his room. Only later did it dawn on him that the name of his faculty rep was Edward T. Cope, and the "ETC" was his initials, not a directive to reclean everything.

Meanwhile, back in the kitchen was Sister Kevin, the prototype of many nuns of the Good Old Days. She would have made a worthy consort for General Patton.

Sister Kevin administered the toast. Not a high-level job, but she made the most of it. Though there were six students per table, each meal began with four pieces of toast. Obviously two more pieces of toast were needed per table—at least for starters.

However, the mystery intensified: Two additional slices were all each table was ever given. A diner could return as often as he liked, but each time one approached Sister Kevin with a suppliant plate, he was given only two pieces of toast.

If anyone dared to ask for an additional slice for that trip, his effrontery would be met by a wordless, frigid glance from Sister Kevin. Meekly, our Oliver Twist would accept his two slices of toast, deliver them to the table, and return repeatedly for more.

The bread was toasted on a rotisserie-like machine. Once around and it was done, after which Sister Kevin would slap on some melted butter. Anyone who didn't want butter was out of luck. Unbuttered toast, like more than two slices of toast per plate, was verboten.

It was a small fiefdom that Sister Kevin had, but she ruled it with absolute authority.

The bells which call you to an exercise should always be obeyed exactly and immediately, as you would obey the voice of God.

—COMMON RULE
Manual of Piety for Seminarians

THE SEMINARY WAS CONFRONTED EACH YEAR with an onslaught of over a hundred (remember, this was the Good Old Days) fourteen-year-old boys, only a quarter of whom would make it to ordination. The seminary survived the presence of all these boisterous adolescent males by means of The Rule, sometimes referred to as The Holy Rule.

The Rule grew up, much as did Canon Law, as a deterrent to offenses against bureaucracy's survival. The Rule was described to the young seminarians as "God's Will," and as such not to be questioned, much less disobeyed.

The instrumentality of The Rule was The Bell. It leaned on the students throughout the day, telling them what it was The Rule wanted them to do at any given hour. The Bell was stationed all through the seminary, in every hall and corridor. It had the subtle nuance of a Klaxon. It could be heard at the farthest reaches of a considerable recreation ground. Whatever other excuse a student might claim, he could not say, "I didn't hear the bell."

The Bell: Woke one in the morning at an ungodly hour to praise God. It was time to wash, dress—later in one's seminary career, shave—and be ready for the next sound of

The Bell: Time now for meditation, time for silent prayer—which, since it was so early, usually was spent extending the sleep period, which was ended by

The Bell: Mass now, but still too early to pray. But one could always depend on

The Bell: Which would summon one successively to breakfast, classes, examination of conscience, lunch, classes, study, recreation, study, prayer, dinner, short recreation, study, prayer, bed, then Grand Silence—which could be broken only at the risk of finding one's neck in a sling.

Unquestionably, it was good discipline. And in the teen years especially, it was probably needed. But in the end, at age twenty-five when other people were married and had responsibility for a family, the seminarian was still responding to bells and asking permission to make a phone call.

As such, The Bell did not encourage maturity. The Rule produced, by and large, disciplined human beings with an extraordinarily extended period of adolescence.

In the minor seminary if The Bell's summons was not obeyed, demerits followed. There were no such things as merits, only demerits. In the major seminary, lack of prompt obedience to The Bell was followed by a confrontation with The Rector—a fearsome prospect.

Demerits were dispensed according to the egregiousness of the crime. Two for being late for something, four for missing the event entirely. Ten demerits in any given quarter sent the offender to the work crew—slave labor that maintained the seminary grounds and buildings. An exceptional number of demerits (the exact amount was never revealed, leaving the ace of spades in the rector's hand), meant a one-way ticket out.

To get demerits, one had to be caught *in flagrante delicto*. Bill Kienzle was frequently guilty of *delicto* and it was regularly *flagrante*. As a result, he worked his way through the seminary. He cleaned handball courts, mowed the lawn, weeded, washed windows, waxed floors, and carried out whatever onerous tasks the ever-nimble mind of the rector could think up. Bill and his fellow criminals spent one whole winter trying to remove a tree stump. Since they were able to work on it only about an hour each day, the stump took on the aspect of the legendary mountain that was brushed once every thousand years by a bird's wing. ". . . and when that mountain has been worn down to nothing, boys, eternity will only have begun."

Armed with shovels and axes, the cohort would daily attack the stump by first breaking the ice that had formed around the base, and shoveling out the water, then taking the ax to the wood. As the winter wore on, they sort of beat the stump to death.

Nonetheless, boys being boys, the temptation to run the gauntlet of The Rule was ever present. Are you brave enough? And if so, are you clever enough not to get caught? Usually, yes to the former; no to the latter. Seminarian Kienzle exemplified both the former and the latter, with an occasional exception. Like the night he and a bunch of brave hearts picked up a bed and, with its sleeping occupant, relocated it to the middle of a corridor.

Shortly thereafter, another lad, oblivious of the relocation, made his way toward the toilet and stumbled over the bed, waking everyone, including the prefect who was the custodian of Order. That worthy's bestowal of demerits on the bed's perplexed occupant evoked loudly expressed oaths from the exasperated victim along the general lines of where the hell did he get off thinking a guy would push his own bed out into the middle of the corridor.

The perfect caper: not one of the perpetrators caught. What bliss!

Bill Kienzle survived the minor seminary's demerit system and the demands of academe to find himself in the heady atmosphere of the major seminary, where never was heard a word about demerits.

The Rule, however, was there, stronger than ever. Since St. John's was a "provincial" seminary, it was governed not merely by one bishop, but by all five bishops of the province. Thus, The Rule became God's Will raised to the fifth power.

The Rule again was enforced by The Bell. Punishment for not obeying The Bell was being hauled before The Rector.

Although this system would later become ineffective as a result of Vatican II, the Church of that day was ranked second only to General Motors as an efficient organization. The efficiency sprang from the virtually unquestioning obedience the laity gave to priests, priests gave to bishops, and bishops gave to the Pope.

The rector well understood how crucial was his role in this chain of operation. He had to mold each seminarian into a priest whose obvious first duty was a multileveled obedience to older clergymen, pastors, clerical bureaucrats, bishops, and the Pope. Finishing far behind, in unhonored, unsung second place, was a priest's obligation to the laity.

That's the kind of priest the rector was to produce, and by God, he was going to do it. Stripped of such weapons as demerits and corporal punishment, the rector had to rely on the whip of his own personality. But there was plenty of that to go around.

The embodiment of the fabled man's man, the rector was the silent guest at all the students' more violent games. The rougher they were, the better he liked them. There was no place for sentimentality in either the rector or his students. He would turn out priests who were not only unafraid to be alone but were at home with loneliness.

Further, contrary to the suspicion of many insecure diocesan pastors, the rector carefully groomed his charges to be as subservient and obedient to their future pastors as bird dogs. There was a simple rule of Canon Law that adequately described the relationship of assistant to pastor. The assistant was "beneath"—"subject to"—the pastor. And the rector's relationship with his students readied them for the worst any neo-Nazi pastor could throw at them.

At the close of each day, after night prayers, and as Grand Silence—again—began, the day's malefactors would single-file it in a line stretching out before the rector to approach him one by one and confess the evil they had perpetrated that day. Confession was based on the honor system and was surprisingly honorably fulfilled. Rarely did the rector look up. His head would be bowed as if he were hearing the sins of all, as one seminarian after another would whisper, "I was late for meditation," or "I was late for lunch," or "I talked during Grand Silence." The rector would not look up. He would merely nod.

Bill Kienzle's presence in that line of sinners was fairly regular. During one particularly bad week, he appeared before the rector six consecutive evenings. At the sixth appearance, the rector looked up at the black sheep—which was an exercise in itself, as the young miscreant was considerably taller than his judge. The rector fixed his victim with a gaze that bespoke agony as if a dagger were being twisted in his heart of hearts. He spoke but one word. *"Again?"*

Appealing to the students' repugnance for sadism was only one weapon in the rector's considerable arsenal. His indignation was terrible to behold. Once, he publicly and erroneously accused a student of cheating. Summoning all his courage, the aggrieved student presented himself at the rector's office that evening to announce, "Father, I demand my rights!"

"You have no rights!" thundered the redoubtable rector.

Actually, for one of the few times in his life, the rector was technically wrong. As graven in Canon Law, and as the students were frequently reminded, if they kept their noses fairly clean, they would be entitled to a Christian burial. But short of that, the rector was correct: The students had no rights. Or so his wondrous, terrible and unpredictable temper was able to cow them into believing.

The seminary by no means churned out clones. Especially in the case of diocesan priests—as opposed to those in religious orders—ordination and afterward found Father Kienzle and his classmates quite different one from another. Still, they were fairly faithful products of what the seminary system intended them to be: latent heterosexuals, denying themselves not only wives and family life, but all conscious expression of sexual activity—creating the impression, if not the reality, of super-hemanship.

Behold the product: the asexual man. Able to go through life with no expressed sexuality, not even any close personal friends. "A part of all families, yet member of none." Just about the only one who drifted easily through life without a spouse. Others might be unmarried, but they were considered odd. For the priest alone, "odd" was natural.

The newly ordained priests were, by and large, men of prayer. And, in fact, that's what the laity expected of them most of the time.

Prayer was a large part of seminary life. Much of it was formal, precomposed prayer. None of the born-again, ecstatic, charismatic type of prayer that is so common today. There was a healthy attempt at instilling rather good forms of meditation—but at hours so early they became more an extension of sleep.

Probably because Mass in the parish could be at a pretty ungodly hour—to mix a metaphor—the morning's first prayer in the seminary was held at something like 6 A.M. It began with a few moments of formal read prayer, followed by what was supposed to be quiet, seated meditation.

One of Bill Kienzle's groggy classmates once broke everybody up when he mistakenly turned too many pages at the conclusion of formal morning prayer. He thus read not the ending of morning but evening prayer: "Let us offer up," he intoned, "the sleep we are about to take in union with that Christ himself took while upon earth."

Nor did seminarian Kienzle get off scot-free. Upon his graduation from the minor seminary, his spiritual director pulled out a file card on which he had cataloged his subject's spiritual life. For the remainder of his days, his subject never quite recovered from the shock of having his spiritual life recorded on a file card.

In any case, the director accused Kienzle of sleeping during prayer. There was no defense: Once, while leading the Rosary, seminarian Kienzle fell asleep. It is one thing to slumber with other scattered members of the crowd during the Hail Marys, quite another to be asleep when responsible for producing the Hail Marys.

Prayer in the seminary might not have been charismatic, but there was a lot of it. The students prayed the Rosary once each day. That is, until the arrival of a new spiritual director. During the month of May the students had traditionally substituted a procession out to Mary's Grotto instead of the chapel-recited predinner Rosary.

The new man suggested, forcefully, that during the month dedicated to the Rosary, his charges might pray the Rosary both before and after dinner. "Any student who doesn't love the Blessed Mother enough to recite her Rosary twice a day during her month may come to me and I will personally excuse him."

It never happened. No one had the guts to 'fess up that he was slob enough not to love the Blessed Mother.

The glue that held it all together was an ingrained sense of discipline and obedience.

The media, especially the movies, caught this image and reflected it over and over. In *The Keys of the Kingdom*, Gregory Peck's priest, in some godforsaken hinterland of China, must first build his church. When his mission is destroyed, rebuilding the church is top priority. He is a man of prayer.

In *Going My Way*, Barry Fitzgerald's priest quietly steps down from his pastorship without a whimper as soon as he discovers this is his bishop's wish. He is a man of discipline. In *The Left Hand of God*, Humphrey Bogart's priest will not touch a willing Gene Tierney even though he is a bogus priest. That's real asexuality.

All in all, the system was effective. Those who survived it, endured it, or remained unenlightened by it, faced ordination convinced that even greater than faith, hope, and charity was obedience. The rules produced, by and large, disciplined humans with an extraordinarily extended period of adolescence. They became priests vainly waiting for that next bell to ring.

Those of us who are priests can appreciate those last few months of preparation. They are the peak of a seminarian's life, the summit of God's holy mountain, the realization of every dream and every hope. The words of ordination are spoken, and a man stands forth a priest forever.

—Father Martin Dempsey
St. Peter Julian Eymard: Champion of the Blessed Sacrament

Despite The Rule, and The Rector, the years at St. John's Seminary were the most fulfilling of Bill Kienzle's youth. For the first time, he said, he became a student. Part of this he ascribed to growing up, part of it to the fact that St. John's was staffed by the Sulpicians, an order that had been founded to teach seminarians.

Granted, he still participated in boyish highjinks—and atoned for them. But he studied and learned to enjoy studying. He walked countless thousands of steps through the gallery halls reading his breviary. And he learned to truly pray. He desired the priesthood with all his heart and soul.

He achieved the subdiaconate, then the diaconate.

On June 5, 1954, William Xavier Kienzle was ordained "a priest forever." He was now "one of those who wield the power not given to angels—to offer God to God."

"I was ecstatic. My feet didn't touch the ground. I went around blessing people, and then I went around looking for more people to bless."

It was, he always said, the happiest day of his life.

So many of its members went on to distinguished military careers that West Point's Class of 1915 was known as "The Class the Stars Fell On." Out of 164, more than a third became generals. Included in this category were Dwight D. Eisenhower, Omar Bradley, James Van Fleet (whom President Truman called "the greatest combat general"), and Joe McNarney, the developer of U.S. antisubmarine warfare.

A large percentage of William Kienzle's St. John's Seminary Class of 1954 likewise went on to distinguish themselves in the priesthood and otherwise. In this category were Edmund Cardinal Szoka, who became archbishop of Detroit and went on to one of the highest positions in the Vatican; and stormy petrel James Kavanaugh, who authored *A Modern Priest Looks at His Outdated Church, A Coward for Them All,* and a number of popular volumes of poetry. Several other classmates became chancellors and chancery personnel. F. Gerald Martin followed in William Kienzle's footsteps in becoming an editor of the *Michigan Catholic.* Martin went Kienzle one better in becoming a monsignor.

It was the pre-Vatican II Church and seminaries that turned out these men, who were refined by the post-Vatican II Church. They straddled two different worlds, but their light still illumines.

It is an interesting question how far men would retain their relative rank if they were divested of their clothes.

—HENRY DAVID THOREAU

IT WAS THE DAY THE CATHOLIC CHURCH ABOLISHED its law obliging Catholics to eschew meat on Fridays. A confident worker in New York's famed Fulton Fish Market was interviewed on the network news. What, he was asked, would this new dispensation do to the fish industry?

"Fish are good," he said. "Fish don't need no help from no law. Fish can stand on their own two feet."

Maybe so, but the absence of that law made it that much harder to identify Catholics without a scorecard. It used to be lots easier to tell who was a Catholic. Little things—like eating fish on Friday— not a guaranteed sign, but a significant indication. Or families with lots and lots of children: either CCs (conscientious Catholics)—or PPs (passionate Protestants).

Catholics, from force of habit, sometimes genuflected in the aisle of a theater before entering their row . . . or inadvertently made the sign of the cross at the end of a movie.

In the Good Old Days, it was easy to recognize a priest. In the church or the rectory, the priest wore a ground-length cassock, occasionally well stained with food particles, and frequently ample enough to provide for a protruding clerical front. On the street, priests were always conspicuous, a study in black—black suits, black shoes, a black chestpiece known as a rabbi, and a roman collar that was always uncomfortable.

The priest was supposed to wear his "clericals" just about everywhere but in the shower. Most of them did. Although one bishop, while admitting that it was ridiculous to expect priests to wear clericals on the golf course, did advise them to wear at least the black jacket and roman collar over their golf togs while they were driving to the course.* Thus they would look like priests, at least insofar as anyone could see. "After all," the bishop asked rhetorically, "what are you trying to hide?"

Today, it's next to impossible, usually, to tell a priest from a businessman or any other man—depending on the priest's taste or lack thereof. And, sadly, they know very well what they're trying to hide.

A succession of small duties always faithfully done demands no less than do heroic actions.

—JEAN JACQUES ROUSSEAU

FATHER KIENZLE'S FIRST ASSIGNMENT WAS AT ST. DAVID'S, a large east-side Detroit parish with its own school. It was the era of full

---

* Priests tended to take their golf fairly seriously. Whenever a member of the fraternity died on the golf course, inevitably the first question from the brethren was, "Which hole?"

churches, full schools, and usually, full rectories. As low man on the totem pole, Father Kienzle had to answer the door and the telephone. Those were the days before the answering machine took over. No matter whether the priests were at table or at rest, when the phone or the doorbell rang, it was answered. After all, someone might need the Last Rites.

When Alexander Graham Bell first said over his new invention, "Mr. Watson, come here. I need you," it was both good and bad news. In the rectory, the telephone was usually bad news.

In Father Kienzle's first parochial assignment, the one capital sin that cried to heaven for vengeance was not having a priest to answer the doorbell or the telephone. How things have changed.

There was no secretary, and the housekeeper—the pastor's sister—was exempted from these chores. Each assistant was assigned to be "on the phone and door," three days a week. For whichever assistant was on duty a simple bowel movement was a luxury before 11 P.M. The phone and the door at that parish were active instruments.

The living room phone had a cord that stretched to the dining room table. Thus the telephone was brought to the table by whoever was on duty. It sat ominously by his plate through the meal. All through dinner, it was "Please pass the phone."

If there was a silver lining to this cloud of communication it was the opportunity to observe others' telephone techniques. That of Father Mullins was fascinating. No matter what problem the caller seemed to have—it was difficult to diagnose difficulties hearing only one side of the conversation—Mullins would invariably sign off with, "Well, do the best you can."

Young Father Kienzle would visualize the caller reflecting on this entirely neutral advice and saying to himself, "The best I can . . . Damn, that's it: I'll do the best I can!"

It was at that table that Father Kienzle developed his own peculiar telephone technique. Partly because he found it embarrassing to share what was essentially a private conversation with bystanders, and partly because he was leaning in that direction anyway, his MO consisted of a series of sounds, which some might term grunts. It was surprising how much could be conveyed by "uh-huh" and "uh-uh." Especially when the conversation was predictable, repetitive, or dull, such sounds—as well as newspapers and even books—got Father Kienzle through meals.

Meals were lively at St. David's. If the phone wasn't ringing, there was table talk, a disc jockey blasting away from the kitchen radio, and the television blaring in the living room. The TV was for the benefit of everyone but Father Kienzle; he sat with his back to the set. So when Matt Dillon was engaged in a shootout or Eliot Ness was closing in on Frank Nitti, the young priest was always startled by the sounds of gunfire.

Since there could never be a moment when some priest was not waiting for the phone to ring, all took turns attending the instrument during the night. The turnover for night duty was monthly, rather than daily. A night call usually was serious business. No one called late at night or in the early morning hours for light chitchat. If it wasn't a wrong number, someone was dead. No one called at night if someone was merely dying.

Those were traumatic times for all involved. Once, near midnight, Father Kienzle was called to the warehouse of a trucking firm and, sure enough, one of the employees was dead. He was, in fact, blue. After a conditional anointing (conditional based on the possibility of there being some life present even though the man was apparently dead), Father Kienzle wandered back into a large waiting room, where some twenty management and labor personnel were pondering the brevity of life. The question arose as to who was going to tell the widow. As one, they all turned to the priest.

She knew as soon as she opened the front door. Why else would a priest come calling at 1 A.M.?

A summons to attend a dead person was not restricted to nighttime. On one occasion, the pastor got such a call just before lunch. He sent his young assistant.

The glass in the front door had been shattered, the work of the police and a concerned son who was worried when he couldn't reach his father, who lived alone.

A crowd had gathered outside. Father Kienzle peered through the still-locked door to see drapery spread on the floor—apparently to cover the broken glass. He stepped gingerly through the opening, and quickly drew back. Some urchin on the sidewalk began chanting, "He stepped on the dead guy's face. He stepped on the dead guy's face."

And so he had.

After that conditional anointing, Father lost his appetite for lunch.

In the name of the Father and the Son, and the—*oh, my God!*

THE SEMINARY PROFESSORS HAD DONE THEIR BEST to prepare each of their charges for life as a priest. Still, there were any number of bizarreries that could not realistically have been anticipated.

In the seminary, the soon-to-be priests had practiced coping with a variety of baptismal possibilities. But few, if any, could have predicted what faced Father Kienzle's debut at the baptismal font.

Those were the days of multiple baptisms. Father himself performed flawlessly. He was just about to breathe a sigh of relief when one of the fathers returned to the baptistry. "Father, there's a lady in church with her dress off."

Oops! Aquinas never said anything about *that!*

Father peered out into the church. Draped over the back of one pew was a blue object of apparel.

Panic reared its ugly head. Punt! Stall for time!

"Why don't you," Father said, with a calm beyond his years and experience, "go place the dress over the lady, and then I'll come and see what the problem is."

He locked the baptistry and warily entered the church.

God! The blue dress was still—or again—back over the pew.

There was no textbook to consult.

Well . . . full speed ahead.

As he neared the area, he could see there was indeed a woman lying in the pew. Fortunately, she was wearing a slip.

So far, so good. After all, he *did* have sisters.

He approached. "Is there something wrong?" he asked. The woman shook her head. He looked in her purse, which sat open. It was filled with prayer books and rosaries.

Father returned to the rectory. The pastor, Father Welsh, was slipping into siesta. Father Kienzle explained what was up—or down. "Call the police," Father Welsh said calmly.

Two police cars arrived with sirens sounding. A crowd gathered.

Father Kienzle returned to the church to find four economy-sized cops standing the woman up while a fifth yanked her dress down over her head. A sixth cop jotted down "just the facts."

Later Father Kienzle learned that the lady was a familiar figure—literally—to the police. She had a couple of hang-ups—religion and sex. And she certainly gave Father Kienzle a memorable first baptism.

❧

Those were the days when it was common to have twenty baby baptisms of a Sunday. After the ceremony the godfathers would approach the priest with either an envelope or a naked fiver in their hands. To their startlement and dismay, Father Kienzle always refused it. He continued this practice until one day, months after he had begun a career of baptizing, the pastor somewhat hesitatingly asked what he was doing with all the stole fees for baptisms.

"I'm refusing them."

The young priest might as well have told his pastor the Pope was a Protestant.

"But . . . but, Father," the pastor sputtered, "that's . . . that's how we eat!"

Oh, that's how.

Either no one in the seminary had mentioned stole fees or seminarian Kienzle had been asleep during that class.

Hear dem bells, can't you hear dem bells . . .

—SPIRITUAL

THOSE WHO KNEW BILL KIENZLE, whether as childhood chum, seminarian, priest-assistant, or pastor, quickly came to know that he had an extremely quirky sense of humor. It evidenced itself at odd times in equally odd ways.

It was midnight of Easter. Over in the church the Easter Vigil liturgy was in full sway. The ceremony began at 11 P.M., and worked its way into the Easter Mass about midnight. The ushers had been instructed to ring the church bells whenever Mass started. Which was fine on Sunday mornings. They had not been told *not* to ring the bells if Mass began in the dead of night.

Mass began, and with that the bells began to ring. And with that the phone rang. "Why are the bells ringing?" the caller wanted to know—not without good reason.

"Because," Father Kienzle—drawing on his Camp Ozanam minstrel experience—explained, "someone am pullin' on de rope."

Those who phoned the rectory, like penitents at confession, generally were on the defensive. Particularly if they were calling to ascertain the time of Mass or services. Most of them, clearly, had had bad experiences. It was not unusual, when calling for such information, to be greeted by a harsh clerical voice raised in righteous rage. "Why do you think we publish a parish bulletin? If you people would pay attention, take home the bulletin and read it, you wouldn't have to waste my valuable time with nonsense calls like this. Or can't you read?"

And all the poor soul wanted to know was when he should come to church.

After having been burned by such an experience, the inquirer generally came up with some cockamamie excuse like, "Pardon me, Father, but I am just passing through town, and I was wondering what time you have Mass at your parish?" Sometimes Father Kienzle could even recognize the caller's voice.

If the phone generally heralded trouble—few called to say that everything was going great—the doorbell was no better.

A surprising number of men and women made their living off rectories. Sometimes, elaborate schemes that could have rivaled *The Sting* developed. One such routine, involving hundreds of dollars, was so elaborate it went right by Father Kienzle without his biting. I think he offered to pray for the man. But many of his confreres were taken in by it.

All such schemes relied on split-second timing. They involved an urgent need that defied all opportunity to verify. At that point, the con artist depended on the priest's charity tipping the scale. The crooks usually won. Thus, thousands of dollars went for emergency food that was never eaten, emergency shelter that was never used, and emergency bills that were never paid.

Usually the caller in need asked only for a dollar or less. These types came by almost as regularly as clockwork. Hitting one parish after another, they got by. Father Kienzle was on door duty the day one such regular—known only as John—stopped by for his usual St. David hit.

One of the other assistants who happened to be passing the door answered the bell, then summoned Father Kienzle. The other priest knew very well what John wanted and could have given him the buck. But it was Father Kienzle's day on the door, so he got the call.

A good deal of gamesmanship went on at the door. In one rectory, a priest, in mufti, admitted a gentleman who wanted to see a priest. "I'll get the priest," the incognito one said, "but he's hard of hearing, so you'll have to speak up." He summoned his assistant, telling him that a hard-of-hearing man was waiting to see him. So there the two stood, priest and visitor, toe to toe, shouting at each other.

One of Father Kienzle's fondest door memories involved a young mother and her little boy, perhaps five. Father opened the door and bade them good morning. "Good morning, Father," said the woman. "Hello, God," said her son.

Once inside, she explained, sotto voce, the boy's singular greeting. "The only way I can keep him quiet during Mass on Sunday is to tell him that's God up there on the altar doing and saying all those things. And I tell him he shouldn't fool around with disturbing God." The boy naturally concluded that if that was God on Sundays, it must be God the rest of the week.

Not wishing to upset the mother's successful ploy, and equally unwilling to add another squalling voice to the Sunday congregation, Father Kienzle did nothing to dissuade the child.

When the two left, the boy said, "Good-bye, God."

"Good-bye, boy," replied Father, trying for his most impressive tone.

Thanks to years of responding to bells, both in the seminary and in the rectory, many's the man who, though he left the priesthood, could not leave the habit of never letting a phone—not to mention a doorbell—ring unanswered.

Nastiness in a priest is worse than thorns on a rosebush and more out of place than horns on a halo; it is one of our sins that Christ died for.

—UNNAMED PRIEST

ALL PARISHES HAD A CERTAIN NUMBER OF TASKS to be performed. As priests aged—paid their dues, as it were—they got first choice among the jobs. St. David's had four priests, a plentitude not unusual in that era. The pastor had retired from just about everything except keeping the books and worrying about finances. Shortly after Father's Kienzle's arrival, the allocation of parochial duties was brought up.

First was the day off. The longest-term assistant picked Wednesday. In this, he showed real class. Wednesday was, by far, the most popular day off. Try to get a doctor or a dentist on a Wednesday. They're all on the golf course with priests and bankers.

The next assistant picked Tuesday. Father Kienzle selected Saturday, which would have freed him from hearing tons of confessions. After a moment of startled silence, they all chuckled over this touch of humor. Father Kienzle then picked a more realistic Thursday.

Next came the selection of responsibilities. The second assistant had already designated himself God's Gift to Youth in perpetuity. So Father Kienzle did miss out on some young people's activities. He did, however, end up with the altar boys and the Scouts. But by the time he completed assignments in later parishes, he had touched just about all the youth bases.

Catechism, or the Confraternity of Christian Doctrine (CCD) classes, seemed the toughest assignment in any parish, from almost any angle. Usually, the children had to attend classes after, or in addition to, their regular classes in public school. Not the most receptive or attentive of audiences. Trying to enlist people willing to teach CCD class was like getting volunteers in the Army. After all, it was their spare time too.

Textbooks were another problem. No one was doing much imaginatively at that time. Mostly, it was the Baltimore Catechism—over and over again.

To be an effective teacher under such circumstances, with such obstacles, one had to be a combination of Milton Berle and Fulton Sheen.

Father Kienzle was lucky. Some young priests were sent to serve under pastors who treated them like dirt, or worse. Detroit had at least three pastors for whom mere irrascibility would have been welcomed by their downtrodden assistants. The meanness of these three clerical tyrants was legendary. Nor were they unique. The story is told of a visit to Detroit of Cardinal Spellman, who, while vesting, asked the young priest assisting him where he was stationed. "I'm an assistant pastor at St. Whatever."

Spellman sneered. "Where I come from, that word [assistant] is a noun, not an adjective."

Actually, in the East, they had an entirely different and more specific word for the lowly assistant. Once, while attending a priests' retreat, Father Francis Connell, the Redemptorist theologian, happened to use the word "curate." He immediately corrected himself. "Oh, I'm sorry. Out here you call them assistants."

"Out here," stage-whispered a big, fat pastor to an equally porcine colleague, "we call them assholes."

Those ordained in the mid-fifties could expect to spend a good twenty years as assistants, moving up, perhaps, from third to second to first assistant. They were like the minor league ball player who is sent to the majors after some years of on-the-job training, after which they got much needed and sometimes welcomed guidance from the old-timers. Nowadays, with the dearth of priests, frequently the oil of ordination is hardly dry before the young priest becomes a pastor. Undoubtedly, he must occasionally ponder the statement attributed to Gandhi: "There go my people; I must hurry and catch up with them, for I am their leader."

In the Good Old Days, assistants generally tended to be kind to one another. They were all in the same boat, and most of the time it was being fired upon.

One of the illustrative tales—undoubtedly apocryphal—of clerical tact involved assistants, three in the same parish.

It happened at Midnight Mass, the good old—and gone—Solemn High Mass. This called for the pastor as celebrant, the first assistant as deacon, the second assistant as subdeacon, and the third assistant as master of ceremonies.

Came the "Gloria" and it was time to sit down while the choir sang.

The three ministers of the Mass sat while the newly ordained third assistant stood to their right. The pastor had his arms folded across his chest, which was liturgically incorrect.

The master of ceremonies leaned over to the deacon—the oldest assistant—and said, "Tell Monsignor to put his hands on his knees."

The deacon whispered to the pastor, "The choir sounds good tonight, doesn't it?"

The pastor murmured that yes, indeed it did.

The deacon leaned back to the master of ceremonies and said, "Monsignor says to go to hell."

St. David's pastor was Porter Welsh, a dear man who had lost a leg to diabetes. Father Welsh's one fear was that he would be relieved of his parish because of his condition. He need not have worried. In an era where priests did not retire, but died with their stoles on in mid-absolution, Father Welsh remained at his post till the end of his life. He was mourned by many, including his priest-assistants.

Father Welsh lay in state in the rectory living room. A candle salesman who stopped by a couple of times a year came to the door. You'd think he'd have noticed that something was different. Clusters of people were entering and leaving the rectory. A funeral wreath hung on the door. Still, the salesman rang the bell as if nothing were unusual. Father Ackerman, not the most solicitous of men under the best of conditions, came to the door. Was the pastor in, the salesman wondered. Father Ackerman, for reasons known to him alone, said yes, and pointed to the living room.

With a happy salesmanship smile on his face, the peddler walked briskly in. Then he caught sight of the corpse.

He didn't even turn around; he backed all the way out through the hallway and front door, all the while murmuring, "I'm sorry. I'm sorry. I'm so sorry."

What a way to go!

THERE IS A PHRASE USED BY OLD-TIME CATHOLICS to describe a good-looking young priest who is the subject of crushes from impressionable young girls: Father What-a-Waste.

Father Kienzle, at six foot three, with wavy black hair, eyes that always saw the humor in life, and a smile that could melt the heart of a stone, inspired not a few such crushes. One day at St. David's a teenage schoolgirl was hit by a car. Father Kienzle happened to be nearby and ran to assist while the ambulance was summoned. He knelt in the street, holding the supine girl's head in his hands, and praying. Students crowded on the nearby sidewalk, and (this was related decades after the event by the mother of one of the onlookers) one girl sighed, "What a way to go!"

The young priest moved through this pubescent admiration totally unaware. It was only many years later—when a former student reminisced about her school days—that he heard with wonderment and disbelief that he had been the object of such feminine adoration. He had never thought of himself as handsome. Actually, thanks to his seminary training, any self-thought was directed toward attaining and maintaining holiness. Consideration of one's appearance other than as it involved cleanliness and neatness would have been prideful—definitely a sin to be avoided.

Some years later, when my parents met Father Kienzle, my mother—who, well into her nineties, still had an eye for a good-looking young man—said, "What a waste!" I was indignant. "Doesn't God deserve the best?" I retorted. My father, whose hobby was eugenics, commented only that the human gene pool was really losing out.

One of Father Kienzle's duties was ministering to female inmates at the Wayne County Jail. Once or twice a month, he would go downtown and offer a short *fervorino* (an encouraging little sermon). The "congregation" was about 95 percent black, and they *really* participated. "Amens" and "Alleluias" came from every side, repeatedly.

The young priest wasn't used to this sort of thing. No one in any white parish he'd ever been in was interrupted like this. Oh, there might be a cough here and there, or parents removing squalling children, or, rarely, someone leaving in a huff. But nothing like this.

Since the ladies were "Amen"ing in the gaps he left to gasp for breath, his only solution was to take deeper breaths and exhale less frequently. It was a harrowing, if novel, experience. In later years, having become acquainted with Flip Wilson's Reverend LeRoy, he said that if he had it to do over he would encourage the ladies. "Now, let's hear a big 'Amen' for the Blessed Mother of Perpetual Help!"

Before the *fervorino*, he would hear confessions. "Now those," he would say in later years, "were *confessions*"—as opposed to the sleep-inducing laundry lists of the super-scrupulous, or schoolkids scared silly by sister.

Around this time, a notorious murder took place, involving Detroit's Chaldean community. A man was found bound and stabbed to death. Nearby was his wife, also bound but very much alive. Her version was that a stranger had broken in, bound her and her husband, then raped her and killed her husband.

Evidence, however, pointed elsewhere. The police version of events was that the wife had been having an affair with a young relative of her husband, and that she and her lover had killed the husband and blamed it all on a mysterious stranger.

The wife and the supposed lover were put on trial for murder. The newspapers gave themselves free rein when it came to purple prose and conjecture, the big question being, Did she or didn't she?

And now on visiting day, who should enter the room where Father Kienzle was seated but the lady in question. Of course he recognized her immediately; after all, her photo was in all the newspapers, and the trial was breakfast table fodder throughout Detroit and environs.

As he told the tale in later years, a fanciful scenario immediately flashed through his mind.

The woman would go to confession to him, he alone would know whether she was guilty. The prosecutor would put him on the stand. He would refuse to break the Seal of Confession. He would then be held in contempt of court, and be thrown in jail, where he would rot his life away, becoming a martyr to the storied seal. A statue of him would be erected next to that of General Kościusko, and parochial schoolchildren would venerate his name.

All these thoughts ran through his mind in a flash. Before he had time to further consider his actions, the woman approached him, knelt, and went to confession . . . in Chaldean.

When she finished, Father Kienzle, not having understood a word she had said, held up his rosary denoting X number of beads. He looked at her inquiringly: Did she understand? She nodded, rose to her feet, and departed.

I do not recall the outcome of the trial. But he was never called to give evidence—so no statue exists of Father Kienzle—in the vicinity of General Kościuszko, or anywhere else.

But I don't *know* five Hail Marys.

FROM TIME ALMOST IMMEMORIAL, those associated with the confessional referred to it as "the box." Appropriate. Most of the confessionals Father Kienzle occupied brought to mind the box in which Alec Guinness was confined in *The Bridge Over the River Kwai*.

They didn't teach architecture in the seminary—but that never stopped the churchmen. It was as if some pastor, having supervised the construction of a church—usually as a monument to himself— suddenly realized, "My God, I've forgotten the confessionals!"

Immediately thereafter, they'd slap some wood and cloth together and stick it away in an apse someplace where it wouldn't get in the way of the Romanesque, Gothic, or Byzantine monstrosity in which it was enclosed.

As a result, there were probably many Catholics for whom going to confession was genuine torture by means of which any sin could be forgiven even without actual absolution.

St. David's had four priests, three of whom heard confessions. (The pastor, having paid his dues, had retired from that ordeal.) There were six confessionals, all of which—thanks to outside help—were staffed with confessors.

By luck of the draw—actually because he was low man on that totem pole—Father Kienzle got the only confessional without a window to the outside world. His box backed into a closed stairwell to the basement. No special problem during winter, but in summer it was hell.

At one point, a salesman dropped by, wondering whether Father would be interested in a portable air conditioner for the confessional. As far as Father Kienzle was concerned, that salesman had just built a better mousetrap.

However, a combination of two problems proved insurmountable.

All confessionals, as a rule of thumb, were built like coffins compacted to contain a body and little else. The salesman's idea of a portable air conditioner was like King Kong's notion of a small banana. By the time that worthy fitted the machine into the confessional, lanky Father Kienzle's feet were halfway up the wall. When turned on, the air conditioner's noise was such that the confessor would have had to communicate with the penitent by megaphone rather than in whispers.

Father Kienzle and his successors were doomed to sweat it out.

A confessional he occupied for a few years in another parish had its own peculiar form of torture. The confessional was heated—as was the rest of the church—by blowers lodged in the ceiling. They would pump down hot air as soon as the thermostat registered a sufficient degree of coldness.

Not a smart idea for a large church. Absolutely insane for a confessional.

During winter months, the confessor would enter the box, bundled against the cold. If the temperature inside the box was nearing the low thirties, one was in pretty good shape. One could just sit there, sliding the doors back and forth; listen, advise, absolve, and shiver. When it reached the point where one's own breath was visible, the blower would activate. Hot air would be pumped down inside the box at about the same rate it was being pumped down inside the entire church.

As a result, one could neither hear, nor be heard in whispers, so everybody's volume was turned up. The confessor began peeling off layers of clothing—the scarf, the coat, the sweater—and loosening the collar.

When the temperature reached the lower eighties, the blower would shut off and the cold air would begin seeping under the door and wending its inexorable way upward.

Back to whispering and reinstalling the layers of clothing.

On one occasion Father Kienzle filled in at a parish whose confessional boasted a Rube Goldberg-type invention for opening the sliding doors that separate confessor from penitent. A rope ran from one door up the wall, across the ceiling, and down the other wall to the other door. Thus, when one door was pulled down, the other went up. (Remember, the priest sat in the middle, with a penitent's enclosure to either side.) The advantage was that the priest needed only one hand instead of both hands to greet the new sinner. Simple.

Except that in this case, the rope had been broken. So each time, instead of pulling one door open, the confessor had to lift the door and hold it open all the while for each penitent.

Whatever the peculiar inconvenience the box itself presented, the essential idea of this event was to construct a setting where a sinner could confess and be absolved while protected by anonymity and a secrecy that could never be violated under any circumstance.

Catholics were carefully taught that they must confess all mortal sins* and/or toss in as many venial sins as could be recalled or seemed appropriate.

Since Vatican II, some successful efforts have been made to correct this approach. But this was the Good Old Days: The Church urged its people to confess frequently with lots of sins. This led to the recounting of long laundry lists of transgressions that had a numbing sameness.

As a result, confessors soon reached the conclusion that most married couples frequently became angry with each other, all parents regularly became angry with their children, and all children

---

* Serious violations of Divine or Church Law, measured by matter, intent, and/or deed, plus extenuating circumstances.

always disobeyed their parents. The result was almost terminal boredom for confessors.

Many penitents tried to cover their tracks when dealing with the numbers of times they had committed sins by adding the phrase "more or less." This became so habitual they even added it to a singular experience. "I was angry with my wife once, more or less."

Only one in perhaps five hundred penitents added a touch of humor to the proceedings. Perhaps one in a thousand mentioned anything at all out of the ordinary.

By far the most daunting experience took place during the scholastic year, on the Thursdays before First Friday. First Fridays, thanks to some promises allegedly made by God to St. Margaret Mary, were favorite days for many Catholics to receive Communion. That generally called for going to confession beforehand. In a parochial school setting, this involved the sisters' herding to the confessional all the children in the school, class after class.

The result: Hour after hour of "I just obeyed [disobeyed] my mother four times, and I just obeyed my father three times, and I just obeyed my baby-sitter twice, and I just obeyed my grandmother once, more or less," etc.

This repetitive monologue, coupled with the confessional's inbuilt inconvenience, from time to time led Father Kienzle to reverie. He would come to with a jolt. At which point, he would have to ask the child where they were in the process. "Have you told me your sins? That's good. Have I given you a penance? No? Well, then, say three Hail Marys and be a good little girl—oh, you're a little boy? Well then, be a good little boy."

Listening to children's confessions—especially those of young children—the priest quickly learned not to interrupt. Most children had their laundry list of sins carefully memorized. Any interruption would stop them cold. In too many cases, this meant they had to start all over again if they were going to get through it at all. So the cardinal rule was: Don't interrupt—even if it didn't make sense. As in "Bless me, Father, for I have sinned. My last confession was one week ago and I missed Mass on Sunday four times . . ." Don't ask. Just let it go, and rely on God to figure it out.

Being a penitent meant being at the mercy of the confessor and thus on the defensive. A Professor of Moral Theology once told of going to confession at a local monastery. He began by stating that it had been a month since his last confession. At which the confessor blew his top and said, "Don't you know, according to Canon Law, a priest must go to confession once a week!?" Not only was the professor familiar with Canon Law, he taught it, and he knew there was no such legislation. Yet he found himself answering, "Yes, Father."

Rarely did a penitent ever get the opportunity to strike back. But once in a while the worm tried a turn. In a downtown parish one noon, the pastor chanced upon a woman who looked particularly disturbed. When he asked what the problem was, she huffed that that was the last time she was ever going to confession in that parish.

"But why?"

"The priest gave me two hundred Rosaries as a penance."

"Two hundred Rosar—! Wait a minute . . . there aren't supposed to be any confessions now . . ." The pastor entered the church. Sure enough, someone was hearing confessions in the front box. The pastor yanked open the confessional door. Inside was a skid row bum—undoubtedly getting revenge for some bad times on the receiving side of the box.

Actually, there were no firm guidelines for dispensing penances. That was pretty much up to the whim of the confessor. Generally, it was a certain number of Our Fathers or Hail Marys, the least common denominator for most Catholics. While the average Catholic might have problems praying—or even locating—the Nicaean Creed as a penance, all Catholics were expected to know those two basic prayers.

This led to a problem with literalness that rarely arose, but it did happen once to Father Kienzle. He had just told a young lad to say five Hail Marys. The boy responded, "I don't know five Hail Marys." The W. C. Fields in Father Kienzle rose to the fore. But . . . the little bugger was technically correct.

"Do you know *one* Hail Mary?"

"Yes, Father."

"Would you say it five times?"

"Yes, Father."

"Fine. Now get out of here."

One priest-confessor in the seminary used to assign an appropriate verse of an appropriate chapter in Thomas à Kempis's *Imitation of Christ* as a penance. It was more difficult to remember the penance than to perform it.

While there were no tight rules of thumb on what exactly to assign as penance, the ordinands were warned, particularly if they would be inclined to give out-of-the-ordinary penances, to at least vary them. If, for example, a priest gained the reputation of always assigning the public praying of the Stations of the Cross for using contraception, other parishioners might conclude, "There goes Mrs. Murphy, making the Stations of the Cross. She and her hubby must've been at it again."

And there would go the fabled Seal of Confession.

One example given to seminarians was that of the new priest hearing his first confessions. At the conclusion, after a long line of penitents had confessed, the tyro exited the box to attend a parish party. During the evening, still excited over his new powers, he mentioned to a circle of parishioners, "The first confession I heard was adultery." A shocked silence greeted his announcement. He could not have known that earlier in the evening, a young woman of the parish had announced, "I was the first one to confess to Father Blank."

The penalty for breaking the Seal of Confession is excommunication. A like penalty is incurred by a priest who cooperates in the commitment of a sin, then absolves the person with whom he committed it. Usually, such penalties may be lifted only by the Holy See in Rome.

Time waits for no Mass.

"GET 'EM OUT, the next crowd's comin' in!"

It was like John Wayne keeping the wagon train moving. But in a big city parish in the fifties, Sunday Mass was scheduled every hour of the morning through to early afternoon. Cataclysmic then was an overly long Mass, particularly in the later, more heavily attended hours. It could cause a traffic jam that might lead to gridlock.

Some priests developed their own styles to meet this demand. One cut the mumbled Latin into a sort of shorthand. Nor did he waste anyone's time with a useless homily. He was clocked at an average twelve minutes for a Sunday Mass—sermon and all. He was much in demand. When he visited another parish on a given weekend, the parishioners would be in a state of culture shock when leaving church after only a quarter-hour. Then they'd begin badgering their regular priests: "Why can't you do that?"

Father Majeski did a lateral arabesque to that formula. He got the basic Mass down to about ten minutes. (With any reverence at all, it should have taken at least half an hour.) But for him that simply cleared the way for miles of sermon time. His sermon topic one noteworthy Sunday was the Bible—the whole thing.

Late in life—in retirement actually—Father Majeski helped out weekends at a suburban parish, still following his tried-and-true formula. The parish's pastor starting getting complaints from his parishioners on the length and lack of depth of Majeski's sermons. The pastor warned him: From now on, nothing longer than fifteen minutes in the pulpit.

Father Majeski noted the warning and immediately dismissed it. The following Sunday, he was just warming to his topic at the fifteen-minute mark when the pastor turned off the loudspeaker. Startled only momentarily, Father Majeski cried out as though the victim of a Roman persecution, "Pull the plug on Majeski, eh? I'll just raise my own volume!" And, undaunted, on he went.

In the end, it didn't much matter how one did it, as long as the congregation was gotten out in time for the next crowd to enter.

It got to be a matter of subtle pride. Once, while visiting New York's Episcopal Cathedral of St. John the Divine—which dwarfed previously visited St. Patrick's, one of Father Kienzle's confreres commented, "I wonder how many times they fill it of a Sunday."

Of course, "they" had to fill it only once. As Father Kienzle said, "We outnumbered them. And we knew what to do about our numbers: Get 'em in and get 'em out."

It also got to be a matter of insanity. What did you do with the 1 P.M. crowd which was followed by nobody? You got them out by 1:45. It had become habit-forming.

Never was Father Kienzle more impressed with this than on his first Good Friday as a priest.

It was in the Good Old Days of the Mass of the Presanctified. Actually, it wasn't a Mass, as there was no consecration. It was a Communion service, using wafers that had been consecrated the day before—Holy Thursday. It also was part of *Tre Ore*, the three hours from noon to three that mark the time Jesus spent on the cross.

Just before noon on Good Friday, a goodly crowd would assemble, most of whom would stick it out to the bitter end.

The Mass of the Presanctified began promptly at noon and, just as every Sunday, ripped through the liturgy at warp speed. The celebrants finished the complicated rites in an hour, breathless and exhausted. They now had two hours remaining—with nothing to do.

It was ad lib time. One would go out and lead the Stations of the Cross. Later, another would go out and read from a spiritual text on "The Seven Last Words from the Cross." Still another would lead our by-now restless but persevering group in the Sorrowful Mysteries of the Rosary.

"What time is it?"

"Five after two."

"How about the Stations of the Cross?"

"We already did that."

"Could we get away with it again?"

"I don't think so."

A Host of problems . . .

THE FIRST THING THE NEWLY ORDAINED PRIEST of those days learned about parish liturgy is that it bore no relation to that of the seminary.

The most impressive liturgy in the Church Year, for instance, is that of Holy Week. Lent is grinding to an end and, with solemn ceremonies, Catholics approach Christianity's greatest feast, the Resurrection.

The most significant of these ceremonies is that of Holy Saturday. First, there was the blessing of the new fire, which symbolizes Christ, the Light of the World. Then there was the reading of Twelve Old Testament texts prefiguring the coming of the Messiah. Then the ritual of blessing special Baptismal water. In the seminary this was carried out with great and impressive solemnity.

In one parish that boasted three priests, each of them started one of these three ceremonies in separate corners of the church simultaneously, and worked toward the middle, where they met in time for the Easter Mass.

In another parish, where the young assistant had carefully arranged everything to go as smoothly as it did in the seminary, the altar boy who was supposed to turn out all the lights for the blessing of the new fire pushed the fire alarm instead of the light switch. For the next twenty minutes, nobody heard anything but the fire siren, since no one could locate the button to turn it off.

One home for Detroit working girls had a German DP priest as its chaplain. Just before ordination, a group of seminarians went down to help with the Holy Saturday liturgy.

They started on the back porch, where the priest had a bucket full of wood for the new fire. The March wind was gusting. Seminarian Kienzle saw no chance of getting that wood ignited so it could symbolize the Light of the World. But the priest had drenched the wood with lighter fluid; one touch of a match turned it into an inferno. They lost the seminarian carrying the censor. He was standing downwind and was enveloped in smoke. To his liturgical credit, he did not move. From time to time, one of the participants would reach into the smoke, feel around, and come out with the censor.

From that point, it went steadily downhill.

Even the seminary—Murphy's Law being universal—was not perfect. Just usually better.

Part of the problem in the seminary was that everything happened so early in the morning. Those who were not morning people seldom were able to participate intelligently.

One of the priest-professors had particular difficulty confronting dawn. One morning, while seminarian Kienzle was assisting him, the priest fell asleep while vesting. Another time he napped after washing his hands at the Offertory of the Mass. He then forgot where he was in the Mass, and went directly into the consecration.

Finishing much earlier than was his habit, he asked his seminarian assistant what had happened. When seminarian Kienzle explained, the priest's response was, "At least it was valid."

Even Father Fenn, the redoubtable rector, one morning fell victim to the early hour. He consecrated the Host, forgot to consecrate the wine, and went on with the ritual.

Now there was a problem. It wasn't going to be valid. The server was a big-boned farmboy from northern Michigan. He looked to his classmates for some clue as to what to do. His buddies indicated, in mime, that he should tap Fenn and tell him. The lad tapped Fenn on the shoulder, rousing him from his reverie. Fenn must have thought it was God; he looked up for the longest time before realizing the tap had come from his seminarian-server.

One of the worst moments with the old liturgy in the seminary came during a Sunday Vespers service that concluded with Benediction. As deacons, the seminarians had the rare privilege of being deputed to touch the consecrated elements. In those days, it was one of the things that clearly separated the clergy from the laity.

One of Bill Kienzle's classmates, Art Childs, was Deacon of Exposition that day. As such, Art was to place the Host, which was in a small container called a lunette, into the monstrance, a large, ornate vessel that properly displayed the Host for adoration.

Something went wrong from the very beginning. The Host didn't look white enough. It didn't look white enough because Art, in his novice nervousness, had inserted the lunette backward, so that the tight-fitting round container was flush with the back door of the monstrance.

What this did was make it virtually impossible to get the lunette out of the monstrance. Art discovered this when he tried to remove the lunette at the end of Benediction.

Being of sound mind, he panicked. After several tries, he attempted to shove the whole monstrance into the tabernacle. This was impossible: the monstrance was larger than the tabernacle.

For some moments, all present thought they'd been condemned to Perpetual Adoration. But cooler heads prevailed, and a deacon with singular fingernails was able to extract the lunette.

The old liturgy had another difficulty: the technical terms that attached themselves to everything.

One day, at Communion in the seminary, a Host fell to the ground. Those were the days, as Garry Wills once described them, when priests fought a War Against Crumbs. Transubstantiation meant that every smallest particle of bread was the living presence of the Lord. So if a Host was dropped, a small white cloth was placed over the spot—which would later be thoroughly scrubbed.

When this Host hit the floor, the priest turned to the deacon and said, "Get the manutergium." The deacon obediently returned to the altar and stood there for endless minutes.

Finally, the priest turned to the subdeacon and said, "Get the manutergium." The subdeacon went to the altar, turned to the immobile deacon and asked, "What the hell is a manutergium?" That question was what had immobilized the deacon.

Finally, the priest went to the altar and picked up the little white cloth.

The story was told—possibly apocryphal—of a theoretical situation posed by a priest-professor as a problem to the seminarians. Bearing in mind the War Against Crumbs, and the solemn horror involved should the Host come to harm, the question was raised as to what should be done if a mouse were to pick up a dropped Host and carry it off into a nearby mouse hole.

After some thought, an otherwise brilliant seminarian responded, "Burn down the church and throw the ashes in the sacrarium."*

An equally punctilious seminarian once posited that in transubstantiation (when the Eucharistic bread is changed into the body of Jesus) there is a cosmic split second wherein the Host is neither bread *nor* body. He was pretty much shouted down, but I can't help wondering whether such an unanswered question might not lead to all manner of heretical or even schismatic errantry.

Consider, for instance, the teenage boy who confesses kissing Susie Simpson for a lengthy period. His confessor informs him that any kiss over three seconds is a mortal sin that, unconfessed, will send the miscreants straight to hell. A kiss lasting less than three seconds is "only" a venial sin—confessible but not hell-consigning.

Never underestimate the power of the youthful mind to seek loopholes. The question was posed—and somewhere, a mare's nest of Moral Theologians is, Sisyphus-like, condemned to pondering the answer—"What if the kiss lasts *exactly* three seconds, no more, no less?"

Ring the bells that still can ring/Forget your perfect offering. There is a hole in everything/That's how the light comes thru.

—Leonard Cohen

(*song*)

The higher in the hierarchy one got, the more complex the liturgical matters became. Nothing was so complex, and thus so apt to go wrong, as a Pontifical Mass presided over by a bishop.

---

* A special church sink whose drain runs into the earth rather than into the sewer system. It is used for washing out chalices and manutergia used in connection with disposal of crumbs of the consecrated host.

The story was told of one acriminious bishop in Baltimore with a temper to match his red vestments. At a Pontifical Mass he would become angered with one minister after another. Each he would suspend on the spot. As each was suspended, the suspendee would enter the sacristy and light up a cigarette, knowing full well that the bishop would eventually suspend so many of his ministers that he would have to reinstate all just to be able to finish the Mass.

When a bishop sat down in the Good Old Days, he didn't just sit down. He had a large white napkin, called a gremial, placed over his lap. The gremial's strings were looped around the arms of the chair so the cloth wouldn't slip to the ground. On one occasion, a master-of-ceremonies turned to the seated bishop and properly announced, "The bishop stands." Nothing happened. Thinking the bishop hard of hearing, the emcee repeated, "The bishop stands." Still nothing happened. Finally, the bishop looked up and said, "The bishop can't stand; he's tied down." The gremial-bearer had failed to unloop the strings.

If this sort of thing could go wrong at the level of seminary liturgies and Pontifical ceremonies, where all the time in the world and most precise preparation were always available, parish liturgies that could afford neither time nor that careful a preparation were inevitably worse.

Father Kienzle's conglomerate recollection of the Sunday liturgy in a series of parishes was of mumbled Latin (much of it was directed to be mumbled), and a constant shuffling, coughing noise from the congregation.

Again, too many things happened too early in the morning. A parish with a 5:45 A.M. Mass was always a challenge to one who was a night owl. One extremely hot summer Saturday night, when immediate sleep seemed impossible, Father Kienzle set his alarm clock in the middle of the floor, so that should he oversleep, he would have to get out of bed to shut the alarm off.

In the early morning hours, it cooled down sufficiently for him to finally fall asleep.

The next sound he consciously heard was the ringing of every bell in the rectory—telephones and doorbells. It was 6 A.M. There was no 5:45 Mass going on because Father Kienzle was supposed to be saying it. He had climbed out of bed, turned off the alarm, and returned to sleep right there on the floor alongside the clock.

Most of the problems with parish liturgies were caused by altar boys—diligent young men, but inexperienced, seldom well trained, and given to instinctive panic. Father Kienzle often wondered why altar boys would light, say, five candles, but when their taper went out, would return to the sacristy to relight the taper rather than just lighting it from one of the already lit altar candles.

His thought was: Probably because no one ever told them they could do that. After all, if one was raised Catholic, one was aware that the cardinal rule was to follow rules. The candle was to be lit by the taper—which was originally lit in the sacristy . . . ergo, *all* candles were to be lit by the taper—and the taper must always be lit in the sacristy.

Makes sense.

One sister in charge of altar boys looked up in shock one morning to see one of her little charges, at the consecration of the Mass, holding the edge of the priest's chasuble in his mouth. Pressed for a reason later, the boy explained, "I couldn't help it, Sister. I only got two hands, and I had to lift his vestment, ring the bell, and thump myself."

One of the lads Father Kienzle carefully trained had never served by himself. Father had taught him only how to serve in tandem. When it came time for the lad to bring a cruet, a dish, and a towel to the altar, instead of draping the towel over his arm waiter-style, he tucked it under his chin.

After another freshly trained lad completed his first serving assignment, the priest he'd served for approached Father Kienzle and complained that the boy had made lots of mistakes. One of those was that he hadn't assisted the celebrant to sit down by draping the back of his chasuble through the gap at the rear of the chair.

"Did you make any mistakes?" Father Kienzle asked the boy later.

"No, I don't think so."

"Are you sure?"

"Well . . . maybe one: I forgot to tuck his tail in the hole."

Then there was the story of the very young lad serving as an altar boy during a liturgy presided over by a visiting bishop. When the time came for the procession, the boy—who had been made temporary custodian of the bishop's miter—was nowhere to be found. A search was instituted. The bishop grew more irate, the host pastor more embarrassed, the nun in charge of the altar boys more concerned, and the congregation more impatient.

Eventually, the mystery was solved. The boy was found in a washroom. He was seated on the toilet, with the bishop's miter on his head.

He had followed instructions to the letter: He had been told not to let the miter out of his possession, and, he explained, "I couldn't hold on to the miter and wipe myself, so I put it on my head."

Nor was it only altar boys who caused problems.

One of Father Kienzle's lighthearted confreres showed up in his usual high humor for a Forty Hours celebration. He partook of the grape in full fashion, only to be brought up short by a request that he assist the Cardinal in preparation for the service. Our man hadn't yet eaten, but had done his bit in emptying a fair part of a bottle into an otherwise empty stomach. He demurred. Finally, assured that, since Cardinal Dearden had been down this road before, his presence would be more ceremonial than participatory, he gallantly rose to the occasion.

While the Cardinal vested, his assigned assistant opened the Cardinal's case preparatory to putting His Eminence's crozier together. (The crozier travels in sections, like a pool cue; one screws the separate sections together to make a whole—in this case the prelate's crook.)

Unfortunately, however, for some reason—whether it was the imbibed bubbly, or whether the screw had been stripped—the now perspiring priest found it impossible to attach the sections of the crook together. The harder he tried, the worse it got. By this time, the Cardinal was tapping his fingers on the counter as his eyebrows grew closer and closer together in controlled gentlemanly dudgeon.

Finally, in desperation, his unhelpful helper turned to the Cardinal, handed him the upper section of the truncated crook, and said, "Why don't you just go in on your knees and pretend you're Toulouse-Lautrec?"

His colleagues dined out on the tale for years.

If parish Masses on Sundays, especially the early variety, were in trouble from the beginning, early daily Masses could be miserable, not to mention very lonely. Frequently, not even the altar boy showed up, which could be a mixed blessing.

At one parish, especially during the bleak winter months, it was Jeannie, the organist, and Father Kienzle at the 6 A.M. Mass. That is, until Jeannie gave birth, after which it was Jeannie and her little daughter, Debbie, and Father Kienzle at the 6 A.M. Mass.

First Debbie was in her crib, cooing and crying away the morning. Then she grew old enough to walk, and her mother's sung responses to Father's sung prayers would come from various sections of the church, as Jeannie wandered among the pews in search of Debbie.

It's all gone now—the old Latin liturgy with its legendary pomp and mystique. As scrambled as it frequently was, when all that Trent-to-Vatican II liturgy went down the tube, the world became a little less rich—for the priests as well as the congregations.

I do and I don't . . .

THERE HE WAS, IN AN ELEVATOR at Hudson's at Christmastime. The tall priest and his roman collar stood out in the crowded cubicle. At the tenth floor, the door opened futilely: Like the Inn of Bethlehem, there was no more room. Outside the door stood a ravishingly gorgeous blonde. Spotting the priest, her eyes widened in recognition. Pointing directly at him, she exclaimed, "He married me!"

The doors closed. Father Kienzle had nine floors to explain to an intrigued crowd that he hadn't really married the girl. He had witnessed her marriage and she was simply confused in her terminology.

Though the wedding in question had taken place only a few months before, Father Kienzle, for whom out of sight was frequently out of mind, undoubtedly wouldn't have remembered the girl had it not been that she was one of the most beautiful brides he'd ever seen.

Weddings and funerals are memorable and/or traumatic events for those who are intimately involved. For the average priest, there are so many of them, at times they cascade in such volume that they tend to blend into one similar wedding or funeral experience.

There are those relatively rare times when a wedding or a funeral involves people well known to the priest. But generally, the involvement is fleeting and the priest can count himself fortunate to remember the pertinent names long enough to satisfactorily conclude the service.

One of the early weddings Father Kienzle witnessed might have been God's way of telling him I never promised you a rose garden.

It involved a couple who were no longer young. He was in his sixties, she in her seventies. He was a crusty geezer. She was trying to hold on to something she'd lost several decades back. John Jones claimed he'd been married several times previously, but in each case he had become a widower. Not only was he unable to produce any pertinent documents, he was highly insulted each time he was asked for them. And he had been asked many times by many people.

The Roman Catholic Church, as anyone forced to go through her bureaucratic channels can attest, is obsessed with documents. For someone with Mr. Jones's track record, documents such as his baptismal papers, confirmation certificate, three wedding certificates, and three death certificates would be required.

When he was in a patient humor—which was not often—Mr. Jones would explain that he had been baptized in England, and the church—with all its records—had been bombed out of existence during World War II. The church that held the wedding records had burned to the ground. And the death certificates were hopelessly lost.

Clearly, there was an impasse. The records were needed. Mr. Jones was not going to cough them up.

As time passed, Mr. Jones became more and more loudly insulted. His righteous indignation could be heard throughout the rectory. Mr. Jones proved to be a bit of a pill that the three assistants passed back and forth. Repeatedly, one or another assistant would make an appointment with the couple for a time that he knew he would not be at the rectory, thus giving one of the other assistants the pleasure of the couple's company.

Father Kienzle lucked out; he saw them least frequently. It was probably for that reason that they were least angry with him. So, after all the compromises had been made, they selected him to witness their wedding.

The wedding went off without undue problem. Father Kienzle saw the couple from time to time afterward. The marriage lasted six months. Mr. Jones, Mrs. Jones one day confided to intimates, was interested in . . . S-E-X.

Although many couples came to Father Kienzle for counseling, he early on became aware that he was, as he put it, limping. After all, what insight could a celibate have into marital problems?

At pre-Cana conferences,* he advised engaged couples to be unselfish with each other. "Now, I know," he would say, "you can't immediately tell if someone is unselfish; after all, that virtue doesn't stick out on one's forehead like a spigot." He felt that if husband and wife were unselfish, they would be able to work out any problems that might arise.

---

* Premarital instruction classes taught by a priest, a physician, and a long-time married couple.

As years passed, having sat through countless pre-Cana presentations given by physicians, Father became quite knowledgeable about female physiology—at least in theory. So knowledgeable that when, as frequently happened, the physician was unable to keep a pre-Cana appointment, Father Kienzle filled in. At such times, he found himself, as he played doctor, diagramming on a blackboard for his audience the various female innards. He was, he later commented wryly, in a state of familiarity with the fallopian tubes.

Whatever you do, don't faint.

ONE HAS THE GENERAL IMPRESSION that those involved in weddings, particularly the brides, were not as nervously emotional in the late sixties and the seventies as they had been previously. It might have had something to do with the feminist movement, but earlier brides did not seem as cool at their weddings. It is much rarer today to find a bride who faints at her own wedding. Not to imply that in earlier days they were dropping like flies; it's just that it was not a singular phenomenon.

For some reason, when a bride did faint, she'd just be stretched out there for the longest time. Seldom did anyone do anything practical in church.

A priest friend of Father Kienzle's much given to expansive oratorical gestures, told of being in a portable pulpit—one on wheels so it could be moved to different sections of the sanctuary. Driving a point home, he made a lunging movement. The pulpit tipped over, launching him forward in a sort of shallow dive. He came to rest draped over the Communion railing. As the sisters in the rear of the church murmured, "Jesus, Mary, and Joseph, help the poor man," and the like, the congregation sat as in stone. Finally, he was able to crawl to safety.

It was unwise for a bride to faint at her wedding. The act had not been part of the rehearsal. In most churches she would fall to a marble floor. That would hurt. She could lie there many long minutes before someone, usually the Maid of Honor, would come to her assistance. That movement would trigger additional help, generally from her new and flustered groom and then the rest of the wedding party.

Another priest friend of Father Kienzle's once asked him, "Have you ever had a bride faint at a wedding?"

"Yes."

"Have you ever had a groom faint at a wedding?"

"Well, no . . . but I've heard of it happening."

"Well, have you ever heard of the *priest* fainting at a wedding?"

Turned out he himself had indeed done just that. Thus giving new meaning to the term "fallen priest."

Even when smelling salts weren't called for, weddings were a hotbed for Murphy's Law.

On one occasion, Father Kienzle, as official witness, arrived at the altar and surveyed a scene wherein everything was proceeding with clockwork precision. The altar boys were in place, the parents had been properly seated and looked pleased with everything. The men of the wedding party were standing like little soldiers awaiting the bride and the bridesmaids, who were hesitation-stepping it down the main aisle.

Father Kienzle suddenly realized he had forgotten the ritual. He would have nothing to say to the couple when they came before him. He leaned over to one small altar boy and said, "Do you know that little black book the priest uses to read prayers and stuff out of?"

"Yes, Father."

"Well, it's on the shelf of the place where the priest puts on his vestments. Would you get it for me?"

"Yes, Father."

Time passed. A lot of time. Everyone had arrived but the altar boy. Finally, he approached—emptyhanded—and whispered, "I can't reach it."

Wedding delayed on account of no ritual.

Probably the worst blunder with which Father Kienzle was associated was a wedding witnessed by a visiting priest. There were so many weddings and funerals that Saturday that help was definitely needed. The priest was a single-minded Austrian. He had never met anyone in the wedding party. Still, all would have gone well except that Father Kienzle inadvertently handed him the wrong wedding license.

The moment of truth came when, relying on the license, he asked, "Do you, John Smith, take Mary Jones for your lawful wedded wife?"

"My name isn't John Smith."

"Yes it is. It says so right here."

They argued awhile until, finally, the rigid Austrian was convinced. Shortly thereafter, he returned to his native country, where, presumably, Teutonic efficiency precluded a repeat of such clerical confusion.

Memorial services are the cocktail parties of the geriatric set.

—HAROLD MACMILLAN

IT COULD BE ARGUED THAT since there are more of them—they come at totally unpredictable times and they are much more likely to involve strangers—more can go wrong with a funeral than a wedding.

Bill Kienzle's introduction to funerals came when he was a very young altar boy. The occasion was the burial of a military man. The lad found the flag-draped coffin impressive. But he was totally unprepared for the rifle squad. So, seemingly, was the widow: At the first volley, she fainted. "Oh, my God, they've shot her!" thought the altar boy.

A lot of ethnicity has been lost in recent decades. Comparatively few people die at home now; even fewer are waked at home. For Bill Kienzle, one such wake remained memorable.

The deceased was his grandma Boyle, a feisty old gal who died in her late eighties. She had lived with—and died at the home of—one of her daughters. It was to that house her body was returned for the wake.

The Irish side of the family gathered in early evening. Hushed and reverent, they quietly awaited the arrival of the priest for the recitation of the Rosary. The priest came, the Rosary was recited, and shortly thereafter the younger contingent of the family, including Bill, a teenager, left for home.

Much later that evening, Bill grew concerned: His parents were not yet home. Finally, he phoned his aunt's house. When the phone was answered, he couldn't make out a word for the noise in the background. The Boyles had broken out the booze and the Irish wake was on, full tilt.

The Polish and the Italian funerals could be equally memorable. The Polish funeral usually concluded with the Polish funeral director saying a few words of condolence in Polish and/or leading the assemblage in a Polish hymn. Then everyone was invited to a luncheon at a Polish hall. Since the invitation was also issued in Polish, it was rare for the non-Polish-speaking priest to find his way to the hall. As Father Kienzle discovered, a guy could get lost.

The traditional Italian funeral involved a lot of very emphatic weeping—usually by the widow and/or mother—independent of the character of the deceased. There seemed to be a sort of script. At the graveside, the widow would attempt to hurl herself into the grave. She was prevented from doing so by the nearest male relative. Father Kienzle felt it would have been disaster had anyone missed a cue.

While weddings are usually scheduled months in advance, funerals take place shortly after someone dies. Which can be anytime.

The priest can find himself presiding over several funerals on a given day.

For the priest, the deceased can be—and frequently is—a total stranger, or at least an unfamiliar parishioner. The sine qua non, not always observed, is that the priest should know the deceased's name, at least for the duration of the funeral.

Otherwise, you get eulogies that run something like: "We can all take hope from the life of . . . this man. It was, in its own way, a promise of something deeper. All of us at St. Mary's parish offer our deepest sympathy to [quickly surveying the congregation to determine if it is likely there is some kind of surviving family present] his family."

It is worse, one priest confessed to Father Kienzle, when the eulogist is not even aware of the deceased's sex.

In the wake of Vatican II, one ancient custom that seemed to be slipping away from the funeral ordeal was the recitation of the Rosary. This was supplanted by a Scripture Reading or the so-called Bible Vigil. One could pretty well tell the traditionalists from the so-called liberals by the choice of Rosary or Vigil for the departed.

In the twenty years of Father's Kienzle's priesthood, he led what seemed to him to be a zillion wake Rosaries. On such occasions, he found a distinct pattern: On the part of most present at the wake, there was a singular dedication to escape the Rosary.

He became aware of this only gradually. When he entered the funeral parlor, any Catholic present knew very well what his roman collar signified: In a few short moments, the Rosary would begin. The priest's appearance led to a flurry of activity. People either shot out a side door, or quickly lined up to bid farewell to the survivors.

Occasionally, feeling particularly puckish, before entering, Father Kienzle would turn up his coat collar, hiding the roman collar. He would slink unobtrusively to the bench before the coffin, kneel, then lower his outer collar with a flourish and loudly begin the Rosary.

"My God, Helen, he's started! We're stuck!"

A religious man is a person who holds God and man in one thought at one time, at all times . . . whose greatest passion is compassion, whose greatest strength is love . . .

—Abraham Joshua Heschel

Father Kienzle's next assignment was at St. Norbert's in Inkster. The pastor, Father Lawrence "Scottie" Graven, was a gracious, good-humored gentleman. If central casting wanted someone who was the epitome of what a pastor should be, Father Graven was that priest. By the same token, if one wanted the ideal place for a young assistant to spread his wings, St. Norbert's fit the bill. Founded in 1951, it was a burgeoning parish, comprising a host of young parents with growing families. In the era when Catholic women seemingly were all either pregnant or had just given birth, "eternity clothes" were the uniform of the day. Father Kienzle was amazed and amused: Whenever a new baby was brought to a get-together, the women—most of whom were mothers several times over—gathered around to coo and crow over the new arrival as if it were the only baby on earth and each woman didn't have a clutch of her own at home.

The parents were roughly the same age as he was. They were active supporters of their parish. They banded together to do land-scaping, build a school, support their church. The feeling was "We're all in this together" and the "we" included Father Kienzle. Several of the parishioners at St. Norbert's remained among his dearest friends throughout his life.

As always, Father Kienzle's Masses were memorable. One of the St. Norbert parishioners, Lou Morand, who years earlier had been in the seminary with Bill, describes him thusly:

"My abiding memory is the absolute dignity he had while saying Mass. No one ever offered a more reverent Mass. He also sang well. He would often use one of the alternate and seldom-used prefaces.

"He was also a marvelous confessor. He related well to the youth of the parish. He and Father Graven worked hand in glove. He also—unknown to any of us at the time—began his newspaper career, serving as editor of the *St. Norbert Messenger* (the parish bulletin).

"He was also most successful in moderating our parish Catholic Family Movement group. And he played a lot of first base for our ushers' softball team. Touch football, some basketball, as well as golf, were also included in those days.

"He made so many of us so happy in so many ways using so many of his talents."

In 1998, with the congregations of St. Norbert's and the neighboring St. Kevin's shrinking, the two parishes merged. In January 2004, with attendance at the combined SS. Kevin and Norbert averaging 80 people and the parish $700,000 in debt, the archdiocese announced that the Inkster church would be closed by May 31, 2004.

Fr. Kienzle: To a swell "Joe" and a real "high-brow." Keep up your fine sense of humor (about the small yellow Sociology papers), and your fantabulous intellect. [signed] Charles H.

—STUDENT INSCRIPTION ON PATRONAGE GRADUATION PHOTO

FATHER KIENZLE WAS SADDENED TO LEAVE ST. NORBERT'S. He had been reassigned to Patronage of St. Joseph, a small, heavily Italian, inner-city parish. It seemed so . . . so cut off, so isolated from the type of parish he had been in. One of Father Kienzle's classmates, Father Maher, was an assistant at Patronage. He showed his successor around the church, the rectory, the convent, the school. The young priest found it depressing.

But the pastor was kindly . . . unlike the pastor of the neighboring parish, who was one of the legendary Nasty Three. At one point, a young woman from Patronage wanted to be married in the neighboring parish, which was her fiancé's home parish. Pastor Nasty sent a letter to Patronage, stating this would be allowed only if he could be assured that the couple would henceforth be contributing to his parish.

Sometime later, one of Father Nasty's parishioners died and because Forty Hours had been scheduled, his church would be unavailable for the Funeral Mass. He sent a letter to Patronage, requesting that Patronage hold the Funeral Mass for the deceased. Father Kienzle, drawing on his quirky humor, wrote back that Patronage would be glad to supply the funeral if Father Nasty could assure them that the deceased would henceforth be contributing to Patronage.

Father Nasty never spoke to Father Kienzle again, not even on the rare occasion when they came face to face.

But the parishioners at Patronage seemed to appreciate this young priest who was so very . . . well, *priestly*. Father Kienzle grew accustomed to inhaling waves of garlic in the church and in the confessional. He grew accustomed to the Italian accents. He even grew accustomed to teaching.

In those days, the priest filled in wherever he was needed. If a parish school was short a teacher, Father stepped in and taught. At Patronage, Father Kienzle taught sociology. His photo album contains a picture of the rectory at Patronage. On the back in a feminine hand is written, "Rectory, 6945 Culver. Home away from home for half a dozen adolescent girls." But one of his teenage students, Carol Fox—now a nurse and a grandmother—saw beyond the Father What-a-Waste sobriquet. On first seeing him enter the classroom, she wrote later, "I said to myself, 'Now here is a man who loves God, life, other people, and himself.'"

Father Kienzle wasn't exactly God's gift to teenagers, but he came close. He listened, but was never buddy-buddy; he always bore himself with total dignity, and though friendly, never forgot that he was a priest. People—even teenagers—recognized and honored this; no one ever tried to cross the invisible line of his priesthood.

Not all priests were expected to relate well to youth. Grouchy old Father Fitzgibbon in *Going My Way* could play the Scrooge and barely tolerate youngsters, but younger priests definitely were supposed to be youth's—especially boy's—best friend. And if you were youngest-priest-on-the-totem-pole, you were relegated—happily, in most instances—to the youth market.

At Sacred Heart Seminary, Bill Kienzle had been active in a variety of theater productions. He had alternated with a classmate, Joe Kitz, as Bouncer in the seminary production of Gilbert and Sullivan's *Cox and Box*. In years to come, whenever *Cox and Box* was shown on television, or aired on radio, Joe would phone—even after he moved to Arizona—to alert his former classmate of the performance.

Father Pomponi, Patronage's pleasant pastor, never lost an opportunity to remind his young assistant that, "The sisters are refusing to direct the high school play this year." The Low Man on the Totem Pole had already learned to say no. But eventually, like the Chinese water torture, the pastor's repeated "reminder" wore him down. So it was that Father Kienzle found himself coaching the students in Patronage's annual musical and dramatic productions.

Not that it was an onerous task. He enjoyed Broadway shows. So, staging *Annie, Get Your Gun* or *Meet Me in St. Louis* was right up his alley. It was an education not only for the students but also for their producer-director. Rehearsing "You Can't Get a Man with a Gun," he mentioned that they would have to figure out some choreography. The students looked at each other blankly. The next time through, Father suggested that they would have to figure out some dance steps. "Oh, *that's* what he meant . . ."

In the scene where Annie's sister drops some keys down the front of her dress and they fall to the floor, the other sister takes them "because you're too flat-chested." She thereupon drops the keys down the front of *her* dress, and again the keys fall to the floor.

That's the way it was *supposed* to go.

But the teenager playing the second sister was—uh—well-developed, and she must've gotten a sturdy bra for the occasion. During the performance, she dropped the keys down the front of her dress . . . and they stayed. Panicking, she looked for help to Father Kienzle in the wings. "What'll I do?" she mouthed. "Jump up and down," he mouthed back.

She did. The keys dropped. The audience howled.

The teenager who portrayed Frank Butler in that production was also the organist for Patronage. He had been an altar boy—a position he gloried in—until the pastor decided to replace the longtime organist. Suddenly Larry—the "green kid"—was *it*. No problem until his first Holy Week came up.

As he recalls, "That first Palm Sunday could have been horrible. I had no idea what Father Pomponi wanted as far as music (Latin of course) went during what seemed like the longest procession with palms in Patronage history. Sure, the *Liber* [Latin book of Mass/devotional music] had several selections available, but I wasn't that versed in all of them. Panic set in.

"At seven-fifteen that morning, Father Kienzle, in cassock and surplice, came up into the choir loft and told me to get vested. Down I went to get my cassock and surplice and together we were the cantors, singing word-for-word and note-for-note (in those days the notes were called neums) all the selections for that processional. How he knew that I needed help, I'll never know.

"I guess that being there at the right time and being willing to 'put it on the line' might be, for me at least, as good a definition of that wonderful Latin term sine qua non as any other.

"When we teenagers were being introduced to rock and roll, Father Kienzle was introducing us to the world of the Broadway musical. When we were learning the names of Elvis Presley and Chubby Checker, we were also learning the names of Rodgers and Hammerstein. While we were 'digesting' three-chord rock-and-roll, we were also being nourished by 'Some Enchanted Evening' and the many beautiful songs from *South Pacific*. We even learned some 'stuff' from a guy named Berlin (*Annie, Get Your Gun*) and still more 'stuff' from Gilbert and Sullivan.

"All of this 'class' immersing came because there was a sine qua non available for some kids at a place called Patronage of St. Joseph by a fellow named William X. Kienzle—our sine qua non. We owe him a great deal."

Larry's older brother had been in the seminary with Bill. He had dropped out for a few years, did some teaching, and eventually was ordained a priest. Larry himself went on to become a high school teacher. He recalls Father Kienzle's sermons:

"What I remember was his brevity. He never seemed to want to go to the 'magic half-hour limit' (if Mass started at nine the sermon had to end by nine-thirty). He seemed to hold the idea that ideas can be presented succinctly. He also seemed to think that there was a bit of intelligence in his hearers, so he didn't talk down to them.

"If he had a model, it was probably Christ, Who did not overburden His listeners . . . as some guy from *Hamlet* put it, 'brevity is the soul of wit.'"

Father Kienzle went on to "write" a show—*Campaign Capers*—scripting new lyrics to songs from Gilbert and Sullivan operettas. The program was a huge success—although at first the students were a bit downcast because the Felician nuns in the audience didn't laugh at any of the jokes in the show. "Don't worry," Father Kienzle assured them. "They have to observe decorum. When they get back to the convent they'll laugh their heads off."

Sports are good and necessary; they prevent the premature and unhealthy pursuit of girls.

—SEMINARY PROFESSOR

BEING ATHLETIC DIRECTOR WAS FAR EASIER than playing impresario. Basically, it involved hiring coaches and financing uniforms and programs.

Sooner or later, the athletic director of each parish came in contact with Cincy Sachs. Cincy was a friendly jock who supplied athletic equipment to most of the parishes in the archdiocese. Though Cincy was Jewish, and knew little about Catholicism, he grew to be close to most of his priest customers.

On one occasion, Cincy visited the rectory to view the body of one of his priest friends. The dead priest was vested, and placed in his hands was the chalice he had used to offer Mass. Cincy viewed the scene for lingering moments. Finally, he asked, in honest ignorance, "Where'd he get the trophy?"

With the advent of Father Kienzle, who had been an athletic light in his seminary days, Patronage began parochial league competition in basketball.

Patronage was a small school with a new program and admittedly a very poor team. In fact, they were terrible. One day, a sportswriter from the *Detroit Free Press* phoned to say that at a game at the University of Detroit the night before, all the sportswriters could talk about was the team at Patronage of St. Joseph.

"How is it possible, Father, that in each of your first five games your team hasn't been able to score ten points?" (This in the era of 100-point games.)

"We're just not very good."

"Well, what is it: You don't have a gym to practice in?"

"No, we've got a fine gym."

"You don't have a coach?"

"We've got a full-time coach."

"All your guys are little, eh?"

"Our center is six foot three."

The obliging writer was trying to find a good human interest angle, but there wasn't any: The team was simply bad.

The next year the team improved slightly. They still lost all their games, but the scores were more respectable.

The final game of that season was against St. Gabriel's, whose team had tied for the division championship but for some reason had been denied a playoff position by the unanimous vote of all the other coaches.

St. Gabriel's was angry. And it had only one game remaining in which to vent its spleen. Poor little Patronage.

St. Gabriel's started the game with a full court press. Patronage had never seen a full court press . . . they had never been close enough in any game to be subjected to a full court press.

They did what came naturally in this time of stress: They kept inbounding the ball to St. Gabriel's players, who kept scoring, and scoring, and scoring.

It became obvious that St. Gabriel's was determined to get at least 100 points. The referees apparently found this unsportsman-like; they began calling peculiar fouls against St. Gabriel's. Everybody tried to stop St. Gabriel's—everybody but the Patronage team; they were still giving away the ball.

By the time the score was about 92 to 12 with only a couple of minutes left, Patronage had only four players on the court. The others were either injured or had fouled out. St. Gabriel's still had their starting five on court.

One of the Patronage four knew next to nothing about basketball, but he was a nice kid. At this point, he was awarded a foul shot.

He didn't know what to do. Of course, the Patronage kids were well aware of his lack of skill. The referee led the lad to the foul line, and pointed at the basket. The kid scored, and the fans went wild. Confetti filled the air like snow, while the St. Gabriel's players looked on in wonderment—and perplexity. But they didn't get their 100 points.

The Detroit Tigers undoubtedly could have empathized with Patronage. On the day that the Tigers ended the 2003 season having lost one game less than the record-setting New York Mets of 1962, Nancy Laughlin's headline in the *Detroit Free Press* exulted, "We're not number one!"

"Gotta keep the young ones moral after school . . . "

—MEREDITH WILLSON
The Music Man

DETERMINED TO SAVE THEIR YOUNG PEOPLE not only from the dangers of the streets, but from that other evil, rock and roll, which was just getting a toehold, many parishes inaugurated youth clubs. They hoped, thus, to protect the younguns from the mod version of Trouble Right Here in River City.

Somewhere along the way, Father Kienzle had started such a group. There was excellent attendance at the first meeting. After the election of officers, which took about five minutes, the floor was cleared for dancing. Father put on a Lawrence Welk record. Everyone sat down. He went from one teenager to the next, asking, "Can't you dance?" Each answered honestly, "No."

The Champagne Bubble music was canceled due to lack of interest. Father capitulated to rock and roll. Loud. After dances, his head would pound on the pillow—six/eight tempo.

The Youth Club escalated fun and games. The object of shuffleboard developed into trying to propel the disk through the wall. The object of Ping-Pong was to make the ball stay up in the rafters. When the group went on a hayride/wienie roast, all the food was consumed in the first ten minutes, after which the youth stood around challenging the adults to entertain them.

Father Kienzle soon learned why their parents had given them willingly into his care. And why, with few exceptions, no parent would ever consent to serve as chaperone.

One evening, while Ping-Pong balls were rattling around in the rafters, and shuffleboard disks were crashing through walls, one lad approached Father Kienzle. "You ought to see what's in the hall."

With such an invitation, Father figured he'd better go see what was in the hall.

He found a miniature premature version of Hell's Angels. Little fellows with leather jackets unzipped to the navel, displaying hairless chests, and tentatively cocky expressions.

"Waddya want?" It was Father's best Spencer-Tracy-as-Father-Flanagan bit.

"We wanna take a look," the little guy said with wavering bravado.

"Well, you've had your look. Now, blow!"

No such thing as a bad boy, eh, Flanagan?

Just beneath the surface, and not well concealed in all this youth activity was the intention to recruit. Most of the time the recruitment was subtle. Sometimes it was overt.

Occasionally, Father was asked to visit one or another parochial school and talk to the students about religious vocations. One such visit was to an elementary school in the inner city. It was about 45 percent non-Catholic and about 98 percent black.

After Father's talk in one class, a singularly uncoordinated young girl stood to ask a question. She dropped her ruler three times. "Fathah, if there is two sisters and they is sisters and they is in the same house, does one of them leave or does both of them stay?"

Father asked her to repeat the question, which she did, amazingly word for word. Finally, Father asked for a translation. Another student supplied: "If there are two blood sisters who are religious sisters and they are in the same convent, can they stay together or does one of them have to leave?"

Father answered in the fashion that would become his ready fallback in years to come. "I don't know."

After the recruitment talk in another class, a young black lad asked, "Fathah, do you gotta be a Catholic to be a priest?"

A better question now than it was then.

❧❦❧

In addition to playing teacher, athletic director, impresario, chaperone, sometime recruiter, and pre-Cana physician, Father was a stand-in when the pastor was away.

It was during his first year at Patronage that Father Kienzle was manning the phone on the evening of my fateful call. In later years, we often wondered what would have happened had Father Pomponi not taken that night off.

PART

2

And God Created an Editor . . .

ACTUALLY, WHO BUTTONS YOUR SHIRT? was not the only question I asked Father Kienzle during my instruction period.

As one evening's session came to a close, I said, "You've got such a creative brain . . . have you ever thought of writing?"

He threw back his head and laughed heartily. "No," he said, "I have no talent for that."

God and the archbishop knew better. And I had the last laugh. In April 1962, the following appeared on page one of the *Detroit Free Press.*

Inner City Priest Named New Editor

By Hiley H. Ward
Free Press Religion Writer

The Archdiocese of Detroit Thursday announced the start of four new parishes and changes in key administrative personnel.

Biggest surprise to Catholic clergy was the naming of a 33-year-old assistant priest in an Inner-City church to be editor of the influential Michigan Catholic.

* * *

The Rev. Father William X. Kienzle, new Michigan Catholic editor, has been at the Patronage of St. Joseph Church for three years. He won attention there for writing original music satires and directing productions for the Patronage of St. Joseph High School.

It all started with a phone call from the archbishop's secretary: "The Boss wants to see you."

Father Kienzle was puzzled and a whit apprehensive. What could he possibly have done—that the archbishop knew about—to merit this attention? If he'd ever thought about it—which he hadn't—he would have assumed that Archbishop Dearden couldn't have picked him out of a crowd of two. Now he was Ensign Pulver coming face to face with the captain after months of anonymous existence in the laundry department.

He knew that each June tons of priests were transferred from parish to parish, from position to position. But assistant priests— pawns in this game—weren't summoned before the throne. That honor was reserved for pastors.

Maybe, he thought, what the archbishop had in mind was to appoint him head of the Music Department at the seminary. After all, he had sung on the Schola Cantorum, knew his way around an organ, and had played piano and drums in the seminary "orchestra," such as it was. Indeed, his nickname in school was "Josey"— after José Iturbi, who had made a popular recording of De Falla's *Ritual Fire Dance*, a work that seminarian Kienzle performed at the drop of a request. Iturbi's job was never in jeopardy.

At the appointed day and time, a mystified Father Kienzle appeared at the archbishop's office as commanded.

Without preamble, the archbishop announced, "We're thinking of making an administrative change. We're making you the editor of the *Michigan Catholic*."

The archbishop kept talking, but Father Kienzle sat dumbstruck and unhearing. Possibly not since the angel appeared to the Blessed Mother had news so struck a deliveree. But where the Blessed Mother at least had the presence of mind to say, "Thy will be done," Father Kienzle sat mute as marble.

He became aware that the archbishop was winding up. " . . . so, if you have no serious objections, we will consider this done." Objections? *He didn't know how to do the job. He didn't want to do the job. He hadn't signed up to do the job.* None of which, he knew, would the archbishop consider worthy of serious note.

Ironically, Father Kienzle had been anointed editor not because of any writing skill.

It seemed that under the previous editor, for some time a bitter schism had existed at the *Michigan Catholic.* The archbishop wanted the wounds bound up. So, as the new editor would later learn, the archbishop's headhunters, in checking out Father Kienzle's qualifications, had asked not, "Can he write?" but "Can he get along with people?"

He could and did.

God said, Let there be light: and there was light. Archbishop Dearden said, Let there be an editor: and there was an editor. If ever there was a case of on-the-job training, this was it. Like the members of Professor Harold Hill's River City Boys' Band, the new editor started in to play without knowing how. And the initial results were about the same. In the former case, the cacophony almost drowned out the melody; in the latter, the misspellings almost obscured the substance.

The new editor used the word mute when what he meant was moot, referred to Pilate as Pilot,* gave someone the "coupe [champagne/dessert goblet] de grâce" instead of the coup de grâce [final blow]. He used illusive when he meant elusive, anxious when he meant eager, and demured when he should have demurred.

Didn't the *Michigan Catholic* have a copy editor? Several. But those were the days when Father Knew Best. It seemed the consensus was that if Father wrote it that way, that's the way Father wanted it. Those days as Father-Editor were the closest he ever came to being infallible.

---

* Obviously a *lapsus calami.*

Mercifully, his colleagues, both in journalism and in the priest-hood, were charitable. It's possible they just wanted to see to what ungrammatical depths he could sink, but not one ever called him on his spelling missteps. The misguided charity was epitomized by *Detroit Free Press* city editor Neal Shine, acknowledged by all to be the newspaperman's newspaperman. (This was before the era of "newspaperperson.") As he passed Father Kienzle's table at the Detroit Press Club, Neal slowed and said, "You're doing a helluva job at the *Catholic*, all things considered." It might not have been the ultimate accolade, but the greenhorn took 'em where he could get 'em.

As the next dozen years went by, his spelling improved, although never to perfection. His editorial "expertise" graduated from purely churchy topics to events that were increasingly rele-vant to all God's children. And for the most part, he learned to write shorter and pithier—even, occasionally, in parables. After all, if they were good enough for Jesus . . .

When Father Kienzle took up his new post, he moved from the rectory at Patronage to the rectory at St. Joseph's on the outskirts of downtown Detroit. St. Joseph's, known as Old St. Joseph's, had at one time served the diocese's German population. St. Joe's, like Patronage, was an old-time churchy church with lots of statuary, and a dark interior.

The pastor at St. Joseph's was Father Bresnahan, an older, red-haired man with an open personality. Father Bresnahan was deeply involved with his pet project, the Gabriel Richard Institute, named after Michigan's early priest-legislator. His involvement entailed being absent from the parish whenever he wasn't offering Mass. As the only other resident, this left young Father Kienzle alone in a cavernous old rectory whose floors creaked and whose doors squeaked, and whose pastor had better things to do than to make repairs or keep the place up.

One night during one of Father Bresnahan's numerous absences, the bathroom light went out, leaving the room pitch-dark. Unable to find a replacement bulb, Father Kienzle put a candle in the bathtub to provide illumination. It was better, he said, to light one candle than to curse Bresnahan.*

The naturally gregarious young priest, though busy learning the journalistic ropes at his new assignment, soon found himself sinking into loneliness. He phoned the archbishop's secretary: Could he move to Sacred Heart Seminary?

The archbishop said yes. And Father Kienzle was back in blessedly familiar territory. He lived in a comfortable suite, dined with classmates and older priests he had known for years, and basked in the camaraderie of his confreres. He enjoyed the theological discussions, clerical gossip, and the general give-and-take peculiar to men who share a close intramural background.

Occasionally, the priests shared meals with the students. Father Kienzle, after years of being God's Gift to Youth, felt he had done his bit and paid his dues.

He found an ally in Father Louis Grandpre, a few years younger, but every bit as loath to play childish games, or temper the conversation to the comparative callowness of the up-and-coming seminarians.

On the days when the dining was to be en masse, Father Kienzle's eyes would meet those of Father Grandpre. Father Kienzle would mouth, "Carl's?" Father Grandpre would nod. The two would excuse themselves, meet in the seminary parking lot, and head off to Carl's Chop House for a steak, a stiff drink or two, and adult conversation.

But normally, Father Kienzle especially enjoyed breakfast in the seminary surroundings. The priests agreed that they, the celibates, were luckier than married men. After all, they could dine on great

---

* A takeoff on the Christopher motto "It is better to light one candle than to curse the darkness."

food, share witty banter and adult conversation, without having to worry about being hit in the face by a spoonful of mush thrown by a screaming baby in a nearby highchair. Which led to one of Father Kienzle's humorous comments—that if ever he were to marry he'd want his wife to be incurably romantic, and sterile.

May you live in interesting times.

—CHINESE CURSE

FATHER KIENZLE WAS LIVING in the most interesting of times. Anyone who was bored in the two decades from the mid-fifties to the mid-seventies was either buried or lobotomized.

In addition to Vatican II, there was the Vietnam "conflict," Martin Luther King's crusade for equality, the Camelot years of John F. Kennedy, the landing on the moon, bra burning, draft-card burning, flag burning, and in Detroit building burning.

Father Kienzle, who professed never to have read more of a newspaper than the front page, the comics, and the sports section, was now expected, among other things, to write editorials. When Father Kienzle advised one of his former teachers of his appointment as editor, the older priest raised an eyebrow and said, "I've been around a long time, and not much surprises me anymore. But this—this surprises me."

A monsignor, on hearing the news via the clerical grapevine, phoned for details. "They didn't spend a dime on you downtown [the chancery] to get you ready for this, did they?"

"No, Monsignor, they didn't."

"Well, then it won't be your fault when you fail." Not *if*; but *when*.

A colleague at the seminary asked, "What will your editorial policy be?"

Father Kienzle didn't even know what an editorial policy *was*. But he learned. Oh boy, did he learn!

Father Kienzle was blessed. He was blessed with a supportive and truly professional staff. From the managing editor, Fran Lenhard,* on down, all were triple-threat players. Each of them could and did write, edit, and proofread. The product continued to improve, and the staff was savvy enough to catch most double entendres before they got into print.

One member of the staff, Jim Stackpoole, later became editor of Cincinnati's archdiocesan weekly, the *Catholic Telegraph*. Jim made the mistake of leaving his staff to put out the paper while he went on vacation. On his return he was confronted with the following headline: ARCHBISHOP CREATES TASK FORCE TO PROBE WOMEN IN CHURCH.

Margaret Cronyn was not only Women's Editor; her column, "Life with the Family," was a reader favorite. Later, when Father Kienzle left, Margaret stepped up to the plate as editor-in-chief and hit many journalistic home runs over the years.

During his twelve-year tenure as editor, Father Kienzle received countless invitations to journalistic junkets. Margaret Cronyn opened the morning mail and routed all pertinent matters to Father's desk. Any invitations were placed atop the pile. Father Kienzle got his morning laugh from Margaret's notations. Across the top of each and every invitation—whether it be to a Catholic Press Conference in Washington or a journalists' tour of the British Isles—Margaret had scrawled, "I'll go, I'll go!"

Father Kienzle was a man of schedule and routine. Not only his upbringing and his father's German genes were responsible; his

---

* Lenhard's word of advice to the tyro editor: Never second-guess yourself.

twelve years of seminary training reinforced this. When one rises to bells, eats to bells, goes to class to bells, prays to bells, studies to bells, and goes to bed to bells, one's system tends to have a built-in schedule. Such a schedule did not welcome the irregularities of travel. Most of the invitations went into the wastebasket.

Margaret Cronyn and her husband, Joe, had seven children. A large family—particularly if it is Irish-American—does not readily lend itself to rigid schedules. Margaret was flexible, adaptable, and had a ready sense of humor. She had to have; each of her children was an individualist. Many the caper that found its way into Margaret's "Life with the Family" column. And once the invitations were addressed to Margaret, things changed. As the former priest-editor later commented, "Margaret always said, 'I'll go, I'll go!'—and when she became editor, she went, she went."

One of the few trips Father Kienzle did take was to the Hawaiian Islands.

From Bill Kienzle's earliest memory, Father Damien had been one of his heroes. As the teenaged Bill Kienzle marched off to the seminary, visions of the apostle to the lepers accompanied him. Never underestimate the power of a saint to inspire.

Where modern-day youth have Eminem and Madonna as exemplars, Bill Kienzle and his contemporaries were imbued with the holiness and purpose of Molokai's Father Damien, Poland's Father Kolbe, and Wexford's Father Murphy.

Father Damien, who one day greeted his flock with, "Fellow lepers . . ."

Father Kolbe, who offered his life in place of a fellow concentration camp inmate who was to be put to death.

Father Murphy, who, after rallying his people against British brutality, was tortured on the rack. Legend has it that though his body was reduced to ashes after the British burned him alive, his right arm, which had been raised to bless his people, remained whole and uncharred.

As a young priest, Father Kienzle traveled to Molokai. He knelt before the cross that is the memorial to Father Damien. The cross bears the inscription: "Greater love hath no man than this: That a man lay down his life for his friends."

He often mused on Father Damien's life and work. He never ceased to marvel at Damien's dedication. I got the impression that he found himself wanting in that he could never have put himself so far away from civilization, as Father Damien had. He could never, he said, have been a missionary priest. But he admired immensely those who were called to that service.

If nothing else, he was a well-balanced person—as priest or otherwise. While in Oahu, he developed a taste for Mai-Tais, saw Don Ho perform, and watched as one of the locals danced up a hula-storm, Tahiti-style. "No haole* could do it," Father's host commented.

In by 10, out by 4

—Sign in cleaning establishment

My checkered career had included stints as a Girl Friday in a detective agency, a legal secretary in New Jersey and Michigan, and a travel agent. With no previous journalistic experience other than writing for my high school newspaper, I applied for a secretarial position at the *Detroit Free Press*.

Timing combined with luck. My application was entered immediately after a long strike had decimated the newspaper's staff. In somewhat the same way that God said Let there be light, and Archbishop Dearden said Let there be an editor, I was picked out of the applicant pool and put in charge of the television listings

---

* white person; foreigner

department. I too was now an editor—of sorts. My job was to over-see the log clerks, edit and copy-edit the weekly TV magazine and the daily TV listings, write thumbnail descriptions of the pro-grams, including the films, and try to make sure there were no errors in the mishmash of local and network schedules.

Not only did our department have daily and weekly deadlines, due to the humors of the intensely unionized printers in the com-posing room we had almost hourly deadlines. This was the pre-computer era. We typed copy, sent it to composing to be retyped on the Linotype, were given galleys, proofread the galleys, and sent them back to composing to be set, and if we were lucky we might even see the final page proof before everything went to press.

I quickly grew to admire and respect the printers and their work. They were true craftsmen in an art that went down the drain with the advent of computer technology. A few were tempermen-tal; a couple could be downright nasty. But most of them were the salt of the earth.

It was a Golden Age at the *Free Press*. The paper was considered the flagship of the Knight organization. The chain's *Miami Herald* brought in the ad revenue that subsidized the *Free Press*'s crusading journalistic image. The poststrike staff was a mixture of old-time professionals, up-and-coming journalistic stars (some lured from other newspapers by the *Free Press*'s reputation), recent journalism grads . . . and a few novices like me.

Mort Persky, in charge of Features, was responsible for my hir-ing. I will always be grateful that Mort saw talent in me that I didn't know I had. His eye for talent brought to the Features Department such writers of excellence as drama critic Larry DeVine, one of the best and wittiest[*] journalists to ever sit at a typewriter; Mike Gormley, a shy young Canadian who reviewed

---

[*] Larry once referred to *Last Tango in Paris* as "the film that made Pauline Kael famous."

rock music and now has his own music management firm; and Susan Stark, a film critic who was arguably the equal of Pauline Kael in quality of discernment.

With people such as these, and those already on board—class writers like entertainment writer Chuck Thurston, Hollywood columnist Shirley Eder, book editor Barbara Holliday, Metro columnists Judd Arnett, Mark Beltaire, and Bob Talbert—Mort Persky had a winning team. This was due not only to the basic talent of these people but also to Mort's talent in inspiring all of us to play over our heads for him. The *Free Press* was the better for it.

One of the hardest-working people in Features was Jeanne Findlater, who helped put the paper's Sunday magazine together. Jeanne went on to become the first female head of a major television station—WXYZ-TV, the local ABC affiliate.

I use the adjective "class" in describing these people, because each was, in his or her own truly inimitable way, above all, decent. At one point, Shirley Eder was asked to write a book about Hollywood, which she knew inside and out. She regretfully turned down the offer, because, she said, "They want me to dish the dirt, and I won't do it." Compare that with the un-integrity of any of a hundred of today's media gossipmongers.

Aware of the rumors about Rock Hudson, I once asked Shirley Eder, "Is he really homosexual?" "Yes," she replied, "but he's such a sweet guy." For once I felt the infamous comment applied: What a waste!

Chuck Thurston made an art out of writing kindly while still managing to be factual about visiting performers. I once asked Chuck to name, in his opinion, the nicest of the performers. His response was immediate: Jimmy Durante, who, Chuck said, was an all-round nice guy.

Chuck's reportage was not reserved for his newspaper column. He was a bull's-eye commentator on life in general. After a fairly zaftig reporter made her way past his desk one day, Chuck was overheard to say to no one in particular, "N——— doesn't buy a new wardrobe—she just gets reupholstered."

Unlike too many later "journalists," most of our writers were not only literate but were grounded in the classics. George Cantor, our boy-next-door travel writer, had spent some years as a sports columnist. During his tenure in that category, he waited in vain for the advent of a baseball player who would be named Chapman and who would hit at least one home run. Because, George said, he had always wanted to start a column with "On first looking into Chapman's homer" (from the Keats sonnet of the same name).

Bob Talbert, while having very definite opinions, never refused to listen to someone else's viewpoint. For some years, his desk was next to mine. Those were the days before answering machines; we each took our own phone calls. I never ceased to be amazed at Bob's open-mindedness and patience. People would phone who were obviously riled about something Bob had written or something they wanted him to write. I never once heard him hang up on anyone. He would listen politely, without argument, and then calmly say something like, "Well, I don't agree with that . . . but thank you for calling and letting me know how you feel."

Bob had a vocabulary that could fry an elephant's hide. But his vulgarisms were used in conversational narrative, never against callers. Film critic Susan Stark could hold her own in this category, and we all got a chuckle the day Susan announced that she was taking up a collection to get Bob Talbert to clean up his language.

Another Free Presser who was less flamboyant, but equally as unflappable as Talbert was photojournalist Ken Hamblin. Actually, Ken, now famous as a talk show host[*] and filmmaker, was one of the most quietly self-possessed individuals I have ever met.

In an era when "soul" was coming into use with regard to black culture, the term was thrown about loosely by those who considered themselves—but were not always—au courant. One day, in the elevator, someone was kidding Ken about the sweater he was wearing, which had a couple of holes in it. Ken sloughed off the

[*] He has been called the black Rush Limbaugh.

comments. When Ken and I were alone in the elevator, I started kidding him. "You and your 'soul,'" I said, gesturing at the holes in his sweater.

Ken, unsmiling, looked at me for a moment, then said evenly, rather like a teacher enlightening a student, "You whites will never understand soul."

Somewhat taken aback, yet aware that there was something here for me to learn, I asked, "Okay, Ken, tell me: What *is* soul?"

"Soul," he replied, "is surviving."

Don't stop the presses!

I NEVER GOT OVER BEING IN AWE of my surroundings. Each morning when I entered the building, I mentally pinched myself to make sure I wasn't dreaming. Here was I, a little country girl who'd never even had a journalism course, and I was an *editor.* And an editor at not just any newspaper, but an editor at the *Detroit Free Press*, which in my mind, was second only to the *New York Times.*

I didn't really consider myself a journalist; I wouldn't have been that presumptuous. My coworkers were journalists; I was an impostor . . . there under false pretenses. If it hadn't been for the timing—putting in my application right after a long, devastating strike—I'd have ended up as a secretary at the beck and call of one of the inhabitants of a middle-management suite.

Instead here I was, hiring my own staff of three, setting standards for a newly revamped *TV Listings* magazine, and trying to act as if I knew what I was doing. At first, I didn't. But, like Father Kienzle, I learned. There is nothing like on-the-job training.

The Features Department, comprising the columnists and entertainment writers, was on the fifth floor. The City Room—the Holy of Holies—was on the third floor. The people in the City Room—they were the *real* journalists. It was, Neal Shine said years later, "a time in the life of the *Free Press* when everybody in the newsroom was a dream of a writer." The old-timers were already legends, the up-and-comers—*investigative* reporters—would go on to write prize-winning articles, find new positions on papers like the *New York Times* and the *Washington Post*, and become editors of other newspapers throughout the country.

Neal Shine, then city editor, headed a *Free Press* team that had won a Pulitzer for its coverage of the 1967 Detroit riots. Years later, Neal would become publisher of the *Free Press*, conquer Hodgkin's Lymphoma, and live through one of the longest, most viscerally nasty strikes in newspaper history. Neal was made of stern stuff; either the cancer or the strike could've destroyed a lesser man. But his Irish genes stood him in good stead. Coming from a people who had survived almost a thousand years of a brutal occupation, Neal, probably the most beloved figure in all of Detroit journalism, survived to retire and enjoy well-deserved golden years with his wife and family.

As I said, I was in total awe of my surroundings. The romance of the newspaper field had infected me. Growing up in the countryside in the pre-TV era, for me radio and newspapers were the mediums of entertainment and information. Poor farmers, we couldn't afford a daily paper. But the O'Reillys, who lived half a mile down the road, subscribed to the *New York Journal American*. My parents, arrant liberals, wouldn't have been caught dead reading such a "right-wing rag." The O'Reillys felt sorry for my sister and me—after all, we were growing up without benefit of the Sunday comics. An agreement was struck: I could walk down to the O'Reillys' farm every Sunday afternoon and pick up the comics. To this day, I am a fan of Prince Valiant . . . and I often wonder how many people, absent Lerner and Loewe, would have known about Camelot if not for Prince Valiant.

After I married, I made up for lost time: Sunday mornings were spent in bed reading at least three newspapers, one of which was the *New York Herald Tribune*. I still remember my sorrow when the *Herald Tribune* died; it was like losing a member of the family.

There are some public events that, though they happened long ago, still have the power to raise extreme emotion. For me, the death of the *Herald Tribune* was one such event. Another—shared by so many Brooklyn fans—was Bobby Thomson's home run.

Jews for centuries had prayed, "Next year in Jerusalem." The Brooklyn version, from fans who so often had seen their beloved Bums end up always the bridesmaid but never the bride, was "Wait till next year!"

And this was "next year"; by early August 1951, the Dodgers were leading the second-place New York Giants in the pennant race by some 13 games. But, in a scuffling, scrapping, snarling, never-say-die effort, the gritty Giants, game by game, pulled out of the pit, until, on the last day of the regular season, the two teams were deadlocked in first place.

Now, on October 3, the Giants came to bat in the bottom of the ninth inning of the last in a so far split best-of-three playoff series. The Dodgers, leading 4–1, were about to take all the marbles on to the World Series. But the Giants, as they had through the recent grueling weeks, fought back. They scored one run and put the tying runs on base. With one out, Ralph Branca pitched to Bobby Thomson—and in one of the greatest moments in sports the "Staten Island Scot" slammed the ball into the stands.

Even now, I can call up the sick feeling that spread through my body as I sat glued to the radio while fellow Dodgers fans shriveled in shock and disbelief at what came to be known as "the shot heard 'round the world."

Decades later, accompanying Bill on a book tour in the Northeast, in a motel at Newark Airport, I turned on the *Today Show* to see the familiar *Free Press* masthead, and heard the announcement of the Joint Operating Atrocity with the archenemy *Detroit News*. I felt as if a mule had kicked me in the stomach. Journalism in Detroit would never be the same. Indeed, with the proliferation of JOAs in almost every major city throughout the country, journalism in the entire United States would never be the same.

Early on at the *Free Press*, I watched as a bunch of high schoolers was shown through our department on an educational tour. The group stopped in front of the desk of Arnold Rosenfeld, who was typing away on deadline. "Tell me," one of the young men asked, "what is the most important thing to know about this business?" Without looking up, without missing a typing beat, Arnold replied, "Knowing who to blame when something goes wrong."

I doubt that Arnold, who went on to became a member of the Pulitzer committee, remembers saying that, but I never forgot the occasion.

Despite all, my romantic idealistic notions of newspaperdom never really left. Each morning when I entered the Free Press Building, I felt that I was one of the luckiest people in the world. As I carried my coffee cup to my desk, I could hear a single Linotype striking away in the composing room. As the day wore on, one by one, it would be joined by the other Linotypes, until there was a steady syncopated clack of background noise. It was like a heartbeat . . . and I gloried in every minute of it. Then, when the giant presses rolled with the early edition, and the building reverberated with their juggernaut momentum, the heartbeat was like the heartbeat of the entire planet. I felt part of that heartbeat. And no words could fully convey the depth of that feeling.

Never open mail with large writing or block letters before lunch.

—CHUCK THURSTON

IN AN ODD WAY, my path as editor was paralleling Father Kienzle's. It was apples and oranges, of course, but we were in the same ballpark so to speak. I was listing events, he was editorializing about them. We each became conversant with newspaper jargon—fonts, widows, overset, galleys. We each learned to crop photos, to write headlines and captions, to cut and punch up, to eschew obfuscation and redundancy.

Father Kienzle, of course, had a publisher to deal with directly. I knew the Knight publisher only from his photograph. Father Kienzle had reams of angry letters to deal with; I had only the occasional fussbudget. Once, in print, I attributed *Show Boat* to Rodgers and Hammerstein, whereas it was, as a reader pointed out, Kern and Hammerstein. She was correct; how could I have forgotten? Another time, one of the TV log clerks, capsulizing *Zorba, the Greek* wrote that "Zorba lives life the way we would all like to." That brought a scathing letter from a woman reader who disagreed vehemently: "That is *not* the way I want to live my life!"

Father Kienzle, on the other hand, heard from Catholics who had such antipathy to Vatican II that they seriously felt that Pope John XXIII, its progenitor, should have been strangled in his cradle . . . and that Father Kienzle should have his collar pulled so tight that his eyes would pop out of his head.

G. K. Chesterton said that if an editor can only make people angry enough, they will write half his newspaper for him. The *Michigan Catholic* staff got to know the "regulars"; the staff could gauge with some exactitude how many letters they would receive— and from whom—after a specific editorial was published. One conservative gentleman in the Toledo area sent so many letters, and was published so rarely that he finally wrote and asked why the editor was keeping *Michigan Catholic* readers from receiving the benefit of his wisdom. Father Kienzle wrote back, "Because yOu write yOur wOrds with all yOur O's capitalized." (Which was so.) The gentleman later took out an ad, offering a collection of "Unpublished Letters to the *Michigan Catholic*" for $1.00.

When it came to dealing with critics, Father Kienzle received a helpful lesson from Otto Preminger.

Preminger was touring the United States to promote his latest movie, *The Cardinal*, an adaptation of Henry Morton Robinson's best-selling novel, starring Tom Tryon in the title role.

In Detroit, Preminger addressed a group of media people. He spoke of how hard a filmmaker works to get everything just right . . . to make the film as good as he possibly can. Then, he said, the film is sent out to theaters all over the country, where all too often it is shown on a screen that is pitted with age and on a sound system that sputters. As a result, the visual and audio quality of the film suffers, which affects the viewer's perception of the film itself.

Addressing his audience directly, Preminger waxed blunt about critics. "If you like my films, I'm glad," he said. "If you don't like them, I ignore you." In Preminger's accent, the verb came out closer to "iknore"; in any case, the disdain was evident.

Afterward, the director came up to Father Kienzle, looked at him approvingly, and endeared himself by saying, "You could have played the part."

Sometimes "No" is an answer.

AT THE TIME THE NOVICE TOOK OVER AS EDITOR, the *Michigan Catholic* had a number of columnists, whose offerings were scattered throughout the paper. Father Kienzle had discovered what an editorial page was, now he would discover what an op-ed page was. The various columns were gathered from throughout the paper and collected on one page. No sooner was this done than it became all too evident that there was not a conservative in the bunch. If Father Kienzle was in the so-called liberal camp, still he would not err in denying the opposition a voice. The search for a conservative—or at least a traditional columnist or two began.

Then there came to the editor what he considered a stroke of near genius. He knew the perfect choice for the traditional-cum-conservative op-ed columnist. It was tantalizing . . . but so provocative that some sixth sense—or an angel on his shoulder—told him that he'd better get an okay from the publisher before going ahead.

He called Monsignor Imesch—Archbishop Dearden's secretary—and requested that the idea be put before the archbishop. Monsignor Imesch promised to approach the archbishop, but he felt that some preparation was required.

All was silence for several days. Then Father Kienzle got a phone call from Monsignor Imesch.

"Bill, I did it. I waited till after dinner when he was relaxed and feeling expansive. He'd had his favorite meal—lamb. He had his favorite drink—a Rob Roy. He was leaning back with an all's-right-with-the-world expression. And I said, 'Your Excellency, Father Kienzle would like to ask Father Coughlin to do a column for the *Michigan Catholic.'*

"He shot bolt upright, slammed his hand on the table, and snapped, 'NO!!'"

In the ecclesial version of Madison Avenue's "Let's run it up the flagpole and see who salutes," Father Kienzle's idea had been shot down without benefit of salutation.

Give advance notice if you are to engage in any form of irony.

—Unknown

Where I was learning not to allow editorialization to creep into the *TV Listings*, Father Kienzle was learning not to take his readers' sense of humor for granted. During one period, he wrote an editorial about the Anglo-Irish problems. Trying to make a point, he utilized satire, setting forth a view of the situation in the north as seen by the English. Of course it was skewed and exaggerated; as I say, he was trying to make a point.

Law and Order, the Wonder of It All

What Northern Ireland needs, most obviously, is law and order. It needs this, most obviously, because it hasn't got law or order.

The ones responsible for this breakdown in law and order are the Irish Catholics of Ulster. They are the ones responsible for the unrest of Northern Ireland. They are the ones who break up patriotic parades celebrating past Protestant victories over Catholics.

They are the ones who protest discrimination directed against them in voting, housing, and work. It is true that they are discriminated against in voting, housing, and work, but then they are not the majority in Northern Ireland. Protestants form the majority.

Protestants know that Catholics destroy neighborhoods. You can see it for yourself in the slums of Londonderry. If they were allowed to live in neat Protestant neighborhoods, property values would deteriorate in weeks, months at best.

If Catholics were content to remain in their own neighborhoods, Protestants would not be forced to invade these neighborhoods during periods of Catholic-caused strife and burn down Catholic bars.

Besides, if Catholics had any respect for property at all, would they be throwing firebombs in factories and offices? Pictures of these atrocities on TV and in newspapers should prove to the world that Catholics have no respect for property and must be suppressed in their attempts to move into good Protestant neighborhoods.

Of course Irish Catholics are not given responsible jobs in Northern Ireland. But that is because, as everyone knows, they are a shiftless people. They do not and cannot hold responsible positions at work.

Protestant members of Parliament would have the good sense and good taste to know their place was at the seat of government, especially during civil upheaval. But elect a Catholic like Bernadette Devlin to Parliament and you'll find her at

Catholic barricades, as you did last week, urging her Catholic constituents on to violence.

Would you like Bernadette Devlin living next to you? Marrying your son?

Catholics in Northern Ireland are second-class citizens. How many centuries will it take them to learn this? How many ways do they have to be told?

There is nothing wrong with this. Ulster Catholics are a minority. If they do not like the way they are treated in Northern Ireland, they can always go south. There they will find hospitality.

What difference does it make that they leave their homes? What difference does it make that they cannot live where they chose [sic]? They are free to go if they wish. And if they go there will be law and order.

Or, they can stay in Northern Ireland if they wish, as long as they are quiet and stop pushing for equal opportunity in housing, jobs, and the vote. If they do this there will be law and order.

In any case, and whatever the Catholics do, England's army is there to enforce law and order. And when they leave, the Protestant police of Northern Ireland will remain to enforce law and order.

What has not yet occurred to enough people either in Northern Ireland or the United States is justice.

This editorial had, in a limited way, somewhat the same effect as "A Modest Proposal for Preventing the Children of Ireland from being a Burden to their Parents or Country," wherein Jonathan Swift, tongue firmly in cheek, suggested that Irish babies be "stewed, roasted, baked, or boiled [or served] in a fricassee, or a ragout."

All hell broke loose. Michigan's Irish, with pens as sharp as their tongues, aimed both at Father Kienzle. They didn't realize that Mary Louise Boyle's son was *not* on the side of the English.

In response, the following week's editorial opened with, "It was a satire. It was a satire. It was a satire." And Father Kienzle went on to explain:

It attempted, through irony, to illustrate the false concept of law and order. The idea was, to get apparently necessarily pedantic, that it is unjust to enforce injustice through law and order.

Clearly, in Northern Ireland, Catholics have been subjected to unjust discrimination for centuries. They have been denied voting, housing, and working rights to which they are, as citizens and humans, entitled.

For years they have petitioned, by relatively peaceful means, [for] the rights which are inherently theirs. The strife and violence that Northern Ireland now endures is the consequence of the Protestant majority's absolute and stubborn refusal to grant them their rights.

The point of the editorial, the purpose of its satirical style, was that the words and manner of Ian Paisley and the reasoning of the Protestant majority of Northern Ireland are the selfsame words, manner, and reasoning of those in this country afflicted with prejudice toward our minorities.

Substitute "black" for "Catholic" in Mr. Paisley's harangues and the general treatment of Catholics in Northern Ireland and you may see more clearly the condition of discriminated minorities in America and, for that matter, the world.

During the past week we have received many, many calls and letters (you don't have to keep them coming) from distraught, angry and incredulous Irish people who missed the satire of the editorial and took it all quite seriously.

They were incensed, and rightfully if one forgets it was a satire, to see Catholics of Northern Ireland called "second-class citizens," "shiftless" and told to leave if they disliked their treatment.

This righteous anger, if it were projected to those needlessly persecuted in this country, might help us better understand what we do to our brothers who are the "wrong" color, creed or origin. No one, be he white or black, can endure insults to his race.

The anger and insult you have felt so deeply for a moment is experienced by others day after day.

Is anything worth that measure of hurt?

Father Kienzle, in making his point, might have mentioned English historian Edward A. Freeman's pertinent statement. Freeman, bemoaning the fact that Irish-Americans had done much to sour relations between his country and the United States, concluded that "the best remedy for whatever was amiss would be if every Irishman should kill a negro and be hanged for it."

The more things change, the more they remain the same. Decades later, then-Oakland County (Michigan) Prosecutor L. Brooks Patterson proposed—undoubtedly tongue-in-cheek*—that one solution for Detroit's crime wave would be to "let half of Detroit kill the other half and then put the surviving half in prison."

Cheer, cheer, for old Notre Dame . . .

WHEN FATHER KIENZLE'S APPOINTMENT AS EDITOR was announced, a fellow priest raised his eyebrows—in an expression similar to that of Ike's on hearing of Truman's firing of General MacArthur—and said approvingly, "He's got balls."

---

* Although with Brooks Patterson, one could never be sure.

Though he was considered too liberal by some, in actuality, he was quite traditional in many ways. In any case, once the editorial visor was placed on his head, he stepped up to bat fearlessly. Over the years, in effect, he moved from near center to left of center, but not radically so. Initially, he felt that it was not necessary for Martin Luther King, Jr., to lead demonstrations; after all, the United States was a nation of laws, and those laws protected everyone, including the Negroes. Later, he came to see the justification for King's actions and admired King's willingness to go to jail for his beliefs.

In contrast, Father Kienzle felt that many of the young people who were taking over universities, throwing rocks, and generally making their presence problematical, were deficient in that after breaking the law, they wanted amnesty.

His feelings came out clearly in an editorial entitled "N.D. and Loyal Sons":

Fr. Theodore Hesburgh, president of the University of Notre Dame, said it "clearly and unequivocally" last Monday. Indeed, he socked it to 'em.

He warned those who would disrupt campus life that they would have: a) 15 minutes to think it over, b) Then face suspension or expulsion, or c) possible arrest.

Notre Dame actually has not been subject to siege as have been so many other American colleges. There was a mini revolution at Notre Dame several months ago and, at that time, Fr. Hesburgh put the matter in the hands of the student government. Which body put down the revolution promptly.

It was from this decision, from consultation with other students, faculty and alumni that the above battle plans were drawn. And we have no doubt at all that Fr. Hesburgh fully intends to follow this a, b, c procedure.

It is good for young men, bent on insurrection, to know the price that must be paid. And even more important for them to pay it.

The New Left is an overwhelming drag on the cause of freedom. They do not deal in thought, they present a series of non-negotiable demands. They do not foster freedom, they deny rights. They do not stand proudly for what they do, they beg amnesty.

Perhaps the New Left should form its own diviversity [sic]. Ruleless, rudderless, without discipline or grades, with neither curriculum nor graduation, with license instead of freedom. It would contribute nothing to anyone and everyone would be poorer for it.

Those acquainted with Fr. Hesburgh know him as a true champion of academic freedom. He has as few hang-ups on freedom as any reasonable man. He will fight, and he has fought, for the free expression of any idea on campus. And Notre Dame has been the scene of some fairly weird convocations.

But when someone says, "This university must stop thinking until it thinks my way," freedom is lost, a greater oppression may come and a school of ideas has become the antithesis of itself.

Meanwhile, back at the academic battlements, the administrations of Columbia, San Francisco, Berkeley, etc., might take a page from the playbook of Notre Dame and win one, even if reluctantly, for the Gipper.

By and large, Father Kienzle's was the voice of moderation. That was his style. Initially, at least, he stayed pretty much inside the box, as evidenced by the fact that the Michigan Knights of Columbus gave him their 1963 Journalism Award.

But there were glimmerings. As time went by, the glimmerings became more illuminative, his voice became more informed, and the envelope did get pushed.

Under Kienzle, the *Michigan Catholic* wasn't a house paper.

—Monsignor F. Gerald Martin

Frequently, a man is known by his enemies. Father Kienzle had broad shoulders, literally and figuratively. He could take the flak not only from readers who left no stone unthrown but also from those members of the clergy who insisted on remaining back in "The Thirteenth, the Greatest of Centuries." One such confrere, a man so portly that his abdomen preceeded him around corners, persisted in referring to the *Michigan Catholic* as "that impediment to thought."

As fate would have it, God called him home before he had a chance either to change his mind about the *Michigan Catholic* or to go on a much-needed diet.

In those days priests were buried in their vestments, hands clasping their chalice. Unfortunately, in this case, Father's stomach protruded to such a degree that his hands refused to stay in position. The mortician fixed that: He stuffed several handy copies of the *Michigan Catholic* beneath the casket lining under Father's elbows, thereby keeping Father's arms in a holding position. Thus Father and his chalice went on into eternity accompanied by "that impediment to thought."

Occasionally, even the publisher—Cardinal Dearden—found fault with his peerless priest-editor. This happened when, after consultation with some theologian confreres, Father Kienzle wrote an editorial accusing two U.S. Cardinals of a form of heresy known as tutiorism. It may have been confusing to the lay reader, but the editor had done his homework, and the handful of cognoscenti who read the editorial knew he had hit the nail on the head.

The Cardinal, however, like Queen Victoria, was not amused. Father Kienzle was called on the carpet.

He went prepared with documentation, including incriminating quotes from the prelates in question. The Cardinal was somewhat taken aback, along the lines of "He said *that?*"

"Yes, Your Eminence."

Still the Cardinal was a member of the Club . . . and two of his colleagues had been attacked in his very own diocesan newspaper: Would Father Kienzle retract his editorial?

Father Kienzle would not.

At this point Cardinal Dearden might well have replaced Father Kienzle with a more compliant editor. It is the rare prelate-publisher who would not have done so. But John Cardinal Dearden, who had arrived in Detroit with the well-earned sobriquet of "Iron John," had a virtue possessed by very few—a virtue much valued by Father Kienzle: He had a rare ability to co-exist with views opposed to his own.

At this impasse, Cardinal Dearden asked merely, "What are we going to do about this?"

Father Kienzle suggested that the Cardinal write an article disagreeing with his editor's conclusions. This would run on page one of the following week's issue.

The article was delivered to Father Kienzle at the offices of the *Michigan Catholic*. In it, the Cardinal called his editor "theologically naive." Shortly thereafter, Father Kienzle received a phone call from the Cardinal, who asked in a tone of some concern, "I wasn't too hard on you, was I, Father?"

The Cardinal could not see Father Kienzle smile. "No, Your Eminence, you weren't."

Another learning experience was being plunged into the periodic negotiations with the unions associated with journalism, which was tough enough for a tyro—but when the *Michigan Catholic*'s maintenance man joined the Teamsters, another faction was added to the fracas.

Teamsters headquarters was within the boundaries of Holy Trinity and the church was their "pet."

Holy Trinity's pastor, Monsignor Clement Kern, ministered to the dregs, the poor, the down-and-out panhandlers. And somehow, whenever help was needed, Monsignor Kern appeared on the scene—no matter the venue. Detroiters still recall with a smile the newsphoto of Monsignor Kern marching with the Bunnies who were picketing the Playboy Club in a battle for higher wages.

Many, both in and out of the Church, considered Monsignor Kern a living saint.

Father Kienzle, who was a largely unwilling player in the negotiating game, discovered that whenever the Teamsters negotiated a new contract, they asked Monsignor Kern to say a Mass for their intentions.

Father Kienzle phoned Monsignor Kern. "Monsignor, will you let me know when you're saying a Mass for the Teamsters so I can say one for the *Michigan Catholic*?" Father knew that his comparative holiness couldn't approach that of Monsignor Kern, but he hoped that his Mass might at least neutralize Kern's—as least insofar as the *Michigan Catholic* maintenance man's Teamster contract was concerned.

If a friend cries in front of me, I consider it a gift.

—UNKNOWN

I WAS WORKING IN A LAW FIRM when Martin Luther King, Jr., was killed. Father Kienzle phoned the next morning. I could tell he was deeply affected. Still, I was surprised when he said, "There are tears streaming down my cheeks." That this highly disciplined and extremely self-controlled man confided this may have evidenced his own surprise.

That afternoon, as I was going to lunch, a black woman got in the elevator with me. Strangers, we did not speak to each other. I wanted so much to hug her and say, "I'm sorry; I'm so sorry."

Instead, we rode in silence to the lobby. To this day, I still feel shame that I didn't express my sorrow to her.

That same type of emotion was with me in the days after the WTC bombings when Americans of Arab descent were being attacked.*

Recalling how I had wanted to apologize to the black woman for what whites had done to the man who was a black Christ figure to his people, I did the only thing I could think of: I bought a bouquet of flowers and took them to our neighborhood gas station. I handed them to the startled Middle Eastern man behind the counter and said, "We've been getting our gas from you for years, but we've never told you how glad we are that you're here."

Then there was the Vietnam War. I can recall early on arguing with Father Kienzle. "How can you back what the United States is doing in Vietnam? We're slaughtering people, and our own boys are getting killed for nothing." I was particularly aware of this because the war had escalated to the point that unless something was done, eventually my son would be at risk.

One evening, my dad, my son, and I got into a discussion of the antiwar demonstrations. I was against the war, but I was also unsympathetic with some of the more extreme student demonstrations. I said to my son, "If you go to jail for throwing rocks, don't come to me for help." My father, who joined in peace marches and contributed to antiwar causes, reached over and patted Mike's knee. "It's all right, Mike; if you get arrested, you call me; *I'll* help you." For the first time I understood the meaning of the term "generation gap"; the gap was between parent and child, *not* between grandparent and grandchild.

Some of my maternal ancestors were Quakers. I had tried to bring Mike up in that pacific culture. As the time grew closer where he would have to make a decision about the military, I told him, "Mike, if you have to go in, I hope you go as a medic. I could

---

* In one case, a Sikh, mistaken for a Muslim, was killed.

live with your death if you died trying to help someone; I couldn't live with it if you died killing someone."

My dearest friend was an American who lived in Canada. "If the time comes, you can stay with Lynn," I told Mike. He shook his head. "No. If it comes to that, I won't run away. I'll go to jail."

I mentally shook my head. I was proud of him, but I thought, "Child, you have no idea what jail would be like; you don't know what you'd be letting yourself in for." Fortunately, he never had to make that decision.

As for Father Kienzle, comparing his early editorials with his later editorials, it is obvious that he made a 180-degree turn on Vietnam. I like to think that I contributed to that, and when it happened, I was relieved for many reasons, not the least of which was that I never was able to understand how such an intelligent man could have such a blind spot. But at the time, he was in the company of many otherwise intelligent people.

If you want to know what kind of a husband a man will make, look at the way he treats his mother.

—UNKNOWN

FATHER KIENZLE LOVED, HONORED, AND RESPECTED his parents. That love was returned fullfold. Not only did his parents love him, they were proud of him, both as a son and as a priest.

Alphonse Kienzle died in January 1967. He was eighty years old and had suffered an intestinal blockage. His son visited him in the hospital. In place of the kind and gentle man he had known, his father under medication was roaring and angry, and had to be restrained in his bed. It was a harrowing sight, one William Kienzle never forgot.

Father Kienzle and his priest classmates concelebrated Alphonse Kienzle's Funeral Mass at Holy Redeemer, where the young Father Kienzle had offered his first Mass thirteen years before. Alphonse's fragile widow, suffering from osteoporosis, was supported by her daughters as she made her sorrowful way down the church aisle behind her husband's coffin.

The night before the funeral, with Alphonse Kienzle laid out in the Hackett Funeral Home, Mary Louise asked her son, "When are we going to have the Rosary?"

Her son, fresh from adjusting to Vatican II's graduation from the traditional to the modern, said, "We're not having a Rosary, Ma; we're having a Bible Vigil."

"But I want the Rosary."

"Ma, you'll like the Bible Vigil. It'll be good; you'll see. You'll like it."

A few minutes later, his mother approached her son with the same question, and was patiently given the identical answer.

Sometime after that, his mother, concerned, again spoke to her son. "You've been here all afternoon and you haven't had anything to eat. Why don't you go get something to eat? It's all right; the girls will be here with me."

In the face of her insistence, Father Kienzle left to get something to eat.

On his return, he discovered that immediately upon his departure, his mother had gone across the street to Holy Redeemer, where she had corralled a Redemptorist, who willingly came to the funeral parlor and led all there in saying the Rosary for Alphonse Kienzle.

Later that evening, Father Kienzle watched as his mother, the only other person now present, went up to the coffin, bent and kissed her husband's still face, and said, "Good night, my darling; I'll see you in the morning."

At which, her stalwart son wept.

One year and six weeks later, Mary Louise Boyle Kienzle, having just finished lunch, stood up to leave the table, and fell forward, dead.

Her son, who had faithfully visited his mother every week and more, led the Rosary at her wake.

When he spoke of his mother afterward, he said simply, "She was always in my corner."

Archbishop: A Christian ecclesiastic of a rank superior to that attained by Christ.

—H. L. MENCKEN

JUST AS SO MANY AMERICANS of a certain age recall where they were and what they were doing when the Japanese attacked Pearl Harbor, when Roosevelt died, when John F. Kennedy was shot, Detroiters remember where they were and what they were doing when they first discovered that Detroit was burning.

The 1967 riots were an education for anyone who had eyes to see, ears to hear, and a heart to learn.

I recall taking the bus to work, riding past uniformed National Guardsmen patrolling with their weapons at the ready. When I got off the bus in the center of downtown Detroit, I had to walk across an open square surrounded by skyscrapers. I felt as if I had a target pasted on my back; anyone in any window of any of those skyscrapers could take me out with a single bullet.

The National Guard was bivouacked on the grounds of Sacred Heart Seminary, which was in the heart of riot country. The priests were reasonably safe from the rioters; their collars protected them. But occasionally, bullets flew, and there were times that the residents of the seminary—including Father Kienzle—hit the deck in fear that a stray bullet wouldn't take note of their collar.

The neighborhood's residents didn't let any grass grow under their feet. Overnight, the face and hands of the statue of Jesus in front of the seminary were painted black. In a reactive move, seminary representatives painted over the black, restoring the Christ's white "skin." Then, cooler, more understanding heads prevailed: Under the heading of We get the message, the seminary repainted

Jesus, again giving Him a black face and hands. And so He has remained to this day.

Detroit's reaction to the burning, looting, and rioting ranged from total sympathy to total antipathy. The Church of course, tried to help those who needed help. Collections were taken up, and food and clothing poured into the Church's inner-city collection points. One of the bishops who was caring but not particularly relevant, stopped by one of these collection points. Inside were cartons and piles of clothing and bedding. On a separate table was a mountain of shoes. Seated at the table was a small black boy, assigned to match each shoe with its mate.

The bishop walked over and stood next to the boy. Thinking to establish some rapport, he asked the lad, "Do you know who I am?" Wordlessly, the boy shook his head. "I'm Bishop ———," our man said.

The lad looked up at him. "No shit!"

Possibly priests should periodically be reminded of the precept that trial attorneys have drummed into them: Never ask a question that you don't already know the answer to.

Saginaw's Bishop Untener spoke of addressing a group of children during a confirmation ceremony. Trying to explain the meaning of Pentecost and the tongues of fire, he asked if any of the youngsters had ever been in a tornado. One lad raised his hand. "And what happened?" the bishop asked. "It blew the f—kin' roof off the house!" was the reply. And somewhere in the audience, two parents undoubtedly tried to slide under the pew, and wondered why they hadn't used birth control.

"What did you do then?" the bishop was asked later.

"We broke into 'Come Holy Ghost, Creator Blest . . . '"

Bishop Untener was one of Bill's favorites. Shortly after being installed the new bishop participated in a baptism ceremony. In conclusion, he held up the newly baptized baby girl to the throng of family and friends. "I'm new at this," he said, "I don't know—I may have ordained her."

Bishop Untener was a bishop who truly cared for his flock and took seriously the mandate, "Feed my sheep." An order went out through the Saginaw diocese: How will whatever action you take affect the poor?"

Bill felt that the mindset of a bishop was a wonder to behold, and he enjoyed telling stories about bishops. Oddly, such stories frequently paralleled those military men tell about their officers. Like the one about the private who called his colonel a stupid jackass. The colonel insisted that the soldier apologize in front of the entire regiment.

"I don't think you want me to do that, sir," demurred the private.

"And why not?"

"Because right now, you and I are the only ones who know that I called you a stupid jackass. If I have to apologize, then the whole regiment will know."

One must remember that bishops are used to having everything done for them. They have ritual assistants, who help them vest, open the Gospel book to the correct page, hold the Gospel book in front of them, direct them when and where to sit, take off their miter when called for, and replace it when called for.

At one such ritual, having gone through the prescribed procedures, the assistant stepped forward to replace the bishop's miter on that worthy's head. Once having done this, he stepped back and—horror of horrors!—realized that he had put the bishop's miter on backward. Many people may not be aware that there are two long lappets, or flaps, that hang down the back of the miter, over the bishop's neck. Because the miter had been placed on the bishop's head hindside before, the bishop now sat with his face obstructed by the hanging lappets.

The horrified assistant stepped forward to rectify his error, when he was stopped in no uncertain terms by the bishop, who said, in a voice loud enough to be heard all through the church, "Leave it alone and let everyone see how stupid you are!"

To Bill, this exemplified the episcopal mindset, wherein "They will think *you* are stupid because *I* am sitting here with flaps hanging in front of my face."

Bill grew to believe that in too many cases, each bishop recommended a man stupider than he himself as a candidate for the club, thus accounting for the "dumbing down" of the episcopacy. There is a German word coined for a similar situation: *Massenverdummung*, in which masses of people become stupid.

Of course, it may be different in future, as the following exchange suggests:

Q. How are bishops chosen?

A. We look for the most righteous, spiritual, most loved person in the archdiocese—and then we call her husband.

In any case, Bill Kienzle felt that the ultimate test for a bishop was whether he could walk with a crozier in one hand and bless his flock with the other. Should you think this is a snap, I pass on his suggestion: "Try it. In the privacy of your own home, pick up a broom, hold it in one hand, and, as you walk through the house, bless the cat and the dog with the other hand." Eventually, he simplified this test to a sole question to be asked of the candidate for the episcopacy: "Can you chew gum and rub your stomach at the same time?"

Nothing in life is preparation for the loss of a child.

—From a statement by the Bessette family

THERE WAS LITTLE TIME TO SIT BACK AND TAKE STOCK. My work at the *Free Press* took up most of my time and a good part of my energy. I was a typical workaholic: staying busy so I would not have to examine and deal with my personal life. Actually, I didn't really have a personal life.

Circumstances had made it necessary for me to leave my teenage son behind. It was the hardest thing I have ever done. I saw him from time to time, and talked to him on the phone. He seemed to be doing as well as could be expected under the circumstances.

Having grown up in a household where my parents fought constantly, I had vowed that I would never put a child of mine through a similar horror. For a while, I had succeeded; until the infamous toaster day, Mike had been surrounded by security, even if it was to a large degree ersatz.

Along the way, like so many misguided wives, I had felt that if only I could have another baby, everything would be all right. My first pregnancy, two years before Mike's birth, had ended in a miscarriage. After Mike, for some reason, I couldn't seem to get pregnant.

This was before the era of in vitro fertilization or surrogate pregnancy. Father Kienzle, trying to be helpful, suggested adoption. He arranged for an interview at Catholic Social Services. Even though Rick and I had the backing of a priest, and a document from Mike's teacher saying that he was the most well-adjusted pupil she'd ever had, the social worker, undoubtedly seeing something that none of the rest of us saw, turned us down. Prescient man.

In the early days of our marriage, Rick's job opportunities had been spotty, so I frequently was the wage earner while he had the role of house husband. The majority of my jobs were high stress. I did not drive, so I took a bus to work . . . sometimes two buses. By the time I got home at night I was exhausted. But as was the case with so many working wives, particularly of that era, there were still "chores" to be done—which left me little or no "quality time" with Mike. Because we needed the money I went to work every day whether I was well or ill. I worked through colds, cramps, strep throat, and tension headaches, as well as a disk problem that put me in a steel brace for six months.

When Mike was eleven, I became nauseated with what I assumed was flu. When it hung on, I visited our family doctor. "I'll bet you're pregnant," he said matter-of-factly. Preposterous! I couldn't be; I'd been trying for years without success.

But, as they say in the old-time sit-coms, the rabbit died.

I was happy, but I had to keep working, at least for a while. As in my previous two pregnancies, the first three months were a nightmare of nausea. My first pregnancy had ended in a miscarriage early in the fourth month. With Mike I had lost so much weight that I had to be hospitalized and fed intravenously. This time, I worked my way through the nausea and the first trimester without incident. Father Kienzle came to the house and read a special prayer for pregnant women over me.

The next couple of months I felt fine . . . almost exhilarated. Then, along about the sixth month, I started spotting. The doctor ordered me to bed, where I stayed still the spotting stopped. I went back to work at a downtown law office. The job was a soft touch; the two attorneys were sympathetic to my condition.

One day as I was taking dictation I felt what I thought were gas pains. I ignored them, typed up the letters, and took the bus home as usual at 5 P.M. The "gas pains" got worse. I phoned the doctor, who told me to get to the hospital as quickly as possible. I got there so quickly that he had not yet arrived. I was placed on a gurney that was rushed through the halls like a scene from *ER*. I could feel the insistence of the baby in the birth canal. "Hold your legs together," a nurse said.

In the delivery room, I was given a spinal. I stared at the ceiling as a stoic-faced oriental intern delivered the baby. I didn't see the baby; but I heard her cry—a weak, unpromising sound. The nurse holding her said, "I'll baptize her. What name do you want?"

"Mary."

My doctor arrived. The intern, engaged in sewing up a tear in the perineum, looked up questioningly: Did my doctor want to take over? "No, you're doing fine," was the answer. The doctor told me later that the intern had done an expert job. He must have; unlike some women who were torn in childbirth I never had a moment's trouble as a result of his handiwork.

Mary lived barely a day. The pain of her loss was such that I would not let myself feel it for fear that I would break down completely. "I can't cry; why can't I cry?" I asked the doctor.

"You will," he said.

He was right—but it took longer than he knew. Some ten years later, I accompanied a friend to visit the grave of her baby in an Irish churchyard. I wept for her sorrow—and then realized that I wasn't crying for her baby; I was—finally—crying for my own.

Sure I believe in fairies. Never seen any, but it stands to reason.

—IRISH PEASANT (TO JOHN KEATS)

I WAS WORKING IN A TRAVEL AGENCY when Carlings Beer aired its TV ads filmed at the Abbey Tavern in Howth. Pubsters of all ages were humming and singing, "We're off to Dublin in the Green." In those days, the airlines subsidized educational trips for travel agents; I could fly to Ireland for a pittance. Like Margaret Cronyn, I said, "I'll go, I'll go!" I made plans for my first trip across the Atlantic.

Once a week after the *Michigan Catholic* was put to bed, the staff lunched out. I was invited to join the group at Carl's Chop House. I mentioned that I would be going to Ireland the end of April. "You'll be missed," Father Kienzle said.

I thought that a somewhat unusual statement, but passed it off as politeness; Father Kienzle was nothing if not polite. And I was so accustomed to the idea of his being a priest, and therefore untouchable that I never would have dreamed of anything even remotely improper. Granted, we were good friends, but not only was he a priest, I was a married woman. Further, he was the soul of probity and correctness. His priesthood was sacrosanct; even close friends never got overly familiar with Father Kienzle.

Accompanied by my friend Karen Webb, I took off for Ireland. As the plane landed in Shannon, I had the oddest feeling that I was coming home. I later discovered that one branch of Mother's family had indeed come from Ireland. In 1727, an ancestor, William Lowther, a young Quaker from Armagh, emigrated with his family to America. What is now Irvinestown, in County Fermanagh, was at one time known as Lowtherville.

No sooner had Karen and I arrived at our hotel in Dublin than we phoned the Abbey Tavern. And before you could say Cushlamachree, we were in Howth, ignoring our jet lag and dining on Dublin prawns. Our dinner was followed by a glorious evening with the Abbey Tavern singers. As we all joined in a rousing chorus of "We're off to Dublin in the Green," I thought I had died and gone to heaven.

After a few days in Dublin, we joined our CIE tour and headed north, to "where the Mountains of Mourne run down to the sea." We sent postcards and letters home and pitied our friends and family who couldn't be with us. We visited what legend said was the grave of St. Patrick, passed by Carrickfergus (named after the first Irish King of Scotland), walked the streets of Belfast—where we stayed at the Europa, which some years later would be known as the most bombed hotel in Europe—and traversed the Glens of Antrim.

We toured the Giant's Causeway, whose basalt columns rise from the sea like an army of headless mushrooms. George Fields, our leprechaun of a guide, pointed out a spot in the middle of the hexagonal columns that he said was the Wishing Chair: Whoever made a wish while sitting in it would have that wish come true.

There is an old saying: Be careful what you wish for; you might get it. I sat in the chair, looked heavenward and said, "God, if Father Kienzle ever needs a best friend, let me be that friend." That was it, no more, no less.

Ireland was everything I could have asked for, and more. The hills were a counterpane of daffodils, gorse, and newborn lambs. Familiar songs and poems came to life before our eyes. We visited ancient Derry on the River Foyle. We came through the

Barnesmore Gap in County Donegal in a snowfall that was like fairy dust. We stopped at Yeats's grave in Sligo "under bare Ben Bulben's head." And then came Mayo and Galway and the bogs and crags of Connemara. I wrote Father Kienzle, "For the rest of my life whenever I close my eyes I'll see Connemara."

On we went, along the majestic Cliffs of Moher that stand against the Atlantic like the edge of the world, then through the moonscape of the Burren, where our bus snaked along limestone cutbacks until we were near dizzy with trying to figure out in which direction we were headed.

Our section of the tour ended in Killarney. While the others took a jaunting car ride, I went out walking one magical evening and found myself in a fairy ring.

I had asked God to make me Father Kienzle's best friend, and had fallen in love—with enchanted Ireland. In years to come, Neal Shine would refer to me as the Closet Colleen.

Psychiatrist researchers have documented a rare malady called "Sight of Sleep Phobia." Those who suffer same reportedly become extremely irritated and anxious when they see somebody dozing off. In their search for case histories, the researchers say they've found an excellent starting point in divorce court records.

—*Detroit Free Press*

I OFTEN SAID THAT IF ONLY Rick had let me get some sleep, we would've still been together. But he was a night owl, and even when I was gaunt with exhaustion, he became infuriated if I refused to stay up with him. If I fell asleep on the couch while he was watching television, he woke me.

Every weekday night he would set the alarm clock for much earlier than either of us needed to get up. Of course the alarm would wake me. And I was expected to wake him, and keep rewaking him until he finally got up. He liked the feeling of being able to go back to sleep secure in the knowledge that I would wake him in time for him to get to work. If I did manage to fall back to sleep and thus not wake him, he was furious.

All in all, I was getting barely enough sleep to sustain me. On one occasion, I actually fell asleep while seated at the dinner table, despite the fact that we had guests dining with us.

Although I had separated from Rick, I had done so only for the sake of my health. I had tried desperately to hold the marriage together at least till Mike graduated high school. Now the years of stress started to take their toll. One day as I was typing, before my eyes double lines appeared on the page. I shook my head in an attempt to clear my vision. Suddenly my fingers, resting on the typewriter keyboard, curled up and refused to straighten. I took a cab to the doctor's office. "Were the double lines side by side or one atop the other?" I didn't know what difference it made and didn't ask. "One atop the other," I said. The doctor prescribed a tranquilizer.

I was uneasy for several weeks, but it didn't happen again. Then one evening, when Father Kienzle was visiting, I took a sip of tea— and suddenly a light exploded in the back of my head. I fell to the floor, literally paralyzed. "Call an ambulance!" I shrieked.

I was taken to a nearby hospital, where an ER doctor, after taking some blood, told me I was diabetic, as my blood sugar was so high. I didn't know—and obviously he didn't either—that under stress, the blood sugar can shoot up. By this time I was vomiting, in projectile fashion. Father Kienzle, standing next to the gurney, was splattered. I would have been mortified had I not been so frightened. I was petrified the doctor would give me insulin, so I kept saying over and over, "I'm not diabetic, I'm not diabetic."

Father Kienzle, trying desperately to think of something reassuring, anything that would help, said to me, "When you get better, I'll take you to Ireland." He kept repeating this. And I thought, "That's nice—but I'm not going to live." Then I lost consciousness.

The following day, Father Kienzle phoned my GP, who made arrangements for me to be transferred to his hospital. By this time, my white blood count had soared. I came to every so often, then immediately fell unconscious again. I was on heavy antibiotics and being fed intravenously. No one seemed to know whether I would live or die. And I was beyond caring.

I survived my ten-day hospital stay, although the diagnosis remained pretty much of a mystery. For insurance purposes, it was listed as gastroenteritis. But the after-effects were to plague me for years. Eventually my symptoms fell under the umbrella of chronic fatigue syndrome.

I would rather have every bone in my body broken than suffer depression again, because I know which would hurt worse.

—ANONYMOUS, QUOTED BY FATHER WILLIAM BURKE
Protect Us from All Anxiety: Meditations for the Depressed

ONCE RICK REALIZED THAT I WAS SERIOUS about our separation, he knew the writing was on the wall. Only then did he go for counseling.

One day I received a call from his counselor: Would I come and talk to her?

I did. Her question was simple—so simple we could've handled it by phone: Was I ever going to come back to Rick? My answer, she said, would have a bearing on the type of counseling she would give him.

I had had a long time to think it over. I felt that if I were to come back, my health would suffer to the point where I would probably die or be institutionalized—or kill him. I told her that. Rick was on his own.

Shortly thereafter—and I'm not sure in which order—he met another woman and decided to file for divorce. Father Kienzle referred Rick to an attorney—a former seminary schoolmate and fellow counselor at Camp Ozanam.

I paid no attention. All I wanted was to sleep.

❧❧

The *Free Press* gave me a fully paid open-ended leave of absence. Not only was this a financial lifesaver; it also helped me emotionally, as it was obvious they were acknowledging my work over the years. But that period remains to this day one of the lowest in my life. My exhaustion was almost total; I could barely pull myself from bed for the necessaries. I had less than no appetite; I was skin and bones. Father Kienzle would stop by at noon and again after work to try to get a few spoonfuls of soup down me. I could barely keep my eyes open, and would drift off almost immediately after what passed for dinner. Father Kienzle would stay till he was sure I was safely asleep, then he would drive back to Dearborn Heights, where he was now pastor of St. Anselm's.

I had double vision and could not read or even watch TV. Also, in addition to tachycardia, I had developed extra irregular heartbeats. On top of all this—or probably because of all this—I suffered—and suffered is the word—acute depression. Blessedly, I was never suicidal—but I didn't care whether I woke up or not.

My doctor treated all these symptoms with a variety of tranquilizers, barbiturates, and vitamin supplements, as well as histamine shots. I, who rarely even took an aspirin for a headache, was terrified of becoming addicted to any kind of drugs. Dr. Pool assured me that my dosage was so infinitesimally low that it would be impossible for that to happen.

Then, one day, at the end of three months, as if by magic, the double vision left one eye.

I could now walk without holding on to the wall—although because there was still double vision in the other eye, I did have to hold my head at an angle to keep from getting dizzy. But I felt ready to return to work.

The image remains of my first day back on the job. Head bent to one side, I walked into the composing room, and was confronted by the army of printers—all walking with their heads bent to one side. I burst out laughing; I felt I was truly among friends.

It took another three months for the double vision to leave the other eye.

I wasn't out of the woods, however. I became subject to panic attacks—with hyperventilation so severe that occasionally I ended up in the emergency room with my back arched, my hands and feet contorted in tetany. I had dizzy spells where I came close to fainting. At times, I was unable to concentrate.

All during this period, Father Kienzle was "on call"—ever ready to help in whatever way he could. To this day, I don't know how he did it—or what I would have done without him. He carried on his full-time work as editor of the *Michigan Catholic*; at St. Anselm's, he said Mass daily—twice on Sundays—heard confessions, officiated at weddings, funerals, and baptisms—and he took care of one very ill lady.

Had someone asked what he did in the evenings, his answer probably would've been that old vaudeville line, "I'm sitting up with a sick friend."

After four years of immersion in TV listings, I transferred to the Features copy desk, where I was privileged to be associated with Dave Smith and later Alex Cruden as well.

Dave, who may have been born with printer's ink in his veins, copy-edited as naturally as breathing. Alex, a collateral descendant of Scotland's Alexander Cruden of *Concordance* fame, was erudite and quietly witty, with the brain of a wordsmith.

Working with Dave and Alex was an education and a half. It also taught me a major lesson: Perfection is impossible—at least in this sphere. The *Free Press*, in striving for perfection, however, gave it the old college try. It was announced that for the upcoming Saturday the entire staff was going to try for the unheard-of: an error-free paper.

The Saturday issue was chosen undoubtedly because it was the lightest issue. Since it had fewer pages, there was less to write, less to edit, less to proofread—ergo, less opportunity for error. The Features Department's Saturday output was one lone page.

All went smoothly. I proofread our one page, Alex proofread our one page, Dave gave it the final eagle-eye exam. We shipped our page to the composing room and sat back with the feeling of a job well done; *our* page at least would be perfect.

Next day, when we read the paper, we found a typo in our supposedly error-free page.

My conclusion was that if a typo had gotten by our dedicated, whizbang trio this was God's way of telling us: "Perfection is Mine alone."

So to those who come up with a "Gotcha!" while reading this book, all I can say is, We tried.

And to those who ask, "What would you like God to say when you enter heaven?" my response is: I hope He will tell me, "I know you tried."

One day I got a call from Rick: The divorce was final; all I had to do was to sign the papers.

It was very civilized. Rick got the house; I got the piano. Rick got custody of Mike; I got unlimited visitation privileges.

My rocky marriage of eighteen years was over. We had married too young; now we would have to finish growing up separately.

I would not have sought thee had I not already found thee.

—Blaise Pascal

If God can put a soul into the body of a baby that doesn't yet exist, why can't he put a body which once did exist back together with its soul?

—Ancient rabbinical source

As a child I had found Catholicism fascinating. But, being raised by atheistic parents, my view of Catholicism was skewed.

Mother's viewpoint was philosophical: Catholics were ignorant, priest-ridden zealots, who turned out babies like rabbits. And the priests encouraged this because the more babies the more the priests could keep the people in bondage to the Church.

Dad's view was simpler: Catholics hated and persecuted Jews, so Jews were wary of Catholics.

Fortunately, like many children to whom books are available, my sister and I read omnivorously. The Bible, if not history, was at least considered literature and as such worthy of perusing. In the public schools of that era, the day started with the Pledge of Allegiance and a reading from the Old Testament—usually the Psalms. To this day I can quote some of my grade school favorites. I doubt that my parents felt there was any harm in our hearing the biblical words; if they had, I feel certain they would have made a fuss.

While still in grammar school, I began to read more "adult" books—mysteries, romances, adventure stories, histories, and biographies, as well as all manner of liberal tracts, some of which traumatized me for years. One in particular I still recall. It was about a lynching that took place down South. The arm of one of the young black men was crushed in a vise and then he was hanged from a tree. A pregnant black woman had her unborn child cut from her womb and the two of them were thrown on a bonfire.

I reread that chapter countless times, in almost breathless horror. How could people do such things? The news that in a nearby backwoods community, the Ku Klux Klan had taken a black woman captive, held her upside down, and poured turpentine into her vagina brought the horror close to home. My parents were considered Communists because of their beliefs. I knew the KKK hated Communists. My father was Jewish. I knew the KKK hated Jews. (Nothing was ever said to us about their also hating Catholics.) I too grew wary. Could some of the people who had tortured the black woman be our neighbors?

Young people tend to be idealistic. If they read books that encourage idealism, they tend to become more idealistic. My childhood favorites included Louisa May Alcott's works. Without realizing it, I began to try to pattern myself after the young people in *Little Women*, *Little Men*, *Jo's Boys*, *Rose in Bloom*, and *Eight Cousins*. They believed in God, they tried to be good, and they put Christian precepts into action.

In later years, the lives of saints such as Joan of Arc and St. Francis of Assisi, books like *Quo Vadis*, *Ben-Hur*, and *Green Dolphin Street* imbued me with an admiration for people who could believe in goodness so strongly that they were willing to devote their lives to an altruistic faith, and even risk torture and death for that faith.

Still, I could not believe in what to me smacked of superstition. I knew there was no Santa Claus, no Easter Bunny. God was in the same category; something people had invented to make themselves feel better about life and death. Jesus was nothing more than a historical figure. And the virgin birth? How could any educated person believe in a religion based on such spurious myths?

Two things happened. One, I met Rick's mother, a devout and pious Catholic. She was bedridden with excruciating arthritis; she had lost a breast to cancer; her husband was an alcoholic; her son had married outside her faith. Yet she never complained; on the contrary, she was the soul of goodness and kindness. Once Rick and I were married, she welcomed me to her home and her family and her life as if I were the woman she would have hand-picked for her son. She was the living example of what a Christian is supposed to be. I never heard her speak a word against anyone; she did not inveigh against the Church that had refused to recognize her marriage, nor against her family who had ostracized her because of that marriage, nor against the God who had allowed her to be afflicted with painful illness. A religion that such a woman believed in must have something to recommend it.

The second thing that happened was that Mike was born. It was a difficult pregnancy and a drawn-out, painful birth. The umbilical cord was wrapped around the baby's neck, and the obstetrician had to wait until the baby was in position before unwinding the cord, so as not to cause damage for lack of air to the brain. After several hours of screaming, I, who had desired natural childbirth, welcomed the anesthetic that bestowed oblivion.

When I woke, the nurse brought Mike to me. I looked at this baby in awe and wonder. And at that moment, I knew—I *knew* there was a God. There had to be a God; otherwise how explain this miracle . . . this living, breathing creature who had started from an invisible seed, had grown inside me, and was now sleeping in my arms.

In later years I read that when God wants to change the world, He doesn't do it with a wave of His arm; He just has a baby be born.

---

*Q*uod promitto perficio (What I promise I deliver).

—LATIN MOTTO

I WAS PLANNING A SHORT BUSINESS TRIP that entailed flying in and out of Metropolitan Airport. Since I didn't drive, I would take a limousine to and from the airport. Father Kienzle said, "I have to be out at St. John's that afternoon; I can pick you up."

An odd little buzzer zinged in my brain. But all I said was, "Okay."

My plane was on time, and so was Father Kienzle—in black trousers and a dark blue polo shirt. I was flabbergasted; in all the years I had known him, I had never seen him in anything but his clericals. In the nine months I had gone to him for instructions, he had always worn a cassock. As I write this, I wonder do priests even have cassocks anymore?

As we left the terminal to walk across the street, he took my hand protectively. My hand trembled in his. What was happening?

He drove back to Detroit in the slow lane. We talked of inconsequential things. Then he said, "I have a confession."

"I know what it is," I said. "You didn't have to go to St. John's."

"How did you know?"

I looked straight ahead. "I just knew." Then I turned to look at him, "So tell me: Why the full court press?"

He laughed at my use of the sports term, and didn't answer my question.

But Javan kept these things in her heart and pondered them.

Father Kienzle was a person of ritual and routine, and a man of his word. If he told someone, "I'll meet you in the middle of the Sahara at 6 A.M. on Easter Sunday next year," you could put money on it: He would be there.

He never committed himself beyond his ability to meet that commitment. One day, we were talking on the phone, and I could hear him take a drag on a cigarette . . . the way a smoker does when he is about to say something.

The words that followed took my breath away. "I think," he said, "I love you."

I was so astounded I couldn't speak. Yes, I had asked God to be Father Kienzle's best friend, but not to have him love me. Never that. His priesthood was sacrosanct. If I cared at all for him—as a friend or more—I would never, could never, do anything to jeopardize that.

He was so superior to anyone I had ever known. So straight arrow, so upstanding, so trustworthy, *so self-disciplined*. I admired the way he honored his priesthood. Privately, I was proud to be his friend. Still, I was fearful that if our friendship were to become public it could cause trouble for him. And now, *he thinks he loves me—!*

It was so typical of him. Any other man would say, "I love you." But cautious, careful, thoughtful Father Kienzle said, "I *think* I love you."

He seemed totally unconcerned . . . undoubtedly because he had a clear conscience; he hadn't done anything that would threaten his priesthood or the Church. Whereas I felt like "the other woman" in a love triangle.

He continued to visit at my apartment for dinner, always leaving early to return to his parish in Dearborn Heights. Occasionally, we would drive to a restaurant in one of the far-out suburbs. And, rarely, to a movie. He introduced me to Gershwin's Concerto in F; I introduced him to Mozart's Symphony No. 40.

When my strength permitted, we lobbed a tennis ball back and forth. Although my swimming was more dog paddle than smooth crawl, he patiently taught me to dive. Though I was petrified to leave the side of the pool headfirst, he reminded me that he was a certified lifeguard. Thanks to him, I eventually was able to launch myself from the diving board. My form left much to be desired, but only once did I belly-whop.

Meanwhile, I was learning more about Catholicism. It was an exciting time in the post-Vatican II Church. And Father Kienzle, as editor of the *Michigan Catholic*, was right in the center of things. I felt privileged to be in the loop—to hear about the behind-the-scenes events, the ecclesiastical discussions, the theological and liturgical changes that were taking place.

The only real change in our relationship was that I had to figure out what to call him. Nowadays, many parishioners refer to their pastor by his first name. At that time, it was comparatively rare. And he had always said that he did not want to be called "Father Bill." "Call me Bill or call me Father Kienzle—but not 'Father Bill.'"

The one place he hadn't been able to enforce this preference was in his parents' home. Where his father's Lutheran family made it a point to call him Bill, his mother's Irish relatives would not let those heretical upstarts get away with such irreverence: They made it an overriding point to call him "Father Bill."

I was very proper, very correct. I had always addressed him as "Father Kienzle"—never as "Bill." I had too much respect for him, for his priesthood. Now how would I address him?

It would feel so strange to call him "Bill"; even stranger to address him as "Dear." Most of the time I settled for no address at all. But eventually, it was just plain Bill.

If someone comes to you entreating aid, do not say in refusal, "Trust in God, He will help," but act as if there were no God, and none to help but you.

—HASIDIC SAYING

BILL LIKED TO TELL STORIES. As a young priest he had envied the older priests. "They had stories to tell; I had none. I looked forward to the day when I would have stories to tell."

By this time he had been a priest for over fifteen years. He had stories to tell. And he had a forum—the editorial page in the *Michigan Catholic*.

I was able to help. I could read the drafts of his editorials and make suggestions—and correct any misspellings. I felt honored to be consulted in such an undertaking.

One day, a news article reported that Charles Evers, the brother of slain civil rights leader Medgar Evers, had been elected mayor of Fayette, Mississippi. The previous white administration, in a fury, before leaving office, had looted the town's treasury, and Charles Evers was now mayor of a bankrupt town. He needed help. "What about your readers?" I asked Bill. "A lot of them wanted to, but couldn't go South for the civil rights marches; here's an opportunity for them to do something about the problem."

Bill placed a call to the town hall in Fayette. A man answered. Bill asked to speak to Mayor Evers. "This is Mayor Evers." The poor man didn't have a secretary; he was answering the phone himself.

Bill asked some questions. Was the news article factual? Yes, the town's coffers were empty. Was it true, as someone had said, that Fayette was the fourth poorest town in the United States? "Yes, I guess so."

"What are the other three?" Bill asked. "I don't know," replied the mayor, "but I'm sure they're in Mississippi."

Father Kienzle's editorial that week ran, not on the editorial page, but on page one of the *Michigan Catholic*. At the time, the weekly had an estimated 160,000 readers. Realistically, each one couldn't be expected to send in money. But if every reader who could spare a dollar would send it to Mayor Evers in Fayette, that could help the town recover from the looting.

I cannot recall the exact amount—and I could be wrong—but if memory serves, as a result of this editorial, contributions somewhere in the upper five figures were sent to Mayor Evers. Bill said it was one of his proudest moments as editor.

Change is bad.

—MERVYN I. CHUMWATER

ST. ANSELM'S, AN UPSCALE SUBURBAN PARISH, was founded in 1954, the year of Father Kienzle's ordination. It stands just off Outer Drive in comfortable Dearborn Heights. On a large greensward in front of the Church is a statue of the Benedictine monk who became Archbishop of Canterbury and was eventually named a Doctor of the Church. Each Halloween, like the shadowy figure who left roses at Edgar Allan Poe's tomb in Baltimore, some whimsical prankster placed a hollowed-out pumpkin over the statue's mitered head.

An assignment as pastor of St. Anselm's would have overjoyed many priests. Father Kienzle was not one of them. He had ruminated on and spoken often of the French worker priest movement, which he felt was worthy of imitation. To live among and work with one's neighbors while ministering to them seemed the ideal as set forth by Jesus. For Father Kienzle, the closest to this ideal were Detroit's inner-city priests, who lived in the midst of the poor to whom they ministered.

Unlike the suburban pastors who dined as guests of the wealthy, golfed at their hosts' country club, and were flown in private jets to exotic vacation spots, the inner-city priests ate on the run at the nearest Coney Island, begged for funds to feed the unemployed and down-on-their-luck, sheltered the homeless, and prayed that their church and rectory roofs would last another year.

Occasionally, Father Kienzle felt that where the poor got the message of Jesus, the well-off just didn't get it. His *Michigan Catholic* editorials hammered away on the duty of the haves to share with the have-nots, in Jesus's name.

But, all too often, he felt, the message went over their heads. How could they call themselves Catholic, how could they call themselves Christian, when they were ignoring the precept "Whatever you do to the least of these you do unto me"?

There was no question that they contributed to their Church. But what did their Church represent to them? Did their Church represent the body of Jesus to be made available to the poor? Or was it, as Father Kienzle once said satirically, that "They pay me to stay on a pedestal"? If Jesus died to save us, was it easier for us to keep Him on the cross than for us to live His precepts?

The parish membership was a mixed bag of auto executives, physicians, tradespeople, attorneys, and other professionals, as well as the elderly retired.

The founding pastor of St. Anselm's had retired southward, taking with him, according to rumor, some considerable parish funds, as well as an accommodating housekeeper. Reportedly, when concerns were voiced to the chancery, the response was, "You wouldn't refuse Father his well-deserved retirement, would you?"

The pastor left behind a basement full of stuffed and mounted animal heads decorating the poker room, and a core of conservative parishioners whom—again, according to reliable rumor—he had had place their hands on the Bible and give oath that they would continue to hold the line against the horrors of Vatican II and ensure their parish would remain ensconced in "The Thirteenth, the Greatest of Centuries."

Now, St. Anselm's was to be Father Kienzle's fiefdom.

He knew the territory. For eight years, since being assigned to the *Michigan Catholic*, he had been a weekend associate at St. Mel's, a nearby parish also in Dearborn Heights.

Father Kienzle phoned the Cardinal's secretary, Monsignor Imesch, with a request: Instead of being transferred to St. Anselm's, could he be assigned to an inner-city parish?

Monsignor Imesch relayed the response. "The Boss says that if he were going to have a pastorate himself, he would choose St. Anselm's."

Father Kienzle got the message, loud and clear: He was going to "Slamslam's." It would be a learning experience for both pastor and parishioners.

Father Kienzle had to feel his way, but he was helped by Father Bob Scanlon, an associate who was relieved to be freed from the chains of the previous pastor's off-the-ends-of-the-earth autocracy.

Still, he proceeded gingerly. Not only was he new to the parish, the evolutionary steps of Vatican II were beginning to be implemented, so there was bound to be chaos in any event.

The makeup of the parish council was heavily conservative. They were heady in their new power. When it became clear that they were not in a collaborative mood, but rather of a mind to take the reins and head the horse right off the cliff, action was called for.

The mettle of the new pastor was proved when he dismissed the council.

"But . . . but you can't do that!" a dumbstruck troglodyte said.

Father Kienzle had checked with his vicar, Bishop Gumbleton, possessor of a degree in Canon Law, and had ascertained that he was well within his pastoral rights. He now assured the gentleman that he not only could do that but indeed had—and added the equivalent of Cromwell's "In the name of God, go."

St. Anselm's set about electing a new, more representative parish council.

Among replacement members was Marge Hershey, a no-nonsense Earth Mother with seven children.

Marge's contribution was to sit at one end of the council table and on occasion comment on the deliberations with a firm "That's bull——." Father Kienzle deemed that more often than not Marge was correct in such assessment.

Just as Father Kienzle had a deep admiration for the work of the nuns, he recognized the worth of women in general. Where, in an early editorial, he had disparaged feminist aspirations to the priesthood, this educable man had gained an awareness that there were some women who would make better priests than some of the men who wore the collar.

On the eve of Father Kienzle's accession, Ramona Kraemer, an active member of the parish, had been asked by the associate pastor to help prepare St. Anselm's for the advent of their new pastor. Mrs. Kraemer was pleased to be consulted on such a propitious occasion—until she discovered that the extent of her contribution would be to spearhead a thorough cleaning of the church and rectory.

She drew herself up and announced to the startled associate, "The women of St. Anselm's are not domestics!"

In later years, St. Anselm's would boast the first female parish council president in the Archdiocese of Detroit—Gene Brazell, whose husband, Bob, was one of St. Anselm's many excellent lectors.

Not all the implementations of Vatican II would be effected as simply as the upgrading of the parish council.

In an attempt to attract young Catholics, many churches instituted what were termed "Folk Masses." Musical combos took over from the organist and the choir. Their performance, as well as the choice of the tunes they offered, was not always agreeable to many of their listeners. One meeting of the St. Anselm parish council was devoted to a spirited discussion as to whether or not "Blowin' in the Wind" would be acceptable to sing at Mass.

On another occasion, after a mod combo had inflicted its musical choices upon the congregation, Father Kienzle was accosted after Mass by an irate elderly parishioner, who poked the pastor in the stomach and said, acerbically, "I want show, I go movie."

In the wake of Vatican II, the lines were drawn: It was The Thirteen Century-ites (Change is bad.) vs. The Implementarians (Whatever is, let's change it.). Father Kienzle said that the only people who were truly prepared for Vatican II were the liturgists; they were not only prepared, they took the ball and ran with it. Which led to the question: What is the difference between a liturgist and a terrorist? The answer (decades before the WTC bombing): You can argue with a terrorist.

The less than totally welcoming response to Change had been borne out as Father Kienzle, having assisted at Communion at another parish, was standing in the rear of the church when an usher, oblivious of his presence, scurried by. As he did so, he said to a fellow usher, "Some kid just peed on the Communion rail." The man continued on his purposeful way, undoubtedly to get some toweling, then added, in a disgusted tone, "It's probably one of the new changes."

Any change in Communion rubrics lent itself to malapropisms and/or spoonerisms.

Before Vatican II, Communion was offered with the Latin formula, "*Corpus Domini nostri Jesu Christi custodiat animam tuam in vitam aeternam* [May the body of our Lord Jesus Christ protect your soul forever]. Amen." (Seemingly the recipient couldn't be trusted to say Amen for himself or herself.)

Whereupon, the communicant could echo, "Amen."

After Vatican II, the formula was changed to merely "*Corpus Christi*," to which the recipient simply replied "Amen."

But the priest was never certain where the communicant's mind was. This was brought home to Father Kienzle one morning as he placed the Host on the tongue of a kneeling woman and pronounced the words, "*Corpus Christi*," only to hear her reply, "Texas."

It was not solely the communicant's mind that was subject to distraction; the priest was also occasionally at risk. As one of the progressive changes in the wake of Vatican II, "*Corpus Christi*" was anglicized to "Body of Christ." And in more familiar or controlled situations, it was not unusual for the priest to use the communicant's name while offering Communion: "John, the Body of Christ," "Mary, the Body of Christ," and so on.

One of Father Kienzle's priest-buddies was chaplain at an all-girls school. The school was run by nuns, the student body was entirely female—even the school's canine mascot was female. So accustomed was this priest to operating in this milieu, that on one occasion, while talking with some of his priestly confreres, he was heard to say, "The other nuns and I . . ."

One morning, the chaplain, who was more or less peripherally aware that some of the students were developing faster than others, went down the Communion line as usual: "Jane, the Body of Christ," "Susan, the Body of Christ," and then, as he offered the host to a particularly well-developed maiden, he heard himself saying, "Christ, the body of Linda."

Father James Macy, then pastor of Precious Blood parish, was also chaplain at Detroit's Sinai Hospital during this transitional time. He was at Sinai early one morning—Communion was given before breakfast in the hospital. Delighted at being able to use the English formula, Father Macy said the introductory prayers and then announced to the somnolent patient in the bed, "The Body of Christ."

"*Corpus Christi*," the patient mumbled.

"Amen," Father Macy replied, as he gave the man Holy Communion. And instantly realized, *It wasn't supposed to go that way.*

Somehow, though, Jesus manages to get through to us if we are willing to receive Him.

There is nothing more apparent in the life of the priest than the manner in which the man is put off and the minister of Christ is apparent at all Masses . . . He offers, he petitions, he thanks, and he adores.

—FATHER MARTIN DEMPSEY
St. Peter Julian Eymard: Champion of the Blessed Sacrament

ONE THING NONE OF ST. ANSELM'S PARISHIONERS could complain about was their pastor's reverence. Those who had eyes to see and ears to hear were warmed by Father Kienzle's celebration of Mass. People came from surrounding parishes to attend.

It was reminiscent of the earlier days at Patronage, when, as one of Father Kienzle's priest-classmates later recounted, "even the undertakers listened to his homilies."

Bill himself said he knew he was cooking with gas if he had the ushers, i.e., if they stayed and listened rather than going out for a smoke.

St. Anselm's was blessed with an abundance of talented parishioners. Many contributed time, money, and themselves to make St. Anselm's a true community of faith. One of the lectors, Roger Rice, had such a magnificent voice that Father Kienzle often thought that if God spoke it would be with the voice of Roger Rice.

Bill considered himself blessed with the excellent lectors at St. Anselm's. It was almost an embarrassment of riches to have readers like Roger Rice, Cy Buersmeyer, and George Lubienski.

It was a mutual admiration society. Recently, Roger, in reminiscing about Father Kienzle, wrote, "No one ever held the Host higher or looked at it more adoringly, lovingly, reverently. I honestly don't know of anyone I have ever met who walked, talked, and acted more like Jesus Christ. I have a sense that he must have looked like Jesus also. In his homilies, genuine love was the core of every message. They were not lengthy, but brief and beautiful in word and thought."

Roger's wife, Betty, recalled the pastor's "gentle, encouraging love," and added, "I thank God for knowing Bill as an instrument of God's peace."

Cy Buersmeyer's recollection is: "Bill was an outstanding homilist. He was brief but to the point, and always helpful. He had a gift for taking the Scripture readings and bringing them home— into your everyday life . . . and especially our obligation toward the poor and weak."

George Lubienski has similar memories: "At St. Anselm's, we all looked forward to Bill's homilies. Not only were they intellectually stimulating, but most importantly they challenged us as Christians to live Christ's message in our own daily lives."

Rosemarie Lubienski recalls: "He would invariably start with a humorous story and then follow with a homily that truly inspired us. In the three decades since Bill left, we have never had a comparable homilist.

"We are supposed to live in the moment, and I think that's what Bill did while he was on the altar. He was very attentive—and very much in the presence of Christ. It was inspiring."

Another parishioner, Jan Smutek, recalls, "No matter how busy I was getting the kids off to school, when I went to Mass every day, he was able to offer, in just a few words, something that was able to help me or give me food for thought throughout the day. In five minutes he would give me something to think about that was meaningful to my life."

One young woman who was a longtime parishioner usually sat in the first row and listened attentively to the sermon each Sunday. Toward the end of the homily, she would fill in a check to be placed in the collection envelope. The amount of the check was based on her evaluation of Father's sermon.

A younger priest, Father Dennis Duggan, recalls, "I remember as a seminarian going out to St. Anselm's and [being] overwhelmed with the cleverness of words from [Father Kienzle]. One seminarian from, I think Dearborn Heights . . . would often just stop in to see 'the Pastor.' Words, sense of humor, idioms and insights made me become a regular reader of the *Michigan Catholic* and a fan of Father Kienzle. Words are formative. I thank God for Bill's words."

Sister Bernadelle Grimm, RSM, was the principal of St. Anselm's school. The sometimes rockiness of the relationship between the pastor and the nun-principal is legendary, having been portrayed in many books and movies, including the performances of Bing Crosby and Ingrid Bergman in *The Bells of St. Mary's*. The extreme was probably best exemplified by Father Duddleswell and the Mother Superior in the British TV series, *Bless Me, Father.*

Sister Bernadelle and Father Kienzle worked out whatever differences there might have been, and Sister became a staunch friend. She heard Father Kienzle mention a clergyman who had such reverence for the Bible that he kept it wrapped in a special cloth—to designate that it was above any and all other books. Sister Bernadelle forthwith presented Father Kienzle with a beautiful square of gold-colored velvet. Thereafter, his Bible was always wrapped in this gift from Sister Bernadelle.

Though Sister Bernadelle was a firm, no-nonsense authority figure, she did not fit the mold of the ruler-wielding nun-teacher. Many of her students recall her with affection. On one occasion, she even stole the pastor's thunder.

Father Kienzle was doing his introduce-the-students-to-good-music shtik, playing bits of recordings of Gershwin and other classical composers for the benefit of some of the younger pupils, who definitely fit the description of a captive audience.

At the conclusion, the youngsters were asked to write their impressions of the musical salon. One cut right to the chase. "Father played some music for us, and then Sister came in and gave us cookies." Father may have brought culture to the classroom, but Sister brought *cookies*.

Father's old rule of never dining at a parishioner's home had long since gone by the board. Just as he had at St. Norbert's, he now became part of the family for several Anselmites. Like the St. Norbert parishioners, many Anselmites became lifelong friends of Bill's. And though he had originally been loath to shepherd St. Anselm's, he came to cherish these new friendships as well.

Although he frequently affected a W. C. Fields mien with regard to children, somehow he retained a rapport with them. Maybe they recognized a kindred spirit in that his responses to questions tended to come from the same country as that of childhood.

As a forty-some priest trying for the Father O'Malley image as he gracefully slipped into middle age, one day he was playing touch football with the grade schoolers. The bell rang for the resumption of school, and none too soon. As a parting gesture, Father punted the ball toward the school. It was not a spectacularly significant kick; it sort of shanked off the side of his foot. However, it apparently was impressive to young eyes. One lad drew near and commented, "Boy, Father, that was some kick." Then he added, "I've always wondered how come you guys are all so good at sports."

"We did that instead of girls."

The answer seemed to satisfy him. Father said it; it must be so.

One winter's day, outside the church, as Father Kienzle stood bundled up in his ground-length wool cape, a passing teenager grinned and saluted him as "Super-priest!" Another day, a parishioner's baby daughter ran up to him and ducked underneath the cape, to peek out laughing, from between his long legs.

He was happy in his vocation; he was fulfilled; he was a role model for young men, a super-father figure to children; he was respected, admired, and welcomed. For the parishioners of St. Anselm, Father Kienzle was everything a priest should be.

And Anselmites were about to get a lagniappe.

One of Bill Kienzle's seminary schoolmates was Eugene "Eugie" Strain. After ordination, Father Strain had gone West to join the Salesians in California. His classmates laughed and said he'd be back when it was time to become a big, fat pastor.

Father Strain was now back. He wasn't big or fat, but it was just about time for him to become a pastor. The only problem was there was no pastorless parish available. Father Kienzle came to his schoolmate's rescue: Father Strain would become copastor of St. Anselm.

Lord, I have loved the habitation of thy house, and the place where thine honour dwelleth . . . But as for me, I will walk in mine integrity: redeem me, and be merciful unto me.

—Psalm 26:8, 11

THERE IT WAS: A NEWS PHOTO of man-about-town Peter Spivak dancing with his bride, a well-known Detroit divorcée. The wedding had been performed by Father William Cunningham, activist priest who had cofounded the famed Focus: Hope, the organization that helped rescue Detroit after the 1967 riots.

Father Cunningham had been a year behind Bill in the seminary. His class had been a bit freer, a bit less strictured, a bit "wilder." "There's a new element here this year that wasn't here last year," the rector would say.

If Neal Shine and his boyhood chum Father Cunningham had run for mayor of Detroit, it would've been a toss-up as to the winner. Father Cunningham could do with impunity what many another priest wouldn't have been able to get away with. But . . . witnessing the remarriage of a divorced Catholic?

Cardinal Dearden was a kind man. Nonetheless, he was, as Bill said, a churchman to his very marrow. The prelate who reportedly had once said to his inner-city priests, "If you open a storefront church, don't tell me," was now forced to act. The matter had become a scandal to the Faithful. And one does not scandalize the Faithful with impunity. Father Cunningham was suspended for a month.

Father Kienzle, who from time to time witnessed the remarriage of divorced Catholics, saw the handwriting on the wall.

Early in his priesthood, a couple had come to him for help. They had been together for fifteen years in a loving and successful marriage. But because one of them had been divorced, their present union was not recognized as valid by the Church.

After consulting Canon Law, Father Kienzle tried to get the marriage legitimized via a "privilege of the faith"—then a complex and costly procedure.

While the investigation was being put in motion so that a determination could be made, Church rules demanded that the couple live as brother and sister. Father Kienzle cringed at this request; he was embarrassed at having to inform the couple of this regulation. He was humbled when the couple said they would go along.

He went back to the seminary to consult with one of his priest-professors. "Don't get involved," the older man told him. "You are there to enforce the rules."

I do not know the upshot of the matter. I do know that Father Kienzle never forgot the couple . . . and he continued to ponder the words of his erstwhile priest-professor. "You are there to enforce the rules." Throughout his seminary days, that precept had been drummed into him and his schoolmates: "Keep the Rule and the Rule will keep you." He was willing to—and did—keep the Church's rules himself . . . but could he inflict them on other people? Had he been ordained a priest of God in order *not* to "get involved"?

Eventually, he had reached his own conclusion: He was a people person—a people priest. He could not *not* get involved. If people came to him for help, his every instinct was to help.

Again he met with his vicar, Bishop Gumbleton, another kind man.

"What will happen if I keep performing these marriages?"

"You'll be suspended."

"I won't accept a suspension."

"It won't be any big deal . . . you'll go on vacation or on retreat for a couple of weeks, that's all."

"I won't accept a suspension."

"Why not?"

"Because that would be an admission that I did something wrong. And the people I've married will think there's something wrong with their marriage—that they're not truly married in the eyes of the Church."

"Then don't do it anymore."

Simple. But he knew that one day a friend would come to him and ask that he witness the marriage of a son or a daughter, in a situation where one or both of the parties was divorced. And Father Kienzle wouldn't be able to turn down a friend. And that would be committing ecclesiastical suicide.

He was willing to—and did—keep the laws of the Church himself; he just couldn't inflict them on other people. As was written of St. Anselm, "his intellectual rigour was softened by the sensitiveness of his mind and the generosity of his heart."

Father Kienzle felt that the whole matter should be up to an individual's conscience. If that individual had been in a bad marriage, and had honestly and conscientiously tried to make the marriage work; if that individual, having gotten counseling and examined his or her conscience, felt that he or she could no longer, *in good conscience*, remain in a bad relationship, then it was up to that individual—not to a Church tribunal—to make the determination.

Granted, since Vatican II, it was easier to get a Declaration of Nullity from the Tribunal. However, Father Kienzle felt that it was like checking into a motel to be told, "There's a shark in the pool . . . but don't worry: It's a friendly shark." There shouldn't be a shark in the pool, period. And to Father Kienzle, the Tribunal was the shark in the Church's pool.

Further, he said, it was obvious that the presumption was in favor of the institution.

Thus started his own purgatory. For a year, he prayed, agonized, pondered, and consulted theologian friends whom he respected. At the end of that year, on Holy Thursday, he spent the day in prayer. By the close of that day, he had his answer.

His decision rocked me. If there was anything in the world I did not want it was for him to leave the priesthood. I racked my brain to try to think of something—anything—that would change his mind. I knew this decision had nothing to do with his feelings for me, yet I had to be certain. If I thought he was leaving because of me, I would refuse to ever see him again. It would break my heart—but I didn't want this on my conscience. He shook his head. "If anything, you've helped me stay in as long as I have."

Still the idealist, I pleaded, "Throw your body in the works."

He smiled. "My mother did not raise me for useless confrontation. Canon Law holds all the cards."

I had one last resort. I would go to the Cardinal and plead with him—tell him, "Do something! You can't let this man go. He's too good a priest."

I didn't. I knew that Bill, a very private person, would resent it deeply. I know now it wouldn't have done any good anyway.

On June 27, 1974, it was announced that seven priests—some of the brightest and the best—would be taking a leave of absence. Two of the men had been Bill's classmates. Another, Father Ramon Betanzos, five years younger, had served at Bill's first Mass; five years later, Bill had given the homily at Ray's first Mass. With one exception, none of these men had known that any of the others were leaving. The exception was Father Tom Hinsberg, who, because he was a columnist for the *Michigan Catholic*, had informed Father Kienzle, the editor, that he would be leaving. Tom's nose was a bit out of joint that Bill hadn't returned the confidence. "You just sat there and never said a word—and then you got out of town and left me to face Nancy Manser!"*

The last wedding witnessed by Father Kienzle was that of Bill Struck and Maria Hercher. It took place at Old St. Joseph's. Maria had been a student at Patronage—one of the adolescent girls for whom the rectory had been a home away from home.

Father Kienzle's last Mass was celebrated on the feast of the Sacred Heart. I cannot even begin to imagine what went through his own heart that day. He never once talked about it, and, respecting his privacy, I never asked. It was between him and God.

Father Strain took over as pastor of St. Anselm's. His new assistant, who liked French Provincial, took over what had been Father Kienzle's living quarters. Bill got a call from the parish secretary. "You should see your old bedroom," she said. "It looks like the Petit Trianon!"

---

* Respected religion writer for the *Detroit News*.

PART

3

Detroit Free Press, Thursday, June 27, 1974

Celibacy Dispute Causes Priests
to Leave Diocese

Seven priests of the Detroit Roman Catholic Archdiocese have applied for and been granted leaves of absence, most because of their disagreement with the church's celibacy requirement for priests.

John Lynch, director of archdiocesan communications, said Wednesday that "most of the seven have indicated a desire to marry," although he could not specify which of the seven.

. . . .

The Rev. Bill Cunningham, pastor of the Church of the Madonna and director of Focus: Hope, called the resigning priests "men of great affection and compassion."

"Because the gospel priesthood is such an enormous challenge, the frustrations will lead many very good men to find some other life that will supply them with the kind of human affection they need," Father Cunningham said.

"The church is hanging onto a myth of celibacy that has no foundation in the real metal of Christian tradition. To call it celibacy and pretend it gives a special purity to a life is profoundly bad theology."

. . . .

The Rev. William Kienzle, editor of the Michigan Catholic for 12 years, has resigned to become editor of the monthly Minneapolis Magazine.

Lynch said Father Kienzle's leave has nothing to do with the celibacy issue, and that it is not a permanent resignation.

July 3, 1974, *The Michigan Catholic*

To the editor:

The announcement that seven more priests have taken leave of the priesthood in the Archdiocese will probably produce a cathartic outrage from a handful of people. Tom Hinsberg, especially, will draw fire—after all, his critics will say, it is obvious that his "theology of liberation" is a thin cover for Marxism. The others can also expect some heavy lumber—"Judases, traitors, deserters, derelicts," etc.

But for most of us, from Cardinal Dearden to the youngest member of the community, the announcement brings mostly pain. We are plunged more fully into death with Jesus. Our sadness and pain cannot be washed away by anger or bitterness. We understand more fully what St. Paul meant when he said that all creation is groaning to give birth to the new life of the Kingdom.

This type of suffering will be repeated time and again until the people of God are able to separate the gift of priesthood from the gift of celibacy, a separation which the bureaucratic Church has not been willing to discuss at the level where it counts most—with the people in the pews.

However, we must not let all of this overshadow the gift of eighty-nine years of service which these men have given to the people of God in this Archdiocese.

Each of them has made a genuine and generous investment of himself in people, bringing new life, faith, hope, love, consolation and peace.

So, to you seven from the oldest to the youngest, to Tom, Bill, Jim, Ray, Gerry, Bill and John, on behalf of all the people who have grown into closer union with Jesus Christ through your ministry, I say "Thank you."

Fr. David E. Weisner
President, Priests' Senate

Never do anything as a journalist that you would not do as a gentleman.

—JOHN BOYLE O'REILLY

AS BILL WOULD LATER SAY, he was less barefoot and pregnant than a lot of priests who left. He'd had a twelve-year career as a newspaperman. He was a personable forty-five; I was forty-one.

Years before, he had jokingly specified that were he to marry, he would want a wife who was "incurably romantic, and sterile." Incurably romantic I was. Sterile? Three pregnancies had resulted in only one living child. Further, my bouts with chronic fatigue syndrome—or neurasthenia, as it was sometimes called in those days—were debilitating and frightening.

When his decision to leave was made, we started looking around. Where would he go? What would he do?

This was an era not all that far removed from the time when the Church, in revoking the faculties of a departing priest, decreed, "Father will cease to function and disappear." Bill, who had kept all the Church's rules as they applied to him personally, would not hang around the archdiocese like an unwelcome wedding guest. He would exile himself from the place of his birth.

Bill would leave both his literal and his figurative home. He was a Detroiter through and through; he had been a priest through and through. But his struggle with the chains of Canon Law had become a struggle for the integrity of his soul. He had gone from being a pre-Vatican II traditional priest who kept all the rules and fitted into his place in the clerical pyramid, to being a post-Vatican II questioning priest, and finally to being a priest whose prayerful attempts to come to terms with the burdens that Canon Law placed on his people—Jesus's people—had led him along the tortuous and torturous path to where he would say, in effect—in the words of another tortured cleric: "Here I stand. I can do no other."

I didn't ask, Would you like me to go with you?

He didn't ask, Would you like to come along?

The questions didn't have to be asked because, although we were two individuals, we were of one mind: Whither thou goest I will go was a given.

The Midwest Research Institute put out a helpful booklet on living conditions in the United States. Using this as a guide, we picked three areas: Minnesota, Massachusetts, and Virginia. They seemed to have the cultural aspects we preferred, and at least two of them had liberal representation in Washington; obviously, the citizens of these two states would not be hidebound conservatives. We would be able to fit in. "There's a place for us, somewhere a place for us," Bill singsonged. The words were from *West Side Story*, one of his favorite musicals.

Bill was still an active priest. He would leave only when he found another job. After all, he would have a wife to support—a wife with a variety of medical expenses.*

We started with the classified section of the *Minneapolis Star*. I clipped any Help Wanted ads that looking promising. One such ad sought an editor for a city magazine. "I can do that," Bill said. He

---

* Cardinal Dearden, in a typical act of kindness, had directed that Bill's hospitalization coverage should be kept in effect by the archdiocese until his lay coverage kicked in.

sent in a résumé, listing his qualifications and giving several excellent references, one of whom was Neal Shine.

As I've mentioned, Neal Shine was the newspaperman's newspaperman. No character in *The Front Page* had anything on him when it came to desire for a scoop.

One day Neal, now managing editor of the *Free Press*, received a phone call from a magazine publisher in Minneapolis. A William X. Kienzle was applying for a job. What could Neal tell him about this Kienzle?

"Grab him!" Neal said.

And—may his name forever be blessed—Neal kept this to himself. He did not send a reporter to dig; he did not slip an item to a gossip columnist; he did not phone Bill with questions. Neal kept his own counsel. I knew then and there that Neal Shine belonged in my pantheon of heroes. Neal Shine proved there could be honor among journalists. And that honor was more precious in God's eyes than any seven-day-wonder scoop could ever be.

Bill flew to Minneapolis, was interviewed, and was hired.

He had some doubts, but he had been beating the bushes for a job, and this one was definitely a bird in the hand.

Bill put off announcing his departure as long as possible. As word got around, the proverbial shock waves rocked his parishioners, both current and previous. Of course in those days when a priest left, his departure was never announced as such; it was always, Father is taking a leave of absence. You could count on the figures of one hand the number of priests who had actually returned to active duty after a leave of absence.

Although it did happen. One we knew in later years had taken a leave and had reportedly hit the fleshpots of New York with a vengeance. Eventually he returned to the active priesthood with his sins seared from his soul, to become one of the most hidebound, rigid priests imaginable. My take on him was that if you were to be burned at the stake, he would earnestly and feelingly pray with you—and then personally light the faggots.

When a priest leaves, the first question asked is: Why? Father Kienzle was straight arrow; it couldn't have anything to do with a woman. Besides, as one of his parishioners said to a friend, "I know he's not leaving to get married because if he were, he'd be marrying me." I came to know that she was not unique. Many priests face similar situations, and it is not only laywomen who fantasize and romanticize about Father. There are others who don't count themselves a total success unless they are able to put another notch in their rosaries.

When human persons love one another, they are stepping into the energy field where little universes of fire are ignited, where chemistry occurs, where something within them will be set aflame . . . In so doing, they are truly communicating with the divine.

—FRAN FERDER AND JOHN HEAGLE
Tender Fires: The Spiritual Promise of Sexuality

WE SETTLED INTO AN APARTMENT IN ST. LOUIS PARK, a western suburb of Minneapolis. Bill went off to work every morning and I tried to get accustomed to being a newlywed. Except that we weren't officially married.

I had known Bill for fifteen years, had respected and admired him, had loved and valued his friendship. But my first marriage had traumatized me, and my years as a legal secretary had scarred me. Something seemed to happen once a couple signed a marriage certificate. One or the other—or both—might be lovey-dovey while they were dating, but let them walk down the aisle and mutual honor and respect too often went out the window. He grew sloppy about his manners; she grew sloppy about her appearance; he yelled at her and slammed doors; she shrieked at him and threw things—each secure in the knowledge that neither of them had to be on their best behavior anymore—because, after all, "We're married—and she(he) can't just walk out on me."

And they couldn't leave; they were locked in—yoked to each other.

Bill loved me; I knew that. I loved him; he knew that. Did we really need what he called the Paper Chase? He didn't. I didn't.

He had said he wanted an incurable romantic. I think that actually what he wanted was someone with whom *he* could be incurably romantic. I wanted to be a strong man's one weakness: I was a bottomless pit when it came to welcoming gallantry, affection, and being placed on a pedestal. Further, I was not just an "other"; Bill admired and valued my brain.

I knew that I could never take the place of his priesthood. I would do my poor best to try to make it up to him that he was no longer an active priest, while knowing that nothing I could possibly offer could come close to equaling the treasure of that priesthood.

❧

There was not a day of our life together that Bill did not say to me, "I love you all there is and all there ever could be—and more than that tomorrow."

There was not a day of our life together that I did not say on waking, "I don't know what I ever did to deserve him, but thank you, Lord."

We felt as "married" as any two people could be.

Then we went house hunting. And it quickly became evident that the documentation involved in home ownership would be a lot simpler if we were legally married. "Shall we?" Bill asked. I hesitated, then nodded.

We planned carefully. We went down to the courthouse—the one whose clock tower is seen in the opening credits of the *Mary*

Tyler Moore Show. It was the Friday after Thanksgiving, when no one was around except one judge on emergency duty. He would marry us, and the extra copy of the marriage record would be destroyed, rather than being filed with the public documents made available for journalistic investigation.

I wore gray—a gray pleated skirt, a gray wool turtleneck sweater, gray suede shoes . . . and a string of pearls. I still have the pearls.

The judge's bailiff rustled up two young secretaries, who were thrilled to be witnesses at a wedding.

The judge spoke the required words, then asked the required questions. Bill replied firmly. I was shaking and unable to speak. Bill took my hands in his and seemingly by force of his love or his will kept me from falling in a dead faint. I finally was able to barely whisper the necessary response. Judge Kane pronounced us married. We were now legal.

That night, thinking of my previous marriage, and of the gift of himself that Bill had saved for me, I said to him, "I'm sorry I couldn't come to you as a virgin." And if, in all our years together, he had never spoken another affectionate word to me, his response provided all the love I would ever have needed. He smiled, and, quoting from *The Music Man*, said only, " 'The sadder but wiser girl for me.' "

Each time I see *Man of La Mancha*, one of Bill's favorite shows, I am reminded that the Don Quixote who saw Aldonza as Dulcinea had a modern-day brother under the skin.

People don't judge a man by his wife, as much as by the way he treats his wife.

—SYDNEY HARRIS

IT WAS WITH MUCH TREPIDATION THAT I HAD LEFT MICHIGAN. I was leaving behind a general practitioner who had been my family doctor for over fifteen years. Who had seen me through pregnancy, hospitalization, and all manner of legitimate as well as hypochondriachal visits. He had brought me along so far and helped so much; how could I replace him in a strange city?

I phoned the Minnesota Medical Society and threw myself on their mercy. I wanted a general practitioner, not a specialist. They gave me three names. I made an appointment with one who sounded promising. He had been a state legislator, who had helped write Minnesota's stringent nursing home laws. He had now returned to family practice.

I gave Dr. Salchert a thumbnail medical history, especially my "neurasthenic" syndrome. I asked him to tell me if he wasn't familiar with this sort of problem, so I could go elsewhere, as otherwise both of us would be wasting our time.

I was reassured when he gave me a rundown on how he would handle my situation. Normally, he said, in the case of a new patient, he would call for a number of tests. In my case, however, I had already had so many tests that he could get from my previous physician any records we might need. "Besides," he added, "with a situation like yours, if I give you more tests you'll just start obsessing more and more about your symptoms and that will be self-defeating."

Back in Michigan, Dr. Pool had patiently treated each aspect of my illness, dealing with each symptom, each manifestation, adjusting prescriptions, dosages, vitamin supplements as the need arose. At various times, I suffered vision problems, intestinal problems, dizziness, hives, spaciness, loss of appetite, inability to concentrate, panic attacks, hyperventilation, tremors, heart irregularities, memory loss, sleep disorders, depression, and exhaustion. The depression and the exhaustion were the most frightening. When a specialist suggested amphetamines, Dr. Pool shook his head. "That's like beating a dead horse," he said.

In Minneapolis, Dr. Salchert provided the medical security I continued to need. Improvement was agonizingly slow, but he was so reassuring that even in the face of periodic setbacks, I felt that there could be light at the end of the tunnel.

But always and above all, there was Bill. He was there for me, every step of the way. He was the sine qua non, the rock I leaned on—clung to—when I grew discouraged, when all looked totally bleak. Without his support and encouragement I truly have no idea what would have become of me.

Every so often, the cumulative effect of my illness overwhelmed me and I wept in frustration: How could I put Bill through this? Occasionally, feeling sorry for myself, I turned maudlin. "Make sure your next wife is healthy," I would half sniffle, half mumble to Bill. In response, he would take me in his arms and say simply, "Put the shoe on the other foot."

He never wavered, never grew impatient, although there must have been times when he wondered whether I would ever be healthy. I know he prayed always.

Little by little, my symptoms eased—although there was the occasional relapse. One day, at home, I grew dizzy, and fell to the floor in a near faint. Fearful of standing lest I fall again, I crawled to the table where the phone was, pulled on the cord until the phone fell on the floor next to me, and dialed Bill at the office.

He was in a meeting, from which he was glad to escape. He came home immediately and pulled me to my feet. A tranquilizer and a foot massage alleviated the tachycardia that sent me into near panic.

But Bill was unable to totally relax; he never knew when the next phone call would come. He said he felt like a runner, on constant three-point stance. Yet he never complained. And he never lost his sense of humor.

Once, in the middle of the night, he rushed me to the hospital for what turned out to be a panic attack. As I was being cared for by the medical staff, the very pregnant admitting clerk was getting the pertinent information from Bill. "What is her religion?"

"She's Catholic."

"Was she baptized?"

"She was 'surprised by the spirit,'" Bill responded.

The clerk sat, tapping her finger on the desk, looking at him humorlessly. Bill got the message. "She's Catholic," he repeated firmly.

Actually, I was and I wasn't. I had never been baptized, never been confirmed, never been anythinged. I had, Bill said on occasion, received what is termed the "baptism of desire." I'm sure this was true. I attended Mass, received Communion, believed in and professed Catholicism. Of course, technically, as far as the Church was concerned, we were "living in sin," and I had no right to Communion. However, trusting in God's great mercy, I was quite willing to let Him sort it all out.

Civilitas successit barbarum (Civilization has replaced the barbarian)

—Motto of Minnesota when it was a territory

Mpls. magazine had undergone a metamorphosis. It had started out as a somewhat shady journal; its new publisher had hopes of turning it into a bona-fide city magazine. Actually, he had visions of himself as a Midwest version of *New York* magazine's Clay Felker. Unfortunately, he didn't have Felker's financial pockets. So *Mpls.* operated on a shoestring. This meant dealing with free-lance wannabe's, many of whom left a great deal to be desired as far as professionalism was concerned. In order to get the required articles in on time, the editor had to wheedle, coddle, and spoonfeed incipient prima donnas.

For Bill, who had existed for twenty years in a Nothing's-Too-Good-for-Father milieu, this was a cannonball dive into ice water.

He soon learned which writers he could depend on. For the rest, it quickly became obvious that it would be easier to write the articles himself than to try to put out a worthwhile publication based on whatever the wannabes turned in. So, as time went by, more and more articles and features were written by Bill—and me. However, since no one wanted the readership to know that this was, in effect, a Ma-and-Pa project, Mark Boyle and Fiona Lowther joined the staff.

Mark Boyle was Bill's maternal grandfather. An important part of Michigan's early lumber industry, Mark Boyle was the man who surveyed a stand of trees and estimated how much lumber would be forthcoming. At his wake, his widow heard two men talking about her late husband: "If he hadn't been such an honest man, he could've died a millionaire."

Mark Boyle died long before Bill was born. After Bill left the priesthood, a cousin sent him a photo of the Boyle family. Bill had never before seen a photo of his grandfather. There was the doughty old man, sporting a bushy mustache of the era—and resembling no one so much as Cardinal John Dearden. The Celtic genes made themselves evident. Obviously, Mark Boyle would be a worthwhile nom de plume.

My pen name was Fiona Lowther. Lowther from the Quaker ancestor who had left Armagh for America, and Fiona after the heroine of Lerner and Loewe's *Brigadoon*. I had always admired Fiona. When she sang "Waitin' for My Dearie," it struck a chord in me. I had come to realize that there was no loneliness like that of being unhappily married, and that it was better to wait—forever, if necessary—than to marry just to keep from being single. I had found my "dearie" and if Minneapolis wasn't Brigadoon, it was the closest thing to it.

As I've said, there's nothing like on-the-job training. What little Bill and I hadn't learned at the *Michigan Catholic* and at the *Detroit Free Press* we learned now. In addition to the editor's monthly column, Bill—or Mark Boyle—wrote articles, did interviews, reviewed stage plays, films, and musical productions, even, on occasion, restaurants, art fairs, and mall openings. He also ramrodded each month's issue of *Mpls.* into publication, handling deadlines with the aplomb of one attuned to rigid schedules.

I wrote articles and did interviews, reviewed books, put together a shopping column, copy-edited, proofread, and, in a throwback to my early days at the *Free Press*, compiled the What's Going on in Minneapolis listings. I also made up movie quizzes and constructed "Minnequotes"—acrostic puzzles.

It was a busy time. We were settling into a happily married life; we were doing work we enjoyed; we were taking advantage of the cultural aspects that Minneapolis had to offer—and there were many. As editor of the city magazine, Bill was invited everywhere and to every event, and I tagged along.

For years, I had heard of the Guthrie—a mecca for serious actors, and for serious theater devotees. We were privileged to be in Minneapolis for three full seasons of what we considered to be the Guthrie's Golden Age—the era under Michael Langham's directorship.

In the past, vacations for Bill had frequently meant trips to New York City, where he and his priest buddies attended Broadway comedies and musicals. Once more he was little Billy, sitting and listening and watching and enjoying as the extended family sang, told stories, and joked and laughed. In later years, one of his priest classmates would say, "Bill lived his life according to musical comedy."

In Minneapolis, Bill could once again indulge his penchant for the theater. In the Twin Cities, wherever somebody nailed two boards together a theater company grew. There was even a nationally known Children's Theater, which staged shows every bit as professional as the best of them.

Aside from New York for Bill, and, later, Dublin for both of us, nowhere did either of us experience the joys of the theater as we did in Minneapolis. Many of the actors we saw there went on to New York, Stratford, TV, and films. We saw Len Cariou as King Lear, Michael Gross as Mephistopheles, Ken Welsh in *School for Scandal*, Blair Brown in *The Crucible*, and Peter Michael Goetz in *Sleuth*. Others included Ken Ruta, Mark Lamos, Nicholas Kepros, James Blendick, Patricia Conolly, Maureen Anderman (who, we discovered, was a Michigan girl), Fran Bennett, and Barbara Bryne. Even now, over twenty-five years later, every so often, I see a familiar face on TV or a familiar name as the credits roll by, and am taken back in memory to the Guthrie.

Coming from Detroit, which boasted a Catholic church almost every few blocks, it was a shock to arrive in Minneapolis and find comparatively few Catholic churches. When we lived in St. Louis Park, we attended Mass at a nearby church in Golden Valley. Until one morning when the cantankerous pastor prayed that the stubborn and selfish athletes would settle their strike and get back to playing football so the rest of us could enjoy our God-given right to attend the games. That's when we switched to the Basilica of St. Mary.

Minneapolis didn't have a cathedral; that was in St. Paul. But it had a beautiful basilica, whose pastor, a monsignor of Irish-Norwegian extraction, ran a reverent ship. Since the basilica was right down the street from the Guthrie, the lector on any given Sunday was apt to be a visiting actor.

One Sunday, the reading was done by a man who could've been Cyril Ritchard's double.

It's Cyril Ritchard, Bill said.

It couldn't be, I said.

It *is*, Bill insisted.

But Cyril Ritchard is Australian, I said, in one of the world's great non sequiturs.

As we drove out of the church lot, we saw the "lookalike" walking down the street. It was a cold day. We stopped and asked if we could give him a ride. He graciously accepted.

It *was* Cyril Ritchard.

We were thrilled. I told him about my unwillingness to believe it was actually he up on the altar. "I know you're Australian," I said, "so I thought it couldn't be you."

"Lots of Australians are Catholic," he said, with some severity.

He told us about his pet dog, who was traveling with him. Then we talked about *Peter Pan*, and his portrayal of Captain Hook. By now, we had pulled up in front of his hotel. Before getting out of the car, he thanked us for the ride. At which point, Bill asked, "Would you do it for us?"

He knew what Bill meant. And he did it! Captain Hook's delicious gurgle bubbled up from Cyril Ritchard's throat, leaving us with an enchanting memory.

Another enchanting memory was the night we attended a performance of *The Music Man* in St. Paul. We sat in the balcony and looked down to the main floor, where the musical's creator, Meredith Willson, sat with his wife. We were touched to see the couple holding hands during the performance.

When Meredith Willson died a few years back, and the beautiful "Good Night, My Someone" was played at his funeral, Bill and I both felt an emotional tug, remembering. I thought too, at that time, of one of Bill's priest classmates, who, with inventive conceptualization, had insisted that the juxtaposition of "Good Night, My Someone" and "Seventy-six Trombones"—the same tune in a different tempo—was intercourse set to music.

Stanislaw Skrowaczewski was the director of the Minnesota Orchestra, which completed its new Orchestra Hall during our tenure. Opening night was not for the wheelers and dealers; it was for those who had built the hall, and their families. The second night was for the reviewers and the celebrities. People were asked to leave their fur coats in the lockers provided so as to preserve the hall's acoustics. We were told that the fur tended to muffle and deaden the musical sounds.

The new Orchestra Hall was just a few blocks from the basilica. One Sunday, after Communion, a man carrying a violin stepped forward on the altar and wordlessly proceeded to play the "Meditation" from *Thais*. In later years, each time we heard the "Meditation," Bill and I would look at each other and smile at the memory of that magical moment.

Not every visitor to the basilica was friendly. One Christmas, a disturbed man broke in. Monsignor Berntsen called the police, then stood watching, unnoticed, as the man proceeded to make a shambles of the altar, decorated for the holidays. It was an educational experience for the monsignor. He was astounded, he said, by the amount of anger that could erupt from a human being.

In another educational experience, a young priest-assistant gave a homily, in which he spoke of his vacation spent camping out in a tent on the shore of Lake Superior. For the first time, he said, he understood the meaning of the necessity for obtaining food and shelter. Bill, who had always referred to the priesthood as the ultimate security, chuckled quietly. "If he wants to know about the necessity for food and shelter, he should leave the priesthood and try to earn a living and support a family."

Of all the things a woman does, her cooking best proclaims her happiness or lack of it.

—UNKNOWN

EVERYTHING IN MINNESOTA WAS AN ADVENTURE. Sometimes on an artistic plane, sometimes laughable, but never dull. Bill, particularly, seemed to have mastered the art of living "in the moment." He never failed to see the humor in life, enjoying it to its fullest.

He was a balanced mixture of private person and people-loving person. He was gregarious at parties, appreciative at the theater, vicarious at sports events, introspective when writing, and reverent at Mass. In the forty-two years I knew him, I almost never heard him use a four-letter word. On those rare occasions, a heartfelt "Damn!" did escape his lips, but I could tell from his expression that the outburst would be cause for penance.

He reserved the verb "love" for God, Jesus, the Church, the priesthood, his family, his close friends, his country, and me. He gently corrected me when I referred to something as "adorable"; God, he said, is worthy of adoration, "things" are not.

The inculcation of the priesthood remained strong. One night I woke to find Bill talking in his sleep. He was absolving me . . . in Latin.

It may have been because we had been friends for so long before we became a couple that we welcomed every experience as a lagniappe—an extra added bonus to our life. Any holiday was celebrated not just as time off but as memorable, fun, a continual reminder that we were blessedly lucky to be together.

And holidays had their residual effect. Take Thanksgiving, for instance.

I enjoyed cooking for Bill. His quasi-starvation years at the seminary had made him an appreciative eater. No matter what I made, or what it tasted like, he declared it delicious, and ate everything down to the last bite. It didn't matter whether it was hamburgers or a standing rib roast; he would taste it, kiss his fingers in the best Gallic manner, roll his eyes heavenward, say, "*Magnifique!*" and proceed to demolish it.

Only once, very early on, did a meal disappoint. I had put together a meat loaf that came out more like a swamp loaf. He ate it, but in future referred to it as the exception that proved the rule. If he marveled over a meal—as he almost always did—and I said, "Aw, c'mon; it can't be that good," his response was invariably, "I told you about the meat loaf."

All of which made me fearless when it came to cooking.

Thanksgiving is known for good reason as Turkey Day. But fearless as I had become, I tried something totally different: New York restaurateur Regine's *Gyuniku Negimaki* (steak and scallion rolls). Bill went through his *Magnifique* routine, and I glowed under the light of his appreciation. I felt very with-it, very half-past au courant, and a quarter-to-avant-garde. Turkey was for fogies; we, though over forty, were solidly part of the Now Generation.

That weekend, going through my coupon envelope, I came across one which stated that Brand X would pay us $2.00 to try their turkey. Too bad Thanksgiving was over. At the supermarket early that evening, the light bulb lit, or, as the British say, the penny dropped: The expiration date on the coupon was that day. It was now 6 P.M.; as long as the envelope was postmarked by midnight we could get that $2.00.

The last pickup at the mailbox outside the market was 6:30 P.M. We had thirty minutes. Never did a *Stop the Clock* contestant move faster; the roadrunner's beep-beep faded in the distance as I flew into action. Assigning Bill to pick out the smallest turkey he could find ("Make sure it's the right brand"), I bought a stamped envelope from the supermarket postmistress, borrowing her pen to fill out the coupon and address the envelope.

It would be gauche to rip the requisite proof-of-purchase label off the turkey while still in the market. Some sense of decorum must be preserved: We would wait till we got the groceries in the car.

There was a new clerk at the checkout counter: Instead of routinely accepting our check in payment, she required identification. Precious seconds slipped by as Bill dug into his wallet for his driver's license.

Once back in the car, we waited as the store's innovative exterior delivery belt moved in slow motion. We could see the carton containing our groceries—and our turkey, our $2.00—inching nearer to the pickup point. Maddeningly, the car in front of us stalled.

At long last, we had the groceries in the backseat. As Bill drove around the corner to the mailbox, I dug down into the bags, scattering items from soup to nuts about like a badger heading for China. Suddenly, there it was: our fat, frozen little friend that would make us $2.00 richer.

The wrapping bearing the proof-of-purchase label was encased in the usual mesh enclosure. I was stymied for only seconds. "The keys! The keys!" I bawled, like Gable giving the command to Dive! Dive! Out of the ignition came the car key and its siblings on the parent ring. Singling out the largest, the house key, I ripped it hard against the mesh, which finally broke, leaving the innards open to attack. And we were stopped cold—literally: The casing bearing the required label was frozen solidly to the bird. Not keys, not fingernails, not coat buttons—nothing could get even a corner of that label up.

"Why weren't you a Boy Scout . . . or a fisherman . . . or a member of the Swiss Army?" I groused, bemoaning the fact that Bill did not carry a penknife. Never in our married life had he been found so wanting!

Bill looked in the rearview mirror to see in the distance the mail pickup truck approaching the next box a short distance down the highway. Though we were in the depths of an Upper Midwest cold snap, perspiration broke out on my forehead. In the feeble rays of the overhead light, I bent to my task once more, breaking a fingernail in my fresh attempt to peel off the label. Using the key again, I was able, in sheer desperation, to gouge a hole—not merely in the casing, but also in the turkey. Poor Tom had never anticipated this manner of skewering when he gave his life for his country's Thanksgiving.

My shoulders drooped. We were beaten. No way were we going to get that label off. Even had we been so brash, there was no time now to dash into the market for a knife.

In the rearview mirror, the U.S. Mail truck neared inexorably. Neither wind nor rain nor dark of night nor frozen turkey label shall stay these couriers from the swift (no brand allusion intended) completion of their appointed rounds.

And then, as the ghosts of Watt, Edison, Bell, Da Vinci, and St. Jude smiled approval, my mouth uttered the words before my brain grasped their meaning: "Quick, give me your American Express card!"

Bill, by now benumbed and slow-moving, fumbled through his wallet. There it was, that beautiful piece of blue! I grabbed it, inserted it into the gouged-out section of the casing—*and lifted off the label intact.* I stuffed the label into the envelope, licked it shut, and dropped it into the box just as the U.S. Mail truck screeched to a halt beside us.

Some weeks later, a check for $2.00 arrived in the mail.

Never again would I smile condescendingly at the maxim that every modern miss had learned at mother's—and Karl Malden's— knee: Your American Express Card—Don't Leave Home Without It.

The ornament of a house is the friends who frequent it.

—Ralph Waldo Emerson

BILL, LIKE MOST MEN, was not a big fan of shopping. That was so whether hunting for shoes or for a house. The real estate agent and I did most of the house hunting, with Bill bringing up the rear.

One day, as we were driving through various neighborhoods, in search of a likely house, Bill stopped the car in front of a "For Sale" sign. "That looks like a good one."

The house was in a nice area, not far from downtown; it looked like it might be affordable, and Bill liked the red shutters. We rang the doorbell, but no one was home. Next day, I notified our agent and she and I went to look at the house. It did seem perfect for us. It was a small, two-bedroom bungalow, with a large, dry basement, a screened porch off the kitchen, nice trees, and a detached car-and-a-half garage off the rear alley.

I reported to Bill, who said, "Let's do it."

"But you haven't seen the inside. Maybe you won't like it."

"I trust you. I'll take your word for it."

If ever there was a case of Speak now or forever hold your peace—!

Financial details were arranged, papers were signed; a closing date was set—and we were homeowners. Bill did not see the inside of the house until we moved in on the day before Christmas.

That night, as we made our way through stacked cartons, trying to find some bedsheets, Bill said, "Now I know how the Holy Family felt . . . it's no fun moving on Christmas eve."

Our first visitor was an old friend of Bill's. Actually, Lou Morand was more than a friend. A seminary schoolmate, Lou was, from mutual ancestors back in the mists of time, also a very distant relative. Lou's father had been the Kienzle family doctor. Dr.

Morand had taken out Bill's appendix. He had also performed the same service for Bill's classmate, Edmund Szoka.

Although Lou's younger brother, Bob, was later ordained, Lou himself decided that he liked girls too much to devote himself to the priesthood. He married Mary Knox, a charming Kentuckian. The Morand family settled in Inkster, where, along with the Fitzpatricks, the Papkes, and the Kamegos, they helped contribute to the growing population of St. Norbert's, where young Father Kienzle was an assistant.

At the time we lived in Minneapolis, Lou was working in nearby Anoka, driving home to Michigan each weekend to visit his family. Lou, having heard that Bill was in Minneapolis, phoned him at *Mpls.* and suggested they get together for lunch.

Lou picked Bill up and as they drove to the restaurant the two began to catch up on events of the past parted years. In the course of the conversation, Bill, in his offhand way, said, "You know, I'm married." In the ensuing silence that spoke volumes, Bill's quiet voice posed the question, "Did you just swerve?"

Shortly thereafter, Lou came to dinner and regaled us with jokes, stories, and reminiscences in his inimitable fashion. Lou's talents included an ability to mimic voices. Occasionally, back in Detroit, those who thought they were speaking to Cardinal Dearden on the phone discovered that Lou had perfectly captured the Cardinal's voice with its soft Irish tinge.

Lou and Mary were active in amateur theater. The family's talent extended to musicals. One of the Morand daughters, Grace, became the lead singer of the popular Chenille Sisters trio.

We were always happy to hear from Lou, as we were never quite sure that he would survive his weekend drives to and from Detroit. He must have led a charmed life despite the fact that the speed limits on the Interstate existed only as a receding blur in his rearview mirror.

Bill did not like surprises. His idea of the opposite of fun was a surprise birthday party. For once, an advertising slogan—"No surprises"—worked. In later years when we traveled, whenever possible we overnighted at the nearest Holiday Inn.

He nearly went into shock the evening his wife came home with a stranger in tow.

Menzies Mc Killop was a visiting Scotsman whose play, *The Future Pit*, was being staged by Guthrie II, the experimental wing of the Guthrie. I had interviewed Menzies for *Mpls.* and discovered he was at loose ends. I invited him home for dinner.

Bill recovered his poise rapidly. Menzies, a bear of a man, endeared himself to Bill with his droll repartee. At one point, Bill was talking about the British films that featured men being piped into battle by kilted Scots playing "the devil's instrument." As the Ladies from Hell (as the kilted warriors were called) advanced, the piper or pipers would be mowed down by enemy fire. As each man fell, the dying wail of his bagpipe signaled his demise.

"Why is it that they always shot the bagpipers?" Bill asked.

"Prrrhaps," Menzies responded in his ruddy burr, "they wrrr music crrritics."

Second Bananas

WHEN IT CAME TO TOURING CELEBRITIES, especially in the television field, Minnesota wasn't exactly on the A-list.

Instead of Jack Lord (*Hawaii Five-O*) we got James MacArthur; instead of David Carradine (*Kung Fu*), we got Keye Luke; instead of Rock Hudson (*McMillan and Wife*), John Schuck; instead of David Janssen (*Harry-O*), Anthony Zerbe; instead of Alan Alda (*M*A*S*H*), Jamie Farr; instead of Mary Tyler Moore, Gavin MacLeod.

Occasionally, there was an exception. We got not only Marion Ross (*Happy Days*), but also Tom Bosley.

Dick Van Dyke at that time was addressing groups throughout the country on the dangers of alcoholism. When he spoke at the Minneapolis Press Club, he commented on how friendly Minneapolitans were. They would see him on the street, he said, come up to him and say, "I'm chemically dependent too." Bill, a smoker himself, chuckled: Van Dyke, during his Press Club appearance, smoked almost nonstop.

Some interviews brought memorable quotes, some for publication, some not. Marion Ross joked that she got the role on *Happy Days* because she was married to the show's director.

Keye Luke reminisced about appearing in a touring company of Rodgers and Hammerstein's *Flower Drum Song*. He had auditioned for the role by singing a genuine, authentic *Flower Drum Song*. He whistled it for Bill. Bill was captivated by its beauty, which was much more flowerlike than Richard Rodgers's melody. Bill asked Keye Luke if he had ever corrected Rodgers's notion of what a flower drum song should be.

"One does not talk to God," Luke replied.

Bill admired Anthony Zerbe for telling his PR people he'd do the countrywide tour only if his wife could come along. One of the topics discussed was Zerbe's role as a bad guy who killed off something like eleven priests in an early episode of *Sarge*. In later years I wondered whether that episode could have been a seed that led to *The Rosary Murders.*

Another wife who traveled with her husband was Mrs. Jamie Farr, an Elizabeth Taylor lookalike. We were entranced when the Farrs told us about sighting a UFO out west.

Also accompanying her husband was Mrs. Gavin McLeod. The McLeods were such a lovely couple that we were saddened to hear of their breakup some time later. However, as I recall, they eventually did get back together.

In the summer of 1974, the Episcopal Church in America ordained its first women priests. Fifty female Episcopal deacons were eligible. All were invited to be ordained. Eleven accepted. Bill interviewed the eldest, Jeannette Piccard, the widow of the famous balloonist. Dr. Piccard, sporting a button that read, "Don't Baptize Women, Ordain Them," assured Bill that she was indeed a priest: "If I consecrate, it is consecrated. If I absolve you, you are absolved. And if I bless you, you are blessed," she stated in a tone that would brook no disagreement. She went on to say that her son said, "I call my mother 'Father.'"

Asked when Catholic women might expect ordination to the priesthood, the Reverend Dr. Piccard replied, "When they get another Pope like John."

Dr. Alla Bozarth-Campbell, another of the ordinees, wrote of the reaction to a theological address she gave to a large group of women religious. "Well," she overheard one say afterward, "I don't mind the clerical collar—but *those earrings!*"

A Minneapolis columnist devoted a couple of sentences to the earrings-cum-collar worn by Bozarth-Campbell's sister-priest, Carter Heyward, one of the youngest of the newly ordained. When I interviewed the Reverend Heyward, she said, "Somehow I feel I've spent my life trying to be God's son, only to realize at last that I am God's daughter."

One of Bill's earliest and favorite interviewees was Bob Keeshan. "Captain Kangaroo is not one show that I've done over and over again for nineteen years," Keeshan said. "It is thousands of individual experiences. I was born this morning for the kid who watched my show for the first time today."

Asked what kind of show he would produce for adults, he could not come up with a format. "Adults are too far gone for me," he admitted. "What's wrong with the worst of TV today is that it's tasteless."

That was in 1974. I shudder to imagine what Bob Keeshan would think of today's TV offerings.

For a December issue of *Mpls.*, Bill interviewed Dayton's* department store Santa Claus, who, like Art Linkletter and

---

* now Marshall Field's

Saginaw's Bishop Untener, had learned that children say the most unexpected things. When one seven-year-old asked Santa for long underwear, Santa wondered why. "Because I want to keep warm," the boy said. "Not like mama. She don't wear any underpants and she freezes her a—— off." Mama's face turned as red as the blue her bottom reportedly was.

Another of Bill's favorite interviewees was cartoonist Dick Guindon. While Guindon was working in New York, it was said that he "cartooned the way [Art] Buchwald writes." He changed his style somewhat after returning to Minneapolis. "Satire doesn't suit the Midwest," Guindon explained. "You have to be more understated." Bill, undoubtedly recalling his own editorial attempt at satire, which had brought Michigan's Irish down on his head, could go with that.

Just ask Detroiters, who for years now have wrinkled their brows over Guindon's views of the Motor City in the morning *Free Press*. Guindon has become almost a satirization of himself as conversation over Michigan breakfast tables is, "Would you explain today's Guindon to me?"

One of my favorite interviewees was the Guthrie's Ken Welsh, who brought a blush to my country girl cheeks when he said, "The stage is a jealous mistress; she doesn't like it when you're off." Welsh has since gone on to garner awards and acclaim for his work in television and filmdom, as well as in the theater. His stage work includes *Hamlet* at Stratford and the role of Johnny in the original Off-Broadway production of *Frankie and Johnny in the Clair de Lune*.

Another interesting visitor was Chief Dan George. Sometime after the film *Little Big Man* came out, the chief was on tour promoting a book he had written.

When Bill and I arrived at the meeting room, which was full of other invitees, the chief was seated in a chair in the middle of the room looking contemplative. No one was speaking to him; few were even looking at him. Either they were so in awe of him, or else they really didn't know who he was. I must confess that even I couldn't think of a thing to say to him. I would do better nowadays.

The situation grew increasingly awkward. No one was saying anything—by this time, we were all just standing around looking at the chief as if he were a subject in Madame Tussaud's Waxworks. The chief sat looking off into the distance.

Finally, Bill, under his breath, said, "This is ridiculous." He went over to the chief, and in a sort of combination bending down and kneeling posture starting talking to him, and got the "interview."

When firefighter-author Dennis Smith was in town, he gave Bill an insight that resurfaced in the wake of the destruction of the World Trade Center. "Of all civil servants forbidden by law to strike," Smith said, "firefighters are the only ones whose services can't be duplicated by nonprofessionals. Others can maintain sanitation; the National Guard or the Army can fill in for police." The public might remember this the next time firefighters ask for a raise.

Among those profiled in *Mpls.* was Tony Dungy, the U-Minnesota quarterback, who was picked as a "face to watch." Dungy went on to become coach of the NFL Tampa Bay Buccaneers and then of the Indianapolis Colts. Al Franken, now television's wonder wit, was another "face to watch."

Joe Selvaggio, a former priest, was the subject of a lengthy article. Selvaggio was described as Minneapolis's version of Robin Hood, who "scrounges from the haves and redistributes to the have-nots." Through his Project for Pride in Living, Selvaggio and his crew of Native-Americans rehabilitated inner-city homes long before Jimmy Carter made a name for himself and Habitat for Humanity.

Mpls. interviewed just about everyone of note, with a few exceptions.

An agent phoned Bill to say that his teenage client, a member of the cast of a then-popular sitcom, would be in town and available for an interview. The idea of spending an hour with a callow youth did not appeal to Bill. He passed. Thus he was never able to say that he had met John Travolta.

He did, however, interview Summer Bartholomew, Miss USA 1975. I got the impression that Bill felt she was a cut above the average beauty queen. I do not recall what her aspirations were, but I'm sure she was all for world peace.

Bill himself gained a reputation as a minor celebrity of sorts. A column in a local utility newsletter in the form of a letter to God said that though the writer enjoyed singing in church, her fellow choristers seemed to find her voice somewhat less than mellifluous. Having heard the saying Who sings prays twice, she was, she wrote, uncertain whether she should continue to sing, or merely mouth the words rather than subject those about her to aural punishment.

Bill, in a pastoral humor, sent the lady a letter on *Mpls.* letterhead. It read: "The saying is 'Who sings *well* prays twice.' I've heard you sing. Don't." He signed it God.

A reply arrived in an envelope addressed simply: God, c/o *Mpls.* magazine. When the unopened envelope was placed on Bill's desk, he had a sudden flash of insight: If Edmund Gwenn in *Miracle on 34th Street* was proven in a court of law to be the real Kris Kringle because the United States Postal Service delivered to him a slew of kids' letters addressed to Santa Claus, then, ipso facto, the editor of *Mpls.* magazine had been recognized as God.

I forbore asking Bill if he could rub his stomach and chew gum at the same time.

Litigious: Of, relating to, or characterized by litigation. Tending to engage in lawsuits.

—*The American Heritage Dictionary of the English Language*

MINNESOTANS ARE SUCH FAIR FOLK. This was epitomized by a Solomon-like decision of Dr. C. Peter Magrath, of the University of Minnesota. Early in Dr. Magrath's presidency, he was confronted with the Great Lettuce Controversy. When faculty and students voted between lettuce picked by UFW or Teamsters, the vote was so close that Dr. Magrath set up a two-bowl policy in the university cafeteria. Patrons could step to the counter and take their choice.

One of the reasons for Minnesota's squeaky clean reputation was that the first word children learned after "Mama" and "Daddy" was "I'llsue"—articulated as one word in the same manner that Southern children pronounce "Damyankee."

Public servants who might otherwise have been tempted to something more than venial sin knew they were walking a narrow tightrope over a volcano. Where inhabitants of other regions were content to vent their spleen via letters to the editor, or possibly furious phone calls, Minnesotans tended to invoke the threat of legal action.

Most editors and/or publishers kept this tendency very much in mind. Bill, seemingly unconcerned, in a review of the film *Mahogany*, tempted fate when he informed readers that it was perhaps the third worst movie ever made. (He did not name the first two.) Such "botching," he said, could not have been easy. "But producer/director Berry Gordy did it. He took all that talent and made another *Springtime for Hitler*. Only [*Springtime*] was so bad it was good. *Mahogany* is so bad it's better than a barbiturate."

He went on to specify chapter and verse, and concluded, "If there has been one kind word written in review of *Mahogany*, it has not been recorded. It got so bad that, some time back, Gordy was threatening to sue the reviewers. He had it all wrong. Anybody who paid good money to see this bummer should sue *him*."

One step below the threat of legal action was the threat to cancel subscriptions. Where a threat to cancel one's *Michigan Catholic* subscription was at most of academic interest to Father Kienzle, the threat to cancel one's subscription to *Mpls.* constituted an attack on our bread and butter. And *Mpls.* readers pulled no punches. Where *Michigan Catholic* readers had threatened to cancel over theological disagreement, *Mpls.* readers threatened to cancel over decolletagical exposure when a busty blonde "disgraced" the cover of the magazine.

Tom, the publisher, was perturbed at the thought of losing even one subscriber, but it *did* get his magazine Talked About—which was one of his primary goals. Tom tended to copy from other city magazines. As a result, *Mpls.* was replete with Ten Bests and Ten Worsts, Chic, Chic-ier, Chic-iest graphs (the ultimate being not "Chic-iest," but "Gauche"), as well as "The Twin Cities' Sexiest" and "The Most Eligible Bachelors" lists.

Of course these elicited letters from the left-out and the erroneously included. It turned out that one of the "most eligible bachelors" was happily married (or at least he was before his name appeared in the listing). Rudy Boschwitz, who later became a U.S. senator, sent the editor a tongue-in-cheek complaint at being left off the "sexiest" list. "I have no idea how you will handle the large number of letters you'll receive from distraught women about the omission . . . but I would suggest you respond by saying it was 'an oversight.'"

One topic that elicited a hailstorm of letters was an article Bill did on the never-ending antipathy between powerboaters and sailboaters. One young buck who became bored with power boating took to sailboating because, he said, "Sailboats are a great phallic symbol for women—the masts. That's why I use my boat for dates." Besides, he added, "nobody steals a sail." It seems that all the motors he ever owned were ripped off.

Anything and everything was grist for the mill. In its annual Doubtful Distinctions listings, the magazine gave itself the Typo of the Year award, noting that in an article explaining how to purchase the least expensive ice cream cone, it had mentioned, "We ordered one single and one double come [sic] for a total cost of 80 cents." Cheap at half the price.

The Gentle, Non-Judgmental Answer award went to one Monsignor John J. O'Sullivan for his reply to the question (published in the *Catholic Bulletin*), "Has the Pope no conscience that he can see the pictures of starving babies and still insist on the

Catholic teaching on birth control?" Monsignor's award-winning answer was: "What a simple, ignorant approach you have to life's complexities!"

The definitive letter to the editor may have been the one written by a seventh grade English class in Edina.

Edina is an upscale suburb of Minneapolis. So upscale that it lends itself to satire, which we now know is iffy at best in the Midwest. In Ireland, all a playwright or a comedian has to do is include a heartfelt "Jaysus!" in a scene or a joke, and the laughs come thick and fast. In the Twin Cities, all one had to do was mention Edina and one was looked upon as a wit.

It was hard *not* to classify Edina as different. For one thing, when the local papers listed garage sales, they were all under one heading: Garage Sales. Except for one separate category: *Edina* Garage Sales.

Mpls. featured a cover story on Edina. It compared Edina to Grosse Pointe, Beverly Hills, and Upper Scarsdale. It was written by a freelancer, with some *Mpls.* staffers contributing. One of the lead-off paragraphs opened with, "Who the hell do those people in Edina think they are anyway? Do they really think their junk is better than mine?"

Mr. Dick Sandeen's third hour seventh grade English class at Edina East Junior High School responded in high dudgeon— Edina dudgeon.

After listing their own chapter and verse of complaints, the students concluded: "Didn't your mother, by the way, ever tell you to keep your trap shut if you don't have anything nice to say?"

The essence of spiritual maturity is the refusal to slam doors.

—RABBI JORDAN PEARLSON

BILL ONCE TOLD ME THAT AS A YOUNG MAN he had been short-tempered, and had had to work to overcome that. It was difficult for me to picture this, as the Bill I knew was amazingly even-tempered. It's been said that many saints achieved sanctity by overcoming vices. I could only assume that his seminary training had helped him to conquer his temper. Maybe that's why they called it "formation."

Further, Bill had inherited his father's ability to laugh off the vicissitudes of life. Alphonse Kienzle, a tall, well-built man, was known for being the neighborhood peacekeeper. If two men were arguing or even actually fighting, it was he who stepped in and defused the situation. I had always marveled at Bill's ability to throw oil on troubled waters, and to reduce aggravating events to humor rather than becoming angry or upset over them.

Although Bill had grown up in a household with two older sisters, he had lived a celibate life for twelve years in the seminary and twenty years as a priest. Now, at age forty-five, it would have been natural for him to be somewhat set in his ways. Not only his training but also his personality was such that routine was second nature to him.

And here he was, having been catapulted out of what he termed the ultimate security into the workaday world, living in close quarters with someone of a different sex, a different background, and a personality that chafed at routine.

Countless cartoons, comic strips, and sitcoms have depicted the male struggle to live with female foibles. Remember the scene in *The Goodbye Girl* where Richard Dreyfuss pulls Marsha Mason's "unmentionables" off the shower rod? Bill's method of dealing with a similar situation was to issue a "Papal Allocution"—postdated for effect—as follows:

(Papal allocution on the occasion of the convention of leaders of Major Religious Orders in Rome. Sept. 28, 1994. Given by Pope Buster I, first American Pope and first married Pope.)

Beloved children! Why have you come to the eternal and sacred city of Rome? Why have you traveled over mountain and sea from the four corners of the earth to this venerable and traditional fountain of Christianity?

You have come, beloved children, to sit at the feet of Our Humble Person and to hear from Our Unworthy Lips (but infallible, remember) the eternal truths which the Church has always taught and continues to teach through Our Ministry as We sit over the very tomb of Our Predecessor, Peter, Prince of the Apostles.

It has come to Our attention, beloved children, that a new and frightening development is taking place throughout the world, which threatens the placid and rightful place of the Natural Law. We refer to the squeezing of toothpaste from the center, instead of the bottom of the tube. This insidious practice is not foreign even from Our own humble palace. In Our own very bathroom, We have found such a tube, disfigured beyond belief. It is too horrendous to think that this nefarious deed might have been perpetrated by Mrs. Pope. But what is one to think?

As the Natural Law has always taught, things go up from the bottom and down from the top. This principle is as certain and unchangeable as the fact that the earth is the center of the universe. (For the denial of which, Galileo Galilei, of unhappy memory, was justly condemned.) Thus, just as the sun revolves around the earth (cf. sunRISE, sunSET in the Enchoridium Symbolorum), toothpaste is squeezed from the bottom of the tube. And this motion is continued until, finally, all the paste miraculously disappears.

We have one further abomination to call to your attention, beloved children, before Our infallibility wears out today. It concerns the hanging and/or depositing of clothing in the bathroom helter-skelter, willy-nilly, hic et ibi. Once again, beloved children, is Natural Law thwarted.

The Law of Nature teaches, and this brand-new law which We are making up right now confirms, that clothing, when not in use to cover the shame of humankind, should be hung in closets. The Creator made bathrooms as places wherein to bathe and other things that are only peripherally relevant to Our infallible power. But, once again, even Our humble palace is not free of this vice. The Papal bathroom, wherein once sat Pope Saint Pius X, is now the depository of feminine undergarments that are unseemly for Our Sacred Person to describe. What is one to think?

But the shadows of the day lengthen, beloved children. Our voice grows weary and Our infallibility is just about used up for the day.

We must save some of it for dinner conversation with Mrs. Pope. As is evident, We have much to colloquy with her about.

One last word, beloved children, especially to Our beloved children from the United States of America. When you return from this sacred, eternal city, over the mountains and waters to your beloved homeland, give Our regards to Broadway.

Given this 28th day of September
Anno Domini 1994
Buster I, Pontifex Maximus

In retrospect, I think that Bill, after thirty-two years of celibate existence in the seminary and the priesthood, rather enjoyed living with a woman's idiosyncrasies—part of the package that came with a marital relationship.

As for the Papacy, Bill said that if he were ever elected Pope he would take the name Buster I, and would move the Vatican to Hawaii.

---

*M*aintenant, elle est comme les autres (Now, she is just like the others).

—GENERAL CHARLES DE GAULLE
(To his wife, at the gravesite of their Down syndrome daughter)

WHEN A HOUSE IS PUT UP FOR SALE, those living nearby are understandably concerned about who their new neighbors will be. But seldom is that concern expressed in the fear that "My daughter could be raped!"

The couple across the alley had finished building their retirement home on the Lake. (Minnesota is known as the Land of 10,000 lakes. Actually, there are more, but Minnesotans aren't braggarts.) One day the FOR SALE sign was crowned by a SOLD sign. Suddenly, neighbors gathered in buzzing clusters. The house had been bought by a professional group that planned to use it as a home for what in those days were termed "retarded" teenagers. Ours was a lovely residential neighborhood, arcaded by tall elms. After a snowfall, the street that curved up our hill resembled a Dickensian Christmas backdrop; one would not have been surprised to see a coach and four rounding the corner, heralded by the coachman's horn. The city's enlightened construction and zoning codes called for a percentage of houses to be in a price range affordable to less wealthy buyers. Other than this quota, the sky was the limit: one huge mansion three doors from us boasted a swimming pool; another was a reconstruction of a Tudor castle.

But with Dutch elm disease advancing—just a few miles away, entire areas were being denuded by the blight—we feared for our neighborhood. We watched, horrified, as the evening news showed us what amounted to small forests being trucked off for burning in an attempt to contain the infestation. Yet when the possibility was raised of banding together to have our elms treated, our neighborhood was unable to reach a consensus, or, more specifically, the inhabitants couldn't agree on what to agree on.

When the snow fell, the city plowed our streets. Unfortunately, most of our garages fronted on alleys. Each snowy winter morn, wheels churned and engines labored, as various patresfamilias stomped on the gas in futile attempts to break forth into the main thoroughfare. Eventually, most were forced to exit their vehicles and strew salt, sand, Kitty Litter, or burlap sacks in front of their tires to gain a get-going grip on the snow-covered ground.

It seemed not to have entered their heads to wield a shovel or chip in to buy or rent a snowblower or the services of a snowplow.

As the new kids on the block, we hesitated to suggest the obvious: that if we were to survive Dutch elm disease with our trees intact, and if our cars were to survive winter with their transmissions intact, we should not just stand there, but *do something*.

Thinking that nothing would succeed like a good example, each time it snowed, Bill and I dug out our section of the alley. Which meant we could now get our car out of our garage. But since no one else had chosen to dig out, we were still stymied. So we shoveled down the alley to the street.

If it snowed every day, we shoveled every day. And though it was winter, no longer was the sound of spinning tires heard in the land. Our neighbors, without any acknowledgment of our efforts, flung themselves into their autos and tore off to the rat race, secure in the knowledge that should it snow that day, still their evening entry would be as trouble-free as their morning exit.

One weekend, we discovered the wealthy attorney whose house lorded it over the alley entrance cleaning off his front sidewalk with a snowblower. Our next-door neighbor, an elderly lady with one of the few garages that fronted on the street, accosted him: "If you have a snowblower, why don't you at least clean off your alley entry?"

"Why should I, when some girl comes down and shovels it off?" That "girl"—over forty—was I.

All of which is merely in preface to illustrate the level of cooperation in our neighborhood.

Now, back to the proposed group home. No sooner had the SOLD sign gone up than the word went out. Faster than you could say "Jesus was a Christian," this collection of liberal do-gooders, who hitherto couldn't get together on anything, were galvanized to action. There were letters and phone calls to city councilmen, attorneys, and newspapers; there were meetings, and there were petitions.

Bill and I were probably the only couple on the block who did not sign the anti-group-home petition.

Our neighbors voiced what we have since come to discover are the usual worries: They'll be noisy, they'll be dangerous, they'll be trouble, they won't keep the property up, they'll bring neighborhood values down—and, always, the bottom line: "My daughter could be raped!"

Bill phoned our councilman and ascertained that the group home people were well within their rights; everything was kosher. He made reference to the situation in his column in *Mpls.*, concluding, "the mentally retarded need us for a more normal environment in which to function. And if we are our brothers' keeper, we need them."

We tried to discuss the matter sensibly with our immediate neighbors. Still, it came down to that theoretically incontrovertible "My daughter could be raped!"—to the point where I began to believe that if the speaker hadn't had a daughter, she would have worried that her pet poodle would be ravished.

The whole thing died not with a bang, but with the proverbial whimper. Six mentally challenged teenagers, along with their young caretaker couple, moved in. They made no noise, no trouble; they bothered no one. And no one, with the exception of Bill and me, acknowledged their presence. The huge house on its huge lot was the quondam Mainland China. No one nodded, waved, or said good morning to its residents. Except Bill and me. Frequently, when Bill came home from work, the teenagers would be playing with a volley ball in their backyard. Bill would say hi to them, and they would respond; occasionally the ball would be tossed back and forth in a friendly across-the-alley exchange. Recalling Bill's active athletic life in the seminary, I was pleased to see that his throwing arm seemed as strong as ever.

As often as I picked flowers from our garden, I would take a bouquet across the alley and hand it to whichever teenager smilingly appeared at the back door. Frequently, the youngsters were seen mowing or raking the lawn. So much for the worry about not keeping up the property. And with the advent of winter, there they were, bundled up, grinning, and—wonder of wonders—shoveling snow out of the alley.

One thing that Minneapolis did not lack for was snow. It started snowing the day we moved in and didn't stop for months—or so it seemed. Having grown up on a farm where the animals had to be fed and watered and the outbuildings had to be dug out, I was used to shoveling snow—enjoyed it, actually. Minneapolis gave me a *lot* of enjoyment. And the doctor said that physical exertion was good for me.

Our garage apron was large, but I tried to keep it snow-free so that when Bill came home he could drive right in.

Winter came and again I was doing my snow-shoveling bit. Bill laughed at the way I shoveled snow. Using the shovel as a sort of blade, he would slide the shovel along, whooshing snow to left and right, and pushing it off to one side. Whereas I picked up a shovelful, carried it off to one side and dumped it, then went back for another shovelful. We each got the job done, just in different ways.

One afternoon, one of the teenagers, who had been watching as I shoveled, called over and offered to do the job for me. I smiled. "Thank you, but I need the exercise." He nodded understandingly, but continued to lean on his shovel and watch me. After some minutes, he said, not unkindly, "Gee, you sure do shovel funny."

It was my turn to nod as I tried to keep a straight face. I hastened out of sight around the corner of the garage, where I laughed till tears came.

Later, I told Bill of having my snow-shoveling technique critiqued by a well-meaning retarded lad. "Well," Bill said, "you *do* shovel funny."

It wasn't the only time I was the object of Minneapolitan commentary.

On St. Patrick's Day, I decided to walk downtown to join the celebration. Dressed in a green wool suit, green shoes, a green hat, and wearing a corsage of artificial violets, and carrying a green purse, I started off.

To reach the Mall from our house, one had to pass through a small warehouse district. As I neared one warehouse driveway, a huge semi started to pull out, blocking my path. I stopped, waiting for it to pass. Though there was no oncoming traffic, the truck halted in front of me. I was a whit apprehensive, but burst out laughing when the driver, looking down at me from his high cab seat, said, "Lady, you lost your parade."

Most of the trouble in the world is caused by people wanting
to be important.

—T. S. ELIOT

AT THE TIME BILL HAD ACCEPTED THE BIRD-IN-THE-HAND JOB at
Mpls., he was aware that there were drawbacks.

Tom, the publisher of *Mpls.*, had previously earned a good living as a live-wire ad salesman. Early on, he had mentioned to us
that an alleged "seer" had told him that he had an "aura of evil"
around him. Tom had laughed it off, but Bill and I got the distinct
impression that Tom's attractive, brainy wife possibly had accepted
this diagnosis as corroborative evidence of what she herself per-
ceived. The couple had separated, gotten marital counseling, and
were now together again . . . but it seemed there might be Trouble
in Paradise.

Tom, like many people who are good at one thing but want to
do something entirely different, seemed to feel that selling ads was
beneath him. We quickly became aware that he had delusions of
being Somebody, hobnobbing with wheelers and dealers and being
a media cynosure. Hiring an ex-priest whose bio was in *Who's Who*,
would, he felt, put a feather in his cap.

This was in an era before the Church started hemorrhaging
priests; people were still in awe of "Father"—even if "Father" was
an ex. Having Bill as editor would achieve one of Tom's main aims:
to get himself and his magazine Talked About.

Like many people who are insecure or who have self-esteem
problems, Tom's viewpoint was analagous to the husband who mar-
ries "above himself" and then denigrates his wife because he feels
inferior to her. Whether this applied to Tom's own marriage I can't
say, but it became increasingly obvious that it was the case with his
employees, including Bill.

Tom did have the talent to attract and recognize good people.
But with each person he hired, Tom had to cope with that person's
excellence—which he obviously felt put his own talent in the shade.

As a result, he threw his weight around, belittled, and was frequently nasty and sarcastic. Many were the times that Bill had to delete Tom's snide comments before returning a rejected manuscript to the author.

Tom tended to hold his punches as far as Bill was concerned, as he was still somewhat in awe of Bill's priestly background. People liked, respected, admired, and enjoyed Bill. Tom suffered by comparison. Bill, through no fault of his own, was becoming a drogue to Tom's amour propre. The mirror on the wall was *not* telling Tom, "You are the fairest of them all."

Unfortunately, I was mostly in the dark about this, as Bill did not want to burden me or worry me. Still, I could see Tom's megalomania growing by leaps and bounds, and I came to sense that life at *Mpls.* was not a bed of roses for Bill.

Tom affected a monthly column—which he always wrote at the eleventh hour, and which was always much too long, so that we would have to kill something else at the last minute in order to find space for the publisher's ramblings. Also, like an ant on a stick that is burning at both ends, Tom didn't know which way to go: He didn't want to look bad, so he insisted that I copy-edit his column—but if I tried to correct an error, he fought me tooth and nail.

In one case, for instance, he referred to "Frankenstein," when he meant the monster, not the scientist. When I changed the phrase to read "Frankenstein's monster" rather than "Frankenstein," Tom refused to accept the change—until Bill calmly told him that people would laugh at his ignorance.

Another time, wishing to appear erudite, he wanted to use a French word in his column. But since he knew no French, he thrust the column with the underlined word at me and said, "Translate that into French." My French was of rudimentary high school caliber; I had no idea how to translate "Balls!" But I dug out a French slang dictionary and made Tom happy because now his readers would think he was sophisticated enough to use a "Pardon My French" term.

Tom chose a Christmas issue of the magazine to list the names of "People I'm not going to talk to anymore . . . space does not permit why, but they know why." He then, like a petulant child, went on to list why. And the publisher being the publisher, space *did* permit.

Things avalanched when I, as tactfully as possible (which turned out not to be tactfully enough) explained to Tom that he would get rich a lot faster if he would get rid of his aspirations to Be Somebody and do what he did best, which was selling ads. By this time, Tom and his wife had separated again, and shortly thereafter, Tom signed himself into a trendy alcoholism treatment center.

Tom had problems, true; however none of us really believed he was an alcoholic. But at that time, being treated for alcoholism was the thing to do—so Tom did it. However, even during his short period in the treatment center (his attention span was severely truncated), Tom repeatedly phoned the office, issuing instructions and demanding that copy be brought to his room at the center. We humored him and went on putting out his monthly magazine.

But I guess my analytical words began to eat at him. There was little he could do to me—although he did phone me one day to tell me I had reached him—but it was obvious I was a thorn in his side.

Bill was a handy goat. Now that Tom's magazine was up and running, Tom advised Bill that his talents would no longer be needed. He had enough respect for Bill not to fire him outright; there would be a phase-out period while Bill searched for another niche, and Tom searched for another editor victim.

Bill accepted the situation with mixed emotions. On the one hand, he was making a fair living; on the other hand, Tom's personality problems made work life increasingly unbearable. "It could have been fun," Bill said later, "but Tom took all the fun out of it." Neither Bill nor the other staffers were free to do their best work.

Where once Tom had relied on Bill's editorial judgment, more and more of Bill's decisions were being questioned. The constraints on Bill were epitomized by an indicative event.

A downtown building housed a well-known Minneapolis music company. Alongside the building was a large parking lot. The music company had commissioned an artist to paint a musical score on the side of the multistory building. It was literally a work of art. So striking was it that Swissair had used a photo of the musical wall as one page of their international wall calendar. Thus it was, in effect, known worldwide.

A cartoon was submitted to *Mpls.* by a freelancer whose past work had been used often in the magazine. The cartoon was, the editorial staff agreed, of *New Yorker* caliber. It depicted the wall with the musical score and the parking lot. In the middle of the parking lot a violin case lay open. Next to the case was the figure of a little man, shoulders bent in earnest performance as he played on his violin from the musical score on the wall.

It needed no caption. It needed nothing but the appreciation in the eye of the beholder. Over a quarter of a century later, I can still see that small figure giving his music to the world of the Twin Cities.

The cartoon went right over Tom's head. When Bill expostulated with him, Tom assembled the entire staff and called for a vote as to the cartoon's acceptability. The sales staff outvoted the editorial staff. The cartoon was rejected. It was left to a disgusted, almost sorrowful Bill to notify the cartoonist of the rejection.

Father Kienzle's erstwhile publisher, Cardinal Dearden, his superior, had shown more respect for the judgment of his priest-editor than did Bill's present publisher.

Had it been left to me, I would have published the cartoon and let Tom rant about it ex post facto. But: "Mother did not raise me for useless confrontation," Bill had told me. So be it. The job hunt began.

Bill's credentials were excellent. But the Twin Cities were full of people with excellent credentials. And Bill's age was against him. Being within waving distance of fifty was not an asset in the job market. Just as would-be authors can paper their walls with rejection slips, we could have papered our home with job turndowns.

I had total faith in Bill and in his talents. But Bill himself was starting to grow concerned.

He had written friends back in Michigan about his situation. And one—whom I henceforth referred to as the Fairy Godmother—threw a lifeline.

Virginia Sommerfeldt was a parishioner when Bill was pastor at St. Anselm's in Dearborn Heights. One of her sons, Dr. John

Sommerfeldt, was a professor in the History Department at Western Michigan University in Kalamazoo. John was the quintessential scholar and academic. At something like seven years of age, he had announced to all and sundry that when he grew up he intended to be a medievalist. "Well," said his very down-to-earth nuts and bolts father, "if anyone needs one, you'll be there." Under Dr. Sommerfeldt's aegis, Western Michigan now hosted an internationally renowned annual gathering of medieval scholars from all over the world.

Western Michigan, in conjunction with the Trappists, had also established the Center for Contemplative Studies, with Dr. Sommerfeldt as its director.

Dr. Sommerfeldt was wearing several hats and could use some help. So the position of assistant director of the Center for Contemplative Studies was created, to handle public relations and to apply for grants to carry on the center's work—which was "to restore its contemplative heritage to Western civilization."

Enter William X. Kienzle, seemingly perfect for the job. Well, yes and no. Bill was great with people—but short of announcing the advent of the ADF collection from the pulpit, he'd never had to ask for operating funds. Once more, he had plenty of rejections with which to paper the wall. In future years, when we watched PBS programs that announced, "This program funded by a grant from—" Bill would say, "I wrote to them. They turned me down."

There was one exception. A phone call came from the office of one of Michigan's senators: the center was being awarded a government grant—predicated on receiving matching funds. My memory at this point is murky; I think possibly Western Michigan itself may have supplied the matching funds. In any case, the center rolled on in its quest to restore to Western civilization its contemplative heritage.

PART

4

When ye depart out of that house or city shake off the dust
of your feet.

—MATTHEW 10:14

LEAVING MINNEAPOLIS WAS TRAUMATIC. We had started our married
life there, we enjoyed living there, we had put down roots there, we
felt at home there. Now we put our house on the market, leaving it
in the capable hands of a real estate agent. We asked that she
inform prospective buyers, "There's been a lot of love in this
house." I don't know whether that was the clincher, but two weeks
after our departure the house was sold.

Moving day was an avalanche. The movers, like army ants, went
through the house, swooping up every object their eye fell upon—
including full wastebaskets. Even Bill, whose patience was written
large in his DNA, was harried. The final straw was when he held
up a hanger containing one of my skirts, and asked, "What should I
do with this?"

I was not blessed with Bill's patience; couldn't he see I was busy!
Recalling my mother's catch-all response to similar questions, I
snapped—quite unwisely—"Stand and hold it."

He looked at me, opened his hand, dropped the hanger and
skirt on the floor, turned on his heel, and disappeared out the door.

This action, which represented the extent of any disagreeable
exchange that ever took place between us, was so rare as to be
almost unique. Bill, like his father, was normally able to laugh off
most arguments or disagreements with a good-natured shrug.

But I was to learn a new rule of thumb: Any marriage that can survive repeated moves can survive anything. At one point, we moved six times in six years through four different states. During this period, one of the country's leading Trappists advised Bill, "You should take a Vow of Stability."

Our marriage was stable as the Rock of Gibraltar; it was our household that was a gypsy camp.

A few years later, we heard that our former publisher, high on drugs, had committed suicide by jumping off Minneapolis's Government Center Building. We were saddened to hear of Tom's death. I think Bill felt Tom was one of his failures—a soul he hadn't been able to save. But God would take care of that.

The Church has 2,414 Canon Laws, and I never met one I liked.
—W.X.K.

WE TRAVELED TO KALAMAZOO in the midst of a teeth-numbing January cold spell. It was during the period that Jimmy Carter, under the gun from Mideast oil suppliers, had issued the edict that thermostats in public buildings should not be set higher than fifty-five degrees.

I know that physical comfort, like so many other things, is frequently psychological. If one is playing or working outside in the spring, a temperature of fifty-five can feel almost balmy. But for some reason, when one is coming from an outdoors whose temperature is twenty or thirty degrees below zero, with a wind-chill factor almost colder than comprehension, fifty-five degrees seems unable to defrost one.

We had lived in Minnesota for two and a half years. We were accustomed to frigid weather. But I was colder in Chicago than I have ever been in my life, before or since. When we got out of the car at one of the turnpike overpass restaurants, the wind hit us like driven knives. I truly felt that my very bones were going to crack from cold. Even now, a quarter of a century later, in the middle of a Midwest heat wave, I still shiver as I recall the trip from Minneapolis to Kalamazoo.

We spent the night at the Holiday Inn on Chicago's lakeshore, which was a solid rampart of frozen waves. Even when we were in our room—which was so small it was almost impossible to turn around without getting carnally involved—I was shaking with cold. The only time I thawed out was when I stepped into a hot shower.

"It's psychological; it's psychological," I told myself. "You've worked on the lawn in fifty-degree weather and been comfortable; why can't you be comfortable in a fifty-five-degree hotel room?"

I kept thinking of an interview Bill had done with Paul Flatley, a former Minnesota Viking. The Vikings' stadium in Bloomington was an outdoor playing field. Bud Grant, the Vikings' coach, was known for not supplying his bench with heaters; he wanted his players to be tough enough to defeat the visiting pantywaists who were not used to being refrigerated while earning their pay. But one of Flatley's teammates seemed impervious. He sat on the bench with a warm, happy expression while his teammates' only heat came from mentally cursing Grant's abstemiousness.

Finally, Flatley discovered his teammate's secret. "I just sit there and think of the best, hottest lay I've had. It works every time."

Bill's position with the Center for Contemplative Studies was tenuous. The Trappist Abbott in ultimate charge of the project was at Gethsemani Abbey in Kentucky. When Bill's name was put before him as a candidate for the post, the Abbott went into reactive mode. Not only was Bill an ex-priest; he had not been laicized; further, he was living in sin; the Church could not recognize the "attempted marriage" of an unlaicized ex-priest.

But the Abbott was a fair man. If Bill would apply for laicization and, once having received it, be married in the Church, all would be well. The Abbott was more than fair: As long as Bill applied to the Vatican for the required laicization, he could then take the position with the center while awaiting the Vatican's response.

My initial reaction was to scream bloody murder. This wasn't the era of the Inquisition; by what right did the Church reach its tentacles into a public university? How dare they!

A cooler head—Bill's—prevailed. In retrospect I can see that the Trappists were probably well within their rights. Indeed, they would have been well within their rights to turn Bill down out of hand. Instead, they had the charity to set what, under the circumstances, were fair conditions.

Thus began the real Paper Chase. My mind blurs at the memory of the documentation required. Not only did Bill have to apply for laicization, but documents relating to my pagan state and my previous marriage had to be obtained. And, as Bill said with regard to trying to prove that I had never been baptized, "It is very difficult to prove that something never happened."

This brought to the fore one of Bill's complaints against Canon Law: The fact that the presumption is always in favor of the institution. Whereas, as Bill was wont to say, "God doesn't need anyone to protect Him [sometimes he said "Her"]." The Church took the view that just because one's parents said that their child had never been baptized, they were not to be believed; after all, they might have ulterior motives. No, there had to be corroborating evidence from someone outside the family—or at least outside the immediate family.

We will close a merciful curtain on that phase of the procedure. I will say merely that my first marriage was one of the Church's simplest cases—what is known as *defectus formae*—where a Catholic "attempts" a marriage to a non-Catholic in a civil forum. The marriage is not dissolved; in the eyes of the Church it never existed. Further, it was ascertained that I had indeed never been baptized, but had grown up as a happily ignorant little pagan.

Bill filled out his application for laicization with more regret than gusto. In the spot where it asked why he was applying for laicization, he wrote down a euphemistic version of "I think Canon Law stinks."

The papers were shipped off and promptly forgotten about. Although the Abbott may occasionally have given some thought to them. But as an Abbott, he had to be aware that the Mills of Rome grind slowly.

Which of you shall have an ass or an ox fallen into a pit, and will not straightway pull him out on the sabbath day?

—Luke 14:5

THERE WERE FEW VENUES FOR ATTENDING MASS in Kalamazoo. After some searching, we ended up at the university's Newman Center. In the wake of Vatican II, a lot of experimentation was going on and particularly in a university milieu this meant a guitar accompaniment and more mod music. Gone were the days when the congregation could join with reasonable fervor in "O Lord, I am Not Worthy,"* or something equally schmaltzy yet singable. Each week before the actual start of Mass the young "music director" taught the congregation a new song. Each week we all dutifully "practiced." But by the time we were supposed to actually participate in singing as part of the Mass most either mumbled, hummed, or just stayed silent. Gimmee that old-time religion!

One heavily midwinter morning with several feet of snow on the ground we approached the entrance to the chapel mentally gritting our teeth at the "practice session" to come. Just in front of the chapel, a car sat racing its motor and spinning its wheels. The driver, a young woman, in turning the corner, had skidded into a snowbank. It was obvious that a good push would free the car. But,

---

* I can still hear Bill—who appreciated Palestrina and Gregorian Chant—muttering under his breath at the second line of the second stanza, "He is *not* the bridegroom of my soul."

intent on heading for Mass, no one had stopped to help extricate the vehicle.

Bill approached the car window and motioned to the young woman, who nodded. Then he and I stepped to the rear of the car and began to push. A passing paper boy interrupted his delivery route to join us. The car shot free. The young woman went on her way; the paper boy returned to his deliveries, and Bill and I entered the chapel.

In years to come Bill spoke of that occurrence, shaking his head over the seeming human inability to put the Christian concept of loving thy brother as thyself into practice.

Granted, in the minds of those headed for the chapel was the thought, "If I stop to help someone, I'll be late for Mass." After all, this was someone else's property. But remember God's law, as passed on by Moses to the people of Israel in Deuteronomy 22.4: "Thou shalt not see thy brother's ass or his ox fall down by the way, and hide thyself from them: thou shalt surely help him to lift them up again."

In the free association of ideas that was so frequent with Bill, that led him to recall coming out of Mass at the Shrine of the Little Flower in the long-ago Good Old Days. Stony-faced, the congregants exited Father Coughlin's den of religion, clutching their copies of *Der Wanderer*, to enter their cars and head out without pausing to give anyone else's car a chance to get in line.

Their version of the Golden Rule was "Do unto others before they do it unto you." Bill referred to them as "God's frozen people."

Yes, Virginia, there *is* a Kalamazoo.

—Anonymous

KALAMAZOO WAS A MINIATURE MINNEAPOLIS. There was a downtown mall—the first in the Midwest, it was claimed. Like Minneapolis, the corporations headquartered in Kalamazoo were community-minded, and contributed time, money, and staff to a variety of cultural institutions, including a symphony orchestra and a superb library.

With Bill busy in academe, my idle hands found mischief: I went into partnership with a local woman and we opened the JK (Javan and Karen) Collection, an olio shop that carried antiques, handicrafts, and books. Our greatest coup stemmed from my instant awareness that an imaginative new illustrated book titled *Gnomes*, published by Abrams, would be a runaway best seller. I ordered as many copies as our budget could afford, and we hit the jackpot. The other bookshops had ordered only the usual number of books; when their supplies depleted, customers ran—literally—into our shop to say, "We hear you have *Gnomes*." Since our shop was on a street that was a direct route between downtown and WMU as well as Kalamazoo College, we had a lot of young people running in.

We also carried Pawprints greeting cards, which were exceedingly popular not only with young people, but adults as well. When the Amsterdam Concertgebouw came to town, some members of the orchestra wandered into our shop. One of the musicians could not speak English, but he seemed to be going into raptures over one of our Pawprints—a card portraying a pig happily playing a tuba. His colleague translated for us: The euphoric one was a tuba player and wanted to buy all the tuba cards we had. Of course, we made him a gift of them . . . and felt we had done our bit for Holland-America relations.

"My definition of happiness is having a doctor who smokes four packs a day."

—Billy Wilder

Bill had smoked since seminary days, sometimes, in more recent years, as many as three packs a day. Now, every morning, when he took his shower, the steam loosened the phlegm, and he coughed.

And coughed. And coughed. His cough sounded like gravel being shoveled. Each cough went through me like a knife. I pleaded with him repeatedly to give up cigarettes. Finally, and for the one and only time in our life, he growled at me. "Leave me alone!"

That did it. "If he wants to kill himself, I can't stop him," I told myself in wifely dudgeon. I never said another word about it—just took the knife stabs every morning.

Once I stopped bugging him, of course he came to his senses. At first, he tried to replace cigarettes with a pipe. I brought him a beautiful pipe from Kapp & Peterson in Dublin. But the pipe burned the roof of his mouth. Eventually, his system rebelled. Everytime he took a drag on a cigarette, he could, he said, feel it throughout his entire body. He put a carton of cigarettes on a shelf in the basement. The last thing at night, he went downstairs, took one cigarette from the carton, smoked it, and then went to bed. When the carton was empty, he never smoked another cigarette.

What he did was chew a lot of toothpicks. A friend commented, "You're not going to die of lung cancer; you'll die of Dutch elm disease"—a line Bill later used in one of his books when Father Koesler gave up smoking.

Coincidence is God's way of winking.

—QUOTED BY MARNEY RICH KEENAN

ONE OF THE PEOPLE WE MET IN MINNEAPOLIS was a P. T. Barnum clone named Bruce Lansky. Bruce and his wife, Vicki, later became famous in the publishing world when Bruce established Meadowbrook Press, whose first publication was Vicki's ultra-best seller, *Feed Me! I'm Yours*.

Bruce, an ad man par excellence, had taken a survey and discovered that there was a solid core of mystery buffs . . . not (at that time) gangbusters, but a solid core nonetheless. He suggested to friends and associates that if they would come up with some good mystery plots, he would pay them for their creations, and then set a stable of writers to fleshing out the mysteries. He had mentioned this to Bill, who, outside of the Father Brown series, had never read a mystery in his life.

In much the same way that I had originally asked Father Kienzle if he'd ever thought of writing, I had several times urged Bill to put together an account of his life as a priest. Finally, probably just to quiet an insistent wife, Bill, who liked to have all his i's dotted and t's crossed before he began anything, wrote a query letter to Thomas Dunne, an editor at St. Martin's Press. Why St. Martin's? Because they had had such success with the James Heriot books—and besides, they were named after a saint.

Mr. Dunne replied, saying something to the effect that chances were such a book would have a limited readership of about six. However, he said, he did sense a degree of humor peeking through the query letter, so he would be willing to read such a manuscript if Bill cared to submit it. His caveat was that he was backed up with manuscripts and it might be many months before he could get to anything Bill might submit.

Since Bill hadn't even written anything yet, this was obviously not a problem as far as Bill was concerned.

He set to writing a book whose working title was *Mother Dresses Me Funny*. This from a greeting card sent to him years before by Margaret Cronyn. On the cover, it said, "I like you . . ." Inside, it said, " . . . even though your mother dresses you funny"—in this case an allusion to the cassocks priests wore in those days.

The manuscript was indeed a manuscript—Bill wrote in pen and ink on yellow legal pads. I typed up each chapter, editing as I went along. After six chapters, we thought there was enough to send off to St. Martin's. But we agreed that something was missing. Bill was a good speaker; he could tell a story with the best of them. However, his anecdotes on paper seemed flat and uninteresting. We put the six chapters aside.

Then we moved to Kalamazoo.

❧⚜❧

I had done freelance editing, including working on one of Meadowbrook Press's books. Shortly after Bill and I arrived in Kalamazoo, Bruce sent me a check for my work. Seated at the table after dinner, Bill idly picked up the envelope containing the check, and recalled Bruce's offer of a stipend for a mystery plot. Bill went into the living room, sat down and started to doodle.

Sometime later, he handed me the envelope. On it he had written the names of ten priests and nuns. "Can you tell me the connection between those names?"

I scanned the names cursorily. "No."

The list was the basis for what eventually became *The Rosary Murders*. Bill had an exaggerated view of my acuity. If I couldn't discern the clue contained in the list, he figured he really had something. Instead of sending the idea to Bruce Lansky, Bill thought he'd take a whack at it himself. After all, who knew more about priests and nuns?

Once having started, Bill wrote in the evenings after work, and on weekends. Then, like the homing horse that smells the barn, during an end-of-January blizzard in 1978, Bill finished *The Rosary Murders*. As usual with his work, I had edited and typed along, so that by the time he was finished, I had only the last chapter to add to the typescript.

He sent it off to the editor at St. Martin's, with a covering letter saying that this was not the book they had originally discussed, but that the humor the editor had recognized was still there.

Then we waited. And waited. And waited.

Four months passed. The American Booksellers Association was holding its annual convention in Atlanta. Since I was co-owner of a store that carried books, I was entitled to attend. We flew off to Atlanta, where neither of us had ever been.

Those who have attended the annual ABA trade show (now the BookExpo America) know how immense the territory of booths is: Hundreds and hundreds of publishers attend from all over the world. Bill made a beeline for the St. Martin's booth, and, as he said, sat like a faithful dog, awaiting the arrival of "his" editor.

When Mr. Dunne finally appeared, Bill introduced himself. Mr. Dunne acknowledged him, and said, "I'm returning your manuscript." Bill went numb; Dunne's succeeding words went unregistered.

It was an early salvo in what came to be known in the industry as the Blockbuster Syndrome. Dunne liked the book. He wanted St. Martin's to publish it. But the other members of the editorial board didn't think it would achieve blockbuster status, so they turned it down.

Bill came looking for me. One look at his face told me the news was not good. "Did Mr. Dunne say you should rewrite it?" I asked.

"I don't know," Bill confessed. "Once he said he was sending it back, I didn't hear anything else."

Wifelike, I went in search of Mr. Dunne. "What should we do about the book?" I asked. "Should we rewrite it?"

"Don't change a word of it," he said. "It's a good book. Just keep sending it around. Somebody will buy it." Probably never had an author's work been rejected while leaving such an open door of hope.

When I reported Mr. Dunne's words to Bill, he perked up a bit. Now we were headed for the Abrams booth, where I wanted to meet the publicist who had sent me the original copy of *Gnomes.*

From my days as a book reviewer, I had quickly learned that one could count the really good book publicists on the fingers of one hand. Carol Schneider was one of those. In a small-world occurrence, Carol later became head publicist at Random House, the parent company of Ballantine, which now publishes the Father Koesler paperbacks.

As we made our way to the Abrams booth, a man who was occupied talking to his companion and hadn't noticed we were in the aisle bumped into Bill. The man looked up; Bill and the man nodded to each other, and we all went on. Bill's brow was furrowed. "I know him . . . but I can't think from where."

We reached the Abrams booth and I introduced myself to Carol, while Bill stood off to one side pondering where he had met the man who had bumped into him.

A dear friend who is a very spiritual person and who always referred to Bill as "That saint you live with," is fond of saying, "There are no accidents." In the Abrams booth was a little person dressed as a gnome. In the next booth was a man with a parrot on his shoulder. It was the Andrews & McMeel booth. The man was Tristan Jones, the Welsh sailor whose book Andrews & McMeel had just published.

It all came back to Bill. The man who had bumped into him was Jim Andrews, who, with his partner, John McMeel, had started Universal Press—the Kansas City syndicate that distributed *Doonesbury, Herman, For Better or for Worse,* and a slew of other comic strips.

Years before, Jim and John had met with Father Kienzle at the *Michigan Catholic.* They were peddling the Catholic columnists published by their syndicate. John McMeel could not only sell refrigerators to Eskimos, he could talk them into buying a lifetime supply of Japanese whale blubber on the grounds that the imported product was better than the domestic.

Jim Andrews's down-to-earth sincerity complemented John McMeel's flamboyance. Father Kienzle was a hard sell, but he could not resist the combination of Jim's earnestness and John's Irish charm. The *Michigan Catholic* had subscribed to their syndicate.

Suddenly, it was old home week. Jim returned to the booth, and introduced us to his wife, Kathy—who recalled sitting in her kitchen and typing Father Kienzle's name on envelopes containing the weekly columns. For Bill and Jim the next two days were full of reminiscences and getting reacquainted.

As the time came for our return home, I asked Bill, "Did you tell Jim about your book?"

He hadn't. I urged him to do so. "If you won't, I *will.*"

"No, I'll do it," he said.

Jim was interested. "Send me the book," he said.

Bill, scarred by the four-month wait from St. Martin's, looked a gift horse in the mouth. "The last publisher kept it four months," he said. "Would you let me know right away?"

Jim, God love him, didn't even laugh at such presumption. "Send me the book," he repeated, "and one week after I get it, I'll let you know."

Bill phoned St. Martin's and talked to a kind employee, who agreed to go through the huge pile of manuscripts, find Bill's, and return it immediately. He was as good as his word; soon, the book was on its way to Jim Andrews.

At the time we sent the typescript to St. Martin's, I had put a bottle of Asti Spumante in the refrigerator to await the book's acceptance. It was still there.

A week to the day after we sent the manuscript to Kansas City, at 5:25 P.M., the phone rang. It was Jim Andrews. "I've read *The Rosary Murders*; we're very excited about it and we'd like to publish it."

Time stopped. All I could think was, "Hold on to this moment. Hold on to it tight. It's a one-time-only. It'll never happen again. No matter how many books Bill writes it will never be like this again."

Then we opened the Asti Spumante.

Beware the fury of a patient man.

—PROVERB

WE BARELY HAD TIME TO ADJUST TO THE NEWS that Bill was going to be a published author when another exciting event loomed: The Center for Contemplative Studies arranged for Hollywood's Lew Ayres to bring his famed film *Altars of the World* to Western Michigan. Ayres would also be showing his film at Oakland University, in Rochester Hills, Michigan. But first he would spend a night in Kalamazoo, and he would be staying with Bill and me.

We ascertained that he was a vegetarian, so we made sure we had plenty of cheese and peanut butter, which his contact said he liked.

Dinner started off somewhat stiltedly, but warmed up when Ayres, who had remarried, and become a father comparatively late in life, mentioned his ten-year-old son. "I even change his nappies," he said proudly. He talked about his days as a conscientious objector in World War II, about serving as a medic, and seeing MacArthur wade ashore in the Philippines—again and again and again until the photographers got all the pictures they wanted. Ayres and his medical group were already on the beach when MacArthur arrived.

He told us about a dream he'd had about an androgynous God who had explained to him why He never interferes with the Natural Law. Ayres, who was at that time sixty-nine, said that he did not fear death; rather, he looked upon it as the Great Adventure. When his death was announced some years later I immediately thought, "Now he's enjoying that Great Adventure."

Lew Ayres's visit was the occasion for the only time I ever saw Bill truly angry. It brought to mind Christ and the moneychangers in the temple.

As mentioned, Bill was a pacific person, with the ability to laugh off things that would send the average person screaming up the wall. He came close to what was said of one of our favorite singers: When an aspirin gets upset it takes two Perry Comos.

Further, Bill was one-quarter Irish. But aren't the Irish known for their fierce tempers? one might ask. Yes and no. Having seen a lot of Irish in action, I had come to realize that one of the qualities of the Irish—believe it or not—is the ability to take a lot without striking back. Over the years—centuries, actually—the Irish had swallowed a lot of guff from the British who occupied Ireland. The Irish learned to take it . . . until pushed beyond endurance. At which point, like cornered wolves, they came out fighting, and the fierceness of their response was indeed something to behold.

This was portrayed graphically in *The Quiet Man*—when Sean Thornton, pushed beyond endurance by both his wife and his brother-in-law, finally allowed himself to fight back. And what a fight it was!

But, as the French say, let us return to our sheep.

Bill and the Center for Contemplative Studies had worked quite hard to bring Lew Ayres and his *Altars of the World* to Western Michigan. Unfortunately, the venue they would have preferred was not available. So they had to reserve a much larger auditorium than the anticipated audience called for. Still, the center would swallow the expense, even if they didn't at least break even.

Ads were placed in strategic media spots, and the coming exhibition was talked up in every corner.

A few nights before Ayres's arrival, Bill and I attended a program at Kalamazoo College. I don't recall the topic, but it must have been relevant. In any event, near the conclusion of the program, the emcee announced that although WMU would be presenting Lew Ayres and his *Altars* film, K College had contracted to also present the film. "But," the emcee announced portentously and smugly, "our showing will be free, whereas WMU is charging for their showing."

What he did not mention was that WMU would be showing the entire film, whereas the K College showing would be only a segment of the film. Absent that information, it seemed clear to all present that it would be foolish to pay to see *Altars* at WMU when one could see it free at K College.

Bill was almost livid. When one hears the phrase "steam was coming out of his ears" it may seem hyperbole . . . but Bill came close. As the program concluded, he said to me, "Wait for me in the lobby."

For the first and only time since I had known him, I was afraid of what he might do. Even though his fury was purposeful and controlled, I honestly feared he was going to sock the guy. But I dutifully walked out into the lobby.

Bill's voice—like Bill himself—was always modulated to the circumstances. Normally, it was low and cordial. But when necessary. he was able to project it without benefit of amplification—like an old-time opera singer. As I paced the lobby, I could hear him verbally accosting the emcee: "You cut the legs right out from under us!" I could tell from the man's weak responses that he found Bill daunting. I couldn't blame him; *I* was daunted.

Fortunately for all concerned, Bill did not sock the guy. I don't know who was more relieved, the emcee or I.

In spite of the appearance of Lew Ayres, the center's showing of *Altars of the World* played to an extremely light house. I don't know about K College's showing. Bill explained the light attendance to Ayres, who felt bad about the situation. Undoubtedly, he too had learned a lesson, and in future undoubtedly made sure that he wouldn't be "playing against himself."

No sooner had Ayres left town than I learned that Bill and I were moving to Texas.

Texas?

The University of Dallas was run by the Trappists. Dr. Sommerfeldt had accepted the presidency of the university. The Center for Contemplative Studies would be moving, lock, stock, and barrel, to Irving, Texas, where the university was located, on a site overlooking the Dallas Cowboys' stadium.

Since Dr. Sommerfeldt would have a full-time job as president of the university, Bill would no longer be assistant director of the center, but director.

But . . . *Texas?*

Neither of us had ever set foot in Texas. We didn't know what to expect.

We flew to Dallas to reconnoiter and find a place to live.

It was *hot*. But it's a dry heat, everyone said. Granted, it wasn't Houston, whose humidity, I later learned, gives its inhabitants a summer-long sauna. But I was a Northerner, born and bred. I was used to trees, and water, and at least an occasional respite from summer heat.

We looked at apartments and finally chose one that seemed as good as any. And we returned to Kalamazoo to close up shop.

The first day back, I ran into our neighbor, a lovely retired widowed schoolteacher. "How is Dallas?" she asked. In response, I burst into tears. She hugged me and said, "It won't be so bad. You'll be all right. Wait and see: You'll get used to it."

Maybe.

PART 5

Remember wherever you go, there you are.

—EARL MACRAUCH

WE HEADED WEST-SOUTHWEST into the setting sun. As we drove
through the rolling approaches to East St. Louis, my imagination
went back in time to the days when the covered wagons had carried
families headed for the Western territories. I pictured the oxen,
thirsty, dusty, foam-flecked, finding within themselves the energy
to pull a little harder, to pick up their hooves a bit more quickly, to
strain their shoulders against the yoke in hopes of reaching the still
unseen Mississippi—whose moist scent found a welcome in their
flared nostrils.

Instead of heading directly for Dallas, we detoured to Kansas City
to meet with the editor who would be handling *The Rosary Murders.*
Jim Andrews and John McMeel had, a short time before, acquired
Sheed & Ward, respected Catholic book publishers. Bill's book would
join a novel by Garry Wills as one of Andrews & McMeel's earliest
offerings. We were honored to be in such company.

Donna Martin was a sweet, petite version of Anne Bancroft,
only, as Bill noted, much prettier. Although Donna was almost as
new at this book business as we were, she was intelligent, talented,
and good-humored. She gave every indication of looking forward
to working with us on *The Rosary Murders.* We felt we were in good
hands, and as the years went by, that feeling would be justified.

Another detour would take us to Oklahoma City to visit a couple
of Bill's former St. Norbert's parishioners. But nobody warned us

about the Flint Hills. No highway sign read, ABANDON HOPE ALL YE WHO ENTER HERE. We had never heard of the Flint Hills.

We would never forget them.

Mile after mile after mile of moonscape brought to mind the English description of Connaught: "No tree to hang a man, no water to drown him, and no earth to bury him." Nothing but some sort of rock or shale . . . well, come to think of it, I suppose it was flint. Not a human being, not an animal, not a sign of civilization. If ever the term godforsaken could be applied to a place, this was it.

After driving through countless miles of lunar landscape, Bill said quietly, "You know, if we died here, they wouldn't even find our bones."

Fortunately, we weren't destined to decompose in that remote area. Oklahoma City rose upon the horizon, looked heavenly by comparison. And the reunion with the couple from St. Norbert's was, as the French say, worth the detour.

Bob had been a special agent when he first met Beautiful Alice, a young secretary in the FBI's Detroit office. He would say later, "I cut her out of the herd." Father Kienzle gave Beautiful Alice instructions in the Catholic faith, then married the couple, who promptly lived up to the Catholic image by producing seven beautiful children.

Bob was tall, rugged, and charming—picture Rock Hudson with heterosexual chromosomes. Bill always referred to him as Secret Agent X-9. When St. Norbert's needed a volunteer to teach CCD classes, Bob stepped in. Where other adults had problems keeping the kids quiet, Bob merely casually sat atop a front desk, making sure his jacket was open and pulled to one side. The view of the regulation weapon that he carried was enough to quiet down the most rambunctious.

The weapon came in handy when Bob and Alice's garage roof needed repairing. The young man hired to do the job somehow seemed unable to finish it. The repairs dragged on. One day Bob came home to find the roofer seated in a lawn chair sipping a glass of lemonade as his eyes followed Beautiful Alice. "How much longer is this job going to take?" Bob asked, as he offhandedly took his gun from its holster and laid it on the lawn table. The job was finished the next day.

Bob and Beautiful Alice—whom Bill pronounced more beautiful than ever—took us to dinner at a restaurant where each table boasted a Stanley Cup-sized bowl of shrimp and whose waiters spent their free time tossing flaming torches over the heads of the diners. I kept wondering what would happen if one of them were to muff a catch, but none did.

From Oklahoma City it was due south to Dallas, and a way of life neither of us could have imagined.

The roof [of Cowboy Stadium] is like Beethoven's [sic] Unfinished Symphony.

—Don Meredith

Mention Dallas—Big D—and many things spring to mind. JFK, the Dallas Cowboys, SMU, the civic rivalry with Fort Worth. We soon had our own icons.

When we arrived, it was memorably hot. How hot was it? It was so hot that Dallasites were buying huge cakes of ice to put in their pools. That fall, Dallasites sported T-shirts that read, "I survived the Summer of '78."

We learned that Dallas houses didn't have basements, but had to be watered every night because otherwise the ground got so dry it would fissure, and the base and the walls would wave good-bye to each other.

When that happened, it was the signal for the Invasion of the Crickets, which, we discovered, were ubiquitous in our section of Dallas.

Our apartment was carpeted in white shag. The crickets were black, and brittle. So brittle, in fact, that the critters in the Dallas Zoo whose normal diet was crickets refused to eat the home-grown product. We were told that the Dallas Zoo imported crickets from Michigan at the rate of half a cent per cricket.

A city boy, Bill could not abide insects. As each cricket poked its antennaed head up between wall and floor, Bill whacked it with a flyswatter. Then he stuffed a wad of tissue into the entrance hole along the baseboard. Being brittle, each cricket fragmented when swatted. Which, unless one wanted a polka-dot carpet, necessitated vacuuming the widely scattered fragments. The wad protruding from each stuffed-up hole made our baseboard resemble a man's shaving-nicked chin stuck with pieces of tissue.

Since it was near impossible to stop up the entire length and width of the living room baseboard, the crickets, in a Gryllidae version of *The Sorceror's Apprentice*, kept coming.

As Bill stepped inside the door on arriving home each evening, his first act was to pick up the flyswatter and go in hot pursuit. Nor did it stop there. Nightly patrols were instituted, consisting of Herr Sterner Stuff stalking his prey through shadowy halls and closet corners, armed with a broom in one hand, a flyswatter in the other, and girded with a dustpan.

In the middle of the night, I would wake to find him headed for the stairway, flyswatter in hand. "Don't you hear them?" he would say. "They're coming up the stairs." And then I would hear Whack! Whop! Thwack!—followed by a flushing sound from the powder room.

Other than the crickets, in our huge apartment complex there was not a living creature to be seen—not a child, not an animal—because who in their right mind would leave the comfort of round-the-clock air conditioning for the joys of stepping out into the equivalent of a blast furnace?

But the "best" was yet to come.

I can't say I wasn't warned.

There it was, bigger than life on the TV news: a feature on the seasonal invasion of tarantulas into Metroplex living rooms. No helpful chamber of commerce had informed me that tarantulas are indigenous to the area (which proves that Texans *can* keep quiet when they don't want to brag).

However, seeing on TV is not necessarily believing; after all, we've seen Hiroshima, the Moon landing, and Nixon—and still there are those who refuse to believe. Why in the name of the Great Pumpkin, then, should a tenderfoot believe that tarantulas are coming to tea?

Having grown up on a farm, I've never gotten used to wearing shoes when I don't have to. When Madam is At Home, the shoes are Off. Such was the state two days later, when, walking through the living room, I felt an odd sensation under my bare heel. My first thought was, "Ugh, I've stepped on a cricket. Yecch!"

I looked down, and if there is an emotion beyond sheer terror, it took over my brain and body. I had stepped on a tarantula. Oh, a small one to be sure, but a tarantula for a' that. And because our shag rug was quite deep, and because I had not fully completed my step due to the sensation of feeling something underfoot, I had not killed it, merely gotten its attention.

There it was, burrowed into the rug pile, waving everything it had that was wavable, and, like Peter Finch's *Network* audience, Mad as Hell.

Bill didn't call me St. Javan of Assisi for nothing: I got a huge paper bag, ushered the tarantula into it, and threw the whole thing out the door. Which, as Bill, informed me, left it free to fight another day.

The tarantula was almost the final straw. Bill phoned several rental offices. If you want to make a Dallasite laugh, ask him or her where in the city one can live bug-free. One agent *did* say he could find such a spot for us. He never called back. Another chuckled heartily and proceeded to give Bill a rundown of the various areas: Richardson had fire ants; south Dallas had scorpions; our area had crickets and tarantulas. It could be worse, he said: The posh Turtle Creek area had rats.

There seemed little or no sympathy for our plight, although our complex did contract for a monthly visit from a fumigator. The young man brought in to treat the House of Horror grinned at my tale of wiggly woe. "Why, ma'am"—a condescending chuckle—"they sell 'em in stores as pets!"

"I know," I replied weakly, "my son's got one in Detroit—but he keeps it in a cage!"

The young man's eyes rolled heavenward. He pressed the button on his death ray, leaving a trail of viscous white fluid in his wake. "Most people think this stuff'll kill 'em," he said cheerily, "but it won't—they just mutate."

I wish we could've mutated. No such luck. After a couple of fumigations brought on nauseating headaches, we learned to vacate the premises and eat out on fumigation day.

Then came the Blue Northers.

I grew up in New Jersey, where, when a hurricane was forecast, we tethered our livestock, sat out the blow, and then went on with our lives. I had moved to Michigan shortly after a series of tornados had caused considerable damage to Flint and surrounding areas. My first months in Detroit were spent wide-eyed with worry whenever a tornado watch was in force. Eventually, I grew to treat the tornado season with the same sangfroid with which New Jerseyites faced the hurricane season.

Now I was in Dallas, a playground for Blue Northers.

My powers of description cannot begin to do proper justice to the Blue Norther.

The Blue Norther is a wind that starts somewhere way north of Texas, and grows in strength and horror as it makes it way down the Rockies, to hit Dallas something like the RAF hitting Dresden.

For some reason, it always seemed to attack in the early hours of the morning—about 3 A.M. I would be wakened by a whooshing gale whose shrieking howl conjured up the phrase the Hounds of Hell. It was impossible to sleep while the sound assaulted the building, which rumbled and shook as it tried to withstand the air pressure. It seemed that each succeeding minute would find the walls crumbling in the face of the wind's screeching power, as the high-pitched whine threatened to confer deafness.

The only good thing about the Blue Norther was that, like a vampire, it disappeared with daylight. I was always amazed to find everything still standing.

SNAFU—Situation Normal, All Fouled Up

THERE MUST BE SOME LAW OF PHYSICS that states that when one thing goes wrong, a whole bunch of other things go wrong . . . maybe it's called the domino theory.

We arrived in Dallas with the clothes on our backs and some more in our suitcases. The rest of our clothing, our furniture, and our household effects were to be delivered by movers whose company was aptly named, in that it took almost as long for our possessions to arrive as it took for the Pilgrims' ship to complete its voyage to Plymouth Rock.

Since we had no furniture, we spent our first night in Dallas at a motel. Next morning, Bill phoned our moving company. And the next morning. And the next morning. And the morning after that. We finally ascertained that because our possessions did not constitute a full load, the movers had warehoused them in Indiana, where they would remain until such time as the company could fill the rest of the van with items earmarked for Dallas delivery.

We rented a bed, we bought a used couch, some drugstore dishes and utensils, and a Cuisinart cooking pot and frying pan. And every morning, Bill went off to his new job at the University of Dallas wearing the same blue sports jacket. After several days, when it became all too evident that phoning the movers would do no good, Bill began to write them. Every day, he sent a full-page type-written letter to the movers' headquarters—threatening, pleading, cajoling. Along the way, sadly, we discovered that we hadn't read the small print: The movers were within their rights.

In our original move from Detroit to Minnesota, the movers had placed my bicycle against an antique bureau, which arrived in St. Louis Park with huge gouges in it where the bike pedals had obviously dug in every time the van's driver stepped on the brakes. There was no problem about repairing and refinishing the dresser—but of course its antique value lost something in the refurbishing.

When we bought our house, we rented a truck and, with the aid of a friend, moved ourselves from St. Louis Park to Minneapolis.

The move from Minneapolis to Kalamazoo was fairly uneventful, except that one of the movers had picked up our "bean jar"—the receptacle in which we kept our household cash—and packed it in a carton—which one was a mystery. We had to replenish the money for our trip. But the bean jar, contents included, did eventually turn up during unpacking—along with the packer's cardboard cutter which had also found its way into the carton. We came out of that move ahead; I still have the cutter.

When, after a full month of spartan living, our furniture, et al., did arrive in Dallas, we discovered that a heavy teak desk had been badly damaged. How that had happened remained a mystery, as the disfigurement was such that if one were to *try* to damage a piece of furniture in that manner, one couldn't have done it. But our movers did it.

Again, a repairman was sent. To this day I wonder whether there is some sort of sweetheart racket going on where the repairers bribe the movers to damage furniture so that the repairers can be sure of steady work.

By the time we were ready to leave Dallas, we had learned some much needed lessons. I phoned the Better Business Bureau and asked for the name of the moving company that had the fewest complaints. We hired that company, which delivered our things on time and undamaged, except for a Baccarat wineglass, which they immediately replaced. I had paid $12 for the glass originally; by that time, it was selling for $16; today, it would cost close to $100. By now, it and its mates have long since broken and have been replaced with less aristocratic pieces.

When the old Roman, Cato, began to study Greek at the age of eighty, a friend asked why he was beginning so formidable a task at such an advanced age. Cato replied that it was the youngest age he had left.

—SYDNEY HARRIS

Naturally I am biased in favour of [students] learning English; and then I would let the clever ones learn Latin as an honour, and Greek as a treat.

—WINSTON CHURCHILL

BILL AND I ENJOYED THE UNIVERSITY OF DALLAS. It was a Catholic university under the aegis of Hungarian Cistercians, who were of a different order than the "silent" Trappists. They had escaped Hungary during the Soviet takeover. I do not recall how they came to end up in Texas, but I often wondered at the contrast between their present situation and their earlier lives.

Mass at the university was concelebrated by the Cistercians, complete with Gregorian Chant. For those of us who feel that Gregorian Chant is God's own music, it was—as they say in Texas—hog heaven. Bill got a quiet chuckle out of the *Pater Noster*, whose second line, with the Latin articulated in the Hungarian accent, came out "*Qvi es in caelis.*"

Since Bill was busy being Contemplative, I was once again left to do my own thing. I no longer had a book-cum-handicrafts shop to occupy me, so I decided to study ancient Greek at the university. That's not quite as much of a non sequitur as it seems. I'd had two years of high school French and one year of Latin. I enjoyed both immensely, especially Latin.

I had always been disappointed that I hadn't had the opportunity to study Latin further, and over the years I had come to believe that in order to really understand Latin one should know Greek.

In any event, I signed up for Ancient Greek. Thus I met Father Placid.

Father Placid Csizmazia (he told me the name meant boot-maker in Hungarian) was a wizened little man with a personality that matched his given name, and a face that was so lined that when he smiled—which was often—he looked like a happy raisin. He also was the quintessential teacher.

Seventeen undergrads and I made up his Greek class. I cannot fully describe the attentiveness with which we listened to him. He taught us not only the Greek language, but also Greek history and culture, as well as the relevant biblical connections. When the bell rang ending class, no one wanted to leave; we sat enthralled, assimilating what we had just heard.

Experts claim that the ideal time to learn a foreign language is up to the age of ten, or twelve at most. As a high schooler, languages had come easily to me. I was now forty-five, with a history of chronic fatigue syndrome, one of whose symptoms was an inability to concentrate. Where once I had run happily through linguistic textbooks, I now plodded, like a cow trying to pull her hooves out of muck and mire.

My youthful classmates seemed to have no trouble with declensions and tenses. One day, I said to one of the young men, "You're all carrying heavy course loads, and doing well at them, and you're also gliding through this Greek class without sweat. How do you do it?"

He grinned at me. "Young brains," he said.

Greek class was three days a week. In between, I studied. I made flash cards, and every time Bill and I went to the swimming pool, we took the flash cards along. Since Bill had studied Greek in the seminary, he was helpful—and encouraging.

I had to work to keep up with the rest of the students. The easier it seemed for them, the harder I applied myself. Some days, after class, I would go into Bill's office, sink into a chair, and sob in frustration.

Many husbands at this point might well be forgiven for saying something along the lines of, "Why are you making yourself miserable? Drop the class."

Not Bill. Among his virtues, noted by so many, were his kindness and his patience. He was the most supportive of individuals.

I'm sure he must have been an ideal confessor. One of his favorite phrases, which I recall hearing many times over the years—directed both to me and to other people—was, "There's not a jury in the world would convict you."

Now, instead of losing patience, or advising me to drop the class, Bill would get up, come around the side of his desk, sit down next to me, take me on his lap, and comfort me. Anyone entering the room while this was taking place could have been forgiven for wondering what was going on. Fortunately, no one ever came in during these sessions.

Encouragement never hurts. I aced my end-of-semester test. My final mark for the class was 4.0. It had been so hard won . . . but I had to temper my pride—for I felt that part of my success belonged to Bill.

Bill did make one suggestion. "Why don't you just audit the next semester? Maybe then you won't feel so pressured." He was right: I did audit, and I was less pressured. I still enjoyed the class . . . however, I wouldn't have gotten a 4.0 for that semester.

After two semesters of Greek, I now felt that in order to properly understand it, ideally I should study Sanskrit. So far, that has eluded me. And, sadly, bearing out the Use-it-or-lose-it dictum, although I still have my textbooks, my dictionary, and my university notes, I have forgotten almost all the Greek I learned—as well as much of the Latin.

But I will never forget Father Placid. He and I corresponded after Bill and I moved back to Detroit. Several times a year I would receive a long letter from him, written in pen and ink in his beautiful hand, telling me about his trips, his projects, his family. His letters were gems of history, culture, religion, and politics. Frequently, he enclosed photos. Eventually, he was able to travel to Hungary to be reunited with students he had taught fifty years before, students who now had families of their own, to whom they introduced their beloved Father Placid.

We continued to correspond until his death a few years back. I felt blessed to have known him. I wish that all students could have a Father Placid in their life.

She's my first and second wife, and I'm her second and third husband.

—W.X.K.

THE VATICAN'S MILLS FINALLY GROUND OUT the necessary rulings. My previous marriage was declared never to have existed, and Bill was to be laicized—or, as the Vatican put it, "reduced" to the lay state. Which, as Bill commented, tells you where the laity rank in the hierarchy of the Church.

We had been married civilly. Now, all being in readiness, it was time for us to be married ecclesiastically.

We flew north to one of God's great gifts: autumn in Michigan.

It is not an exaggeration to say that I was in almost total ignorance of the events that surrounded our marriage in the Church. Just as Bill had relied upon me to pick the house for both of us in Minneapolis, I had signed papers almost blindly, relying on Bill to know what he was doing for both of us. He made the arrangements for our marriage to be "regularized."

On the appointed day, Bill and I met his sister Anne, and her husband, Art, who would be our witnesses, outside Our Lady Queen of Hope on Detroit's west side. Anne, doing honor to the occasion, sported not only a mink stole, but an orchid corsage, and Art wore a natty suit. I think Anne was a whit taken aback when she saw Bill and me attired in everyday clothes—Bill in sweater, sport shirt, and chinos, me in turtleneck, skirt, and loafers. However, like the loving and dutiful sister that she was and had always been, she kept her own counsel.

As for Bill and me, having lived as husband and wife for the past four years, this ceremony seemed almost gratuitous. But it would dot the i's and cross the t's.

Actually, it was the two other events that would take place prior to the actual ceremony that were of greater moment.

Bill would sign the final laicization papers, accepting reduction to the lay state, thus freeing him to marry in the Church. And I, who had passed forty-five years as a technical pagan, would be baptized.

The witnessing priest for the ceremony would be none other than Bishop Thomas Gumbleton—who a few years before had advised Father Kienzle to stop performing illicit marriages or face the consequences.

While Anne, Art, and I awaited the arrival of the bishop, Bill and the elderly pastor disappeared into the sacristy, where Bill would be officially signing his priesthood away. After some long minutes had passed, I turned to Anne and said, "If he comes out wearing a collar, I'm leaving." I could tell from Anne's expression that she feared I might just be serious, so I reassured her that I was not about to leave her brother waiting at the church.

A few minutes later Bishop Gumbleton arrived and proceeded with the bare bones called for by Church Law. In after years, Bill and I credited Bishop Gumbleton—a member of the Flying Priests hockey team—with performing a hat trick that day: laicizing Bill, baptizing me, and witnessing our marriage. I felt honored to have the bishop officiate at our wedding, and, although Bill never said so in so many words, I know he did too, as both Bill and I believed fervently in the bishop's work for peace and humanity.

It was one of those days that satisfied everyone involved: Bill and me, Anne and Art, the Roman Catholic Church in the person of Bishop Thomas Gumbleton—and certainly, the Trappist Abbott, who could now sit back and relax, secure in the knowledge that his director at the Center for Contemplative Study was in good standing with the Church, not to mention God.

In days to come, when traditional Catholics assumed that Bill, as a married ex-priest, was not in a state of grace, I was pleased to be able to inform them that we were totally kosher.

Some years down the road, when a rabbi friend asked me what I considered myself to be, I responded, "A Jewish Catholic."

"You can't be both," he said. "You have to be one or the other. Nobody can be both Jewish and Catholic."

"Jesus was," I said.

In the old days, those who hit bad times would scratch "GTT" on a fence and leave. "GTT" stood for "Gone to Texas"—a land of beginning again, a chance for a new life. "But what can I do?" a suicidal grad student wrote to a friend, "I'm already *in* Texas."

—U<small>NKNOWN</small>

A<small>LTHOUGH</small> B<small>ILL AND</small> I <small>ENJOYED</small> the University of Dallas immensely, neither of us was enamored of Texas. It was hot, it was dry, it was full of insects, and the Texas culture seemed to revolve around guns, leather, and he-man sports. Admittedly, we never did visit Austin, which I am told is an oasis of enjoyable living. And we never did totally figure out the wet vs. dry rules. If I recall correctly—and I'm not certain of this—social clubs were allowed to sell drinks to their members. So, in dry counties, a stay at a hotel made one a "member" for the length of one's stay, thus allowing one to drink in the hotel's restaurant.

To Bill the wet-dry rules were analagous to the tortuosity of Canon Law. If your lawyer—Canon or Texan—was clever enough, you could get around almost any legalism.

Texans themselves were another story. They were warm, welcoming, and laid-back—and frequently humorous. An elderly teacher told us that her parents had emigrated from Oklahoma in the early part of the century when, she said, people asked, "What was yer name afore ya come?"

Texas tested our marriage. Bill had signed on with the center for one school year. He had put out feelers back in Detroit and had been promised a job the following summer doing public relations for one of Detroit's Catholic hospitals.

As the first month in Dallas went by, and the heat seared my brains, I grew increasingly miserable—so much so that Bill suggested that I might want to go back to Detroit and wait for his arrival a few months down the line. I considered it for about ten seconds, but there was no way I was going to be separated from him. We were in this together and together we would stay.

The heat wave of '78 gave way to something Dallasites were unaccustomed to: winter. The Christmas–New Year's holidays found a good part of Dallas affected by a major ice storm. Our own neighborhood was without electricity for three days, but some areas were blacked out as long as ten days. Which led to another of Bill's favorite headlines, which appeared on page one of the Dallas *Morning News*: OFFICE OF EMERGENCY PREPAREDNESS NOT YET READY.

Like the other residents of the Dallas–Ft. Worth Metroplex, we made do. Our apartment had a fireplace, so we bought firewood at the local market, and roasted hot dogs on a stick. We kept wondering why the burning logs didn't warm the room. Then we discovered that the flue was broken. We reported this to the management and were told it would be taken care of. It wasn't. We reported it again. Again we were told it would be taken care of. Again it wasn't.

Some six months later, after we had returned to Detroit, we received a letter from the apartment complex's secretary, who had since moved back to her home in another state. She had liked us very much, she wrote, and had felt so terribly sorry for us, because, she said, when we reported the broken flue, she knew, but couldn't tell us, that the management was never going to fix it.

We didn't have a lot of time to worry or wonder about much in Dallas. So many things were going on. Bill was occupied at the Center for Contemplative Studies, I was trying to keep up with my Greek class, and every so often a communication from Andrews & McMeel would arrive, necessitating proofreading or promotional planning in connection with the book. Originally, we had given the book the working title of *The Rosary Murders*. That was a dreadful choice, Jim Andrews said, and couldn't we come up with something better? We sent in three pages of suggested titles—including *Buy This Book*. But none of them hit the mark and since no one seemed able to come up with something preferable, it remained *The Rosary Murders*.

Actually, that appealed to Bill's sense of simplicity—a sense honed by an artist whose work had graced the pages of *Mpls.*, and who had helped lay out the magazine. Lloyd Crider and Bill had hit it off from Day One. Lloyd believed in reducing things to their simplest possible element. So when I referred to the book review column as "The Book Nook," Lloyd simply styled it "Books."

Lloyd had further endeared himself to Bill by throwing an annual booze-and-chartreuse bash each August to commemorate Nixon's resignation. "Because that was the day," Lloyd would say, "they got the bastards!"

Since it never rains but it pours, the final galleys for *Rosary* arrived just before the holidays, during the same period when I was studying for the final Greek exam of my first semester. I proofread during the day and boned up on Greek at night, while my nerves grew tauter and tauter. Since I had no time to cook, one night I put a frozen pizza in the oven and forgot about it until I realized smoke was coming out of the stove.

I opened the oven door to find a cricket, like the proverbial cat on a hot tin roof, hotfooting it from spot to spot on the pizza. I think it was trying to avoid the hot cheese and tiptoeing from mushroom to mushroom. Horrified, I tried to pull the pizza from the oven, and in doing so, managed to drop it, cheese side down, on the floor.

My cup of woe had runneth over: I threw myself into the corner of the kitchen, where I sat, curled up in a fetal position, sobbing. Bill entered, and stood indecisively for a moment, not knowing whether to pick me or the pizza up first. After a few seconds, he picked me up, we picked up the pizza together, and then went out to dinner.

If you want to make God laugh, tell Him your plans.

—SISTER MARY OF THE COMPASSION, OP

THE UNIVERSITY OF DALLAS had been good to us. In reciprocation, we donated our aggregation of books on Ireland to the university library. Thus was established the Boyle-Lowther Collection—Boyle in honor of Bill's Irish ancestors, Lowther in honor of mine.

It was not easy. Parting with some of those books was like ripping off one's skin. One of the few we kept was a biography of John Boyle O'Reilly, one of my heroes. Later, we were able to locate another copy and send it on to the library.

Many of the books had been given to us by Irish friends, as well as by fellow Hibernophiles. Almost each book had a story behind it. Donating such books was akin to turning one's children over to an orphanage. But the university was planning an Irish Studies program, and we wanted to be part of it. We never regretted our contribution, and have since added to the collection, as have many others.

The university, like most universities, always needed money. Among other things, they hoped to build a science center. During this time, T. Cullen Davis was on trial in Fort Worth. Davis had previously been acquitted of murder in the shooting deaths of the daughter and the boyfriend of his second wife. He had subsequently been caught in an FBI sting and was now in jail, charged with solicitation to commit murder.

Davis, one of the richest men in Texas,* had as much arrogance as he had money, but he was ingratiating enough to capture the sympathy of Texas juries in more than one trial. However, his ace in the hole was Richard "Racehorse" Haynes, a high profile lawyer who made Melvin Belli, Percy Foreman and F. Lee Bailey look colorless. A reporter once asked Haynes if he was the best criminal defense lawyer in Texas. "I believe I am," Haynes said. Then he added, "I wonder why you restrict it to Texas."

Years later, in a speech to the American Bar Association, Haynes described his MO: "Say you sue me because you say my dog bit you. Well, now, this is my defense: My dog doesn't bite. And second, in the alternative, my dog was tied up that night. And third, I don't believe you really got bit. And fourth, I don't have a dog."

----

* The character of J. R. Ewing in the TV series *Dallas* was said to be based roughly on Davis.

The trials of T. Cullen Davis generated the notoriety of the Claus von Bulow or O. J. Simpson trials of later years, at least in Texas. Among other things, Davis was known for the grandness of his charitable contributions. An enterprising nun on the staff of the University of Dallas reportedly wrote to the jailed Davis telling him that if he would contribute a science center to the university she would pray—not for him, but for "Racehorse" Haynes.

Once more, Haynes came through for his client. A mistrial was declared and the State of Texas didn't have enough money to take Davis back to court. This deliverance was referred to as Texas Justice.

The day came when, good-byes said, the movers having come and gone, and our car packed to the gills, we left Dallas and headed north, crossing the border at Texarkana. This time there were no detours. Michigan was calling.

In my early years in Michigan, whenever I traveled outside the state and was asked, "Where are you from?" my response was, "I'm from New Jersey, but I'm living in Michigan."

Nine months in Texas had been an evolutionary experience. When we finally crossed the border into Michigan—trees, grass, water!—I wanted to kiss the ground. From that day forward I was a Michigander.

We had left Michigan five years before, not knowing what lay ahead of us. Now, having lived in Minnesota, Kalamazoo, and Dallas, we were back in Coleman Young's Detroit. We still didn't know what lay ahead.

We rented an apartment in Lafayette Towers, where I had lived before leaving for Minneapolis. It was near downtown, had a beautiful view of the Detroit River, Belle Isle, and Windsor, and was at the entrance to the expressway that Bill would take to work.

Imagine our surprise to discover that a new CEO had taken over at the hospital. Wanting to start with a clean slate, he had fired the existing staff—including the executive who had hired Bill. Which meant that, somewhat like a shirttail monsignor relegated to nonmonsignorship with the death of the Pope, Bill was now in employment limbo.

While we were trying to catch our breath in the face of what seemed to Bill a catastrophe, we were visited by our insurance agent. Henry Meurer, Jr., was the son of the attorney I had worked for at the time my baby died. That day, Henry Junior helped not only by giving us expert insurance advice, he lightened Bill's load considerably by suggesting something that Bill had never considered. When Bill bemoaned the fact that he had lost his new job before even starting it, Henry looked vaguely puzzled. "What do you need a job for? You can make a living writing books."

The Rosary Murders had just hit the bookstores. And indeed, while we were in Dallas, Bill had started researching a sequel, *Death Wears a Red Hat*. Henry's suggestion affected Bill something like the thunderbolt that dumped St. Paul off his horse.

"Do you think we can do it?" he asked me after Henry had left.

"Of course," I said blithely. I believed in Bill. *He* could do anything.

Sr. Anna Catherine Emmerick has said that the Lord let her know that even if something which was previously forbidden is later allowed by Bishops on earth it is still held bound in heaven! He does not recognize lacization [sic] of clergy or of religious who have taken their final vows! She said 'they are in delusions of their own making & will merit a most harsh punishment after death.'

—Excerpt from a crank letter

In 1979, an ex-priest was still an object of more than usual interest. Particularly an ex-priest who had written a murder mystery. The public was interested, the media was interested, and Catholics—especially conservative Catholics—were definitely interested. There was a lot to be straightened out, particularly with regard to the conservatives.

Interviewers would ask Bill, "Why did you leave the Church?"

Bill would explain that he hadn't left the Church, he'd left the priesthood.

"Well, why did you leave the priesthood?"

"I left because there are 2,414 rules in Canon law and there's not one of them I like."

Or he would reply, "I could keep the rules myself; I just couldn't inflict them on others."

"Were you excommunicated when you left?"

"No, I was laicized."

"What's that?"

"I was 'reduced to the lay state.'"

The call-in shows were fraught. I would sit in the control booth with the show's producer, while Bill and the host took calls from sometimes irate listeners. Initially, the nastiness of some of the callers had me gritting my teeth. But I soon learned that Bill was quite capable of dealing with them.

It was obvious the son had inherited his father's peacemaking talent. He had a way of turning aside and/or disarming even the most vicious caller.

Instead of being confrontational, he would respond with something like, "You could be right. Please pray for me." Or, "I'm sorry you didn't like my book. I hope you like the next one better."

It was the same with crank mail or nasty letters. Where I would have shot back an argumentive missive, Bill sent thoughtful responses that somehow touched a chord in the recipient. Many times he received a pacific and even apologetic reply to his response.

Bill explained to me that Catholics had grown fearful. So much had happened since Vatican II, and their world was being pulled out from under them. They reacted by striking out at anything they saw as the cause of such an upheaval—or anyone they felt had contributed to or epitomized such an upheaval.

Bill was a handy scapegoat. But somehow, he managed to reassure them, or at the very least neutralize them. I was so proud of him. "Blessed are the peacemakers, for they shall be called the Children of God."

Some Catholics seemed particularly bitter about our marriage. The fact that we had been married in and by the Church, rather than allaying their anger, seemed to intensify it. We realized that undoubtedly these were people who had come up against Canon Law's "No's" in their own life and thus resented the fact that we had been able to—in their eyes—circumvent those laws, where they themselves had not been able to.

The threat was always there. One day, an anonymous letter came in from someone who was obviously bitter about our marriage. I don't remember it verbatim, but it concluded along the lines of "I've seen you two in St. Mary's [old St. Mary's downtown, where we attended Mass], sitting there looking so holy and all. I'm keeping my eye on you."

I wasn't concerned, but Bill was, more for me I think than for himself. In any case, we changed churches, alternating between Holy Rosary on Woodward and SS. Peter and Paul, the Jesuit church on Jefferson.

Still, it could be nerve-wracking. At one autographing, the bookstore hired a guard to stand watch. Once, Anne and I accompanied Bill, taking turns standing at his back as he autographed. On another occasion, I was standing just a few feet from Bill, trying to make sure that no one approached him from the rear. I turned my head for a split second, then turned back to see a man who seemingly had appeared out of nowhere, standing over Bill's back. Fortunately, he was just a fan waiting for an autograph. But it gave me a clear indication of the difficulty of guarding someone from potential danger. My hat is off to the Secret Service.

Bill remained calm, cool, and collected. He liked people, and always seemed to enjoy meeting them and talking with them. Years later, however, he told me that in those early days when he got dressed to go out on public appearances, he felt, he said, like a matador suiting up to meet his possible death in the bullring.

They [Basques] eat anything that hops, sprouts, swims, trots, slithers, creeps or flies . . . Basques have always regarded prodigious quantities as mandatory . . .

—HERBERT BAILEY LIVESEY

THE CONTRAST BETWEEN OUR LIFE IN TEXAS and our life in Michigan took some getting used to. While we were decompressing, Bill continued to research *Red Hat* and I happily made the readjustment from Neiman-Marcus to J. L. Hudson. It was so good to be "home."

One of the many joys was meeting Bill's seminary schoolmates—those who had left before ordination, those who had been ordained, and those who had left the active priesthood. Bill had corresponded with several of them since leaving, most notably Ray Betanzos, one of those who had left the same day Bill had.

Ray, now a professor at Wayne State University, had visited us in Kalamazoo, occasioning a state of near-panic in me.

Ray was a full-blooded Spanish Basque, a marvelous athlete, an incredibly brilliant scholar, academician, philosopher, and linguist. He was conversant in something like seven or eight languages, most of which he spoke fluently. Additionally, he was one of the world's most inventive punsters. Although on one occasion, he was outdone by one of his students, who asked him politely to please not stand in the classroom doorway. When asked why not, the student responded, "Because we don't want all our Basques in one exit."

At the time Ray visited us, a WMU professor had recently written a life of Christ, wherein he dealt with, among other things, the question of whether St. Peter had indeed been crucified upside down. As I recall, the author, after much research, concluded that the upside-down-crucifixion was more legendary than factual.

It seemed unlikely, he said. Consider: The centurions had already set the upright part of the post and attached the crossbar. Now, just because some crazy old man wanted to be crucified upside down, would the centurions go to all the trouble of extracting the post, redigging, and reinserting the post, with the crossbar at the base . . . just to satisfy Peter's whim? Hardly.

Ray's comment on the disputed point was *"Quod cruxi, cruxi."* It was a play on Pilate's *"Quod scripsi, scripsi* [What I have written, I have written]," uttered when taken to task about the sign—"INRI [Jesus of Nazareth, King of the Jews]" he'd had placed above Jesus's head on the cross. Ray's pun, though it does lose something in the translation for the lay listener, never failed to break up any theologian who heard it.

At one period, a string of correspondence between Ray and Bill and me had reduced composers' names and titles of musical compositions to canine-sounding names, e.g., Johann Sebastian Bark. This went on for some time, until finally we all felt we had plumbed the depths of the subject, in a conclusive two-page, single-spaced epistle listing such favorites as:

Mozart's *Post Hund* Concerto (K.9); Smetana's *The Bartered Briard*; Verdi's *Mastiff Ball*; Moussorgsky's *Boris Dogounow*, and *Pinschers at an Exhibition*; Lalo's *Symphonie Espaniel*; Elgar's *Saluki d'Amour* and *Pomeranian and Circumstance*; Ravel's *Pavane for a Dead Pinscher*; and many other more esoteric entries, including the "Concerto in D" by Hydrant (adapted by Sousa as *The Washington Post*).

Bill's contributions, since he was au courant with contemporary music, included "Dachshund Through the Snow"; "The White Cliffs of Doberman"; "Pug of My Heart"; "Basenji Mucho"; and Elvis Presley's "Don't Step on My Blue Tick Hound," as well as Weill's *Threepuppy Opera*. Bill's beloved Gershwin was also represented with *Corgi and Bess*.

The final collection concluded with *"Morituri te saluki . . .* from upon a *Peke in Darien."*

In addition to their national game, pelota (jai alai), their fervid love of freedom, and their tongue-twisting language, the Basques are noted for their ravenous appetites. Over the years, I had heard many stories of Ray's fabled eating prowess. Like the time that Ray, having just finished a full-course dinner at the seminary, had proceeded to eat a full carry-out dinner that a confrere brought back from a Phoenician restaurant.

Thus my near-panic at Ray's impending visit: How could I be sure to have enough food on hand? I solved the problem by overkill: I served not only huge steaks, but also a plateful of chopped sirloin burgers. Ray did not totally deplete the vittles; Bill and I dined on leftovers for several days.

Ray had married a sweet, beautiful teacher, Kathleen (Kay) McNamara, and they had a daughter, Mary, whom Bill dubbed Little Mary Sunshine. Beth, Kay's young daughter from a previous marriage, rounded out the Betanzos household. From time to time, Kay's mother, a dear, elderly lady, came to visit. As the years passed, Mrs. McNamara grew more and more forgetful, which led to oft-repeated tales of humorous incidents.

When working at home during the summer, Ray spent a good part of his time at a desk in the basement, from which he would emerge for meals, or to rejoin the family group. One day, Kay took young Beth to spend the weekend with Beth's father. Kay's mother and little Mary went along for the ride. All went well until, having delivered Beth to her father's house, Kay was driving back home. Her elderly mother grew increasingly perturbed. "Where's the little girl?" she asked repeatedly. Each time, Kay patiently explained that Beth was going to spend the weekend with her father. Her mother would fall silent and then, a few minutes later, "But where's the little girl?"

Kay stopped the car and turned to her mother. "Mother, Beth is with Ken. Ken and I were married, and Beth is our daughter. Ken and I are divorced now. But he's her father, and she's staying with him."

"He's her father . . .?" asked Mrs. McNamara.

"Yes," Kay replied.

"Then who," her mother asked, "is the man in the basement?"

Ever after, we all referred to Ray as The Man in the Basement.

Well married, a man is winged.

—Henry Ward Beecher

As I met more of Bill's ex-priest friends and former seminary schoolmates, I grew more impressed. These were good—even holy—men, kind, intelligent, caring people. The Church's loss became sadly evident. There were times when I felt bitter over the loss of some of the brightest and the best. Bill had left the priesthood because he did not see eye to eye with Canon Law. Over the years, when asked if he would return to the active priesthood if the Church no longer required mandatory celibacy, his response was unfailing: "Not unless they get rid of Canon Law and go back to the law of Christ: Love."

Most of the others had left the priesthood to marry. I was doubly impressed with their wives. These were strong, intelligent, warmhearted, relevant women, loving of their families and of humanity, and giving of themselves. This told me a lot about their husbands: Here were men who were secure enough in their own masculinity not to feel threatened by a strong woman. Men who were, on the contrary, at ease with and grateful for their wives' strength, excellence, and talents.

In this present decade, when those with their own agenda blame pedophilia, ephebophilia, homosexuality, and all manner of priestly scandal on the seminaries, all I can think is that it was the seminaries that turned out the magnificent priests of Bill's era. Many of those men are still active—ministering to their flocks in the face of everything the news media and their own wagon-circling hierarchy can throw at them.

And so many of the men who left the active priesthood are loving husbands and fathers, who, though not on the altar, continue to give of themselves to their parish, their Church, and their community.

Many of the wives are ex-nuns. Actually, Kay Betanzos and I are two of a minority; we used to joke about having badges made up that read, "I am not an ex-nun."

Once when Bill was on a radio call-in show, the female producer, sitting with me in the control booth, asked if I were an ex-nun. When I replied in the negative, she said, "That's too bad—if you were, we could have you and your husband back for a show together." For one of the few times in my life, I was literally speechless. All I could think was: I've been Girl Friday in a detective agency, a legal secretary, a travel agent, a newspaper editor, a book reviewer—how is it that I have nothing of interest to say unless I happen to be an ex-nun?

But I discovered early on that there is a salacious undertone to some people's interest. Nuns and priests. Priests and sex. Sex and priests. Priests and women. Celibacy. Chastity. Buzzwords and phrases that pique the prurience of even the most otherwise circumspect.

On talking with the wives of ex-priests, I discovered that many had had the same experience: an awareness of extreme interest on the part of the laity. It was like being under a magnifying glass. If the wife of an ex-priest was attractive, people said, "She seduced him out of the Church." (One man, who should have known better, described me in almost those exact words—"she seduced him out of his cassock"—in the presence of Bill and me and a roomful of our business associates.) If the wife was not particularly attractive, it was almost as if people were disappointed: "What on earth did he see in her?"

It would have been funny if it hadn't been so tragic, but in a few short years, the events that started the insidious crack that would lead to open scandal brought things to the point where if a priest was involved with someone, the chancery merely breathed a sigh of relief if the offender's partner was female.

A relevant story that made the rounds seemed from all reports to be fairly factual. A Detroit priest who had played fast and loose with his promise of mandatory chastity was sent off on retreat. On his return, he was accepted back into the fold, with the admonition, "Just don't date anybody from your own parish."

People must help one another; it's nature's law.

—JEAN DE LA FONTAINE
Fables

ONE OF THE BASIC DIFFERENCES between Bill and me was my inability to ask for help. I always thought it was due to my farm upbringing. When one grows up in the boondocks, one learns to be self-sufficient. If there's no one else around and something needs to be done, you do it yourself. If you don't know how to do it, you figure out a way to get it done.

This held over even into my marriage. If I needed something from a top shelf, I climbed up on a step stool and retrieved the object. Many is the time Bill walked into the kitchen to find me balanced precariously, holding something breakable, as I backed down the step stool. "Why didn't you ask me to get that? I'm tall; all I have to do is reach up."

If something needed to be moved, rather than asking Bill for help, I figured out how to effect the leverage, so I could do it myself. Though Bill always described me as petite, my years of mowing grass, lifting egg crates, and carrying food and water to the livestock had left me with healthy arm, shoulder and abdominal muscles.

Bill never ceased to be amazed at my physical strength. When not laid low by illness, I was a poster child for the benefits of youthful exercise. Not only had farm work toughened me, but a talent for softball and basketball all through my school years had contributed to a healthy stamina. Granted, I had a heart murmur from a childhood case of what the doctor termed "incipient rheumatic fever" so I wasn't a distance runner. Nonetheless, I could walk the legs off an Olympic centipede. Even Bill, a whole foot taller than I, was hard put to keep up with me. "You're walking too fast," was a frequent refrain.

In *Till Death*, Bill described Lil as "surprisingly strong," adding, "On those occasions when a heavy object was too hefty or bulky for him to lift alone, Lil bore the load every bit as equally as he." I knew he was thinking of his petite wife when he wrote those words.

In earlier times, when I heard the Reverend Jesse Jackson preaching to young blacks that "There's nobody standing in the schoolhouse door anymore," I would think to myself, "Today's young people should have grown up on a farm." I thought of the blacks I knew who hadn't let anything stop them from reaching their goal. If a mountain stood in their way, rather than wasting precious time trying to move the mountain, they found a route around the mountain, and continued on their way. There were times when I couldn't help feeling that a lot more young people could have achieved their goal had they spent more time with their eye on the goal rather than getting sidetracked by the impediment. Maybe if they had tried to do it themselves rather than expecting someone else to run interference . . .

Nonetheless, I envied Bill's easy way of picking up the phone, calling a friend, and asking, "Can you help me with [whatever]?" I assumed it came from his years in the priesthood when, as he used to say, "Nothing was too good for Father." People rarely turned down a request from a priest.

Those who have read Bill's books may recall that each of them contains an acknowledgments page. Bill's research entailed questioning a lot of experts, and he was always grateful that the people he called for help gave it so readily. Among this group were a number of members of the police department.

Jim Grace, a detective lieutenant in Kalamazoo, was the son-in-law of Virginia Sommerfeldt, the lady I referred to as the Fairy Godmother. (When Virginia's daughter, Mary, told her mother that she was pregnant with her and Jim's first child, her mother responded, "Hail, Mary, full of Grace.") Bill relied on Jim to vet the manuscript of each of his books for any mistakes in police procedure. There were a few, but, thankfully, Jim caught them.

Later, Bill would call on many members of the Detroit Police Department, all of whom, like so many others Bill asked for help, were unfailingly gracious and ever ready to answer questions and make suggestions.

Law enforcement people also freely shared tales of their experiences. One particularly intriguing account came from a polygraph expert who told Bill of a subject he had tested: The man had been ripping pages from a paperback edition of *The Rosary Murders* and mailing them to his mother-in-law.

Not only the local variety, but Ireland's *gardai* and London's Scotland Yard were cooperative and helpful in answering Bill's questions and offering suggestions, when Bill was researching *Shadow of Death*. It was an assistant at Scotland Yard who taught us a new word—bumph—when she put together a folder of pertinent information for Bill.

In Ireland, Superintendent Sean Gallwey, the epitome of Kojak-style toughness, and Superintendent Thomas J. O'Reilly, gracious to a fault, spent an afternoon answering Bill's questions in spite of the fact that a rare (for the Republic) murder had taken place in the south only the day before.

Shortly after our return to Detroit, we heard that the Police Department budget was unable to provide bulletproof vests for the police. Bill thought maybe he could help. Neal Shine's brother Bill, a member of the department, suggested that we talk to Deputy Chief Bannon. So one afternoon, I headed for Police Headquarters at 1400 Beaubien, a well-known address in Detroit.

I was directed to the fifth floor, where I explained to someone in uniform that my husband would like to buy some bulletproof vests for the police. I was turned over to an attractive policewoman, who asked if she could help me. As I started to again explain the purpose of my visit, I realized that not only was the lady being exceedingly polite and exceedingly kind—but it was evident that she thought she was dealing with a street kook with delusions of grandeur.

In an attempt to disabuse her misconception, I mentioned *The Rosary Murders* and the name William X. Kienzle.

Her face lit up. "I was a student at St. David's when Father Kienzle was an assistant there." And Sergeant Mary Marcantonio took me in to speak with her boss, Deputy Chief James Bannon.

Deputy Chief Bannon had a somewhat different viewpoint than I had expected. It was improper, he felt, for private citizens to provide equipment to the police force. If the department needed equipment, the city should provide it.

However, he said, he had long felt that there was a need for some sort of medal or award for deserving officers. If Bill wanted to contribute funds to design such a medal, the department would be pleased to accept the gift.

It was done. We were told that the Police Department got their medals—and, eventually, the city did provide their bulletproof vests. Mary Marcantonio became one of our dear friends, and every so often she and I laughed as we recalled our initial meeting when she thought she was dealing with somebody who wasn't quite all there.

One of many helpful members of the Police Department was Lieutenant Barbara Weide, who literally "wrote the book" on homicide investigations. Another was Commander Judy Dowling, a friend of Mary Marcantonio. Judy and Mary came to lunch at our Lafayette Towers apartment on the day after I had had several facial moles excised. With my face black and blue and full of stitches, I resembled a female version of Dr. Frankenstein's monster. When I opened the door to admit Judy and Mary, Judy looked at me and with a perfectly straight face, asked, "Has he been beating you?"

Bill and I felt that the police see so much horror and ugliness that it's a relief for them when they can joke about something like that.

When asking for help with research, Bill discovered that frequently one person led to another. If it was a legal question, the police handed him off to the prosecutor's office. Thus he became acquainted with Andrea Solak and Tim Kenny, two stellar members of the prosecutor's staff. Andrea, like Barbara Weide—and so many other successful women of that era—had to be twice as good as a man in order to become successful in a male-dominated field.

We were privileged to see Tim in action in court, and were impressed with his even, low-key demeanor. He was the opposite of the flashy, verbally assaultive attorney; it was obvious that all Tim ever wanted was to get to the truth.

Tim Kenny is now a highly respected Circuit Court judge. Chances are that he will someday sit on the Michigan Supreme Court.

One of the most helpful—and colorful—experts Bill consulted is Dr. Werner Spitz, who was, at the time of their first meeting, Wayne County Medical Examiner. Dr. Spitz, Professor of Forensic Pathology at Wayne State University, is known worldwide for his forensic expertise. He has been consulted in many well-known cases, including that of the assassination of John F. Kennedy, and New York City's "preppie murder." Dr. Spitz's textbook on medico-legal investigation, now in its fourth edition, remains the prime reference for anyone in that field.

Some of the characters in Bill's books were made up out of whole cloth; others were based on composites. Some were patterned on specific people; others were only thinly disguised. Anyone who ever met Dr. Spitz would immediately recognize Dr. Willie Moellmann.

Nelson Kane, city editor of the *Detroit Free Press*, could only be Neal Shine. Likewise, Pat Lennon could only be Pat Chargot, who continues as one of Detroit's most intelligent newspaper writers. Bob Ankeny—styled Ankenazy in the Father Koesler series—formerly of the *Detroit News*, carries on as one of journalism's true professionals with Crain's *Detroit Business* weekly. At this writing, Bob has just received a "Most ABLE" award for commitment to excellence.

Though the characters of Walter Koznicki and Zoo Tully came entirely from Bill's imagination, yet they are among the realest of the real for me, and for many other readers. For years, when I went to bed at night, I felt all was well because Inspector Koznicki was on the job.

The character of Zack Tully was suggested by Peter Spivak. When the black Zoo Tully discovered he had a half brother who could pass for white, we all thought we had the makings of a great TV series. We even wondered if we could copyright the idea. Then one day we looked up to find James Earl Jones and Robert Duvall as a black cop and his white half brother in the film, *A Family Thing*.

Undoubtedly some people figured Bill had filched the idea.

It is interesting how different writers writing at different times in different places can coincidentally come up with the same plot.

Dead Wrong was based on an actual occurrence in Bill's mother's family. Bill elaborated on the original event to come up with a convoluted tale of revenge. Sometime later we saw the film *Widow's Peak*, starring Mia Farrow and the beautiful Natasha Richardson, and were startled to discover that its denouement was reminiscent of *Dead Wrong*.

Since *Widow's Peak* was scripted by the incredibly talented Irish dramatist/author Hugh Leonard, Bill felt he was in the best of company.

Bill, in his whimsical way, could also retaliate against the bad guys by giving some of the villains names similar to those who had done him wrong, as it were. One such character, in particular, had a different background and a different name, but everyone in the Detroit presbyterate knew who he was: He was the monsignor who, when he heard of the "irregular" marriages Bill was witnessing, said to Margaret Cronyn, "I've got the bastard now."

Oddly, even though he was one of the rankest ever, as with so many of the villains in Bill's novels, one ended up feeling sorry for him. Bill had a talent for humanizing even his killers. The French have a saying: "To understand is to forgive all." And on coming to the end of one or another of Bill's books, one could understand and—as Father Koesler did—forgive.

For Bill—as did Father Koesler—truly believed in the words he once read on a cloister wall: When you die you will be judged by love.

PART
6

Never correct a man's grammar in bed.

—Dodie Meeks

Over the years the question most frequently asked of me was, "What's it like being married to an author?"

I can't answer that. All I can say is what it was like being married to Bill Kienzle.

Bill was incredibly easy to live with. He was patient, good-humored, loving, and caring. As for our "partnership in crime," I was in my element: I have always been a compulsive clipper and researcher. I felt that I was fulfilling a purpose anytime I came up with a pertinent or relevant newspaper or magazine item that aided Bill in his plotting.

Bill himself was thorough in his research. Our phone bills and our luncheon bills peaked during the period just before he started each book, and remained at a healthy level throughout the actual writing, as Bill spent hours in discussions over specifics with various "experts."

Not every piece of information found its way into the book. Sometimes it was "deep background" information. In researching *Requiem for Moses*, Bill visited first a crematory, then a topless bar. He did not invite me to accompany him to the bar. Undoubtedly, he knew I would have declined. However, he *did* invite me to the crematorium. I declined that invitation, telling him, "You Germans are always trying to get us Jews in the ovens!"

As a made if not born editor, I was devil's advocate—best friend and severest critic—with regard to Bill's writing. This was so particularly when it came to things Catholic. As a convert raised in religious ignorance, I felt free to ask Bill to explain terminology or ritual for the benefit of those readers who were unfamiliar with Catholicism. It was not unusual even for some Catholic readers to say, "I never knew that."

One such example is the misuse of the term "the Immaculate Conception." Many readers—including some Catholics—assumed this referred to Mary's maternity of Jesus—the Virgin Birth. Actually, the Immaculate Conception refers to Mary's conception as the daughter of Anne and Joachim, free of all original sin. Thus the prayer that begins, "O Mary, conceived without sin . . ." Mary's appearance to Bernadette Soubirous at Lourdes was particularly noteworthy for her announcement, "I am the Immaculate Conception."

A friend who was a jurist in Denmark read Bill's books first in English, then in Danish. She informed us that the translation was excellent. Thus Bill was able to write an appreciative letter to the Danish translator.

Translations can be a bugaboo. Not for nothing do the Italians say, "*Traduttore, traditore* [the translator is a traitor]." In one of Loren Estleman's private eye books, a character pulls a gun. In the French edition, instead of saying "Freeze!" he says "*Voila!*" Something is definitely lost in that translation. At one point, a French publisher wanted to publish a French-language edition of one of Bill's books. However, the publisher wanted to make considerable cuts. Oddly, though France is considered a Catholic country, the publisher felt that there was too much Catholic content in the book.

The agent who had made the tentative sale was not happy when Bill turned down the request; it queered the deal. When we mentioned the situation to our Danish friend her response was immediate. Since Denmark is a Protestant country, the Danes knew comparatively little about Catholicism. It was for exactly that reason, she said, that so many Danes enjoyed the Father Koesler series, as it enabled them to learn things about Catholicism that they otherwise would not know.

Ironically, many years later, when I studied German, I picked up a German edition of one of Bill's books and discovered that the translation was full of deletions; they had freely edited out countless segments.

That was the difference between the Germans and the French. The French asked for permission; the Germans didn't ask—they just went ahead and did it.

❧❀❧

Bill wrote, slowly, thoughtfully, and with precision. I kidded him that he wrote like God handing down the tablets. Bill found rewriting onerous. Rather than outright questioning a statement or suggesting a change, I learned to rewrite a sentence or a section and offer it for his approval.

When editing, I worked with a dictionary and a thesaurus at hand. I checked each word Bill had written to ensure that each was the specific word he wanted. If I had any doubt, I inserted an alternative or alternatives in subscript for his approval or selection.

In *Mind Over Murder* I described the ship's purser as a "nautical concierge." Bill snorted. "Father Koesler wouldn't even know that word [concierge]," he said. He rewrote the phrase as "seagoing watchdog," and was content.

By the last two or three days before each final typescript went to the publisher, Bill had been rubbed raw with my questioning of every comma, semicolon, adverb, and adjective. At that point we knew it was better just not to discuss the typescript. Neither of us wanted to say anything that would hurt or leave a scar.

As time went on, he grew more at ease with my corrections and/or suggestions. While his initial response to most things was "I don't think so," often by the next day, after thinking it over, he would go along. And I learned it wasn't necessary to pursue a point—because I had the world's best backup—Bill's editor, Donna Martin. Donna and I were pretty much on the same wave length when it came to Bill's writing. So if Bill rejected one of my suggested changes, I let it go, knowing that Donna's eagle eye would catch the problem. And, Bill admitted, he couldn't fight both of us.

A negotiating session between Bill and Donna was entertaining and instructive. Bill liked to write as he spoke, which occasionally meant using incomplete sentences. At one point, he was particularly proprietory about a paragraph that consisted in its entirety of one word: "Whatever."

Donna took exception to this usage, and the discussion began. In a conclusion that a diplomat well might envy, Donna "gave" Bill his one-word paragraph in return for his acquiescing to her rewriting a phrase in a later paragraph.

Donna Martin was one of the best things that ever happened to us. Just as I would wish that all students could have a Father Placid, I would wish that all authors could have a Donna Martin. She was warm, witty, tactful, encouraging, and had a delightful sense of humor. Over the years we heard so many horror tales from other authors about their editors and/or publishers. Each time, we felt almost guilty because we had been so blessed with Donna Martin and Andrews & McMeel.

When Donna retired, after twenty years as Bill's editor, her place was taken by Dorothy O'Brien, longtime managing editor. Bill, a person who lived by routine, was near traumatized: How could he possibly get along without Donna?

Dorothy could not help but be aware of this. She stepped in and in unfailingly good-humored fashion was able to reassure Bill that he had not been deserted.

I repeatedly told Bill that if I were to predecease him I would want him to remarry. His response was always, "If something happened to you, I would curl up in a little ball and blow away." For me, when Dorothy took over as Bill's editor, she provided proof that Bill could indeed adjust to at least an editorial version of a second wife.

Imagination . . . is a way of illuminating the facts.

—Alfred North Whitehead

I had not known Bill in his youth. All I had seen was the thoughtful man with an interesting mind. So it had made perfect sense for me to ask if he would ever consider writing. Whereas, those who had known him earlier never would have believed that he would someday have a literary career.

Thus the priest who, on Father Kienzle's appointment as editor of the *Michigan Catholic*, said, "Not much surprises me, but this does."

In later years, readers of his mystery novels wondered how such a pacific man could write about murder. "Look at the Bible," Bill would reply. "Lots of sex and murder."

For my part, I attributed his storytelling ability to genetics. In the ancient Celtic culture, the *seannachie*—the teller of tales—and the bard—the poet-historian—were welcomed and venerated above all others. Music, poetry, and storytelling were an integral part of Celtic life. In Wales, according to legend, if a man went bankrupt the only possession that was exempt from foreclosure was his harp. No matter how much he owed, his ability to make music could not be taken from him.

If asked to name a German writer, the first—and in some cases the *only*—name the vast majority of Americans could come up with would be the Brothers Grimm. Jacob and Wilhelm Grimm collected the ancient legends and folk tales of their Teutonic heritage, and gave the world some of its most beloved fairy tales.

And then there was Charles Perrault, the French poet-author who gave us *Puss in Boots, Cinderella, Little Red Riding Hood,* and *Sleeping Beauty.*

So here was Bill Kienzle, the repository, on his mother's side, of the Irish and French genes, and on his father's of the German genes. How could he help but be a storyteller?

When asked by would-be writers how to plot a story, Bill explained that all one had to do was ask, "What if . . . ?" Then, he advised, throw out the first four or five "What ifs." What was left—the fifth or sixth "What if"—would advance the plot in a more creative way than if one had gone no further along the "What if" path.

Bill's fans enjoyed sending him plot ideas. Usually, the younger the suggester, the more imaginative the suggestion. Bill's response was a grateful, "That's a good one—but that's *your* book." Several young readers suggested that what Father Koesler needed was a dog. One suggested that what Father Koesler needed was a youthful assistant. "You mean like Batpriest and Robin?" Bill responded.

An Ann Arbor nurse, who had been a chemical officer in the Army, wrote that *The Man Who Loved God* had provided inspiration that helped him figure out an important clue as to how HIV/AIDS may operate, and how to treat those afflicted. As a result, he went on to write "The Unified Theory of AIDS: Reconciling Duesberg, Root-Bernstein, and the HIV."

A West Coast woman married to an ex-priest who was dying, wrote that after reading a relevant part of one of Bill's books she had contacted the local chancery and her husband was able to be reconciled with the Church before his death. The reconciliation allowed him to die in peace and gave her much needed solace.

When Bill's cousin, Mary Anne, phoned the copyright office in Washington, D.C., to ask about copyrighting her poetry, she spoke with a helpful gentleman who, on learning of her relationship, told her that reading one of Bill's books had given him enough information so that he was able to "give himself a divorce in the internal forum" and was happy with the result.

Critics who doubted the realism of Bill's books had no concept of some of the things that go on in real life.

The story that most appealed to Bill was told to him by the divorced wife of a deacon. She and her husband had gone through the training necessary for him to become a deacon and for her to properly fill the role of the deacon's wife. She was told that in order for her to do this, she must be "supportive and nonpublic."

All well and good. Unfortunately, her husband subsequently divorced her and was about to marry the ex-wife of an ex-priest. (As Anna Russell would say, "I'm not making this up, you know.")

The lady planned to write a book on the soap opera-ish situation. She had already designed the book jacket. Her training had impressed upon her that as a deacon's wife she was to remain supportive and nonpublic. So, the book jacket would display a jockstrap—which, she said, was supportive and nonpublic.

As Bill was wont to say, one need not add the word "scorned" to the phrase "Hell hath no fury like a woman."

Catholic church innovations pass through three distinct stages. First, the new thing is false; second, even if it were not totally false, it is extremely dangerous; finally, the church has always held it to be true.

—FATHER JOSEPH GALLAGHER (CITING JOAN ESTRUCH)

BILL CONTINUED TO BE ALTERNATELY AMUSED and bemused at some of the wilder shores reached by Church teaching and what people—even some of the clergy—erroneously thought was Church teaching.

As a young priest, his take on the Church's version of the Facts of Life for young people was, "Sex is dirty: Save it for the one you love."

One of Bill's priest classmates predicated everything on Natural Law. For instance, he insisted that spaying or neutering pets was against the Natural Law.

Bill knew which of his buddy's buttons to push. When Bill received a new golf bag as a birthday gift, he left the plastic covering on it, game after game. "Aren't you ever going to take off that plastic?" asked his legalistic buddy.

"Nope," said Bill calmly, "it's against the Natural Law."

It was this same priest buddy who inveighed against a married priesthood. "Do you want to take Communion from the hands of some guy who's been messing with his wife?"*

Once upon a time, in the Good Old *Old* days, priests were allowed to be married. However, a rule was promulgated that they had to wait a full day after their husbandly duties before going about their priestly duties. As more priest-husbands performed their conjugal duties more often, the days when a priest was available for

---

* One might just as easily question whether one wanted to accept Communion from the hands of anyone who's been using his hands in connection with lavatorial cleansing.

Eucharistic tasks grew further and further apart. This led to fewer Masses. As a result, the Faithful suffered, receiving Communion less and less frequently.

In today's world, periodic abstinence is an acceptable form of family planning. The Church of olden times might well have called for periodic abstinence in order to preclude improper handling of the Eucharist. Instead, the Church went whole hog: In order to assure that properly pure priests would be available to offer daily Mass, celibacy was made mandatory.

Or so I've been told.

In any case, we now have mandatory celibacy, and fewer and fewer daily Masses.

Back to the old drawing board.

With regard to Church Law, Bill's contention was that no matter what, when, and if the Church might change, it had no word for "oops." Therefore, he concluded, if any innovation were to be introduced, it would be prefaced by, "As the Church has always taught . . ."

About the time that *Humanae Vitae* first sent tremors through the People of God, Bill was presented with a mind-boggling example of Church-Think. A parishioner with an imaginative mentality bestowed by both Irish ancestry and longtime association with the ad industry related his experience with Family Planning.

He had no problem with the Church's stance on Family Planning. But he was of a curious and exploring nature. Along those lines, he couldn't help but wonder what it would feel like to use a condom. He had posed his query to his old-line confessor. "My wife is presently pregnant, so I wouldn't be contravening nature by using a condom. Under the circumstances, would it be all right just this once for me to use a condom the next time we have intercourse?"

Undoubtedly, such a query had never been raised in any of the seminary's Moral Theology classes. The elderly confessor had to start from scratch on this one. Finally, the bingo ball fell into the slot. "Yes, you may use a condom this once—but make sure it's perforated first."

Then there was the Basque Jesuit, Antonio Maria Arregui, who taught moral theology in the 1920s. His forte was the moral reasoning involving the distance from which it is proper to view mating animals. Observe too closely and it becomes an occasion of sin. The future Pope Paul VI, a seminarian at the time, was taught that all depended on the size of the animals: One could observe from close up flies copulating, but mating elephants could be viewed only from a distance. As the writer who recounted this said, "Think about it: From there, Paul VI went on to write *Humanae Vitae*."

Nor is the Roman Catholic Church unique in imposing inane legalisms on its flock. Consider denominations that forbid men and women to worship together. The women are segregated, lest male worshipers become "distracted." Leaving one to wonder how such groups' homosexuals are expected to worship without distraction.

Critics are like eunuchs in a harem: they know how it's done, they've seen it done every day, but they're unable to do it themselves.

—BRENDAN BEHAN

Reviewing is definitely a form of hate mail.

—ALEXANDER THEROUX

WHEN PANDORA OPENED THAT INFAMOUS BOX and loosed its ills and woes upon the world, the one saving grace within was a winged creature called Hope. I've often wondered whether Sir James Barrie based Tinker Bell on this mythological sprite.

With the joys and sorrows of authorhood, the ratio is decidedly reversed. In this inverse ratio, one main sorrow can be as ghastly to the author as Hope is salvific to the world.

What is that sorrow? you ask. The answer is: the Critic, sometimes called the Reviewer.

Father Koesler was blessedly fortunate: By and large, reviewers welcomed him, and the encomia were plentiful. Part of this might have been analagous to a variety of old jokes about the man who takes his dog into the bar and offers to have the dog do tricks for his drinks. The dog proceeds to play the piano—very badly. When people complain, the dog's owner responds, "But how many dogs can play the piano at all?"

When *The Rosary Murders* first came out, to my recollection, no other priest, or ex-priest, had written a mystery novel. So we were never quite certain whether the reviewers were being more kind than percipient. After all, how many priests could write mysteries at all?

Publishers Weekly, the bible of the industry, over the years, continued to be either kind and/or percipient—with a couple of exceptions. We could live with that. Indeed, Bill could live with any reviewer who didn't care for his books for any objective reason. He had a radar sense, however, for the critic who made it quite obvious that his/her dislike had nothing to do with the book; it was the fact that Bill was an ex-priest that rankled.

While editor of the *Michigan Catholic*, Father Kienzle lunched one day with one of the moneyed wheeler-dealers who contributed heavily to the archdiocese. An ex-priest had recently come to this man in search of a job, which it was well within the man's power to arrange for. Instead, the man related gleefully, he had turned the ex-priest down. As far as he was concerned, he said, he hoped the ex-priest would end up face down in the gutter.

This type of mentality could rear its ugly head when least expected. When *The Rosary Murders* came out, it was nominated for a TABA in the Best Mystery category. TABA was an acronym for The American Book Awards. At the time, it was quite an honor even to be nominated. Nowadays, when a publisher merely has to fill out a form and submit a book, almost any book can be termed an award "nominee."

Bill and I, as well as his publishers, were thrilled that *Rosary* was one of the five nominees. When John MacDonald's *The Green Ripper* took the prize, Bill felt it was no disgrace to lose to such a top writer. We even got a laugh out of it, as every so often an emcee would introduce Bill as author of *The "Rosemary" Murders* and would also refer to John MacDonald's *Green "Pepper."*

In any event, since *Rosary* had been a finalist for the TABA, we took it for granted that *Rosary* would likewise be nominated for an Edgar in the Best First Mystery Novel category. The Edgar—named after Edgar Allan Poe, considered the father of the American mystery genre—is awarded annually in several categories by the Mystery Writers of America.

We flew to New York for the annual awards banquet. On our arrival, we discovered that *Rosary* had not been nominated. We were disappointed, but even more so, mystified. If *Rosary* was good enough to be nominated by TABA in the Best Mystery category, why was it not worthy of consideration by the MWA as Best First Mystery Novel?

The mystery-within-a-mystery was at least partly solved by a Catholic friend who also attended the banquet. A member of the awards committee who had been seated at our friend's table made no bones about the fact that as far as he was concerned, it would be a cold day in hell before any ex-priest was rewarded for anything.

How much sway this gentleman had we never knew. But his diatribe provided a possible clue as to why *Rosary* was a nonentity . . . or rather, a nonentry as far as the Mystery Writers of America was concerned.

The bad taste in our mouths was not improved when we learned later that although the MWA affected a "The winner is . . ." stance, it was a sham. In actuality, the awards recipient was notified ahead of time that he had won. Whether this is still the case, I have no idea; Bill—recall kindergarten and the Boy Scouts—dropped out of the MWA, never to rejoin.

Years later, *The Rosary Murders* was included in the *Chicago Sun-Times* list of the top twenty-five mysteries of the first ninety years of the twentieth century. Once more, Bill was in good company.

Some years back, a gentleman by the name of Jim Dance was associated with the Detroit Public Library. Jim not only wrote book reviews, but also hosted a radio program about books. Jim's theory was a civilized one: If he didn't like a book he didn't mention it. He didn't want to take the time/space from good books just to tear down bad ones. Sadly, Jim is no longer with us; he died some years ago.

The difference between Jim and the less than professional reviewers is that some of the latter are either would-be authors, or authors who review books in their own genre. In either case, they tend to resent another author's success and use a review as an outlet for their dissatisfaction with their own comparative lack of success.

Fortunately, their number is not legion. But authors—successful or not—tend to be extremely thin-skinned. This is understandable: How many of us want to be told that our dog is ugly or our baby is a brat? There may be a few authors who couldn't care less what critics say, write, or think—possibly William F. Buckley, Jr., is one. But for the vast majority of authors, a nasty review, especially if it is unfair or based on a false premise, can stick in the craw indefinitely. For such an author, his or her waking hours may be spent not in creating, but in responding to such criticism.

Those who have dared to question Father Andrew Greeley's godly literary rank, for example, are sure to find themselves on the receiving end of a broadside of epistolary buckshot. According to Father Greeley, any criticism of his efforts as far as his fellow priests are concerned, is predicated on "priestly envy."

Having crossed literary swords once or twice with Father Greeley, Bill's reaction was, "Envious?! On the contrary, when I wake each morning, I thank God I'm not Andrew Greeley."

Early on, an English mystery novelist of note reviewed one of Bill's books rather scathingly, intimating that Bill's work was second-rate. Normally, Bill would have shrugged that off. But he was piqued by the reviewer's veddy British implication that Bill should not aspire to breathing the same air as his betters. Bill's response was, for him, near unique: He wrote to the author, telling him he was the equivalent of a jerk. Amazingly, in later years when the same author put out a book on mystery writers, he referred to Bill's work in complimentary terms. Thus positing that he was not as much as of a jerk as Bill thought he was.

The crimes of an unprofessional or second-rate reviewer can not only ruin an author's disposition; they can also ruin a book for the reader.

After Bill had come up with an involved mystery containing a number of red herrings, a reviewer actually gave away the plot and the crux of the mystery in his column. On reading his review, I was near speechless with disbelief. I recovered my verbal powers sufficiently to phone the man and expostulate with him. He was totally taken aback and couldn't understand why I was so upset.

Then there is the reviewer who says, "The author is full of hogwash; such and such couldn't possibly happen." After Bill spent months in researching and tracking down voodoo practitioners, one Detroit reviewer pooh-poohed the existence of voodoo in Detroit. All she was doing was betraying her own ignorance.

Interestingly enough, when Bill went to the Detroit Public Library in search of reference books on voodoo, he was taken to a literally empty bank of shelves. In response to his quizzical expression, the librarian informed him that they couldn't keep the voodoo books on the shelves because they all get stolen.

Another reviewer mocked Bill's portrayal of the police; their language was too clean . . . after all, everybody knows that police can speak only in four-letter words. Bill checked with several members of the Detroit Police Department, and was particularly reassured when a homicide detective of long-standing told him that it is the articulate and gentlemanly police who get the most confessions. For some reason, he said, it seems that the bad guys tend to have more respect for and trust in the civil-speaking rather than the gutter-speaking.

Jim Grace, the Kalamazoo police detective, was as smooth and articulate as any diplomat. Likewise, Sergeant Roy Awe, a member of Detroit's Homicide Division. Had Bill put four-letter words in the mouth of a police detective, he would not have been true to the picture he had in his mind of Jim, Roy, and many other members of the police force.

Still another reviewer complained along the same line that the football players in *Sudden Death* were unrealistic because they didn't

243 ♦ JUDGED BY LOVE

use a lot of profanity. Although boys will be boys, and oaths seem to drop from too many male lips with the ease of an exhaled breath, still, many of these men are college graduates who belong to religious athletic groups. As such, four-letter words do not take over their sporting life.

When Bill was researching *Sudden Death*, he phoned the Detroit Lions, asking for a behind-the-scenes look at the team. The response was "Buy a ticket to a game." A short time later, Bill mentioned this opposite of red carpet treatment to Peter Spivak, the retired judge who had his finger in many pies and on the pulse of the city at the same time.

"Funny thing," said Peter, "I just bought into a football team." It was the Michigan Panthers, Detroit's entry in the borning USFL. Peter arranged for Bill to spend a few days at the Panthers' training camp in Daytona Beach. Bill had played football in the seminary. Although he accepted Peter's offer calmly, I knew it would be a thrill for him to get a firsthand look at the game and the players, many of whom had been NFL fodder.

The players—and the coaching staff—entered into the spirit of Bill's work, answering questions, making suggestions, and coining titles for the upcoming book. Two I recall were *Fourth and Dead* and *Terminated with Extreme Prejudice*.

One of the players was Chris Godfrey. I later discovered that he had been a freshman at De La Salle when Mike was a senior there. Bill patterned one of the football heroes of *Sudden Death* on Chris, both as to appearance and general athletic history. Chris was an offensive lineman . . . a very good one. He and the other Panthers—quarterbacked by Bobby Hebert—were so good as a matter of fact, that they took the USFL championship that year. Chris went on to play with the New York Giants under Bill Parcells. The Giants won the championship that year.

Then, for some unfathomable reason, Parcells decided the Giants no longer needed Chris Godfrey. That season saw quarterback Phil Simms go down under repeated sacks. Each time he went down, I would say, "That wouldn't have happened if Chris Godfrey were there."

Eventually that became a byword whenever any quarterback was sacked: "That wouldn't have happened if Chris Godfrey were there." It got to the point where, if I groaned aloud when the Red Wings were scored on, or a Texas Leaguer dropped for a hit against the Tigers, Bill would chuckle and say, "Yeah, I know: That wouldn't have happened if Chris Godfrey were there."

Chris ended his playing career with the Seattle Seahawks, then went on to study law at Notre Dame. He may be the only player to have a championship ring from both the USFL and the NFL.

If the concentration camps and the gas chambers were all imaginary, then please tell me: Where is my mother?

—Billy Wilder
(whose mother, stepfather, and grandmother
died at Auschwitz)

IT WASN'T ONLY THE UNINFORMED REVIEWER who occasionally questioned the authenticity of Bill's books. Readers too can be filled with disbelief. One woman wrote Bill complaining about his mixing priests and alcohol: "I've never been in a rectory, but I know they don't drink that much." Bill replied simply, "Well, I have been in a rectory—and they do drink that much."

Another woman wrote that she had grown up in Germany during WW II, and all that stuff about the Holocaust was just lies. She expressed this in such forceful terms that it was obvious she believed what she was saying. For some time after, when Bill addressed various groups, he read her statement aloud. It never failed to elicit gasps from his listeners.

Yes, there are people who still believe the earth is flat. And lots of them will go to their death refusing to believe that two and two are four.

We eventually found a way to deal with the criticism. I read the reviews, filed the carping ones in a scrapbook, and gave him only the good ones to read. But, as he said, "a hundred good reviews can't make up for one bad one."* Being low-key, and aware that somewhere in the archives were a bunch of carping critiques, he tried not to let the laudatory ones go to his head. Every so often when a particularly complimentary review (or letter) came in, he would read it, hand it back to me, and say satirically, "I don't have to put up with this." But I could tell that he was pleased.

At one point, Bill had an idea for a book jacket. Instead of the usual complimentary blurbs, he thought it would be fun and revelatory to put together a bunch of contradictory sentences from reviews. Where one reviewer would say something like, "Really captures the language of the police," another reviewer would say something like, "His police talk like choirboys." Where one reviewer would say, "His writing is smooth and readable," another would say, "His writing is uneven and does not hold the reader's attention." He actually did have such a collection in his files. But he couldn't talk his publisher into going along with the idea.

Another reef to beware of is the interviewer who can't get things straight. A frequent cause is the inability to read one's own notes.

During Bill's tenure as editor, the *Michigan Catholic* printed an article that was somewhat uncomplimentary about Cardinal Dearden's successor as head of the National Council of Bishops. The Cardinal was embarrassed. He sent Father Kienzle a letter telling him that he felt the article was in "execrable taste." In later years, Bill—who had not written the article in question—referred to the Cardinal's letter as the Execrable Taste Award.

Sometime later, another controversy arose as to the advisability of the paper's accepting political ads. The problem was thrown in the Cardinal's lap. He wrote his editor, stating that he trusted

---

* John Steinbeck said, "You never get over the ability to have your feelings hurt by deliberately cruel and destructive attacks. Even if you know why the attack was made, it still hurts."

Father Kienzle's judgment in the matter, and would leave it up to his "excellent taste." Naturally, Bill referred to this letter as his Excellent Taste Award.

Years later, during a speech, Bill related these events. However, when an account of the speech made the local paper, the Cardinal was quoted as having felt the article was in "inexorable" taste. The article went on to quote Bill as having received the "inexorable taste" award.

In another interview, the reporter quoted Bill as saying that he and his seminary classmates "got high." We were completely mystified over this, as (a) it never happened and (b) Bill had said nothing of the sort. But undoubtedly to this day, there are those who nod their heads knowingly in the sure and certain belief that Bill and his seminary buddies did inhale something stronger than cigarette smoke.

Interviewers frequently asked how Bill's former priest colleagues felt about his books. As far as we knew, they all seemed to enjoy them immensely. Whenever Bill needed information on the current status of the priesthood in Detroit, or on a current presbyterate situation, there were no end of priests who willingly contributed—although not for attribution.

Bill was quite careful not to include them in his acknowledgments, as he did not want them to be the object of episcopal recrimination.

Among those whose help Bill did acknowledge were several nuns, including his old friend, Sister Bernadelle. At the time of his ordination, Church rules called for a priest to be ordained for five years before being allowed to hear the confessions of nuns. The archdiocese must've been short of candidates, as Father Kienzle received a dispensation to hear such confessions before his first five years were up.

From childhood on, he had respected the dedication of the nuns. In manhood, he quickly grew to realize the contribution the sisters had made. He often said that it was the nuns who were responsible for the health of the Church in America. It was the nuns who had set up and backboned the U.S. parochial school system. It was the nuns who had educated the laity who became the parents of succeeding generations of practicing Catholics. Were it not for the "coolie labor" of the nuns the Catholic Church in America would have been without the graduates who fed into this country's seminaries to provide succeeding generations of priests.

I didn't know enough about that to agree or disagree. But I clearly recall that it was the sight of the wimples and habits of the nuns—as well as the roman collars of the priests—in the forefront of the civil rights marches of the sixties that had increased my attraction to Catholicism.

Even the "bad guys" seemed unconcerned if they recognized themselves in Bill's books. One particularly venal character, when told by a fellow priest, "You should sue him [Bill]!" seemed complimented to be the subject of such a characterization. "He said I'm a strict bastard!" he crowed.

One of Bill's most treasured possessions was a letter from Cardinal Dearden (Cardinal Mark Boyle in the Koesler series), congratulating him and confiding that he had tried to solve the mystery of *The Rosary Murders*, but had been misled by one of Bill's red herrings.

The Cardinal was basically a modest, even on occasion shy, man. Where many prelate-publishers let it be known that 'twere a good thing if their photos dotted the pages of the archdiocesan paper, Dearden had preferred to remain unacknowledged. Prior to one of the Cardinal's trips to the Vatican, his then editor thought it would be a good idea for the *Michigan Catholic* to run a photo of the Cardinal boarding his Rome flight at Metro Airport.

The Cardinal demurred. Father Kienzle persisted. Cardinal Dearden had more Irish in him than his editor; he also outranked him: He would agree to have his picture taken at the airport if Father Kienzle would agree to be in the photo.

Editorial desire for a newsworthy photo won out over the editor's own modesty. As I write this, I can look up at a photo that has hung on the Kienzle wall from our earliest time together. There is the Cardinal, at the foot of the plane's boarding stairs, looking benignly pleased with himself. Also in the photo: Monsignor Imesch (the Cardinal's secretary), Monsignor Karey (who had recommended Father Kienzle for the post of editor of the *Michigan Catholic*), and, hat in hand, a thin-lipped Father Kienzle. The victim of the Cardinal's blackmail does *not* look like a happy camper.

After the photo was taken, the Cardinal turned to Father Kienzle and with a straight face suggested that as long as they were there, the photographer should take several separate photos of him [the Cardinal], one at the foot of the boarding stairs of each airline that serviced Detroit Metro. That way, the Cardinal told Father Kienzle, tongue in cheek, you'll have a photo to use in future no matter where I go. There were those who would not have believed the Cardinal capable of such whimsy.

Shortly before the Cardinal's death, Bill and I spent an evening with him at a small dinner party hosted by Jane Wolford Hughes (Joan Blackford Hayes in *Shadow of Death*). He spoke of his earlier days in Pennsylvania, and it was obvious what a superb teacher he had been. He was, as Bill said, a churchman to the marrow of his bones. Yet the Cardinal had that prime virtue, so admired by Bill, of being able to coexist with views opposed to his own.

In the words of an unknown author in another context, to the word "gentleman" Cardinal Dearden gave an austere and spiritual meaning. When he died, Bill and I felt that the Church—sadly—would not see his like again.

The only thing better than taking a trip is coming home.

—UNKNOWN

ANTAEUS, A VILLAINOUS CHARACTER in Greek mythology, grew weaker each moment he could not touch the earth. He was eventually dispatched by Hercules, who picked him up and held him up in the air until he grew weak, at which point Hercules strangled him.

I was somewhat the same way with regard to Ireland. If I didn't get my every two-to-three-year Ireland "fix," I waxed puny, as they say down South.

One year when a long bout of bronchitis kept returning me to the doctor's office, I asked him what else I could try to get rid of it. "Go to Ireland," he prescribed. "The minute you get off the plane there your bronchitis will disappear."

He was right. I did go and the bronchitis did disappear.

Bill, who called me Bridey Murphy, gave me a similar prescription while we were in Minneapolis. At one point, he suggested that it was time. I did not want to go without him. But he could not get away. So, with a great deal of misgivings and not a few tears, I took off.

It was a good news–bad news trip. The good news was that the minute I got off the plane in Dublin, I felt rejuvenated. I breathed that aroma of peat fire that once inhaled is never forgotten, visited with friends, and sank back once more into the soft murmur of the Irish brogue. One grows so accustomed to the quietness of Irish speech, that on returning to the United States after a week or two in Ireland, the comparative loudness of normal conversation assaults one's ears like a medieval torture bell.

The bad news was that I missed Bill . . . missed him so much that my phone calls home turned into a series of sobs. I cut short my "medicinal" trip and flew back to Minneapolis, where Bill was—as he'd said he would be—waiting at the airport to "scoop me up."

Once we returned to Detroit and there was no nine-to-five job to prevent travel, we traveled. The first thing we did was take a two-week Caribbean cruise on the *Veendam*. I was pleased to discover that the *Veendam* was the refurbished and renamed SS *Argentina* I had boarded during my days as a travel agent some twenty years before.

It was Bill's first cruise, and he enjoyed it immensely. The only drawback was that Bill and the French Caribbean did not mesh. This antipathy was epitomized by his experience on one of the islands—where, walking on the beach, we were suddenly surrounded by a group of noisily insistent urchins, each of whom seemed to want us to go visit "their" beach some distance away, a trip that would have entailed taking some sort of surface transportation, for which the urchins would, I am sure, have received some sort of kickback.

I tried not to laugh at the image of this tall man beset by all these little people, like Gulliver among the Lilliputians. The humor of the situation escaped Bill, beleaguered by a horde of *gurriers* chattering away in a totally unintelligible patois. Finally, he could take it no longer and—in a near unique loss of his storied cool—he threw his hands in the air and spun around, yelling, "No! No! No!"

Possibly it brought back the memory of the day at Camp Ozanam when the junior counselors had surrounded him prior to tossing him into Lake Huron.

I took pity on him. "Go back to the ship. I'll meet you there when I'm finished sightseeing." Done and done.

On the other hand, in St. Croix, Bill was fascinated by the local patois, which was an amalgam of several languages. On a sightseeing walk, he and I stopped in a neighborhood food market to pick up some fruit. As I finished paying for the purchase, I looked around for Bill. He was standing, entranced, listening to a couple of the locals converse. I think it was his musical ear that was attracted, as their speech had a singsong quality. I got the impression that even had they spoken pure English, one would've had to listen hard and get in the swing of things in order to understand what they were saying.

We returned from our cruise much rested, relaxed, and ready for whatever else was to come.

People are to Ireland as champagne is to France.

—Unknown

FROM TIME TO TIME I TEASINGLY REMINDED BILL of the promise he had made in the emergency room of Harper Hospital: that he would take me to Ireland.

I wanted so much to show him the Ireland that had so endeared itself to me, the country not only of one branch of my family, but also of one branch of his own family. I wanted him to see all the places I had seen and enjoyed. He bowed to the inevitable, and once more I was "off to Dublin in the Green," this time with Bill in tow.

It was the first, but not the last trip we would take to Ireland together. They have all merged in my mind, so that at this point I cannot say exactly where we visited on each trip. I do remember every village, every town, every drive, every point of interest, every historic spot.

Some of these places Bill incorporated in one of his books, *Shadow of Death*, wherein Father Koesler visits Ireland, spending a few days in County Sligo. There he is subjected to "the coldest bathroom in western civilization" at Teach Murray,* in Gurteen.

I wanted to show Bill the spot where I had sat in the Wishing Chair—and had been given so much, much more than I had asked for. We headed north, across the border.

En route, we stopped off in Armagh to see the cathedral, where according to legend and the old song, lie the ashes of Brian Boru. We entered the cathedral and stood contemplating the ancient interior that was home to so much history. We moved slowly past the pews, with Bill drawn inexorably to the altar. I turned my head for a moment, then turned back to locate him in the dim interior. I was startled to see him embracing a total stranger—at least to me.

---

* *Teach* is the Irish equivalent of the French *chez*.

Each summer the Archdiocese of Detroit sends a priest to study in Ireland. Father Ed Prus was that year's priest-recipient. Neither Bill nor I had been aware of the program. We had come some 3,500 miles to encounter in a Protestant cathedral in the north of Ireland, a beloved Detroit priest considered by many to be a living saint.

We made arrangements to meet Father Prus again in Dublin and then went on our way, heading for the Glens of Antrim, famed, like so many other sites in Ireland, in song and story.

As we were settling in at our small hotel on the Antrim coast, we learned that there had been a breakout that day from the Maze Prison. Our driving the next three days was fraught, as we met roadblock after roadblock set up by the British. At the first road-block, an officer walked up to our car, and politely asked to see Bill's license. As Bill reached into his pocket to comply, the officer's hand went down to his sidearm and he stepped back. At that moment, several soldiers, weapons at the ready, rose up from behind a stone wall alongside the road. From then on, whenever we were driving, I held Bill's license on my lap for all to see. That way, no one could fear that he might be reaching into his pocket for a gun. It would have been ironic for us to have gotten shot due to such a misapprehension.

Although we were both solidly on the side of the Irish national-ists, at the same time, we felt much pity for the English soldiers. They were *so* young, and obviously as scared as they were young. I kept thinking: They shouldn't be here; they should be back home in England, playing soccer and walking with their girlfriends in the park. Undoubtedly that's where they would've preferred to be—and that's where the Irish nationalists would've preferred them to be.

We did all the touristy things and all the special things. We toured Bushmill's and "minded the mead" at Knappogue's banquet; we stayed at Dromoland Castle; we drove the Ring of Kerry and the Ring of Iveragh. We rode the jaunting car through Killarney's Lakes; we visited St. Canice's in Kilkenny, Cashel in Tipperary, the cathedral in Galway, the ruins of the monastery in Boyle, and Powerscourt in Wicklow. We spent an evening at the Abbey Tavern and another at the Abbey Theatre; we saw Blarney Castle and walked through the druid grove; we strolled Fota Wildlife Park; we breakfasted at the Arbutus Lodge (where Bill and the chef compared scrambled egg recipes), lunched at Myrtle Allen's, and had dinner at Knockmuldowney's; we visited Mother McAuley's Mercy Center; we went through the museum at Maynooth; we stopped off at the Trappist monastery in the Knockmealdown Mountains; we saw old friends and made new ones; we enjoyed the Dublin Theatre Festival; we rode the DART everywhere.

On our many visits, Bill and I experienced the best Ireland has to offer: its people.

One evening we took the DART north to visit friends in Howth. On arrival, we realized we did not know what time the last train left for the return to Killiney. We walked up to the head of the train, where the engineer was leaning out the window. "What time does the last train leave tonight?"

He grinned, as he gave a typically Irish answer: "At eleven-thirty . . . but you'd better take the eleven-fifteen so you don't miss it." Bill grinned in response.

We strolled in the general direction of our friends' home and stopped at a garage to ask for directions. The young lone attendant gave us specific directions, concluding with, "It's right behind the Such & Such Hotel. You can't miss it." We thanked him and strolled on.

Shortly, we became aware of quick footsteps behind us. We turned, and there was the young man, running to catch up with us. "I forgot to tell you: The hotel just changed its name. It's now called the So & So Hotel. I wouldn't want you to be confused and not be able to find your friends."

It was so typical of the Irish. The young man had left the gas station unattended and had chased after us to make sure that we would not get confused and lose our way.

Our experiences in Howth were just a small part of what further endeared Ireland and its people to both Bill and me. "*Cead Mile Failte*"—a hundred thousand welcomes—is not an empty motto. The friendliness and helpfulness of Ireland's people across the board lingers long after one's return to the United States This was epitomized by a visitor who recalled being told by an Irish hotel employee, "Madame, I exist only to make you happy."

As with inhabitants of many countries who have suffered impoverishment, the Irish are embarrassed to be found wanting. An American ordering a drink at a pub in the Irish hinterlands one summer asked, "Do you have ice?"

"Only as it's in season," was the reply.

Even the *gardai* (police) seem to have gone to charm school. A tourist once asked a *garda* what a yellow line on the side of the street signified. "It means no parkin' at all," the *garda* said.

"And what do the double yellow lines on that side of the street signify?" the tourist asked.

"Oh, they mean no parkin' at all, at all."

In a memorable visit to Dublin, thanks to our dear friend Jack Byrne, we were treated to a performance of the premiere run of *Translations*. On another visit, Jack arranged for us to attend Joe Dowling's magnificent production of *Juno and the Paycock* which would shortly have New Yorkers raving. I felt that *Translations* was the most moving experience I had ever had in the theater, whereas Bill felt that way about *Juno*.

Among the actors we particularly admired was the young man who played Dolty in *Translations*. The day after the performance we were lunching in Bewley's Cafeteria on South Great George's Street, when we looked across the room and saw the same actor waiting in line. We went up to him and told him how much we had enjoyed his performance. He smiled shyly, and, obviously pleased, thanked us.

Sometime later we saw the film *Excalibur* and thought we recognized a vaguely familiar face. As we sat through the concluding cast credits, we found that it was indeed the young man we had seen in Dublin—Liam Neeson.

Discovering Ireland was almost as much fun for Bill as it had been for me. Although he did not like to travel, it was the getting there that he did not care for; once "there"—wherever "there" was, he did enjoy himself—with the exception of the French Caribbean.

In Dublin shortly after the publication of Bill's first book, we went to Trinity College's magnificent library to see the famed Book of Kells. The gorgeously illuminated version of the Bible is kept under glass to protect it, with one page turned each day so as not to wear it out.

After we looked at the Book of Kells, Bill wondered whether the library carried *The Rosary Murders*. Trying to assuage what I felt sure would be his disappointment, I reminded him that this was a college library in a foreign country, and as such there would be no reason for it to carry an American mystery novel. Nonetheless, he asked the librarian to check. She disappeared and returned in a minute or so to tell us they did indeed have *The Rosary Murders* on the shelf.

Henceforth, when Bill spoke of his visit to Ireland, he made sure to tell his audience that he had visited Trinity College, that Trinity's Library had the Book of Kells and *The Rosary Murders* " . . . and one of them is under glass."

At that time, the Irish had a somewhat exaggerated view of the wealth of some of its American guests. This was brought home to us when, after one of our later visits, an Irish friend reported reading a newspaper account of our recent stay, which referred to Bill as the millionaire writer. Nothing could have been further from the financial truth.

Actually, we did "own" a little bit of Ireland. We had bought a time-share week at Fitzpatrick's Castle in Killiney, just south of Dublin. Since a writer's income is frequently feast or famine, we found that too often when we had the time to travel, we didn't have the money, and when we did have the funds, we didn't have the time.

Whether it was due to lack of time or lack of money, I cannot recall, but our first year of ownership did not find us at Fitzpatrick's. Margaret ("I'll go! I'll go!") Cronyn and her husband, Joe, went in our stead, and sent us photos of "our" apartment.

However, when we finally did visit Fitzpatrick's, we found it a joy. From the living room of our time-share apartment, we could look out over Dublin Bay. At night, the lights of Dublin twinkled like jewels. I can still see them in my mind's eye.

We attended Sunday Mass at the little church just down the street from Fitzpatrick's. Bill was both charmed and fascinated as he sat through his first Mass in Irish.

He was also delighted to discover a bishop who could laugh at himself. Bishop Brendan Comiskey's weekly column in a Dublin newspaper caught Bill's eye. The bishop wrote of giving a homily on marriage. He reported that after the Mass, as he stood to one side while parishioners exited the church, he overheard a man say to his wife, "Margaret, wouldn't it be wonderful to know as little about marriage as the bishop?"

Ireland captivated Bill as it had me. Like so many Americans of Irish ancestry of that generation, Bill had felt no particular affinity for that ancestry. His family was Americanized; they didn't talk about the history of the country that had seen too many of its young people leave never to return. The sad memories of the "American Wake" were known all too well to those left behind; those who would die without ever again seeing the beloved faces of their departing children.

Coming from an ethnically mixed family, and knowing little of his mother's Irish ancestry, it was not unexpected that Bill identified more strongly with the ancestry of his father. Indeed, during the seminary's annual German-Irish tug of war, Bill Kienzle always pulled from the German side, never from the Irish.

This identification was to hold true for many years. When word came that a German edition of *The Rosary Murders* was to be published, Bill exulted. "It's the Fatherland!" he explained.

Now he had discovered the "Motherland" and he never ceased to marvel at the beauty of the country, and even more at the hospitality, generosity, kindness, and good humor of its people. He would evermore take pride in his Irish ancestry. This came through clearly when, in *Shadow of Death*, an Irish woman relates the history of her country's struggle for freedom from the English—who may have occupied Ireland, but never conquered the unconquerable Irish.

Death always comes too early or too late.

—SAYING

WE WERE AT DROMOLAND, looking forward to meeting up with John and Susan McMeel, who were also vacationing in Ireland. The call came through from John in Dublin: Jim Andrews—at age forty-three—had died suddenly of a massive heart attack. We made immediate arrangements to fly to Kansas City for Jim's funeral.

It was a sad flight. We sat silent, thinking about Jim's wife, Kathy, and about their two young sons who were now fatherless. The memories washed over Bill in waves. The day that Jim Andrews and John McMeel had visited the *Michigan Catholic* office, and talked a young priest-editor into signing up with the baby Universal Press Syndicate. The day Jim had literally bumped into Bill at the ABA convention in Atlanta. The afternoon that Jim had phoned Kalamazoo to tell a thrilled and grateful writer that he was going to be a published author. The many supportive and encouraging phone calls from Jim. After reading the manuscript of *Death Wears a Red Hat*: "You're a publisher's dream. You made me laugh and you scared me." After receiving word that *The Rosary Murders* had been nominated for a TABA award in the mystery category: "I am so proud of you."

Bill and I had always felt that God had brought him and me together. Part of God's plan. We both felt that God had brought us to Atlanta in order to bring Bill and Jim together. Part of God's plan. Now, Jim was dead, and we had to believe that that too was part of God's plan. We had accepted the joy; now we would have to live with the sorrow. We mourned his loss, to his family, to his partner, to the publishing world, to all of us.

There is no psychiatrist in the world like a puppy licking your face.

—BEN WILLIAMS

WHEN OUR ACCOUNTANT SUGGESTED that it made sense taxwise for us to buy a house rather than staying in an apartment, the search began.

This would be our first house since leaving Minneapolis. Once more, Bill left it up to me. Kay Betanzos had gone into real estate, and she was the soul of patience as we trekked from neighborhood to neighborhood, from suburb to suburb. Like Goldilocks we finally found one that was just right.

It was down a long lane, in a quiet, woodsy area of Southfield. The property consisted of a fenced acre and a half of towering oaks, bordering a golf course on one side and a tributary of the Rouge on the other. The house itself was not large or fancy, but it was comfortable.

Since I had grown up on a farm, it was nice to be out in the country again. Then I remembered: On the farm we'd always had dogs. Now, here we were, out in the boondocks. If Bill was away, I'd be all by myself, and while I wasn't overly concerned about my safety, there was no one within screaming range. Conclusion: We needed a dog.

Bill was not a pet person. But he saw the sensibleness of my suggestion. I didn't want a purebred with inbreeding problems; I wanted a mixed breed that would be intuitive and territorial. We started reading the ads. And Chappie came into our life.

In an occurrence that, sadly, takes place all too often, a family had sold their house and moved, leaving their pregnant German shepherd behind to fend for herself. A kindhearted woman down the block had found the dog under the porch of the empty house. Despite the fact that this woman's husband had been laid off for sometime, and despite the fact that they had several small children, she took the dog in. When the pups were born, the bitch, who had been near starvation, was unable to feed them for more than a short time. Her foster owner mixed formula and fed the pups. When they were four weeks old, she put an ad in the paper.

We had no problem picking out the pup we wanted. The minute I picked up Chappie, she nuzzled against my neck. That was it for me. On the way home, in the front seat of the car, she crept over to Bill and rested her head on his thigh as he was driving. That was it for him.

Despite the fact that Bill was willing to play daddy to a dog, he was not thrilled by the idea. He had agreed on one condition: That he get to name the dog. Little did I know he had a name picked out before we had a dog picked out.

We called her Chappie. But her full name—coined by Bill—was Chapp E. Quiddick. Because, he said, he felt the same way about having a dog as Ted Kennedy must've felt about That Bridge. Sometimes we called her Chap-Chap, and occasionally Bill referred to her as Ms. Quiddick.

As Chappie grew, the circles around the eyes, the thick hairy coat, the bushy curving tail bespoke husky paternity. Chappie would be big and she would be strong and she would have sled dog stamina.

Normally, pups are not totally weaned until they are at least six to eight weeks old. This gives them the opportunity not only to get sufficient nourishment, but also to interact with canine siblings. Chappie no longer had siblings; all she had was us. She used Bill's fingers as teething rings. For weeks, his hands looked as if they'd been caught in a meatgrinder.

Then one day words came out of Bill's mouth that I had never thought to hear. "I think Chappie needs another dog—you know, to keep from being lonely." After recovering from my astonishment, my first thought was, "I wonder what he'll name the next one."

❧❦❧

On my first trip to Ireland in 1967, I was standing across from a row of tall firs, waiting to board a tour bus, when suddenly a lanky, shaggy-haired animal unlike any I'd ever seen came from between two of the firs and slowly walked toward me. It was my first view of an Irish wolfhound, and I had never forgotten it.

Now I phoned animal shelters around town. No one had an Irish wolfhound. We started searching the ads. One day, there it was—just what we were looking for: an eighteen-month-old Irish wolfhound mix.

When we walked into the owner's house, a little dog was yapping at our feet. And then suddenly, through the door came this tall, calm, regal creature. Bill, who had never seen an Irish wolfhound, looked somewhat startled. Startled was a weak word for his expression when the dog walked over to him, stood up and put her front paws on his shoulders, looking eye to eye with him.

We should have smelled a rat when the owner said she wanted to keep the dog for a few days so she could give her a bath before selling her to us. We agreed and made an appointment to pick her up the following week. Bill was still in a somewhat bemused state as we drove home. I knew he was thinking, "How did I ever get myself into this?"

The following week we returned. The dog had not been given a bath. We were the ones who were going to take a bath: Instead of the original asking price of $50 the owner now wanted $100.

Bill said afterward that if he hadn't felt sorry for the dog, he would've walked out the door at that point. But we paid the $100 and took the dog. Bill opened the back door of the car and she climbed up on the seat and sat there looking for all the world like a monarch about to review her subjects.

This led to an immediate name change. Her papers—which came from a pet shop—listed her as a wolfhound-shepherd mix. Her name was Sadie. We grimaced. Visions of a plump, mouthy aunt, or of Dogpatch's Sadie Hawkins flew to mind. Not this regal creature. Instantly, she became Lady. And a lady she was throughout her days.

Instead of going directly home; we went straight to the veterinary clinic. That's when the expenditure really started. Lady had fleas, she had ear mites, and she had horrendous worms, which impeded her ability to assimilate nourishment.

After the initial vet visit, we took her to the Pampered Pet for a bath. The manager told us they charged according to how much trouble they had with the animal while washing it. "In for a penny, in for a pound," we thought. But when we came back to pick her up, the charge was their lowest rate. Lady had indeed been a perfect lady.

We were soon to discover that the Irish saying about their wolfhounds—Gentle when stroked; fierce when provoked—fit Lady to a T. We also discovered that wolfhounds are called "the heartbreak dogs." They are the tallest canine breed and because of their size rarely live past seven years. Because Lady was a mixed breed, however, our vet told us she might make it to eight years.

Lady's meeting with Chappie was a howl. She stepped out of the car to be greeted by this ragamuffin of a pup who seemed not at all in awe of her. Indeed, Chappie, not having seen any legs other than Bill's and mine since leaving her mother, now had four hairy legs to run back and forth through. Which she immediately did, giving every evidence of what would become her reaction to everything: Isn't this *fun!*

We had a small, grimy greenhouse off the kitchen. Chappie slept in the greenhouse. Since she had been weaned unconscionably soon, we felt we didn't want to add insult to injury by trying to housebreak her right away. We had strewn newspapers on the greenhouse floor to train her, and she was a quick study. But when she went outside, instead of doing whatever she had to do there, she immediately headed back into the greenhouse and did it on the greenhouse floor—just as she had originally been taught. Bill chuckled. "Nothing learned that must be unlearned," he said.

We took the dogs for walks several times a day, Lady strolling majestically, Chappie stumbling over her own feet, and tumbling every which way. One of the farm dogs I'd had as a child was a greyhound mix. She had been sheer beauty to watch as she chased rabbits in the fields—occasionally, unfortunately, catching one. I kept waiting for Lady to run. But she didn't; she merely plodded along at our heels, seemingly content just to be part of the family.

We knew that she had been kept in an apartment during her earlier days, as her owner had worked full-time. Eventually, we realized that she didn't run because she had never run. She didn't know how to run.

We tried to teach her to run. We threw balls. We tossed food. We called her from a distance. To no avail. It was two weeks and still nothing more than a sedate stroll. Then I had an idea. I knew that Irish wolfhounds are very protective. I told Bill to walk Lady out to the far corner of our property while I stayed by the house. When they got to the fence and turned around, I yelled her name and jumped up and down, shrieking as if I were being threatened. Instinctively, Lady took off as if shot from a cannon, heading straight for me.

At the last minute, she pulled up short, looked at me with a dawning expression, looked back at Bill, then turned and headed toward him at a lope that alternately speeded and slowed. For many minutes, she didn't stop. She ran in circles, in a straight line, back and forth, along the fence, from one of us to the other, as Bill and I watched with tears in our eyes. As Bill said, "The wolfhound had discovered her nature."

Chappie was irrepressible, Lady long-sufferingly patient. Lady had pretty much achieved her full growth, but Chapp was growing like a lion cub; actually her paws were the size of lion paws. The vet would look at them, shake his head and say, "She's going to be a big one." Eventually, she grew to somewhere between 125 and 135 pounds. We never knew exactly, because we couldn't get her to stand still on the vet's scale.

Lady wasn't quite as heavy, but she was a head taller than Chapp. When it came to speed, Lady was the sprinter, but Chapp had the long-haul stamina.

We had an ancient sofabed that we had bought from the house's previous owners. It was full-size, dark blue, and sat along one wall of our dining room, which was just off the garage. The sofabed became Chappie and Lady's "family room." And like so much in their canine lives, there was a routine to their interaction with regard to the sofabed.

If Chapp clambered onto the couch first, all was well as she curled into the corner at one end, leaving an open space in the middle, and the other end of the couch for Lady. However, if Lady got there first, she took the middle of the couch.

Normally, Chapp was totally undaunted by Lady. However, Chapp needed her "space" and with Lady taking up the entire center of the sofa, Chapp felt infringed upon. While Lady sat there totally unconcerned, Chapp's angst sent her in search of Bill or me. We quickly learned what was expected of us. Either Bill or I would leave what we were doing, go into the dining room, walk over to the couch and—since she was too heavy for either of us to move— call Lady off it. Lady would clamber down from the couch, Chappie would immediately clamber up and take her home corner. Lady would then climb onto the other end of the couch. And peace would reign until the next time.

All in all, the two coexisted amazingly well. Until one day when Bill and I returned from an outing to be greeted by Lady alone. Chapp was nowhere in sight. When I finally found her hiding under the back porch, I gasped. Her head was bearlike—twice its normal size. Her eyes were blood-red and swollen. Her normally jaunty walk was a stagger. Lady looked on seemingly unconcerned.

As we prepared to run Chapp to the vet, the mystery was partly solved by a neighbor. He had seen the two dogs fighting. Since we always locked the gate when we left, he had been unable to get into the yard. He had yelled at them and thrown several snowballs in an attempt to interrupt their battle. It must have done the trick, as Lady had backed off just enough to allow Chapp to break away and disappear.

A wolfhound's jaws are exceedingly strong. At first the vet thought that Lady had taken Chapp's head in her mouth and clamped down. But he came to the conclusion that somehow Lady had caught Chapp's collar in her mouth and twisted it—thus garroting Chapp so that the blood vessels in her head and eyes had near exploded.

Chapp was treated for shock and given a diuretic. Lady remained noncommittal. We couldn't know how the fight had started, but a good guess would be that Chapp had hectored Lady beyond endurance, at which point Lady had struck back. Whatever, after that, unless the dogs were being taken out of the yard, we left their collars off. Chapp had survived one garroting; we wouldn't take a chance on a second.

The problem was that Chapp liked to dig out. Many was the night we returned home to be met by Chappie trotting down the middle of the street as if it were her own private path. Since both dogs were now without their collars in our absence, there would be no identifying Chapp if she got picked up or worse yet, run down. It got to the point where, every time we came home after being out for the evening, as we neared our street my stomach would tighten in fear that when we turned the corner, we would come upon a dead or wounded Chappie lying there.

When we first got Chappie as a pup, an acquaintance said, "Huskies are notoriously independent; you'll have to take her to obedience school." Having grown up with dogs, I felt quite capable of training Chapp myself. Chapp was indeed independent—as independent as they come. However, she was extremely intelligent, and, like any good dog, wanted to make her masters happy. So, as I told Bill, all we had to do was to let her know what we wanted and she would do it.

QED.

Each time we found Chapp running free after digging out, we would repeat, "Bad Dog!" several times, with extreme disapproval. But I could see that Chapp didn't understand what she'd done wrong . . . or what we wanted of her.

We tried putting huge rocks all along the fence. Chapp dug out beneath them. I wondered whether maybe digging was genetically inherent in huskies—from their having to scoop out a place to bed down under the Arctic snow. One day Bill watched as Chappie, digging furiously like a roadrunner version of a backhoe, half covered Lady, who was standing nearby, with a blizzard of flying sand. Finally, Lady had had it. She walked over and shouldered Chappie down on her side in the hole she had dug. It didn't faze Chapp for even an instant. Her feet continued to work, as, lying on her side, like the Energizer bunny she continued to dig.

Matters came to a head when one Sunday morning we were kept from going to Mass because Chappie was missing. We split up to search the neighborhood. Finally, I found her trotting happily down the golf course. She was covered with mud from having scootched across a swampy stream. I called her, but she refused to come. So I took off after her, turning my head frequently to make sure I wasn't the target of a golf ball.

By this time, Bill had caught up with us and left to get the car, as there was no way we could get Chapp back under the fence. The final straw was trying to clean the mud off her and trying to clean the car's backseat after we'd gotten her home.

Our neighbor, who raised German shepherds, had several kennel-sized runs. After "Bad-Dogging" Chapp repeatedly, I put her in one of the kennels and left. I checked on her periodically. Each time, she was just lying there, looking at me like a pouty child being punished. After a couple of hours, we brought her home.

She never dug out or ran away again.

Undoubtedly, Chapp considered her penning an indignity. Her canine brain could have had no comprehension that the incarceration was a lesson to protect her from possible future injury or death.

Which might lead one to wonder about vicissitudes in our own lives. Is it possible that bad things happen to us to keep even worse things from happening to us?

Should we recognize such events not as afflictions, but rather as God's teaching tools providing us with learning experiences that will enable us to live better, happier, safer, more worthwhile or even holier lives?

❧❀❧

Both dogs had been trained not to run through the open gate when we took the car out. It had been comparatively easy to train them, especially Chappie, who lived for snacks. All I had to do as Bill drove out was stand by the gate and say, "No!" forcefully, and offer biscuits when the dogs stayed inside in front of the open gate.

Lady, however, had her own way of letting us know how she felt about this. One day, we went through the routine as usual: I unlocked and opened the gate, and stood there saying, "No!" as Bill drove out. I gave each obedient dog a biscuit, and closed the gate. Both dogs started to walk back toward the house. Then Lady stopped, turned slowly and deliberately, gave me an unfathomable look, and with barely a running start, took a couple of steps and serenely sailed like Pegasus over the closed five-foot gate.

When she touched ground on the other side, she turned and walked back up to the gate and stood looking at me as if to say, "You don't have to treat me like a child; I can get out any time I want to."

---

*F*eed me, I'm yours!

—Vicki Lansky

Just as Bill had felt that Chapp needed another dog for company, he anthropomorphized further with regard to the dogs' food. He felt that their pellets were too dry and that they needed some moisture with their meals. Chicken soup was the answer. The Teutonic thoroughness came into play. Twice a week, Bill made chicken soup from scratch. The ingredients were organic chicken, garlic, parsley, onions, peppercorns, celery, and carrots. After simmering for several hours, the soup was strained, with only the chicken meat retained. Daily, each dog was served pellets à la Kienzle, i.e., with soup and pieces of chicken added.

From time to time we felt sinful, thinking about children who were starving throughout the world while our dogs ate like royalty.

Somehow, we both came to terms with it, although I would not be surprised if God were to call us to account for it.

Since we lived in woodsy surroundings, a variety of fauna was ever-present. Usually, the animals were fast enough to escape the dogs, but when Lady and Chappie teamed up they were deadly. One night just before bedtime, a ghastly shriek reached our ears. We dashed outside to find a newly dead rabbit dangling from Lady's toothy jaws. A similar fate was met by any number of squirrels and rabbits, as well as a raccoon, and even a pheasant.

Possums fared somewhat better. So adept was one at playing dead that Lady actually dropped it without realizing that it was very much alive. As I held Lady back, the possum slowly got up and ambled off. Lady's startled expression was probably the canine equivalent of the fisherman's "You should have seen the one that got away."

On another occasion, we let the dogs out for their before-bedtime run only to hear loud barking from a distant corner of our acreage. Since we had no floodlights; we each took a flashlight and headed for "the back forty."

We had gone only a few steps from the door when we heard the phone ring. Remember the bells. Remember the rectory. If a phone rings, answer it. Bill turned back.

I kept going, and came upon a scene akin to a woodland version of the Crocodile Hunter.

Lady and Chapp had cornered a possum, which stood in the glare of my flashlight beam, teeth bared and nowhere to go. I didn't want the dogs to kill it, nor did I want it to get those wicked teeth on either of the dogs . . . or me, if I got too close. But yell as I might, I couldn't get the dogs to back off, and since there was only one of me, I could hold only one dog at a time . . . especially since neither of them wore a collar. *Whereinhell was Bill!?* I shrieked for him at the top of my lungs, while trying to prevent animal mayhem.

Finally, I saw his flashlight beam coming through the trees. I yelled at him to hurry. He got Lady, I got Chappie, and the possum got away.

Smoke was coming out of my ears. How dare he leave me in the face of who knew what *just to answer a phone?!* It could have been a fox, a bear, a skunk, somebody with a gun—! My ire was not assuaged when I learned that the call had been a wrong number.

His formation director—and Father Welsh—would have been so proud of him: A phone had rung, so he had answered it.

If you have men who will exclude any of God's creatures from the shelter of compassion and pity, you will have men who will deal likewise with their fellow men.

—St. Francis of Assisi

SOMEHOW, WHEN BAD THINGS HAPPENED, they usually happened in cold weather. Chapp and the squirrels declared war on each other from Day One. For Chapp, fun consisted of dashing out the door the minute it was opened, and heading for the nearest squirrel. Since the house was surrounded by trees, the squirrels were in little danger; safety was always just a step and a bounce away.

But Chapp never gave up. As she flew out the open door, some dozen squirrels would take off, each corkscrewing up the nearest escape tree. Chapp would circle the tree, pacing back and forth like a character from *Peter and the Wolf*, while the squirrel chattered irritatingly from just out of reach above her head.

On one occasion, we heard a noise as if buckshot or BBs were being fired at the metal garage door. We hurried to the door to find several squirrels up in a nearby walnut tree, tearing pieces of bark off and hurling them down at Chappie, who for once wasn't quite sure if this was fun or not.

On another occasion, the routine started as usual—Chappie chasing, the squirrels running—and then the comedy turned to drama. One of the squirrels had run up a fir tree so fast that, with

Chapp hot on its tail, it had gotten caught in the crook of a branch. When it tried to escape from its predicament, it slipped and now hung by its tail from the wishbone.

Chapp kept trying to jump up into the tree, each time further panicking the squirrel, who, although it was high above Chapp's head, was obviously terror-stricken.

I ran out and dragged Chapp inside, then went out to assess the situation. The squirrel was definitely caught in such a manner that it was not able to work its way free. It hung there undoubtedly saying its version of squirrel prayers.

At this point, something made me look up. There, circling purposefully above the oak trees was a huge hawk, undoubtedly slavering for dinner.

As usual, I ran for Bill.

It was a bitterly cold and windy November day, with snowflakes coming down as if God couldn't make up His mind whether to send us sleet or a blizzard.

Bill carried the stepladder from the garage to the fir tree. But when he climbed the ladder, we could see that even with his height and his long arms he would not be able to reach the squirrel.

Our friend Chris Murray had given us a tall extension ladder, the kind professional carpenters used. Bill and I dragged the ladder over to the fir, fighting the wind and snow in our faces. We tried to set the ladder up against the fir, but it was so heavy it kept sliding down.

We could see Chapp's interested face peering out of the dining room window. We could see the squirrel's frightened eyes rolling, as it twisted slowly in the wind. And we could see the hawk, circling, circling, circling.

Leaving Bill to stand guard, I went inside to phone for help from Animal Control or the Humane Society . . . or *some*body. I finally reached a human being at one of the animal rescue shelters. I explained the problem. There was a lengthy silence. Then: "Would you run that by me again?"

I couldn't blame her. After all, if someone phoned and told you that a squirrel was caught in a tree, you might well be forgiven for responding, "Yes, and I suppose you have a fish caught in the water."

I ran it by her again. Finally, she said, "I'm sorry; we just don't have the personnel to send anyone that distance for a squirrel."

We were on our own.

Fans of Al Capp's *L'il Abner* may recall Fearless Fosdick, who was forever getting into extreme Perils of Pauline–type scrapes. As each week's climax approached, L'il Abner and the fans reading over his shoulder were left breathless, wondering how their hero would get himself out of this one. I recall one such situation, with Fosdick bound hand and foot about to be thrown out of a plane by the villain. How would he get out of this?

How indeed?

The following week's strip started with these words (or something vaguely akin thereto): "Having escaped from the plane, Fosdick went in pursuit . . ."

At this point, I cannot say to you, "Having escaped from the tree, the squirrel went back to its nest."

I asked Bill to again set up the stepladder. I handed him a saw and pointed at the fir. He looked at me and said, "You've got to be kidding." I shook my head and pointed up at the hungry hawk. Bill shook his head and, saw in hand, climbed the stepladder.

He got as high as he could, bent over through the branches, and started sawing the tree trunk. The spot where he was sawing was some two to three feet below where the squirrel was hanging.

As the saw broke through the trunk, the entire top part of the fir toppled, crashing to the ground. I had an image of the squirrel being crushed. But in falling, the top section of the fir had twisted, freeing the squirrel's tail. The squirrel hit the ground running. I imagined the hawk snapping its talons as it hissed the raptor equivalent of "Drat!"

When the time came some years later to sell our house, we had to explain to the new owners why they would be looking out their kitchen and dining room windows at a truncated fir that looked like a child's unfinished drawing.

Everything in life is somewhere else, and you get there in a car.

—E. B. WHITE

I WAS FORTY-SEVEN WHEN WE MOVED TO SOUTHFIELD. We were not only far from the delivery of the *New York Times*, we were even farther out of the bus routes. If I wanted to go somewhere I would have to depend on Bill. He was perfectly willing to stop whatever he was doing to chauffeur. But I did not want to do that to him. It was time for me to learn to drive.

I had watched my father teach my mother to drive when she was forty. It was not a happy memory. The car stalled, Dad swore, Mother wept. She did eventually learn to drive, but it was not the family's finest hour.

Later, rather than going through the same thing with Rick, I decided to take lessons from a driving instructor. When he started the lesson by putting his hand on my knee, I had the good sense to call it quits.

But it was time.

Bill was the soul of patience, and I got my license without incident. Shortly thereafter, we decided to buy a new car. Bill suggested a stick shift. I was a bit dubious, but he and the salesman took me for a test drive and I managed somewhat jerkily to survive. The convincer was when Bill said, "If it doesn't work out, we'll bring it back and turn it in for an automatic."

So Javan and her new license went out to practice on a stick shift. After a couple of weeks of jerking and bumping, I came home one day, stomped into the house, slammed the door behind me, threw the keys on the table, and said, "I hate that car!"

Bill, who had patiently listened to this sort of thing for some time now, quietly asked, "What's wrong?"

"What's wrong?! The mayor of Southfield is putting up signs at every intersection in the city—and they all say the same thing: 'Javan Kienzle stalled here.'"

"That's it," Bill said quietly, but firmly. "We're turning it in for an automatic."

That got my Irish up. I thought of all the stupid, brainless females who had driven a stick-shift car over the years. If they could do it, I could do it!

I kept going out to practice every day, and every day I kept stalling.

Shortly thereafter, Dad came for his annual visit. Remembering his lack of patience with Mother's attempts to learn to drive, I didn't expect any great degree of help from him. I did, however, mention to him the trouble I was having with stalling. "If only I understood what was happening in the car," I said. "I just don't know what's going on when I step on the clutch."

Dad, who admittedly had mellowed over the years, took a piece of paper and drew some pictures. He illustrated what happened when one stepped on the gas, the clutch, the brake. I can't say that I never stalled again . . . but every time I stepped on the clutch I could see the diagram that Dad had drawn. Soon I was driving with a greater degree of assurance, and shortly, I was indeed driving without stalling.

On our trip to Ireland the following summer we rented a car. Not only did it have a stick shift, but the steering wheel was on the right-hand side, and the stick shift was to the left of that, making everything, in effect, backward as far as the U.S. driver is concerned.

Bill and I took turns driving, and I acquitted myself well; we drove all over Ireland without once stalling or bumping into anything.

Most of life's blows fall when you're happy.

—J. P. Donleavy

We lived in Southfield ten years. It was bucolic. In the summer the oak trees kept us cool; in the fall we raked leaves and burned them; the view from our picture window in winter was a Christmas card come to life; in the spring, we were surrounded by baby woodland creatures and wildflowers.

It was a routine but happy life. Bill wrote, I edited. I accompanied Bill as he gave speeches, did autographings, and made media appearances. We joined our circle of friends in theater, symphony, and sports outings, and shared a round robin of dinners and get-togethers.

Mike lived with us for a while, then moved to California to get on with his own life.

Occasionally we traveled, mostly on book tours. Every two or three years, we had the enjoyable task of flying to Kansas City for business meetings with the Andrews & McMeel family.

We attended Mass at Divine Providence, a cozy "national" church at the foot of our street. I thought it fitting that I, the granddaughter of a Lithuanian Jew, was now receiving Communion at a Lithuanian Catholic church. The pastor, Father Krisciunevicius, offered a reverent Mass and worthwhile homilies.

After Sunday Mass we went to the Kingsley Inn for the best brunch in town. The inn was owned by the Zawideh family. Jerry, one of the sons, was on-site manager. The food was excellent, as was the service. We got to know the "regulars." At Christmas we exchanged cards with the staff.

All was good.

Henry Wadsworth Longfellow wrote, "Into each life some rain must fall." The rain was heading our way, but it wasn't Portia's "gentle rain from heaven"; we were about to get hit by a gullywasher.

PART

The absolute best thing for me is to have the book bought and never made into a movie.

—E. L. DOCTOROW

A SEPARATE BOOK COULD BE WRITTEN about the selling and the filming of *The Rosary Murders*. Probably one of the main reasons such a book was never written was that we both wanted to forget about it. Even now I would rather skip it. But since our lives were so disrupted by the situation, and Bill was so scarred by it, an account of his life should include at least an outline of the events.

Bill and I were with some out-of-town friends at the London Chop House. The Bobby Laurel trio was featured. As a boy, Bobby, who lived in the Holy Redeemer neighborhood, had practiced on the Kienzle piano.

Father Kienzle had witnessed the marriage of Bob and Janet, who now had several children and lived in Detroit. Bob was a popular performer and a talented composer, with many connections in the entertainment industry.

During a break, Bob came over to talk to us. Bill mentioned that he had written a book and was looking for someone to film it. He asked if Bob knew anyone who might be interested.

Bob was galvanized into action. The next time we saw him, he had started his own film company. He bought the film rights to *Rosary*, retained Bill Buffalino as attorney, and hired Dutch Leonard to do the screenplay.

We met with Bob, and Dutch and his wife, at the Caucus Club to discuss the arrangements. All was going well.

Shortly thereafter, Shirley Eder bumped into Rock Hudson at the Chop House, where Bob and his trio were still appearing. She asked Rock if he knew Bobby. Hudson grinned. "Yeah, I know who he is. I went to Swanson [a Hollywood agent] to buy the film rights to *Rosary Murders* but he told me, 'You're too late; some kid from Detroit bought it two weeks ago.'"

Fans who caught Donald Sutherland in the film version of *Rosary* may now consider how Father Koesler would have fared as portrayed by Rock Hudson.

We were all learning, but not necessarily together.

For Donna, Bill's editor at Andrews & McMeel, the acquisition of *Rosary* had meant first of all, setting up an auction for reprint rights. When the hoped-for big-bucks bids didn't come in, Donna called a more experienced friend in the industry, who informed her that paperback houses didn't (in those days) bid high for mystery novels. Donna hung a sign on her office door that read, "Crime doesn't pay."

Bobby was learning that it was not easy for the new kid on the block to raise money. He was also learning, as he put it, to swim with the sharks. Hollywood was full of sharks. Hollywood is still full of sharks.

Bill was learning that though he had kept his own priesthood sacrosanct, he would have the battle of his life to try to keep Father Koesler's film priesthood sacrosanct. Lawyers in Michigan, California, and Kansas City argued over this point for eighteen months.

It all started when Bob discovered that in order to raise funds for filming, the investors had to be assured that he had "creative control." Once again, we met Bob for lunch. He explained to Bill that the rights to creative control had not been included in the contract that Bill had signed giving Bob the right to film *Rosary*. Further, Bob said that since he had mortgaged his home to raise money for the film, he could lose his home if he didn't get creative control from Bill.

I don't know that any of us fully comprehended at that time exactly what creative control entailed. But Bill must have had an inkling; he did not want to sign off on it. I in my ignorance talked him into it. All I could see was Bob and Janet losing their home. The thought made me ill. At my urging, Bill, despite his strong reservations, and without receiving an extra cent, signed over the creative control that Bob said he needed.

In retrospect, I think of Will Rogers's line: Would you rather be the guy who sold the Brooklyn Bridge—or the guy who bought it? I've concluded I'd rather be the guy who bought it.

Bill and I bought it.

I don't feel as stupid as I once did. Irwin Shaw, who had a lot more experience than either of us, had included "creative control" in the rights he sold when *Rich Man, Poor Man* was made into a TV miniseries.

What we—and Shaw—discovered is that whoever has creative control has the right to use the characters in a sequel or sequels. Shaw sued, unsuccessfully. A sequel to *Rich Man, Poor Man* was filmed, using Shaw's characters, but not Shaw's plot. In the case of Father Koesler, Bob's film company now had the right to film a sequel to *Rosary*, using Father Koesler, but not using Bill's sequel, *Death Wears a Red Hat.* We were informed that Bob's film company, Take One Productions, had no right to any of the sequels to *Rosary*—those plots were still owned by Bill. But Take One could put Father Koesler into any plot they wished, written by anyone they wished.

Bill trusted Bob; we weren't worried about him—it was those sharks he was swimming with.

Someone once asked James M. Cain how he felt about having his book ruined [by Hollywood]. He said, "No, they didn't ruin the book; it's right there on the shelf."

—Related by Donna Martin

Bill's only leverage in keeping the character of Father Koesler unsullied was that Hollywood wanted creative control. Bill would give them creative control if they would promise (a) that Father Koesler would remain alive* and well, in good standing with the church, and celibate and chaste; (b) that the police would not do anything illegal; (c) that the reporters would not do anything illegal. Bill and I got a taste of what Bob was going through in his swim with the sharks. The lawyers grew more bellicose; their communications waxed increasingly nastier. At one point, one referred to Bill as a "spoiled brat."

After months of wrangling, with Bobby growing more and more desperate, an agreement was reached as to what was termed a "virtue clause." The lawyers for the film company would not agree to (b) or (c)—which tells us Hollywood's view of police and newspaper reporters. They would agree to (a)—except that they deleted the word "chaste." When Bill protested, they asserted that celibate and chaste are the same thing. Bill insisted that they weren't, and held firm on this point, which the other side finally conceded.

Sometime after the affair was settled, we saw a relevant item in the newspaper. It seems that while these negotiations were going on, one of the Hollywood lawyers involved was also going through bitter divorce proceedings. In that settlement, the judge awarded the couple's Rolls-Royce to husband and wife on alternate weeks. We concluded that the nastiness directed at Bill was expressed during whichever weeks the lawyer had to go without his Rolls.

Nor did the situation ease even as the picture was being filmed.

The first we knew of the filming was when we read in the *Free Press* that the Happy Gang from Hollywood had hit town.

Bill and I had, over the years, cast *Rosary* in our minds. We pictured Michael Moriarty as Father Koesler, Ken Ruta of happy

---

* More than one author has walked this pitfalled path. In 1939, MGM decided to kill off Tarzan's Jane, and actually filmed her death scene. When fans raised a ruckus, and Edgar Rice Burroughs threatened to sue MGM, the studio refilmed the scene. Jane was wounded, but survived—and Maureen O'Sullivan got a hefty raise.

Guthrie memory as Inspector Koznicki, Brenda Vaccaro and Richard Dreyfuss (they were both much younger then) as Pat Lennon and Joe Cox.

The actual cast comprised Donald Sutherland in the lead role, with Charles Durning as one of the priests, Josef Sommer as Koznicki, and Belinda Bauer as Pat Lennon. Joe Cox was barely in sight. Just as we had feared, Hollywood tried to make Pat Lennon a love interest of Father Koesler. This was exactly the reason Bill had fought so hard to keep the character of Father untainted.

Further, scuttlebutt had it that the Seal of Confession would be abrogated in the film. A newspaper account reported that the pastor of Holy Redeemer, where *Rosary* was being filmed, had threatened to throw the film company off the property unless they deleted a scene wherein the Seal of Confession was being fractured.

Thinking to be helpful, and for absolutely no other reason, Bill wrote the director, saying that he was available for consultation in any way that could be of assistance. The response was another nasty note from the Black Hats Brigade, making it quite clear that Bill was to cease and desist sticking his nose in, and disappear as far as the filming of *Rosary* was concerned.

Bill concluded that the director didn't want the author running around the set yelling, "What are you doing to my baby?"* Under the circumstances, Bill grew increasingly convinced that something was rotten in the state of Denmark. He asked to see a copy of the screenplay.

We discovered that it would be easier to get a copy of the blueprints to the presidential bunker. No way was the author to get his hands or his eyes on the script.

---

* Hugh Leonard recounts how, on the set of *On Golden Pond*, Katharine Hepburn, on spying the story's author on the sidelines, grabbed his arm and firmly conducted him off the set. "We didn't look over your shoulder while you were writing it," she said. "We don't want you staring at us while we're working."

Bill sued to see a copy of the script. The Bad Guys fought back, claiming restraint of trade.

St. John—the patron saint of writers—took pity on us. Someone peripherally involved in the filming was able surreptitiously to get a copy of the screenplay and put it in Bill's hands.

We were horrified and disgusted to discover that the script contained a scene outside a men's room stall whence came the sounds of flatulence.

This evidences the mental age of Hollywood's would-be giants, who would overreach themselves if they managed to achieve a sophomoric level of so-called humor. It was never explained how this scene would advance the course of the plot. We concluded that a film director is like a dog that urinates on a tree, a lamppost, a hydrant, in an attempt to imprint the area as *his* territory.

Fortunately, Bobby, as producer, was able to hold the sharks off and see to it that the offending scene was quashed. Otherwise the world would have been treated to noises purportedly from Charles Durning's posterior.

Occasionally an indicative story would find its way to Bill.

Like the scene being filmed where a bunch of police cars pulled up en masse and screeched to a halt in front of the spot where the action was taking place. The police consultant advised the director that wasn't how it was done. The director insisted that's how he wanted it done. The consultant argued with him.

Those who have seen real-life police pull up to a real-life situation know that they park their cars in such a way that they can drive off instantly if need be, rather than trying to maneuver around nearby vehicles.

The consultant's arguments were slapped down by the director. Then, in the midst of the scene's filming, a passing motorist with, eerily, a rosary dangling from his rearview mirror, lost control of his vehicle, which crashed through the set periphery.

It took some time to disentangle the police vehicles, which were facing every which way like a crazy quilt. At which point the police consultant quietly commented, "*That's* why we don't do it that way."

There may be no such thing as heaven for a director. After all, even if one does go through the Pearly Gates—and for many of them that would be after a l-o-n-g period in Purgatory—he (or she) discovers that God is totally in charge. There is no way the director can control or manhandle *that* script. Imagine the frustration of not being able to imprint the scene. So, in effect, for such a director, heaven must be hell.

Bob and Bill met occasionally on neutral ground. Bill knew that Bob was beset on all sides; Bob knew that Bill wanted not only to preserve their friendship, which had been battered and perverted by the Hollywood villains, but to preserve the purity of the Father Koesler character. Bill left each such meeting feeling that their friendship was still intact. But Bob was being subjected to myriad pressures. Bill could only pray—literally—that Bob would be able to hold out and not break down under Hollywood's steamrollering.

By the time the world premiere took place in August 1987 at the Fisher Theatre, just about everybody in Detroit and environs had either been on the set or knew somebody who had been on the set of *The Rosary Murders*.

Bill and I received an invitation to the black tie benefit. We turned the invitations over to our lawyer, Pete Bellanca, and Father Tony Kosnik, a theologian friend of note. They would attend and vet the film to make sure that the "virtue clause" had not been abrogated.

The director, with delusions of Freddy on Elm Street, had added a "Boo!" scene that had absolutely nothing to do with the book. Elmore Leonard had been hired to write the original screenplay. But it was obvious the director had superimposed his spurious talents on Dutch's excellence. We were told that the film's credits listed the director's name as author of the screenplay, with Elmore Leonard in second place.

And though the director was legally constrained from anything overt along the lines of sullying Father Koesler's priesthood, he figuratively thumbed his nose at the author: He heavy-handedly inserted a scene and a few lines that made it appear to the prurient-minded that Pat Lennon and Father Koesler had had a one-night stand. So slyly was it done that it would have been difficult to prove in a court of law that he had crossed the line.

The consensus was that the envelope had been pushed, but not sufficiently to call for legal action.

Shortly thereafter, Donna, Bill's editor at Andrews & McMeel, caught the film in New York City along with her teenage son. Where the Pat Lennon character looks at Father Koesler over morning coffee in a diner and says something like, "Hi, Tiger," Donna's son turned to her, shook his head, and said, "Who are they kidding?"

The best thing about the film version of *Rosary* was Bob Laurel's evocative score, containing the song, "In Your Eyes," adapted from the first movement of Brahms's *Symphony No. 2*.

Every creature is a word of God and a book about God.

—Meister Eckhart

Because our dogs were so large—and so coddled—when we left home for any length of time, we hired a dog-sitter. This worked until we returned from Ireland to find Lady a shadow of her former self. She had decided to rebel against our absence and refused to eat during the last few days of our absence. It's a good thing we hadn't taken a round-the-world trip. Chappie of course lived to eat; we could've gone to the moon without affecting *her* appetite.

About this time, Chapp developed a limp. When it didn't go away after a reasonable period, it was off to the veterinary clinic—where our money went instead of going to the bank.

We felt very fortunate to have found Dr. Jeff Feld and his staff. Not only was he a superb diagnostician, he had a whimsical humor that somehow seemed to match Chappie's.

When it came to being touched, Chappie was a hellion. As a pup she had developed a bad ear infection. The machinations we had to go through to get drops of medicine in her ear would have taken the prize on the Funny Animals show. I had to sneak up on her while she was sleeping and drop the medicine in her ear. Once I was just about to squeeze the dropper when Chapp leaped to her feet: She had heard Bill's car coming down the lane.

Cutting Chapp's toenails was an exercise in improbability. It took place over a period of several hours. First we waited till she was stretched out, snoozing. Then I would sidle up to her, holding the nail clippers, while Bill approached, holding several dog biscuits. Our timing had to be perfect. As her attention was focused on the biscuit in Bill's hand, I would get the clippers in position and as she took the biscuit in her mouth, I clamped down on the toenail.

The sharp yowl that emerged let us know she was *not* a happy camper. We would back off till she calmed down and started to snooze again, and then it was back to Square One. Until all the toenails had been clipped.

Lady of course gave us no trouble at all. Bill used to say that we could cut Lady's feet or ears or tail off and if she thought that's what we wanted, she would lie there and let us do it. It's a good thing she felt that way, as, periodically, because of the layers of leaves in our huge "yard," Lady's toes and nails suffered fungal infections. Treatment necessitated soaking her paws in an iodine solution two or three times a day for 15 minutes at a time. Lady bore the treatment with total equanimity. Bill and I took turns saying, "It's a good thing it isn't Chappie." We would've had to immobilize *her* with knockout drops.

Giving Chapp any sort of injection was always problematic. Not only was it difficult to corner her for the procedure, but having stuck the needle in, one had to be prepared for a loud vocal protest. On one occasion, I was in the hall at the clinic when one of the vets was giving Chapp a shot. Her yowl was unmistakable. Dr. Feld, unaware that I was within hearing distance, chuckled, and said to no one in particular, "Good old Chappie."

Bill's favorite Chappie/Dr. Feld interchange took place when Dr. Feld was suffering from a miserable cold of long duration. Chapp needed some sort of shot, and Dr. Feld was not in a humor to play games with her. After a couple of peremptory attempts at injection, Dr. Feld leaned over on the examining table, and as Chapp—thinking she had escaped attack—came out from under the table, Dr. Feld merely bent down and jabbed her in the rump.

Giving the dogs pills wasn't too problematical. Chapp, omnivore that she was, gulped down anything we put inside a piece of liverwurst. Lady, however, was more discriminating. We would carefully enfold the pill in a liverwurst globule, and Bill, with years of experience at dispensing Communion, would insert the globule in Lady's mouth. Then we would watch as Lady rolled the globule around in her mouth, swallowed it, and spat out the pill.

Finally, I'd had it. I tilted her head back, dropped the pill down her throat, held her mouth closed, and stroked her throat . . . ulp. Worked every time.

Although Chapp's limp hadn't cleared up, we assumed that it was probably something akin to dysplasia. Chapp was half shepherd, and now weighed some 135 pounds. She had the husky's barrel chest and the husky's independent spirit. Her favorite game—besides chasing squirrels—was taking a huge tree limb in her mouth and prancing, head held high, across the yard. The first time she did this, Bill said, "There goes Guy LaFleur." We never stopped seeing Chapp as one of the Montreal Canadiens proudly bearing the Stanley Cup across the ice.

We kept several old towels near the door. When the dogs came in from the rain or snow, we dried off their paws. As usual, Lady accepted this without complaint. With Chapp, however, it was a wrestling match with sound effects. One day, Bill set the recorder and captured Chapp's very vocal protests. When we played back the tape, all I could think of was Egypt's King Farouk, whose car horn played agonized howls of dogs being run over. (I try to be Christian and forgiving, but when I think of Farouk it's difficult.)

As Chapp's complaints grew more voluble with succeeding dry-offs, we felt it was time for a visit to the vet.

Dr. Feld, superb diagnostician that he was, knew immediately what we were dealing with. Hoping against hope, he took X rays. Chapp's right shoulder was riddled with bone cancer.

Dr. Feld could treat Chapp with palliative measures, but sooner or later the cancer would eat away, leaving only lacelike bone. One day Chapp would take a step and what was left of the bone would shatter. It would be horribly painful, and when it happened she would have to be put down immediately.

We weren't sure how much time Chapp had, but as long we could keep her comfortable with a good quality of life we would. Chapp seemed unconcerned, and with the palliative care she was not suffering. As usual, her appetite was unaffected.

We enjoyed her as much as ever, while being aware that ever would shortly be coming to an end.

Bill was scheduled to make several appearances in Portland, Oregon. We didn't want to leave Chapp with anyone else, so for once, he would travel without me.

We spoke on the phone daily. When Chapp started spending the entire day sleeping on the couch, I knew the time was getting close. She still got up to eat dinner, but climbed off the couch very gingerly. The dog whose ultimate curiosity made it impossible for us to open the refrigerator door without having her head appear in the kitchen door now stayed on the couch even when the refrigerator was opened.

One other factor was involved. I knew how much Bill had come to care for Chappie. She had been with us eight years—from chewing on his hand in young puppydom to outright biting his hand in panic when he was trying to free her from a live electric wire she'd gotten tangled in. She had given us such joy, so many laughs, and in her inimitable way, a world of love. I didn't want Bill to have to watch her being put down.

I made two rib-eye roasts. She so enjoyed chewing on the bones. In the past, we had discovered that the normal amount of canine tranquilizer didn't slow Chapp down. Now, Dr. Feld instructed me to give her a double dose, and if that didn't work, to give her some more so that she not be her usual berserk self when facing a needle.

Next morning, I gave her one of the bones, and the tranquilizer. She laboriously climbed up on the heavy wooden picnic table, where she frequently slept in the sun. She sat there with the bone between her paws, chewing on it. She still seemed too lively for an injection, so I gave her some more tranquilizer, and the other bone. The tranquilizers seemed to be taking effect. Her eyes, always so bright and inquisitive, dulled and seemed to shrink, leaving her lower lids loose and almost gaping.

When Dr. Feld and his partner, Dr. Sayles, appeared at the gate and walked into the yard, Chappie clambered down from the table and walked over to them. My heart was like a stone.

We got her to lie down, and Dr. Feld tied some gauze around her snout. I was sorry he had to do that; I knew how much Chapp hated it. But even as tranquilized as she was, we couldn't take the chance that she might lunge and bite one of the vets. Dr. Feld inserted the needle, and I held Chapp and talked to her. As the fluid entered her veins, she slowly lowered her head between her paws and left us.

Bill and I had talked it over and decided we wanted Chapp buried in our acreage where she, with Lady's acquiescence, had been mistress of all she surveyed. That morning, I had dug her grave—in the exact spot where she had been digging when Lady had toppled her on her side.

Now, Dr. Feld and Dr. Sayles and I carried Chapp to the hole and lowered her gently into it. Even with three of us carrying her, she was incredibly heavy. I thought, "This is the definition of dead weight."

Dr. Feld asked if I wanted them to stay. I shook my head. I would take care of Chapp myself.

After they left, I stood by the hole and howled. I threw my head back and howled like a banshee. Then I started filling in the grave.

And howled even harder. I thought, "It's a good thing we're back in the woods; anyone hearing me would assume I was being murdered."

When the hole was filled, I drove to a nearby nursery, where I bought enough flowering plants to completely cover the grave area. I planted them on the spot where Chappie's body lay beneath the sand. Then I phoned Bill in Portland.

At Vatican III the bishops will be bringing their wives—and at Vatican IV the bishops will be bringing their husbands.

—CONTEMPORARY JOKE

JUST AS MANY BLACK PEOPLE meeting one another identify wordlessly, so it was with the priestly fraternity. It mattered not whether one was active, inactive, retired, laicized—or even, in many cases, whether one left the seminary prior to ordination. The identification was there. The camaraderie was there. It was as if one looked at the other and silently said, "I know."

This began to change in the wake of Vatican II. Father Kienzle used to joke that when priests gathered, they should wear a variety of T-shirts. Some would read, "Vatican II," others would read, "Council of Trent." Still others would read "Vatican III."

Nonetheless, at heart, the confraternity remained an indissoluble club. With extremely rare exceptions, whether a priest was Council of Trent or Vatican III, some things never changed. Always there was the memory of seminary days, the time of shared formation.

Undoubtedly, groups like the Marines, the Navy Seals—or those who have been in POW camps—share a similar identification: I know who you are because I know what you went through to get here.

This response is an undying one. This was brought home to me on a memorable occasion.

One of Bill's classmates, George Weber, was an outstanding student and an excellent athlete. He went on to become a missionary priest in Africa, then headed Maryknoll in upstate New York.

Eventually, George left to marry a Maryknoll nun. George and Julie had three children. They all moved back to Detroit in the late 1980s. Bill and George had corresponded, and now we invited George and Julie to dinner, along with Jim and Irma Macy.

It had been almost forty years since Bill and Jim had seen George. I didn't know what to expect. But when George and Julie walked in the door, it was as if the three men had seen each other only the day before. Their conversation was as one picked up after an interrupted phone call. It was one of the most beautiful things I have ever seen. It affected me so deeply that I went into the kitchen and wept at the wonder of it.

Sadly, tragedy entered George and Julie's life. One of their sons, standing in line for tickets to a rock concert, was hit and killed by a car that went out of control. Some years later, George and Julie divorced. George returned to work with the poor in Africa; Julie married again—to an ex-priest. She continues her work at a local cancer institute.

It seems that whether priests and nuns stay in or leave—whether they are "active" or "inactive"—they remain God-oriented and people-caring. And who is to say that is not what God had in mind for them all along?

Life is ten percent what happens to me and ninety percent how I react to it.

—Lou Holtz

LIVING DOWN A LONG LANE back in the woods meant digging out of winter snows. It also meant long walks to get the morning paper, and to pick up the afternoon mail. I got the mail; Bill got the paper.

Bill's priestly routine had involved frequent and scheduled prayers. After he left the priesthood, he continued for many years to read his breviary daily. Though I didn't know it at the time, during each morning's paper journey, he repeated the refrain of "St.

Patrick's Breastplate," the beautiful prayer composed by the beloved Irish saint:

> *Christ be with me, Christ before me, Christ behind me,*
> *Christ within me, Christ beneath me, Christ above me,*
> *Christ on my right hand, Christ on my left,*
> *Christ when I lie down, Christ when I sit, Christ when I arise.*
> *Christ in the heart of everyone who thinks of me,*
> *Christ in the mouth of everyone who speaks of me,*
> *Christ in every eye that sees me,*
> *Christ in every ear that hears me.*

At least one more line should have been included: *Christ in every patch of ice.* One morning, Bill's feet went out from under him. As he fell, his body twisted, and his right shoulder—the same shoulder he had dislocated in a seminary football game years before—took the brunt of the fall.

Bill had told me about the original dislocation—how he had sat up for nights, unable to sleep for the pain. He had been in his twenties then, able to "offer it up."

Now he was sixty and not only was the pain excruciating, but his arm motion was affected. Diagnosis: Injury to the rotator cuff. Cortisone didn't help. The pain continued until finally an orthopedic surgeon was the only recourse.

After the procedure, the surgeon gave his report. He had found evidence that the original injury had never fully healed. The fall had aggravated the old wound. The rotator cuff, he said, was, in effect, destroyed. It was not even possible to sew it up; the flesh was so thinned that the needle or thread would simply have ripped right through. All the surgeon could do was to debride the wound, staple the incision, and route Bill to rehab.

The story is told of the inhabitants of a lonely island who were informed that a tidal wave would inundate the island the following morning. There was no possibility of rescue. All on the island would be drowned.

Immediately the islanders split into three groups. The first, and largest group, spent the night in living it up, under the "eat, drink, and be merry for tomorrow we die" theory. The second group spent the night in fervent prayer. The third, and smallest, group gathered along the shore, trying to learn to breathe under water.

Bill, pragmatic almost to a fault, would have been in that third group.

At this point, Bill could barely raise his right arm. But remember the small group trying to learn to breathe under water: Bill's self-discipline rose to the fore. He signed up for rehab at St. Joseph Mercy Hospital in Pontiac, where he was fortunate to be assigned to an excellent physiotherapist. Bill, using the mnemonic of all the western movies that mentioned Durango, had no difficulty in remembering the therapist's name: Durando.

Mr. Durando and Bill made a good team. Bill did his exercises faithfully and regularly, and with each visit Mr. Durando brought him along to the next step. Bill started out supporting his right arm with his left hand, then went on to raise his right arm shoulder-high without support. After time, he could raise his right arm above his head. He could reach up into the closet, grasp his hat, and though he couldn't place it on his head, he could toss it into the air and, like the jugglers on the *Ed Sullivan Show*, move his head into position so that the hat in falling would settle onto his head.

Eventually, after months of rehab, Bill regained something like 90 percent of his motion and strength in his arm. There would always be that weak spot in his range of motion. But he could live with that. Especially since it did not impede his ability to hold a pen and write.[*]

---

[*] Everything was grist for the author's mill; Bill incorporated a shoulder injury to Father Koesler into *Body Count*.

A few years later, I talked him into trying out for a senior citizens' baseball team. This was where he discovered the limitations of his injury. He wound up and threw the ball—except that instead of going to first base, it headed out into right field. Whatever he needed to control the ball was missing. His senior baseball career was over before it began.

He was grateful for two reasons. As a youth, Bill had been highly competitive in sports. As a senior citizen, he was looking only for exercise and camaraderie. He had assumed that the group would be playing ball for the fun of it. On arriving at the tryout field he quickly became aware that "These guys are dead serious . . . they want to *win*."

Although Bill was used to dogs, he was not used to playing in what George Bush referred to as deep doo-doo. The outfield was liberally dotted with dog defecation. It didn't seem to bother the other old-timers. But Bill could not envision himself handling a baseball that had been picked out of a pile of manure.

Thanks to his rotator cuff, he could retire gracefully from the field of play with his honor intact—and his hands clean.

Where there's smoke . . .

WE ENJOYED OUR HOUSE IN THE WOODS. Especially in fall, when we raked endless carpets of oak leaves into piles. Chappie would wait until a pile was big enough and then she would dive into it, scattering leaves in all directions. Oak leaves do not compost as readily as other leaves. In the early years, we burned them. Eventually, so many people were burning leaves that the city fathers frowned on that. So we dumped wheelbarrow loads over the fence into the woods that separated us from the golf course.

All went well until one winter when Bill dumped some fireplace ashes along the fence. It turned out that the ashes must've contained some embers. Before we knew it, we had a fire on our hands. We hooked up hoses, carried pails of water, and soaked down the piles of burning leaves. We were assisted by our neighbor, a chiropractor who had just moved in and seemed quietly amused at the situation.

We thought we had the fire out. However, next day, there it was again: thick smoke wafting over the neighborhood. This time we phoned for the fire department. Since the property was so far from the road, they had to literally go to great lengths in hooking up their hoses and extending them back to the woods. Finally, after soaking the entire area to a fare-thee-well, they pulled away, having saved the trees and doused the fire.

Or so it was thought.

Next day, our doorbell rang. On the front step stood a fire-fighter, smiling at me. "Are you two at it again?" he asked. I had no idea what he was talking about until he pointed up at the smoke, again wafting through the air.

I assured him that we hadn't started anything new; that obviously the same old hidden fires had again leaped to life.

The fire crew pitchforked the smoldering leaves, spreading them around so that the water from the hoses could saturate sufficiently. Finally the Great Kienzle Fire was put to sleep once and for all.

In future, we would let the leaves stay where they fell. Except for the roof, which still required cleaning if the gutters were not to get clogged.

My acrophobia precluded my climbing onto the roof. Which meant that either Bill handled that chore or we hired someone to do the job. Till now, he had always felt quite capable of doing the job himself.

But what with his shoulder problem, I felt that maybe his clambering about the roof wasn't the smartest thing to do. One day as I looked up at Bill, roving the roof with a leaf blower, I thought, "I can't let this go on." It must have been ESP, for he looked down at me and said, "We need a simpler life."

I started looking for an easier-to-care-for house.

Here we go again . . .

We were spoiled. We had the advantages of country living while being near several major traffic arteries. What we wanted now was something that would be easy to take care of. After years of living under tall oaks, I wanted someplace with some sun so I could have a garden. Someplace where, when I went out the door, I could interact with neighbors.

Bill wanted whatever would make me happy. So, as usual, I did the house hunting.

One Sunday afternoon, en route to visit a friend who lived several miles north of us, as I turned a corner, I noticed an OPEN HOUSE sign with an arrow pointing across the intersection. Driving along, I wondered whether it was worth turning back for. It was in West Bloomfield, an area we hadn't even considered, as the homes in that area seemed much too large for our needs.

A little voice said, "This could be *your* house."

For the one and only time in my life, I made a U-turn and went back.

I pulled into the driveway of the ranch home, which didn't look unacceptably huge. The front screen door was open. I stepped inside and felt, I think this is it. I walked into the kitchen/dining room area. The patio doors overlooked a pretty little lake. Just as Chappie's neck-nuzzling had instantly won me over, it was the lake that did it. I *knew* this was it.

After talking to the agent, I headed home to talk to Bill. He was watching a football game. When I asked him to come look at a house, he was reluctant. But he put on his shoes and got in the car.

I thought, "If we're supposed to have this house, he'll like it. If we're not supposed to have it, he won't."

He liked it.

❧❀❧

He was the kind of person where you could go away and leave a million dollars on the coffee table and when you got back there would be a million dollars plus interest.

—Unknown

The body lay on a bier in front of the window. It was December, and bitter cold. What little heat there was came from the fireplace on the other side of the front room. Margaret Kelly Murray was, in accordance with her last request, dressed in blue.

Later, in a coffin draped with the Irish tricolor she and her husband, dead these thirteen years, had championed, the body of Margaret Kelly Murray was borne to rest in Gurteen Cemetery, County Sligo, Ireland. Attending the obsequies were all ten of her living children (she had given birth to thirteen), including the six from the United States: Tom from Oklahoma; Chris, Vince, Frank, Nancy, and Peggy from Michigan.

Till her dying day, Margaret Kelly Murray, even into her eighties, had done her own cooking, cleaning, and housekeeping, despite poor health and the loss of a leg, amputated ten years before. She knew what had to be done and she did it.

Margaret Kelly Murray was buried on Saturday; on Monday her son Chris was back at work in Detroit. He knew what had to be done and he did it.

Christopher Martin Murray came to the United States from Ireland in 1954 to visit two of his brothers, who had come earlier to visit an aunt. "I never intended to stay," he said many years later. "Now I would never leave."

In 1955, the U.S. military was drafting men. Not only citizens, but even visitors were subject. The U.S. Navy wanted Chris, age nineteen.

What Uncle Sam didn't know was that, like many people from Ireland, Chris couldn't swim. On that tiny island, so custom has it, men fight everything but their fate: If the sea is rough enough to tip a man into the drink and leave him boatless, it is perforce too rough to struggle against. Swimming merely prolongs the inevitable: Better to offer up a last prayer, submit one's soul to God and one's body to the deep, and go down like a stone to Davy Jones.

Legend has it that this line of thinking led to the varied patterns of the Aran or Irish fisherman's sweater. In olden times, each family had its own pattern. If a man drowned—and many did—by the time his body washed up on the beach, there was no knowing him; identification hinged on his unique sweater pattern.

Fishermen's sweaters were not Government Issue; the Great Lakes Naval Training Station chose to teach the Irish lad to swim.

A bad time was had by all, but young Chris finally made it. "I had a helluva time learning, but I went around the pool once on my back, and that qualified me as a swimmer."

The sailor never went to sea, however, but was flown to Subic Bay to join the Seabees in building a U.S. naval base. Which is how one military chapel in the Philippines came to have handmade confessionals lovingly carved by a son of Erin.*

Three years later, Chris was back in Detroit, again a civilian. "I was glad to get home; I never wanted to make a career of the Navy." But he was still working with wood—wood modeling at Ford's engineering division. It was a good job, and he enjoyed it. Then the 1958 recession hit and Chris was laid off. "They did me a favor—although at the time I didn't know it." To keep the wolf from the door, Chris started remodeling houses. Eventually, he got his builder's license and then started his own custom building business.

---

* When the base was closed a couple of years ago, I found myself wondering whatever had become of those confessionals.

Meanwhile, Chris became increasingly active in the Detroit-area Irish community, to a degree that he became known as the Irish Godfather. Eventually he hosted the *Irish Fireside Show*, a live radio program that aired every Sunday. During the program's early years, some listeners found the program too innocuous. Gradually, the reverse came to be true: The station took to issuing a disclaimer after each broadcast. Once, after Chris and a medical guest had discussed abortion on the air, an irate male listener called to tell Chris, "I wish to Christ you would end up pregnant some day!"

In the almost ten years we lived in our Southfield house, many improvements had been made—all thanks to Chris, who had become an important part of our life.

Chris had held the contract for repairs at Lafayette Towers, where I had lived before Bill and I went to Minnesota. The Towers manager, a member of the Gaelic League's Irish-American Club, at one point invited me to be one of the judges for the club's annual Rose of Tralee contest. Chris was president of the club, which sponsored the annual Irish Festival as part of Detroit's summer ethnic riverfront celebrations. Chris was very much in evidence during the festival.

I had always been impressed by his professional demeanor and his obvious feeling for the land of his birth.

When Chris heard that Bill was going to Ireland for the first time, he phoned and—much as Peter Spivak had said, "Funny, but I just bought into a football club"—said, "My brother Gerry and I have a pub in Sligo. Would you like to stay there while you're in Ireland?"

We would and we did. Sometime later, Father Koesler stayed at the same pub, experiencing, as Bill wrote, "the coldest bathroom in western civilization."

Chris's oldest son, Tom, then a teenager, was handling pub duties for the summer. Bill and I were as impressed with Tom as we were with his father. Bill, who rarely offered a comment unless requested, volunteered, "He is a very special young man—the kind that you could give your money, your car, and your house keys to without worrying."*

It was when we met Chris's wife, Mary, and the rest of the Murray clan that we got the full picture. Mary Carty Murray is one of those rare people in whom one senses pure goodness. Picture Melanie in *Gone With the Wind*—but a Melanie with spirit, humor, and grit. In later years, I would say to Chris, "Mary is a saint." Chris would reply with a grin, "Yes, and it's livin' with me that's made her a saint." Their children concur.

Like all who know her, Bill loved Mary. He once told me, "I could never say no to Mary Murray. If somebody wanted something, all they'd have to do would be to tell Mary to ask me, and I couldn't say no."

Chris was for us a guardian angel. I am totally challenged mechanically, electronically, and technologically. Bill was even more so. Early on, he replaced a wall plate, and when he was finished with the job, the switch read "NO" and "FFO." He was, we agreed, lucky he could tie his shoelaces. Obviously anytime repairs were needed, an outsider was required. At such times, Chris would interrupt his work to come over and either fix what needed fixing, or put someone on the job to fix it.

Over the years, Chris, his family and/or crew, put in eaves gutters, tiled the dining room floor, refinished the basement, and completely gutted and replaced our bathroom. When a raccoon chewed a huge hole in the roof, resulting in rain flooding the dining room, Chris was there to repair the damage immediately. It was Chris who, when we needed a ladder, gave us the professional carpenters' ladder.

And it was Chris's sons who moved a truckload of oak logs from our old house to our new one. Every time we used our fireplace we thought of the Murrays.

---

* Today, Tom is co-owner of three pubs: Conor O'Neill's in Ann Arbor, Michigan, and in Boulder, Colorado; as well as Brendan O'Neill's in Cleveland.

I wrote an article about Chris and submitted it to the *Free Press* for publication in the St. Patrick's issue of the Sunday Magazine. The then-editor refused it on the grounds that Chris was nothing more than a Mick who was smuggling IRA criminals into the United States. The editor would accept the article only if I would include "all that smuggling stuff."

His view was totally erroneous. Chris was not involved in any "smuggling stuff." When I told him of the editor's statement, Chris laughed, shook his head, and said, "Don't I wish I had such power." But at that time, the general public's perception of the Irish was very much IRA-colored; the article was never published.

A home is not a mere transient shelter: Its essence lies . . . in its quality of representing, in all its details, the personalities of the people who live in it.

—H. L. MENCKEN

WE ARRANGED FOR A BRIDGE LOAN, put our Southfield home up for sale, and moved into our new home on Dollar Lake.

We discovered that we could not get continued insurance on our Southfield house unless it was occupied. Fortunately, our neighbors had recently sold their house and were waiting to move into their new condo, which was still unfinished. They rented our house, thus satisfying the insurance company's requirements, and helping us to meet the payments on the bridge loan until the house was sold some months later.

One of the many blessings throughout our married life has been our neighbors. I can truly say that we have never had a bad neighbor. On the contrary, many of our neighbors have added immeasurably to the joys of our home ownership.

❧❀❧

Our new house was a four-bedroom ranch with a huge walk-out basement. It was on a lot and a half sloping down to a lake that we shared with twelve other homeowners, mallards, wood ducks, Canada geese, herons, an occasional loon, snapping turtles, and even for a while, swans. And there was the usual assortment of wildlife—raccoons, possums, skunks, and groundhogs. One day, Bill looked up, startled, to see a deer run between our house and our next-door neighbor's.

Once more, we enlisted Chris Murray's aid. Chris, his son Patrick, and Chris's brother Vincent ripped up old carpeting and put in oak floors, replaced all the bedroom windows and the patio-door wall, installed a bay window over the kitchen sink, and another in my workroom, which overlooked the lake. I felt like Tennyson's Lady of Shalott, except that she was doomed to see life only through the reflection of a mirror, whereas I could spend hours sitting on the window seat, looking out at the lake and the wildlife, without having to worry about the spell being broken. Of course I didn't get much work done.

One morning I was in the basement while upstairs Bill was showering. I became aware that water was dripping down onto the floor. An SOS went out to Chris. Like a 911 paramedic, Chris strode onto the scene. He discovered that the base of the shower had been improperly installed, and the entire floor beneath had rotted. It was only a question of time before, as Chris put it, "Bill's feet and legs would've been wiggling in front of your eyes in the basement."

Chris and Vince rebuilt the floor and installed a new shower. Bill, who did some of his deepest plotting in the shower, could return to his literary concocting without having to worry about dropping feet-first into the basement.

Again, life fell into a routine. After morning Mass and breakfast, Bill played the piano, answered letters, exercised, and showered. After lunch, he played solitaire, which, along with showering, was his tool for plotting. Then he worked on the current book until dinner. During dinner, we talked over the news, the day's events, and a zillion other things. Bill occasionally adverted to a *New Yorker* cartoon depicting an obviously longtime married couple, one of whom was saying to the other, "We never talk anymore." After one of our daily gabfests, he would grin and say, "We never talk anymore."

It brought to mind an anecdote of Hugh Leonard's. He and his first wife were seated in a restaurant near a couple who were eating dinner in what seemed angry silence. Finally, the woman threw down her fork, looked at her partner in barely contained fury, and said, "Once and for all: Are you going to tell your wife or shall I?"

After dinner—just as after every meal—Bill adjourned to the bathroom to floss and brush his teeth. Although we had the advantage of having had, for some twenty years, one of Michigan's best and most talented dentists, James Barone, DDS, Bill wanted to make sure that his teeth would always be with him, so he cleaned his teeth faithfully after each and every meal.

He stuck strictly to this regimen no matter what. Only once was he almost derailed. One evening, after a speaking engagement, we were guests at the home of the program's host, who happened to be a dentist. When offered hors d'oeuvre, Bill politely declined, explaining, "I've already flossed."

"Go ahead and eat," his host urged. "I've got a dental chair in the basement, and I'll clean your teeth for you when you're finished."

Unless we were going out for the evening, after dinner—and after Bill's dental ablutions—we moved to the den, to wind down by watching television. Actually, Bill watched television; I did crossword puzzles, wrote letters, or clipped newspapers. Unless there was an NFL game on. In which case, Bill's entertainment was derived more from my shrieks of joy or agony as the Detroit Lions or some other team drove me ecstatic with admiration or wild with frustration. "That wouldn't have happened if Chris Godfrey were there!"

My concern for the Detroit Lions impelled me from time to time to write to their coach, Bobby Ross, giving him the benefit of my football expertise—which consisted mainly of suggesting that the Lions players study films of Vince Lombardi's Green Bay Packers—"Dowler split to the right, McGee out to the left"—as they ground out juggernaut yardage.

Mr. Ross was a gentleman of the old school: Overlooking my chutzpah, he replied courteously to each and every one of my letters. He may not have brought a championship to Detroit, but, as Bill said, Bobby Ross was a class act.

Undoubtedly, the reading public tends to envision authors spending the night living it up and/or jet-setting all over the globe. Bill was content with a life of quiet routine, and I was content to be with him, wherever. Normally, I went to bed after the news; Bill after David Letterman—with an occasional side trip to Jay Leno.

But always, he tucked me in, kissed me good night, and never failed to say, "Call your angels to you."

As for New Year's Eve, we stayed home, happy to leave the roads to the dipsomaniacs or the designated drivers. Usually, Bill would have to wake me to wish me a Happy New Year.

Because we no longer had a fenced-in area, we could not let Lady run free. We did take her outside on the lawn without a leash, until one day, chasing a squirrel, she ran into the street right in front of an oncoming car. I shrieked at her to stop, but her eye was on the squirrel. The driver of the car slammed on the brakes so hard he fishtailed. Still, the front fender broadsided Lady just hard enough to bowl her over. The driver glared at me. I didn't blame him. On the contrary I was grateful for his alertness. Had he not slammed on the brakes, we would've had either a dead or badly injured wolfhound.

Bill and I took turns taking Lady for a walk around the lake daily. She would be leashed until we got off the main street and onto a back unpaved road with little or no traffic. Then she could amble freely without worry of being run down. The sight of such a huge, unfamiliar animal frequently caused cars to slow as the drivers gawked at her. Occasionally, a car would stop and the driver would ask, "What *is* that?"

Lady had surpassed her seven-to-eight-year life expectancy. Frequent visits to the vet kept her up to snuff, and Bill took very seriously his duties as co-owner of this rare and loving creature.

One winter an ice storm of extreme magnitude covered the ground in what appeared to be a mantle of glass. Fearful that Lady would fall and break one of her long, spindly legs, Bill spent the better part of one morning breaking up the ice so she could walk outside safely. He continued to cook his made-from-scratch chicken soup for her. She continued to sleep on the floor by his side of the bed.

A Mass is a Mass is a Mass—*not.*

I WAS THE EARLY BIRD and Bill was the night owl. When we moved to West Bloomfield, we visited several nearby churches in search of a daily Mass. I, who rose earlier, sought a reverent Mass. Bill, I think, sought a Mass where he could worship and meditate in peace.

When Father Halfpenny was made pastor of St. Vincent's in Pontiac, I welcomed his presence. He had presided at Joe Cronyn's funeral and had done such a beautiful job that I told him afterward, "I hope you're still around when I go so you can do my funeral."

Father Halfpenny offered a reverent Mass and gave excellent homilies. The only problem with St. Vincent's was that Mass was rarely held at the same time two days in a row. One morning, when I arrived to find the church door locked, I was returning to my car when I heard a woman's voice: "Are you here for Mass?"

"Yes," I said.

"Well, we're having a communion service in the business office today."

"I wish they'd make up their mind about having Mass here," I groused. "It's never in the same place or at the same time."

"You must understand," she lectured me, "there is a priest shortage, and you know our pastor is also editor of the *Michigan Catholic* . . ."

I bit my tongue. Later, Bill said, "Why didn't you tell her, 'I knew one of those'?"

But it was pointless. I knew only too well there was a priest shortage and that Father Halfpenny was doing the best he could under the circumstances.

Still, I wanted to be able to attend Mass daily without having to worry about whether it would be held or not. A friend mentioned the Monastery of the Blessed Sacrament, the home of an order of cloistered Dominicans. Daily Mass was at 7 A.M.—every day. Though the monastery was a little over six miles away, I could attend Mass and still be home before Bill left for his later Mass at a church in Orchard Lake. Sometimes, if he got up early, he came with me to early Mass at the monastery.

I found a home away from home at the monastery. Father Weber, the celebrant, not only offered a reverent Mass, but his homilies were gems. I once asked him if he would put them into a book. He shook his head. He spoke totally extemporaneously. This was doubly sad because when he died a few years later, only the nuns and the few daily communicants had had the opportunity to experience the treasure of his homilies.

When the Blessed Sacrament was raised in the monstrance after each morning's Mass, many of those attending remained in the pew to worship. I did not want to leave; I felt I could stay there forever. I knew now how little Billy Kienzle had felt as a boy at Mass.

After the majority of the worshipers left, the extern nun locked the chapel door; those remaining had to leave by a side door through the monastery office. Bill kidded me: "If they lock you in, they get to keep you." I joked back that if anything happened to him I would become a contemplative nun.

The Masses that Bill attended became increasingly unsatisfactory. A frequent celebrant seemed to have some personality problems. The day that he announced to all present something along the lines of "If it weren't for the Jews there would be no abortion," he reached Bill. Bill thought, "This man is dangerous." Bill wrote the pastor—the erstwhile occupant of the "Petit Trianon"—of his concerns, but the response was less than satisfactory. Because of the priest shortage, pastors had to make do and tried to hold on to whatever warm body they could.

This situation presaged the later public pedophilia scandal, which was exacerbated for the same reason: Because of the priest shortage, the Church, instead of ousting pedophiles or dealing with the problem, used them to fill in as needed. Had there been enough priests to go around . . .

One might be forgiven for wondering which would be worse in the eyes of God: a married clergy, a female clergy, or a pedophile clergy? Is it more important for your children to be safe or is it more important for them to see an unmarried man on the altar? The hierarchy gave the people in the pews its answer. Obviously it's been more important for the children to receive the host from male celibate hands even if the children have had to suffer sexual abuse at those same hands.

Many rote Catholics tend to take their cue from the Church. So if, due to the priest shortage, churches are shut down, and Masses are fewer and farther between, what does that tell the people in the pews?

It tells them that the Church considers manmade rules more important than the Eucharist. If the Eucharist were important the Church would see to it that daily Mass and the Eucharist were available, even if it had to be offered by someone other than a male celibate clergy. If, however, there are so comparatively few male celibate priests that daily Mass becomes every-other-day Mass, or even every-other-week Mass, a growing percentage of Catholics might be forgiven for thinking, "Well, if the Eucharist is that unimportant, why should I bother being present to receive it at all?"

One of Bill's favorite books was *Mr. Blue*, Myles Connolly's futuristic tale of a very different priest figure. *Mr. Blue* was first published in 1928,[*] the year of Bill's birth. The paperback edition was first published in 1954, the year of Bill's ordination. In alluding to *Mr. Blue*, Bill predicted—only half-jokingly, I fear—that someday

---

[*] The year of the dragon—a propitious year in the Chinese calendar.

there would be so few priests that Detroit would have one Mass a year, held at Tiger Stadium.

Bill switched to St. Colman's, whose pastor, Father Kendzierski, offered a reverent Mass, and whose parishioners were a welcoming group.

So between the monastery and St. Colman's, Bill and I finally had our daily Mass, even if we usually attended separately.

Life is a bus ride . . . All of our struggling and vying is about seats on the bus, and the ride is over before we know it.

—ERIC HOFFER

IT'S BEEN SAID EVERYONE WANTS TO GO TO HEAVEN, but no one wants to die. An Anglican friend mused that if heaven is all it's cracked up to be, why don't we all commit suicide? Still another view is that we start to die the day we're born.

Look at the student in the weeks prior to graduation, the seminarian prior to ordination, the bride-to-be prior to her wedding, the mother-to-be prior to birth, the traveler prior to his round-the-world trip. Each is at one and the same time filled with happiness and yearning for what is to come. Such people go through each day with joy and extreme anticipation . . . enjoying both the now—what is—and the future—what is to be. This is known as life. If we believe in heaven, we can enjoy living at the same time as we prepare for dying and what comes after.

Along with grief, sorrow, and pain, the death of a loved one brings intimations of one's own mortality. If after forty it's patch, patch, patch, after fifty it's watch, watch, watch, as one after another is taken by disease or sudden death. In the former case we can prepare for death; sometimes we even consider it a blessing. In the latter case, death often comes as a wrenching shock.

As years passed, Bill lost his parents, his two sisters, former pastors and seminary professors, a growing number of seminary classmates and priest buddies, as well as former parishioners.

As it does to most of us, each death took a chunk from Bill's heart. And with advancing years, the dearer the departed, the bigger the chunk.

When Bill's sister Anne died in a nursing home after a long struggle with illness complicated by a broken hip, memories of his childhood and later years came flooding back. Annie, eating the fat on his meat, the yellow of his egg, the stewed tomatoes—all the things a young boy thought were too yucky to put in his mouth. Annie taking him for walks. Annie taking him to Mass. Annie standing at the foot of the stairs rubbing her head after he'd "bombed" her with a toy gun. Annie, proud as punch of her brother the priest, proud as punch of her brother the author.

We had joked that Annie, who took such good care of herself, would outlive all of us, even her younger husband.

Next to go was Bill's sister Pauline. She had turned on the water in the tub, and lain down on the bed as she waited for her bath to fill. She never got up. The water streamed through her apartment and out onto the sidewalk. The police were called. The police called Bill. It could have been a scene from one of his Father Koesler mysteries. The police decided death was due to natural causes.

Now he alone of his family was left. How many times over the years had he offered Mass for the soul of a departed parishioner? How many times had he eulogized the deceased? How many times had he comforted the bereaved family?

I asked him once what was the hardest thing he'd ever had to do as a priest. He didn't have to think more than a few moments. "Help a parent bury a child."

His parents had buried a child. But that was before he was born. He had buried his parents and his sisters. Did he now have intimations of mortality? Not yet; those he had lost were so much older than he.

The chariot wheels of time rolled on.

Never underestimate what it takes to watch someone you love in pain.

—ERMA BOMBECK

RAY BETANZOS WAS LOVED AND ADMIRED by all who knew him. The joke was that each person felt that he or she was Ray's best friend. When Ray married, he told Kay he wanted a house that would always be welcoming. And so it was. Their home was open to all—a large extended family, friends, neighbors, relatives from near and far, friends and classmates of Beth and Mary, former seminary schoolmates of Ray, coworkers of Kay.

Bill, being somewhat reserved, did not feel the same way about an open house. We had dinner parties, which were less spontaneous than the gatherings Chez Betanzos. But whomever we invited, Kay and Ray were always at the top of our guest list; we knew they would fit in with anybody and everybody. Each December, we hosted a Christmas get-together with Ray and Kay, Jim and Irma Macy, and Art and Patti Schaffran if they were available.

Jim had entered the seminary the same day as Bill; he had left the priesthood the same day Bill left. Jim married Irma, a vivacious, talented former IHM nun. Their son, Josh, was about a year older than Kay and Ray's Little Mary Sunshine. Art Schaffran had left the priesthood a couple of years before Bill to marry Patti, a petite, peppy blonde, who was as much of a Hibernophile as I was. I always took it for granted that our little group would all toddle happily off into the sunset together.

In the summer of 1989 Ray took a sabbatical from Wayne State. He, Kay, and Mary left to spend a year in Salzburg, where Ray and Kay hoped to eventually spend part of each retirement year. We missed them. Undoubtedly our phone calls to Austria upped the value of the telephone stock considerably.

In the summer of 1991, Ray, Kay and Mary returned to Europe for a month. Ray was working on a book about *Franz von Baader's Philosophy of Love*. He had been invited to address a Baader seminar at Munich's Philosophische Theologie. Kay and Mary attended Ray's presentation, pleased at the recognition of his work. The three of them then went off to tour the Eastern Bloc countries.

They planned a return to Austria in August 1994. Ray would take a six-month sabbatical from Wayne State to update his research on Baader. Although Ray had complained that spring of indigestion and back problems, he dismissed them as part of aging. Arrangements were made to rent a house in Vienna and to lease a car.

In July of that year, they visited Kay's sister on Little Glen Lake. On the golf course, Ray found himself in pain. He tried to play through it. Eventually, the pain was so severe he was talked into going to Munson Hospital in nearby Traverse City.

We received a phone call from Kay. When Bill answered the phone, Kay asked that I get on the extension. She told us that Ray had stomach cancer. They would be returning to Detroit that day, and Ray would be operated on at Henry Ford Hospital. She asked us to pray.

The following months were a nightmare of hospitalization, chemotherapy, radiation, surgery, with all the attendant side effects. Ray, normally the most patient of individuals, was short-tempered with pain and discomfort. He grew increasingly thinner and weaker. All of us tried to pique his appetite. I took rice pudding and tapioca pudding over every few days. The huge Betanzos refrigerator was full to overflowing with friends' offerings.

Ray continued to lose weight. Not only did he have no appetite; if he was able to force down even a few spoonfuls of food, nausea followed. One day, his sister Pat, having been unable to talk him into taking some soup, fled the room in tears.

Specialists were consulted; oncologists tried everything they could think of. Meanwhile, we prayed. Rarely had so many people in so many places prayed so earnestly for anyone who was not a celebrity. Every Sunday, like a circuit rider, I would seek out a different church, adding Ray's name to the list of those being prayed for. From time to time I would weep against Bill's chest, as he held me and assured me that if we all prayed hard enough, our prayers would be heard.

When Ray needed blood transfusions, there was no dearth of eager donors. Bill and I and Ray shared the same RH negative blood type. I checked with my doctor: Would my past CFS preclude my donating blood? I was assured that it wouldn't. The hospital arranged for us to give blood and earmark our donations for Ray. After each transfusion, a bit of Ray's strength would return for a week or so.

Ray never lost his sense of humor. One day, after a nurse had left the room, Ray, weak and miserable, lay with his eyes closed. "Did you notice how pretty that nurse is?" Bill commented. Ray opened his eyes, looked at Bill, and said, "I may be sick . . . I'm not dead." Bill was reminded of the long-ago seminary professor who had told his soon-to-be-ordained students, "You can look; just don't touch."

Two older priests, Monsignor Matyn and Monsignor Sherzer, were among the many praying for Ray. They knew him well, knew how intelligent, how strong, how athletic he was. "There's such a thing as being too strong," Monsignor Sherzer said. We knew he meant that frequently it just prolongs dying.

The sands of time ran out. By February 1995, the cancer had spread through the lymph system to the lungs. Though the doctors felt Ray had only a short time left, nonetheless, they would try one last desperate procedure.

Bill had promised to give a eulogy at a memorial for a former parishioner. We were assured that, based on the doctors' information, Ray had at least a few weeks left. When we returned home, a message on our answering machine informed us that Ray had died.

It had happened much sooner than the doctors had expected. We were grateful that Ray was at last out of his agony. But for Bill and me, denied the opportunity to be with Ray at the end, hold his hand, pray our good-byes, there was no closure.

Again, for Bill, the longtime memories: youthful high-jinks in the seminary; Ray on the handball court, on the football field; Ray serving at Bill's first Mass; Bill offering the homily at Ray's first Mass; Ray as a young priest, with his matinee-idol good looks—so handsome, Kay had joked, that the first time she saw him, when he turned toward the congregation at Mass, she gasped.

For the rest of us, the memories of Ray, greeting us at the door with a smile that welcomed like an embrace; Ray punning; Ray laughing; Ray golfing; Ray living up to his Basqueness by devouring whatever was placed before him; Ray discussing theology; Ray caressing Little Mary Sunshine; Ray looking pridefully at Kay— "My Kate: Isn't she something?"

The priests came in droves to Ray's wake. They exchanged reminiscences till late night forced them back to their rectories. Ray's Funeral Mass was held at the Shrine of the Little Flower, Father Coughlin's former fiefdom. Ray's classmate, Bishop Harrington, was the celebrant. Mourners packed the church; priests packed the altar.

Bill gave a eulogy. He recalled how, after receiving a transfusion of Bill's blood, Ray had phoned him from the hospital. "It's funny," Ray had said, "but I feel like writing a mystery." And Bill, who was so in awe of Ray's brain, had replied, "Just run it through your system and give it back to me so I can get some of your smarts."

Another eulogist was Jack McNamara, Kay's brother, who spoke of Ray's love for his gentle daughter. "I would never argue with Mary," said Jack, "because, being half-Basque and half-Irish she might blow up my car." We all knew it was hyperbole; Little Mary Sunshine lived up to the nickname Bill had given her.

Mary was nearly eighteen, with a mixture of her mother's generosity and her father's intellect, her good looks inherited from both the Basque and Irish ancestry. Almost six feet tall and strikingly attractive, Mary had already done some modeling. When her proud father had shown her portfolio photos to an old friend, the man, a retired FBI agent, looked at Ray and said quietly, "Betanzos, you're in deep sh-t."

I had loved Ray dearly. We shared puns, phoned each other to try to figure out the *New York Times* crossword clues, compared notes on favorite operas. I had helped Ray edit his books on Dilthey and Baader; Ray had helped Bill with all but the first of the Father Koesler books. He had answered questions about history and theology, about grammar and punctuation, about Latin and German.

In one of the early books, Bill, having forgotten most of his seminary-learned German, had Dr. Willie Moellmann exclaim, "*Gotterdammerung!*" Ray, tactful soul that he was, tried not to laugh. "I think what you want is *Verdammt!*" he said. "What you've got Dr. Moellmann saying is 'Twilight of the Gods.'"

Ray would read the original typescript and offer suggestions and corrections; he would reread the galley proofs and find errors we had missed. Henceforth, when we needed help with the books, where once we had been able to call Ray and get all the answers, we would now have to consult half a dozen people—and frequently still not get the answers.

"The soul of Jonathan was knit with the soul of David, and Jonathan loved him as his own soul."

—1 Samuel 18:1

I had gotten in the habit of meditating each morning on awakening. A few days after Ray's death, I was lying in bed, looking out the window, not really focusing on the trees, the sky, and the sunshine. Bill was still asleep; I was peripherally aware of his regular breathing, and of the birds twittering outside. I was going through my meditation practice, focusing on my own breathing and trying to empty my mind.

Suddenly, I heard Ray's voice. I recognized it immediately. Odd; he sounded frustrated, irritated—almost angry. Ray was one of the kindest people on earth. The only time I had ever heard such a tone from him was on the rare occasion when he inveighed against nihilism. Ray felt that nihilism was a sin, and he would, as they say, argue Christ off the cross with anyone who professed anything that even resembled nihilism. It was such a bête noire for Ray that to this day I cannot see the word in print without thinking of him.

Ray spoke just three short sentences. And by "spoke" I do not mean that his voice was heard in the room. Rather, it was heard in my head—something like when one "hears" a tune or a song in one's head.

His first words were "I can't get through." This was said in a tone of extreme irritation. So unlike the kind, soft-spoken Ray we all knew and loved.

I knew instantly that he meant he could not get through to Kay. I don't know how I knew this; I just did. Before I had a chance to ponder it further, he spoke again. "Don't look back." Now I knew—again instantly—that this was a message for Kay. He was telling her not to second-guess herself about his medical treatment or anything she felt should or shouldn't have been done.

The third and last thing he said—and one that might be considered the most mystifying, was "Put your arms around it." Strange . . .

And yet I understood immediately what he meant. I had always heard that one has to embrace grief in order to get through it and surmount it. What Ray was saying to Kay—using me as a channel—was, "Embrace the grief. Don't fight it; put your arms around it." In that way, she would be able to surmount it.

That was all. Just those three short sentences. I lay there for a moment, totally bemused. Then I reached for the pen I always kept on the nightstand. The first piece of paper I picked up was a small mail order catalog. I wrote the three sentences on the back of the catalog. That way I wouldn't forget them—although there was little chance of that.

I walked around all morning in a fog. Finally, at lunch, I told Bill of my experience. I compared it to the biblical, "Lord, I believe; help Thou mine unbelief": "I know it happened," I said, "but I don't believe it."

Bill pondered for a short while. "I think you did hear Ray," he said finally.

I phoned Kay to give her Ray's message. Kay is a natural skeptic; I knew she would find it difficult to believe. But the message had been for her; I had been only a conduit.

A few days later, in Borders, a book caught my eye. It was about communications from the deceased—a book I would not normally have looked at twice. I started to leaf through it. Once more something caught my eye: a description of such communications. It seemed that frequently when a loved one dies, the survivor is filled with so much grief that the grief becomes an impediment to communication. In which case, according to the book, the deceased will contact a member of the family, or a close friend—and when this happens, frequently the first thing that the deceased says is "I can't get through"—Ray's exact words.

I would have had no way of knowing any of this in advance. But it made a believer out of me. Although I'm not sure if it convinced Kay.

Bill, as usual, kept his emotions to himself. But a few days later, a photo appeared on his writing desk. It was a picture taken at Sacred Heart Seminary of a bunch of high school boys. Prominent among them was a young Ray Betanzos, face broken into infectious laughter. From time to time over the following years, I would see Bill, pen in hand, pondering the next words in his manuscript as he sat gazing at the friend with whom he had grown from boyhood to manhood.

Slowly, gradually, he detached himself, breathing less and less . . . then was he off and free . . .

—HELEN NEARING

BILL'S ONETIME PASTOR, Lawrence "Scottie" Graven, was now a monsignor. Born in Scotland of Scots-Irish parents, Scottie would charm Bill with stories of "The wee hoose in the heather," of his father, who made clay pipes, and his mother, who worshiped tenor John McCormack.

Young Lawrence had been a student in a Scottish seminary that was visited by the then-Queen Elizabeth—the future Queen

Mother who would die in 2002 at age 101. The queen had stopped in front of the youth and addressed him: "So you're going to be a priest."

"Yes, ma'am."

"Then be a good one," she said. And he was.

When Monsignor Graven was forced to retire for health reasons, he went to live at Lourdes, a combination retirement, assisted-living, and nursing home that gave priests preference on its waiting list. Lourdes, run by the Oxford Dominicans, was and is the Cadillac of retirement communities.

Over the years, Bill regularly visited Monsignor Graven at Lourdes. The two men put their storytelling skills to good use—Scottie telling Bill the same old tales Bill had heard over the years, and Bill telling Scottie the same old tales he had told many times before. "They're good stories," Bill said, "and a good story is always enjoyable, no matter how many times you've heard it."

Monsignor Graven suffered from arthritis. Doctors had prescribed a series of exercises for him in order to keep his joints limber. Bill chuckled at Scottie's impish response when a nurse asked, "Monsignor, are you turning your head?"

"Only when you go by, honey," replied the irrepressible monsignor.

Bill was a very measured person. He did not act precipitately. He did not like surprises. He was not "fast on his feet." He liked to have time to think things over.

One morning, when Bill was in the shower, a phone call came from Lourdes. It was a nun who knew of Bill's faithfulness in visiting Monsignor Graven. She called to inform Bill that the monsignor was going downhill and had only a few days left. She thought Bill would want to know.

I gave Bill the message in the shower. I assumed he would be going out the following day to see Monsignor Graven. I was startled when, a few minutes later, Bill, fully dressed, prayerbook in hand, headed out the door, saying, "I'm going to Lourdes."

I don't know whether it was the experience with Ray, or just a sixth sense that told him not to put off the visit. When Bill arrived at Lourdes, the monsignor's condition had deteriorated. It was obvious that the end was much nearer than previously thought.

Bill sat alongside Scottie's bed, took the monsignor's hand in his own, and started reading from the prayerbook. He spoke aloud the *Nunc Dimittis*—the beautiful night prayers that begin, "Now lettest Thou Thy servant depart . . ." Scottie's hand pressed Bill's ever so slightly. He seemed to fight for breath. And then he was gone.

In Bill's files is a treasured letter from Monsignor Graven. It was in response to a letter Bill had written, telling him, "My years with you at St. Norbert's were the happiest in my priesthood." Scottie's letter reads in part, "The years with you at St. Norbert's were for me also the happiest in my priesthood."

Shortly thereafter, Neal Shine's mother died. After her funeral, outside the church, Bill stood talking with some of his priest classmates, including Father Val Gattari. Father Gattari asked if Bill had heard about Monsignor Graven's death. "Yes," Bill said, "I was reading to him when he died."

"That's a new way of killing somebody," said Father Gattari, "reading him to death."

He looked at life and got the joke.

—UNKNOWN

EVERY SO OFTEN I would give Bill a book to fill in some of the blanks in his mystery-reading education. One such book was William Irish's *Deadline at Dawn*, a classic that was adapted loosely into a 1946 movie starring Susan Hayward.

The plot involves an innocent man scheduled to be executed for murder. His only chance of escaping the electric chair is for someone to investigate and uncover the truth that will exonerate him and save his life. The doomed man depends on his best friend to do this . . . to drop everything, put his own life on hold, and follow each and every lead in hopes of stopping the execution.

Bill was quite taken with the story. When he finished, he sat thoughtfully for some time, pondering who among his friends could be depended upon should he find himself imprisoned under a death sentence. Who would drop everything, put his own life on hold, and follow each and every lead to save him?

The first name that came to mind was Chuck Papke.

Chuck and Sue Papke were St. Norbert's people. Father Kienzle had been there for them in good times and bad . . . when their three children were growing up, when they lost a baby, when Sue had almost died. They had remained the closest of friends over the years. When I first met Chuck and Sue, Chuck was on his worst behavior—a feisty, salt-and-pepper-haired agitator—the type who, if you said black, would say white just to get your goat. I couldn't figure out what Father Kienzle was doing with such an irritating friend.

After we moved back to Detroit, I got to know Chuck and Sue. Although Chuck from time to time reverted to being Peck's Bad Boy, his bark was worse than his bite. I grew to recognize and appreciate his good points. I admired Sue for being able to remain so even-tempered in the face of her husband's agitprop.

For many years, Chuck and Father Kienzle golfed with John Kamego, a clone of *JAG*'s Admiral Chegwidden. John, whom they called the Commander, had been a naval aviator in World War II. He remained in the Reserve after his tour of duty, and was in public relations at Michigan Bell. Chuck worked for Ford Motor Co. On holidays like July Fourth and Labor Day, Bob Fitzpatrick—Secret Agent X-9—completed the foursome. At other times, Chuck's son Mark, an expert golfer, joined the group to show them how to play the game.

After the outing, the guys would return for a cookout, alternating from year to year between the Papke, Kamego, and Fitzpatrick homes. Long years later, on each July Fourth and Labor Day, Bill would phone his friends to reminisce about those Good Old Days that they all missed.

Occasionally Chuck joined Father Kienzle in a game at St. John's, where Bill introduced him to any other priest who happened to be on the course, as "Father Chuck," adding, "He's more of a father than you or I." However, if the bishop happened to play by, Chuck went into the bushes to hunt for his ball.

Chuck also joined Father Kienzle for some of the priests' pickup basketball games. Most of the priests were pretty big guys and Sue worried that Chuck might get accidentally clobbered. As a protection, she always hung a medal of the Immaculate Conception around his neck beforehand. Father Kienzle remarked that she had never given *him* such a medal. On his next birthday, Sue presented him with such a medal—along with the ugliest necktie she could find.

Sue's parents had a country cottage. They gave Father Kienzle a key. He, Chuck, Sue, and their children spent many happy times there. Sue, thinking she was doing Father Kienzle a favor, arranged for him to fill in for the local pastor during their stay. The Papkes got up early each morning to attend the Mass that Father Kienzle offered. Many years later Father Kienzle informed Chuck and Sue that he liked to sleep late and that he wasn't required to offer Mass on vacation.

Shortly before Chuck's retirement, Bill and I visited him at his office high up in the RenCen in downtown Detroit. My acrophobia was in full sway, and as Bill and I rode up in the glass elevator, I buried my head in his chest. At one point I thought to be brave and lifted my head, to immediately shriek with fear as my brain and my innards instantly told me this was a big mistake.

A voice came over the elevator's intercom: "Is everything all right up there?" It was reassuring to know that somewhere a guard was keeping tabs on what was going on in what I had come to feel was a torture chamber.

On the way down, I put my head inside Bill's jacket and did not look up until I felt the elevator come firmly to ground.

❧⚘❧

In spite of regular checkups, which gave no hint of any problem, Chuck's health became problematic. Eventually his physical condition deteriorated to the extent that he could no longer keep up at work. He took an early retirement from Ford, and he and Sue headed north where they built a house on Little Glen Lake. By the time a percipient physician came on the scene, Chuck had suffered irreparable heart damage. Chuck, once tireless on the golf course, now could barely make it through even a few holes.

Weakened though he was, Chuck took on another project. He and Sue volunteered to work with young children who needed a loving relationship with parent figures.

Chuck's trip on what Bill referred to as the final glidepath was slow but inevitable. But instead of bitterness, or anger, or struggle, Chuck, in a spirit of acceptance, waxed philosophical.

The ever-feisty guy who would have argued with the devil himself spoke of his impending departure as if he were going on a long-anticipated trip. In effect, he was. In earlier days, Chuck had on occasion taken issue with Church Law. At one point, he had told Father Kienzle quite matter-of-factly, "Confirmation is a minor sacrament." Nonetheless, both he and Sue were totally faith-filled. They faced Chuck's situation with equanimity.

Bill visited with Chuck for the last time shortly before his death. He marveled at Chuck's calmness, peacefulness, and total lack of fear. Bill said he had never seen anyone face death with such grace.

To Chuck it was simple: He had lived a good life; he had kept the faith, and he looked forward to being with God in heaven.

Bill gave the eulogy at Chuck's Funeral Mass. Bill had lost his parents and his sisters. He had lost Ray, who had been part of his life since seminary days. Now, he had lost the dear friend who had been part of his life since the early days of his priesthood. Halfway through his reminiscences, his voice broke and he stopped to regain composure. Later, Chuck Junior said, "I didn't think he'd be able to go on."

In all the years I knew Bill, it was the only time I ever heard his voice break.

The world is a book and he who stays at home reads only a page.

—St. Augustine

Between my wanderlust and Bill's book tours, his preference for his own bed and bath was sorely tested. Like the author who hated to write but liked having written, when it came to travel, Bill didn't want to go but liked having been there.

A busy book tour is akin to the If-this-is-Tuesday-it-must-be-Belgium syndrome. More than once, I wakened in a strange hotel room, wondering where I was. At such times, I would reach for the phone book on the nightstand to ascertain which city we were in.

On one such trip I woke not only in the dark as to where I was—but also as to my name. It is a fearful feeling not to remember one's own name. Those with neurological problems have been known to worry from time to time about "losing one's mind." I had always heard that as long as you know your own name you have nothing to worry about along those lines. But now I couldn't remember my name!

I turned over in bed, to see Bill lying asleep next to me. Everything fell into place: "That's Bill Kienzle," I thought. "And if that's Bill Kienzle, I must be . . . Javan."

I don't know how long it would've taken me to realize who I was had I been in bed alone.

In addition to our Caribbean cruise and our trips to Ireland, Bill's book tours took us to a variety of places. These included London, where we met with English publishers. British editions of

Bill's first three books were published by Hodder & Stoughton; several subsequent ones were picked up by Severn House.

We enjoyed London, primarily for its historical aspects. Both of us, for different reasons, were particularly eager to visit the Tower of London.

One of my ancestors, Sir Richard Lowther, had escorted Mary, Queen of Scots, on her fateful journey from Scotland to London. Accused of being implicated in the plot to put Mary on the throne in place of Elizabeth I, Richard Lowther was thrown into the Tower. At that time, he had thirteen children. As heads rolled around him, he somehow managed to prove his innocence, and after a lengthy imprisonment was eventually released. He returned home to father his fourteenth child—my umpteenth-great-grandfather. Had Richard Lowther been executed, you would not be reading this book.

For Bill, the Tower was where St. Thomas More had spent the last days before his beheading at the order of Henry VIII. In the courtyard, as the Royal Warder was giving us a capsule history of the edifice, Bill asked if we could see St. Thomas More's quarters.

"Here," the warder said quietly but firmly, "we refer to him as *Sir* Thomas More."

"What," Bill later commented, "the English kill a saint?!"

An extension to one of our Irish trips brought us to Scotland. We spent a few days in Glasgow with Menzies Mc Killop, with whom we had corresponded since his visit to the Guthrie many years before. Menzies's hospitality once more bore out the Celtic "hundred thousand welcomes." In addition to showing us around Glasgow, he hosted us to a day in Edinburgh. A wet day—rain came down as if it would never have another chance to fall. Undeterred, we visited Holyrood House, the Castle, and the art museum, where we sat and gazed at Gainsborough's *The Honorable Mrs. Graham*.

We took the train to Aberdeen, where we had reserved a car for the forty-mile drive to Ballater. We would be staying at

Craigendarrach, a time-share resort on the River Dee. Aberdeen is known as the Rose City and it lived up to that sobriquet. Though it was almost November, each and every spot of earth bore blooming shrubs.

We spent the next week traveling through the Highlands. There are no words to do justice to the breathtaking beauty of Scotland's Highlands. We were grateful that we had the opportunity to enjoy them. We pitied all those who would never have that opportunity.

The day before our scheduled departure, we woke to an unexpected blizzard. The main road from the Highlands to Glasgow goes through a narrow pass at Glenties. During winter, it is not unusual for the pass to be snowed in. The resort phoned Glenties. The road was still open, but we would have to leave immediately.

Bill drove and I prayed. We made it through Glenties amidst the swirling snow. Bill's foot never left the brake on the downgrade.

Glasgow itself was still blessed with beautiful autumn sunshine. We drove out to Loch Lomond, where we strolled the lakeside gardens, then boarded a sightseeing steamer.

It was windy on the Loch, but I went topside to enjoy the view. When I came back down, I discovered Bill sitting all alone in the public cabin, singing—at the top of his lungs—"'Oh, you take the high road and I'll take the low road . . .'" He figured—correctly—that the sound of the engine would cover the sound of his voice.

It was my idea to later add this experience to Bill's last book, wherein Father Koesler recalls his visit to Loch Lomond.

Over the years, we visited most of the major cities of the United States. Each had something to recommend it. Three of our favorites were very different.

Boston is so full of history that one can almost feel it oozing from the bricks. It is difficult to walk the streets without thinking, "One if by land and two if by sea . . ."

San Francisco is for people in love. For Bill and me, the honeymoon never ended. Often, over the years, we recalled sitting in the Top of the Mark, watching the fog roll in over the Golden Gate

Bridge. A waitress bounced up to take our order. "Hel*lo*, happy people," she chirped. *Pace* Tony Bennett, we didn't leave our hearts in San Francisco; we brought the memory of San Francisco home with us.

We felt that it was literally impossible not to get a good meal in San Francisco—or in New Orleans. No matter whether one dined at a top restaurant, or a hole-in-the-wall, the food was superb.

Before brunching at Commander's Palace, we strolled the restaurant's beautiful gardens. Suddenly, a wolf whistle split the air. I whirled. If a bird can register amusement, the mynah bird in a nearby tree did. I guess he got his kicks from whistling at passing females.

It was in New Orleans that I first ate Oysters Rockefeller. The restaurant was ancient, and so was our waiter. The restaurant had a tradition, which seemed to be sometimes observed and sometimes not. When a diner ordered a flambé dish, the lights were dimmed and the waiter served the dish to the accompaniment of a French folk song.

I ordered cherries jubilee, and we got the whole treatment: the lights dimmed, the cherries flamed, and our creaky waiter stood by our table and, in his high cracked voice, offered the chanson.

Shortly thereafter, a middle-aged couple at a nearby table also ordered cherries jubilee. Their tall, youthful waiter presented the dish, but without the accompaniment. The male member of the couple expostulated. "Aren't you going to sing to us?"

The rangy waiter halted, looked thoughtful, then shook his head. "All I know is the Notre Dame Fight Song," he said finally.

Occasionally, we exchanged our Irish time-share week for a week elsewhere: Traverse City, French Lick—and Collingwood, Ontario, where we visited Big Chute, a marvelous lift that carries boats from the Lake Superior level up to the inland canal level. It is a site that is definitely worth the detour.

Bill and I always enjoyed Canada. Toronto particularly holds a special place in my heart. It was in Toronto that I first received Communion—from a Jesuit, no less. And it was in Toronto that Bill once again proved his gallantry.

We had gone to a performance of *Aida*. I was wearing a new pair of high-heeled shoes. By the second act, my feet were so sore that I slipped out of my shoes. By the time Radames and Aida ran out of breath in their underground tomb, my feet had swelled to the point where I could not get my shoes on.

Walking barefoot was never a problem for me. I exited the theater carrying my shoes. As we stood waiting for the light to change, the street-cleaning truck went by, scrubbers awash, spurting water all over not only the street but the curb as well. Without shoes, my feet were going to get *soaked*.

Bill didn't hesitate. He scooped me up in his arms and, ignoring the amused glances of passersby, carried me and my shoes back to the hotel.

In later years, we joined the Nomads, and traveled with the group to Quebec City, one of the continent's wonders. It is incomparably situated atop a bluff overlooking the St. Lawrence. Like Aberdeen, every spare spot of earth is covered with flowers. And unlike Paris or the French Caribbean, the Gallic residents of Quebec City could give the Celts a run for their money when it comes to hospitality and helpfulness.

We attended Mass, which was in French. And just as the Irish Mass had charmed Bill, the French Mass did likewise.

I tried to utilize my high school French whenever possible. The Québecois welcomed my attempts. This in spite of the fact that, in the famous phrase, I speak French *comme une vache Espagnole* [like a Spanish cow]. I came across only two Québecois who did not speak English. One, a gardener outside one of the museums, was extremely helpful. It was he who told me of a section of the museum that few people visit because they don't know about it. When I didn't understand all his directions, he acted out the words for me, in a form of charade.

When I told our waitress at dinner that my husband did not understand French, she laughed and said, "Oh, I'll teach him." It was fun to hear the two of them "conversing." It went something like:

"I giv-ay *vous le menu*."

323 ❖ JUDGED BY LOVE

"Oui. Merci beaucoup."

"Vous are *très* welcome."

"Can . . . will *vous* bring-ay *moi* some *cafe?"*

"Bien sur, Monsieur."

"Merci beaucoup."

"Maintenant—now, 'ere is *vôtre* beel. I giv-ay *vous* the beel. *Vous* giv-ay *moi* le money."

"Oui."

Travel is definitely educating. After all, unless we had visited a Kansas restaurant that offered Prairie Oysters how would we ever have discovered that the phrase is a euphemism for calf testes?

In Ius Voco Spurius [Sue the Bastards].

—LATIN SAYING

ONE OF BILL'S FAVORITE SITCOMS was *Barney Miller.* From time to time he wondered aloud why there couldn't be a TV series about a parish based on a similar premise. Eventually, after getting together with some priest buddies who were pastors, he worked out a pilot, fleshed out some characters, and submitted it to Jeanne Findlater at WXYZ-TV, the local ABC affiliate.

Jeanne submitted the project to ABC-TV in Hollywood. They turned it down.

A few years later, we were dumbfounded when ABC-TV with a great deal of hoopla touted their new series about a parish that sounded suspiciously similar to Bill's project.

Bill was not only angry; he was sick at heart. But not for the reasons one might have supposed.

When we returned to Detroit from our five-year wilderness sojourn, Bill discovered that the inner city priests were not taking their salaries; rather, they were turning the money over to those in need. They used their salaries to feed, clothe, and shelter the poor of their parishes. In other words, they were doing as Jesus had directed when he said, "Feed my sheep."

The priests themselves were living abstemiously, getting by on a pittance. Some were driving on bald tires. Others were surviving on hot dogs and beans. Many wore threadbare clericals.

Some of these men were Bill's classmates . . . members of the Class the Stars Fell On. Bill, whose desire it had been to be assigned to the inner city, felt that these men were on the front lines in the battle against poverty. Bill enlisted the aid of his buddy Father Grandpre, and they set up the Core City Parish Fund.

Bill donated any money he received from his public appearances to this fund. When he addressed various groups, he mentioned the work of the Core City priests. As a result, occasionally one or more of his listeners would contribute to the fund.

As the years passed, there were many times, particularly if a public appearance required a long drive or an overnight stay, when Bill would have preferred to stay home. But, feeling that God had given him this means of making a contribution, he accepted all invitations that offered an honorarium that he could pass on to the Core City. Public appearances can be very draining, especially if they involve one-on-one conversations with crowds of people. Though Bill enjoyed meeting the public, I have, on occasion, seen him gray with exhaustion during a long trip that involved several speeches, and/or autographings. But he always fulfilled these obligations uncomplainingly, holding before himself the image of the dollars that would flow into the Core City Fund as a result.

If the books were selling well enough, Bill wrote an additional check to the fund, which was overseen by Father Grandpre. Annually, just before Christmas, Father Grandpre divided among some nine or ten inner-city priests whatever money had accumulated in the fund during the year.

The proviso of course was that Bill's connection with the fund remain anonymous. Father Grandpre withstood repeated grilling from the recipients, but never gave Bill away.

Bill hoped his projected TV series would not only be accepted, but that it would be a success so that he would be able to give the proceeds from such a series to the inner-city priests, whose flocks needed help so desperately.

It was for this reason, and this reason alone that he went to court in an attempt to force ABC-TV to acknowledge that they had stolen his idea for the series.

Like *The Rosary Murders* contretemps, the resultant events could make up an entire book. Suffice to say that the judge threw the case out of court, stating, "There's nothing new under the sun."

Sadly, the controversial TV series was eventually cancelled—to our sorrow, as both Bill and I felt that it was a realistic and excellent depiction of inner-city parish life.

PART

8

Humor is one of God's most marvelous gifts . . . Humor reveals the roses and hides the thorns. Humor makes our heavy burdens light and smooths the rough spots in our pathways.

—SAM ERVIN

BILL'S FRIENDS WHO HAD KNOWN HIM as Father Kienzle were pleased that he had found marital happiness. "Soulmates," they said of us.

Many times over the years, Bill and I marveled over our being brought together. We felt it had to be God's will. Otherwise, how could a religiously ignorant farm girl from New Jersey and a pious, dedicated priest from Michigan have met—much less established a happy combined life?

I often said that if I had tried to create a husband for myself, I couldn't have done half as good a job as God had done in giving me Bill. As the years went on, I began to worry. His whole life seemed wrapped up in me. I worried about what would become of him if something happened to me. At one period, I had mentioned it to a stress counselor. "Javan, did you ever stop to think that where, in the past, Bill ministered to a flock, he is now ministering to just one: you. Everything in him that previously focused on helping so many people in so many different ways, has been narrowed like a laser beam to focus on you."

She was undoubtedly right. I found myself wondering whether this wasn't one of the reasons for priestly celibacy. I know that many married clergymen* of other faiths carry on their vocation successfully. Yet most Catholics consider their priests "above" other clergymen. One of the reasons they do is that they are aware of what their priests have given up for their vocation.

As more and more of Bill's friends and former parishioners and classmates passed on, I tried to get Bill involved in things that would give him an outside interest if something were to happen to me. After all, it was I who had had a lifetime of illness, I who was most apt to go first. He was the one who was healthy—almost sinfully so. His annual medical checkups left his physician in a dilemma: There was so little wrong with him that the clinic had to be creative in filling out the medical forms so that the insurer would cover the tests.

Bill's father had died as the result of a bowel obstruction. Annual colonoscopies revealed Bill had intestinal polyps. An early one was so huge that it could not be removed all at once; part of it was excised, the wound allowed to heal, and then the other half removed. But with each succeeding year, thanks to an excellent diet and the proper vitamin-mineral supplements, the incidence of polyps grew fewer and their size much smaller. To the degree that after his last colonoscopy, the doctor informed him that the next exam could be scheduled for two years, rather than annually.

Bill, remembering his father, was loath to go that distance, Finally, under gentle prodding from me and the doctor, he agreed to an eighteen-month hiatus.

Bill as a patient was what might be termed a card. His quirky sense of humor occasionally got him in trouble. Early on, as he was being prepped for a comparatively minor surgical procedure, the doctor appeared at Father Kienzle's head to answer any last-minute questions. He informed Father that the procedure required only a local anesthetic. The doctor, a physician from the Orient, went on to introduce himself: "I'm Dr. Wong."

---

* I know there are successful married clergywomen as well. It's just that "clergypersons" grates on my ear.

"Is that wight?" the patient responded. Dr. Wong obviously did not appreciate the patient's wit; a general anesthetic put him beyond any further punning for the duration. Father Kienzle came to in the recovery room. A nurse was bending over him. "What is your name?" she asked.

The irrepressible patient replied, "My name José Jimenez." The nurse walked away. Father heard her say to another nurse, "He doesn't know his name yet." As a result, he was sentenced to an extra hour in recovery mode.

It is said that the personality exhibited by individuals who have had too much to drink is their basic personality. Since Bill was highly self-disciplined, and not given to extremes, I saw him tipsy only once. There was no change in him, only an intensification of his sweetness, lovingness, and humor.

It is said that likewise, the personality exhibited by individuals coming out of anesthesia is their basic personality. I don't know whether this is so. All I know is that Bill was almost hysterically funny when coming out of anesthesia.

The first time I was aware of this was immediately after his first colonoscopy. The drug used for this procedure is not a heavy anesthetic, rather more of a relaxant; some people remain drowsily awake during the procedure. Bill was one who was semi-somnolent. As he was being wheeled out of the procedure room, I could see his lips moving. I bent down close to his head and listened. He was singing, "Merrily we roll along, roll along, roll along . . ."

I recall little he said during the post-procedure period, except that at one point he kept calling his nurse, "Kemosabe." When Dr. Tootla came around to explain whatever he had done, Bill asked questions. Dr. Tootla answered Bill's questions, but told me, "He won't remember any of this." True. Nor did Bill remember telling the doctor, "You are a lovely man." Actually, Bill remembered nothing he had said.

❧❀❧

One never knew what form Bill's humor would take. I don't think he himself knew; his active brain merely responded to a given situation.

During a meeting with members of the accounting firm that was engaged to help us navigate the myriad mazes of royalties, it was suggested that Bill and I should incorporate for tax purposes. Agreed. When asked to pick a name for the corporation, Bill responded, "GOPITS*." All present—including me—looked quizzical. GOPITS, Bill explained, was an acronym for Great Offertory Procession in the Sky—where, he assured us, we would all be going eventually.

One of the button-down accountants leaned over and tapped my arm. "I don't think he's taking this with the proper degree of seriousness," he said—seriously.

When it came time to have business stationery imprinted for GOPITS, Bill, undoubtedly thinking of the entertainment media knaves, chose the spurious Latin phrase, *Illegitimi non carborundum*, a version of "Don't let the bastards grind you down."

Christianity has not been tried and found wanting; it has been found difficult and not been tried.

—G. K. CHESTERTON

I HAD RECENTLY FINISHED READING A BOOK about the golden age in Spain. It was an era when the humanistic concepts of the Koran held sway. As a result, the Jews, Muslims, and Christians coexisted in peace and harmony. Bill and I had been discussing this with Dr.

---

* I later discovered that this acronym was the brainchild of Ramona Kraemer, the lovely lady who had once proclaimed that the women of St. Anselm's were not domestics.

Tootla, who invited us to his mosque for the celebration of the breaking of the Fast of Ramadan.

It was to be an ecumenical gathering, since it was one of the unusual periods when Ramadan, Christmas, and Hanukkah juxtapose.

It was a snowy, slushy day. Bill dropped me at the mosque entrance, and went to park the car. I was wearing a dark, mid-calf length jumper and had a scarf over my head. As I entered the mosque and looked around, uncertain how to proceed, several people approached me in succession, offering their hands in greeting, and directing me toward the gathering hall. I did not feel out of place; rather I felt supremely welcome, although I knew none of those present, as Dr. Tootla had not yet arrived.

The evening was a warming experience. The buffet was delicious. The presentation by three speakers—the Imam, Father John West (the archdiocese's ecumenical representative), and a woman rabbi—was fascinating. A question-and-answer session followed. I was particularly impressed by Father West's ability to consistently connect the common ancestry of the three religions.

I also found noteworthy the beauty and the poise of the Islamic women. All present were invited to participate in the separate-but-equal prayers, which were held in another part of the mosque. Bill went along with the men, but I stayed at the table with our host's wife, an American of non-Islamic background. I was having some trouble with my scarf. I asked her if there was some secret to keeping it on my head. "Use a long scarf," she advised.

My memory of that evening, in an odd way, brings to mind the validity of Bill's struggle with Canon Law. If one were to follow the precepts of Moses, Jesus, and Muhammad, as set forth in the Torah, the Bible, and the Koran, undoubtedly peace and harmony would have a much better chance of prevailing. Instead, we have the Talmud, Canon Law, and Shariah—the manmade rules that are used as weapons by fundamentalists, rules that have come to supersede—in some cases even abrogate—the Commandments, Jesus's law of love, and the Golden Rule.

If we had purely and lovingly followed the Torah, the Bible, and the Koran, instead of burning people at the stake, beheading them, and blowing them up we could well have been on our way to establishing another Eden. Instead, we have become a three-headed hydra, too often spewing poisonous hate at each other.

And He Who sits in Heaven weeps.

As the vet said when it was over, the trouble with dogs is that we outlive them.

—UNKNOWN

LADY WAS MY RIVAL as head of the Bill Kienzle fan club. She adored Bill. If her eyes had been arms they would have embraced him every time she looked at him. When the two went out for walks, Lady was in her element. The two tall creatures seemed made for each other.

Bill missed Chappie, but where both dogs had held a spot in his heart, now Lady inhabited that spot totally. Whenever she fell ill, the ride to the vet's was a silent one. I could tell that Bill was mentally girding himself for bad news. The Heartbreak Dogs had a normal life span of some seven years. Lady was now far past that span. But on one occasion, when Dr. Feld hooked her up for an EKG whose reading went via phone to a canine cardiologist in New York City, the specialist was amazed at the strength and consistency of Lady's heartbeat; he couldn't believe this was a thirteen-year-old Irish wolfhound. Dr. Feld dubbed her the Miracle Dog.

All in all, she was fairly healthy. But any time she fell under the weather was cause for concern. One Halloween she started acting strange. She moved her jaws oddly and displayed her teeth in an almost constant rictus grin. She seemed not herself. We phoned the vet. Dr. Feld was out of town, but his partner, Dr. Sayles, asked a pertinent question. "Has she been eating anything unusual?"

I almost laughed. Bill, with his Teutonic routine, always fed Lady the same thing at the same time, without deviation. No, she hadn't eaten anything unusual. Off we went to the clinic. Dr. Sayles examined Lady and took some blood for testing. The only thing that showed up was a slight liver problem. Dr. Sayles advised us to keep an eye on her and to call him if we noticed other symptoms.

That evening I went to the étagère near our front door to ready the donations for the Halloween Trick-or-Treaters. Dr. Sayles had been prescient: A pound of chewy orange-and-black candy had disappeared. Even though it had been on a high shelf, Lady had managed to reach it. That explained the odd jaw movements and the rictus grin: she had been trying to dislodge the caramel from her back teeth.

The aftermath was a trail of orange-and-black paper-wrapped stools in the wake of Lady's post-Halloween excursion. I guess that was her form of trick-or-treat.

Eventually, Lady developed gastroenteritis. Dr. Feld prescribed an antifungal pill, and an even stricter diet regime. Where previously Lady had been fed once a day, she now would be fed twice daily, the same time every day, and with her food at room temperature. Her intestines, which had received an early traumatization from the worm infestation of her youthful days, must now be coddled.

Coddling was second nature to Bill. He had always been particular about the dogs' feeding. When daylight saving time went into effect in the spring and reverted in the fall, the dogs' feeding times were always adjusted in fifteen-minute increments over a period of four days. After all, Bill said, Chappie's stomach knew it was feeding time; she wouldn't understand having to wait another hour.

Our social life was scheduled around the dogs. No matter where we were, one of us was always home at five to feed them. In earlier years, when we traveled, a dog-sitter stayed at the house during our absence. But after one trip, when we came home to find that not only had Lady not eaten the past few days, but had licked herself sore, we decided to forgo lengthy travel for the nonce.

Late one April, Bill had a public appearance before a library group at a motel in Monroe, Michigan, some forty miles away. The date had been set months before. As we started out, the weather was very iffy, with the good possibility of heavy snow. By the conclusion of Bill's speech, the snow had turned into a blizzard. Our hosts offered us a motel room.

We had left our garage door open, so the dogs would be able to get outside during our absence. The garage was quite comfortable. There was a large carpeted area behind a wide, heavy storage cabinet, so they would be protected from the wind. Chappie, of course, with her husky heritage, reveled in cold weather. Sometimes I would see her lying on her belly on the ice-covered garage apron. Lady had the wolfhound's thick, rough coat. Had we spent the night in Monroe, the dogs would've been fine.

However, Bill felt that they knew we were due home and that they would worry, possibly even feel deserted and fear that we weren't coming back. So we started for home.

As I write this, I feel my shoulders tense in memory. It was a major blizzard. Vision was practically nil. We inched along the Interstate, praying that we would not be rear-ended by a semi. From time to time, we could see off to our right another in a series of semis that had skidded off the highway, each lying on its side like roadkill.

Bill drove—or rather steered the car—as I leaned forward, shoulders hunched, peering through the curtain of snow, trying to guide him. It was with extreme relief that we reached the civilization of Telegraph Road—streetlights, gas stations, restaurants.

The dogs were pleased to see us. They could have had no comprehension of what we had gone through to make sure that they weren't left alone to worry that night.

On another occasion, we attended a wedding. It was an ecumenical ceremony, presided over by a Syrian Orthodox priest and Bill's priest-buddy, Father Louis Grandpre. The service was lengthy. We sat near the back of the church so that Bill could leave unobtrusively in order to go home and give Lady her required 5 P.M. feeding. After which, he returned to the church for the remainder of the ceremony.

Between the medication and the diet regimen, Lady's health stabilized. But it became increasingly obvious that it was just a matter of time. Just as we had with Chappie, we wanted to keep Lady with us as long as she was comfortable and had some quality of life.

One morning, Bill and I looked at each other and both knew this was the Day. Lady had slowed down considerably; her appetite was almost nil; there was no joy in her eyes. We phoned Dr. Sayles, and prepared to take Lady on her last journey. Before we assisted her into the car, we took her picture. There she stood, as if posing for a statue.

I remembered the first time she had hopped up on the back seat, sitting there like a queen. Now she lay on the backseat with her head in my lap—still a queen, but an old, tired one.

Lady had always lived up to her name. Unlike many dogs, she never licked. She would come close, sniff delicately, but never lick. Now, as if reassuring me, she weakly licked my hand. It was as if she were saying, "It's all right. I know it's time. Don't worry. It's all right."

Dr. Sayles and the staff were blessedly supportive. Bill sat on the floor and held Lady's head in his hands. I sat next to her and petted her. And then it was over. Our Miracle Dog had lived to thirteen and three-quarters years—almost double her allotted span.

In later years I often thought that it was mutual devotion that had kept her alive—her devotion to Bill, and Bill's devotion to her.

Chapp—a creature of the outdoors—had been buried behind our previous house. We decided that Lady, who was never far from Bill's side, would be cremated and her ashes kept with us. From that time on, whenever we adjourned to the basement during a tornado alert, Bill made sure to carry Lady's ashes down the stairs with us, so that no matter what happened, we would all be together.

Each Palm Sunday Bill brought home a new supply of palms, which he placed strategically around the house, and even in our car. One day I asked him about that. He replied that the palms were a protection against tornados. Since he had always been quite capable of making up stories—which I always fell for—I didn't know whether I was having my leg pulled. When I questioned the premise, he smiled and said, "Have we ever been hit by a tornado?"

No, we never had. But I couldn't help thinking of the old East Indian prayer, "Keep this house safe from tigers." We'd never been bothered with tigers either.

He who loves animals as well as people doubles his life's grief time.

—PEARL SWIGGUM

WE WERE NOW, for the first time in twelve years, dogless.

Having grown up on a farm, I was accustomed to losing animals. If a dog or a cat died or had to be put down, it was always replaced with another. But each death left a scar on my heart. I can remember the cat that woke me, giving birth under the blankets at my feet. I remember when she, and her kittens, died in convulsions from feline enteritis. We had to disinfect all the outbuildings and wait six months to be certain that no more germs remained.

To this day I can tell you the names of every one of our farm dogs, including the one who took on a mountain lion when it made off with a neighbor's puppy. I was a baby at the time, but when I grew older and asked why part of Gwennie's tongue was missing, I was told the story. Gwennie later developed a painful cancer. In those days if a dog had to be put down, it would be shot. As for cats, most farmers usually drowned them. When our cats had to be euthanized, they were put in a covered barrel with a rag soaked in chloroform, which was then available without prescription from country druggists.

But Mother had read that larger animals like dogs found the chloroform method very fearful. Gwennie had come to Mother as a stray before her marriage. She did not want to subject Gwennie to such a fate. She called the state police, who sent out a trooper.

Mother chained Gwennie in the backyard. My sister and I didn't know why, but we were sent off to a neighbor's house. As we were walking down the road, we heard shots. It took the trooper, whose marksmanship left much to be desired, three bullets to still the mighty heart of the chained animal. Mother wept for years at the memory.

When Mike was young, Rick and I had gotten an Airedale pup for him. Mike and Cindy were a twosome. When Cindy developed cancer, the vet treated her with palliative and life-prolonging drugs. One day Mike came home from parochial school to announce, "Sister said that animals don't have souls, so Cindy isn't going to heaven." He was more than disturbed; he was perturbed.

I phoned Father Kienzle, inadvertently waking him from a mid-afternoon nap. I posed Mike's problem. Groggily but firmly Father said, "You tell Mike that if he needs Cindy for him to be happy in heaven, she'll be there."

Then I had to try to diplomatically explain to Mike why what "Sister said" was *not* so, and what Father Kienzle had said *was* so. It was not the first, nor would it be the last time, "the experts were in dispute."

When it grew time for the inevitable, Rick and Mike took Cindy on her last ride to the vet's. Mike sat in the waiting room while Rick and Cindy disappeared through the office door. When some minutes later, Rick came out alone, Mike—who since baby-hood had *never* cried—burst into tears. On the way home, he con-fessed that all along he had been praying for Cindy to live. Now that his prayer had not been answered, he gave up on God.

We decided to replace Cindy. We left the choice up to Mike. Not only did he get another Airedale pup, he named her Cindy II. Eventually, she too had to be euthanized.

Many years later, as a young man, Mike got a third Airedale pup. She disappeared from the backyard—undoubtedly stolen, as she had been tied up with the gate closed. She was never found.

Sadly, these experiences only intensified Mike's disbelief in God. But not in pets. Over the years, he has rescued and adopted a whole series of stray cats, and now cares for an additional bunch of feral felines. He even made medical history when he saved the life of a stray that was suffering from FIPS.* Mike treated the cat with some sort of garlic nostrum. It survived and was written up in a veterinarian magazine. Unfortunately, when he used the same nostrum on another similarly sick cat, it died. It took Mike a while to track down the cause. He discovered that the company that made the garlic mixture had since added alcohol to it, which had had an adverse effect. Furious, Mike went on a crusade, calling the company to account. I don't know whether they ignored his anger, or whether they have since reinstated their previous formula.

Though I was still sorrowing over the loss of Lady, I was ready to take on another dog. But Bill was crushed. First Chappie, now Lady. I had a feeling that the deaths of so many he cared for—whether human or four-legged—had worn him down, and Lady was the final straw. He steadfastly refused to consider getting another dog.

Mike knew how beloved Chapp and Lady had been. He phoned to ask, "Will you be getting another dog?"

When I explained that Bill just couldn't bear to be hurt any more, Mike—who had experienced so much hurt in the loss of his own pets—said, "But, Mother, they give so much love."

I was glad that although he no longer believed in God, he still believed in love.

When I told Bill what Mike had said, he looked thoughtful. Then he said, "I can't go through the pain of losing another dog. Maybe when we're in our mid-seventies, we'll get a small dog that we can be sure will outlive us."

As the months went by, Bill and I continued to experience the pull to be home at 5 P.M., which had been the dogs' regular feeding time. To this day, if I am away from home at 5 P.M., I am still aware of that pull, somewhat like the lunar pulling of the tides.

---

* Feline Infectious Peritonitis.

Hear our humble prayer, O God, for our friends the animals. Especially for animals who are suffering; for any that are hunted or lost or deserted or frightened or hungry; for all that must be put to death. We entreat for them all thy mercy and pity. And for those who deal with them, we ask a heart of compassion, gentle and kindly words. Make us true friends of the animals and so to share the blessings of the merciful.

—ALBERT SCHWEITZER

WHENEVER I LEFT THE HOUSE, as I drove off, Bill always said the same prayer. It was along the lines of, "Please don't let her find any animals in trouble."

It's an odd phenomenon, but well-adjusted people seem to attract maladjusted people. People with needs see people whose lives seem to be running smoothly and think, "If I can attach myself to that circle, my life will run smoothly too." There are also people who seem to attract animals in trouble. I seemed to be a magnet for animals who needed help. Or maybe they were a magnet for me.

No matter where Bill went, when he said, "I'll be home at such and such," you could set the clock by him. Unfortunately, it was not the same with me. I would set out with the best of intentions, and before you could say ASPCA, there I was, confronted by an injured dog, a stray cat, a staggering raccoon, a lost duckling.

One day, I held up traffic on a main road to rescue a huge snapping turtle whose shell had been lacerated by a passing vehicle. I've seen snapping turtles in action; I didn't want to lose a finger. I got a box and a shovel out of the trunk and, assisted by another Good Samaritan, was finally able to push the turtle into the box and deposit it alongside a nearby lake.

Not once did any of the waiting drivers blow a horn or complain. They just sat there watching the little slice of life unfold, and then proceeded on their way. When I returned from my errand, I looked for the turtle, but it had undoubtedly gone back to the muck whence it had come. I hoped the muck was healing.

When I got home, Bill said, "I can never figure out why it takes you so long to do one errand."

"Guess," I said.

He shook his head. "St. Javan of Assisi was at it again."

Yup.

We had SLOW: DUCK CROSSING signs made to protect a mallard family that inhabited our lake for half of every day, but for some reason insisted upon crossing the busy street for the other half of the day.

One weekend, I picked up a Doberman mix that was lying in the road. It didn't seem to be injured, but since this was when we still had our two dogs, I couldn't take it home. I threw myself—and the dog—on the mercy of our ever-helpful vet. He would keep the dog until the animal rescue league opened the following Monday.

The next week I did a fill-in column for a vacationing Bob Talbert. I mentioned the dog and the helpful vet.

A woman in another part of the state read the column. She recalled that her best friend, whom she had lost track of years ago, had had a son who wanted to be a vet when he grew up. She phoned Dr. Feld. "Are you ———'s son?"

Shortly thereafter, she flew to Florida for a reunion with her old friend whom she hadn't seen in years.

Ripples.

Nor did I even have to leave the house.

One morning I took some clothes to the basement to put in the washer. As I walked through the laundry room, I thought, "Oh, a kitten is lying on Bill's T-shirt." A few seconds later, I stopped and did a double-take worthy of Cary Grant. *We didn't have any kittens.*

A baby raccoon was curled atop the pile of soiled clothes.

The mystery was solved when Animal Control came out and discovered several more raccoon babies in our attic. No mother in sight. She had probably been killed by a car during the night, and the hungry baby had crawled down in search of food.

But just in case the mother might still return in search of her babies, we left them in the attic, along with some humane cage-traps. Hourly that day, I clambered up into the attic, feeding the little ones with an eyedropper.

Next morning, every cage was full—but the occupants were all males. No mother in sight. Animal control took off with the whole crew, leaving some additional cage-traps. When they returned next day, the traps were full—again with males.

I asked about the babies. "Oh, we picked up a mother raccoon in another area, so we gave the babies to her, and she's feeding them." It might have been a kind white lie; I was grateful to take it at face value.

Each summer, our patio was visited by critters. Occasionally, it got a bit hairy when the skunks stopped by, as there was nothing between us and them but a screen door. But they behaved themselves and we never suffered for their presence—except once, when Lady was still with us.

I had taken her out for her before-bedtime walk. Suddenly, she took off into the open yard next door, and disappeared under our neighbor's deck. The next thing I knew, she emerged and came barreling toward me. As she reached me, I smelled a horrid odor as if something were burning.

Our farm dogs had frequently tussled with skunks, but I had never smelled anything like this. I thought Lady had gotten into some sort of chemical. We dumped her into the car and took off for the all-night emergency clinic, which, fortunately, was only a mile away.

The vet on duty was almost apoplectic when I brought Lady in. "Get her out of here!" he shouted. I did. He then came outside and handed me a bottle of some sort of smell-riddance liquid.

We took Lady home and started the cleaning process. Yuck! The car stank, we stank, and Lady *stank*. Fortunately, only one side of her head was affected. I shudder to think what we would have gone through had her body been sprayed. As it was, we had our hands full.

We tried tomato juice, detergent, and lots of water. A very unhappy Lady spent that night in the garage.

Next morning, I called every animal agency I could find. I even called the Detroit Zoo. Nobody had any suggestions other than tomato juice. Finally I phoned Mary Marcantonio at Police Headquarters. Mary had a Labrador retriever; maybe she knew something we didn't.

When I told her the problem, she said, "Let me check with the Indiana farm boy." A minute or so later she came back on the line. "Use a mixture of baking soda and milk, and then wash that off with water. You may have to do it several times."

"Who is the 'Indiana farm boy'?" I asked.

She laughed. "Deputy Chief Bannon. He grew up on a farm in Indiana."

Mary further suggested putting open bags of charcoal in the car and anywhere else that the smell was lingering.

Both suggestions worked. Lady, seemingly none the worse, was able to rejoin us in the house. We did keep the charcoal in the car for a l-o-n-g time before the smell finally dissipated.

Among the visitors to our patio was a huge feral tomcat. He was extremely skittish; I couldn't get anywhere near him. For over six months, I put out food every day, sat at the other end of the patio while he ate, and talked to him quietly. As winter approached, I worried more and more about him. I set out a huge heavy plastic recycling bin so that he could eat protected from the elements. But he always disappeared before dark.

One evening, I was able to slap a cover on the bin and capture him. He went ballistic. His claws protruded through the side holes, and his yowls set one's hair on end. We put the bin in the car and carted him off to Dr. Feld.

Sadly, a test showed that he had feline AIDS and would have to be euthanized. I was miserable. This animal had trusted me enough to let himself be captured, and now I was going to have him put down. I wept as Dr. Feld assured me it was the kindest thing to do. "He would have died a horrible death," he said.

No wonder Bill prayed that I wouldn't come across any animals in trouble. God didn't always answer that prayer.

Please don't give me any more books where the dog dies.

—Nine-year-old voracious reader to his grandmother

I was heading along Eight Mile Road, the boulevard that is the demarcation between Detroit and its northern suburbs. Eight Mile Road was notorious to area residents: Those accustomed to Detroit Mayor Coleman Young's proclivity for four- and twelve-letter words had flinched as the mayor, in an inaugural speech, addressed Motor City malefactors with, "All you muggers,* hit Eight Mile Road."

It was a cold, windy day; sleetlike snowflakes hit the windshield with increasing ferocity. I was en route to a medical appointment that had taken a long time to get and was a long distance away.

As I approached a traffic light, I noticed in the median a small dog curled up against the cold. When the light changed I circled the island, trying to ascertain if the animal was injured. I stopped the car and walked toward the dog, speaking in a low voice that I hoped was reassuring.

Repeatedly, the dog looked alternately at me and then into the distance, as if expecting someone—someone who was supposed to return and pick her up from the spot where she had been dumped. As I neared her, she stood, backed up, and bared her teeth. Using my folded coat as a shield, I tried to get closer. She continued to retreat, snarling.

I opened the front and rear doors of my car and walked a short distance away. After some hesitation, she clambered up into the driver's seat.

She continued to alternately bare her teeth and bark as I approached the car. I inched closer. She retreated to the passenger seat. Still using my coat as a buffer, I slowly slid into the driver's seat and carefully put the car in gear.

---

* To this day, there are those who insist that Mayor Young said "mothers," rather than "muggers."

As we entered traffic, she shook herself, giving me and the car's interior a muddy shower. Obviously she had been out in the sleet for some time. She seemed grateful for the warmth from the heater and gradually settled down, although she whimpered every so often. She didn't seem able to get comfortable. I continued to speak quietly to her, and she now accepted my touch.

When I stopped for a light, I ran my hand over her body to check for injuries. She was skin and bones. She winced as I came to a huge swelling and a raw jagged wound.

I stopped at two veterinary clinics but neither could locate a convenient animal shelter. Time was getting short. Mercifully, the second clinic agreed to keep her while I kept my appointment.

When I returned to pick her up I knew there was only one place to take her: Our vets had been so good over the years in caring for stray and injured animals. They did not fail me now. Their examination, X rays, and tests told a story of starvation, mutilation by other animals, and some sort of BB or bullet lodged in her. Her eyes and ears were infected; her heart was enlarged; her spine was arthritic, and there were growths in the abdominal/lung area. Her feces consisted of bones—evidence that without decent food she had barely survived by scavenging.

Even with the very best of care, her life expectancy was only a very few months—and wretchedly agonizing months at that.

There was only one thing to do. I held her as Dr. Chang inserted the merciful needle. She was out of her misery. I wept. She had been dumped along the highway to survive on her own. She had tried. And she had kept coming back to where she had been dropped—waiting, waiting, waiting for the person whom she thought cared enough about her to return.

I couldn't let her death pass unnoticed. I wrote her story.

It seemed so flat. Somehow I wasn't getting my point across. I asked for Bill's help.

"You've written it like a diary entry," he said, after reading it. He scribbled a couple of sentences. "Here . . . try this."

Bill's additions altered my account from a mere chronology; it was now a message to the dog's one-time owner—the master the pitiful creature had been waiting for when I came upon her. I added a couple of paragraphs and sent the account to the *Free Press*.

It was published under the heading, SEE SPOT DIE. I received many letters and contributions in response to that account. It had been my story—but it was Bill's suggestion that made it work.

He had added an opening sentence, and the same words in closing: "I had your dog put to sleep the other day. You gave me little alternative."

It was obvious who the writer in the family was. I was the live-in editor.

One of the letters I received in response to "See Spot Die" was from Wendy Lewis.

When Wendy was seven years old, she saw a pet shop burn down. She vowed then and there to devote her life to saving animals. With the aid of her parents, a cooperative veterinarian, and sympathetic friends, Wendy has fulfilled that vow.

Wendy, a beautiful young woman, from high school on put every penny aside from various jobs, in hopes of buying property in the Michigan countryside as an animal haven. When she fell short, her parents remortgaged their house to make up the necessary balance. Now, Wendy and her significant other have acreage and outbuildings sufficient to house many homeless dogs and cats, as well as a full-size pig and three horses.

The pets that find their way to Wendy's Animal Orphanage are those who have been mistreated, dumped, deserted, or have become homeless for a variety of reasons. Some of them are eventually adopted out. Some are too old or too disabled for adoption. They are fed, kept warm, made comfortable, and cared for tenderly.

The orphanage survives on contributions from people who recognize the sanctity of Wendy's work. For 12 years Wendy rented a booth at the Royal Oak Farmers Market. Every weekend, Wendy, assisted by volunteers, was at the market, selling antiques and flea market items. Many of these items were donated, with all proceeds going to help support the animals.

Wendy, who is of an artistic bent, now designs works of art, including garden benches, planters, and sculpture, as well as unique items for inside the home, all created from reclaimed antique iron. The proceeds from the sale of these pieces go to support the animals—and to reimburse her parents for their mortgage payments.

If Wendy were not so dedicated, she could easily be a wealthy gallery owner. Instead, she eats on the run, wears cast-off clothes, and takes no vacations—every cent goes to rescue and care for the derelict creatures that too few others care about.

Wendy provides food for the pets of the elderly who are otherwise unable to provide for their animal companions. She also arranges for the spaying or neutering of pets for those who cannot afford the procedure.

It is not unusual for Wendy to get a phone call in the middle of the night about an injured animal or a stray. In such cases, she gets up, gets dressed, and goes out in search, sometimes driving many miles and arriving home long after sunrise.

Bill admired Wendy greatly. He marveled over her dedication and looked upon her as a living saint. In late fall of 2001, we stopped by Wendy's booth at the Royal Oak Farmers Market. Bill said, "Wendy, if I ever get to heaven, I'm going to tell God about you."

"Just find out about Jinny," Wendy replied. Jinny was Wendy's beloved dog, who had died some time before.

Had I not picked up the little dog that snowy day, had the *Free Press* not published the account of her life and death, we might not have met Wendy. Because we did, Bill and I were able, over the years, to contribute to Wendy's work, in the form of both salables and monetary donations.

It may be an eccentric theology, but in a way, that little dog became for me a canine Jesus figure—dying in order that many other pets could be saved. I never ran this concept by Bill. If I had, he undoubtedly would have looked at me thoughtfully and said—as he did so often over the years—"You have an *odd* mind."

There's a tenacity that the dead have on the living that no living person has on you. The dead are truly gone. The only way you have to keep them is to think about them over and over again.

—Survivor of a plane crash victim

It had been three years since Ray's death. All who knew him continued to miss him. Each time Bill and I drove down Woodward, we hearkened back to the many years of driving to Kay and Ray's home, to be met at the door by Ray's warm, incomparable smile.

Kay had borne up nobly. Years before, watching Rose Kennedy bury yet another one of her sons, Bill had commented on her dignity and poise. "Irish women have been burying their sons for centuries," I said. "They've had lots of practice." I was thinking of the countless beautiful young men for whom the British scaffold had been the altar on which they had offered up their lives in the struggle for Ireland's freedom.

Kay's McNamara genes had stood her in good stead. After Ray's death, she had gone on with her life, still the gracious hostess, still the supportive mother and inspiring grandmother.

Colleen, Kay's eldest daughter, had moved with her husband to Arizona, where she was a nurse on an emergency helicopter. Beth, the boisterous middle child, had gone to college in Colorado, then moved to Alaska, to work on a master's degree in Genetics. She married Owen Guthrie, the son of a noted paleontologist. Mary, once the apple of Ray's eye, kept up her studies while pursuing extracurricular activities such as church work and helping inner-city AIDS sufferers.

Kay often had a faraway look in her eyes. We all knew that many nights she cried herself to sleep. But her friends grew increasingly hopeful, as, slowly, Kay began to emerge from her cocoon of pain, grief, and loss to walk ever more steadily on the upward path to a peaceful life.

Kay's girls, though spread out, were now all in Michigan. Colleen, divorced and remarried, was a cardiology nurse in Ann Arbor. She, her husband, and her two daughters, Megan and Brittany, lived in Hartland. Beth and Owen and their two girls, Eleanor and Fiona, lived in Marshall, a picturesque village just off the Interstate in western Michigan. Mary was a student at the University of Michigan, where, as a young priest, her dad had studied for his PhD in History.

It was Memorial Day. Kay headed out to Colleen's for a family cookout. Beth would be coming from Marshall; Mary would be coming from Ann Arbor.

Kay arrived at the Hartland house to be met by Colleen, who was carrying Eleanor in her arms. Colleen said only, "Owen is in the garage. You'd better go see him." Mystified, Kay headed for the garage, where Owen was waiting.

Beth, Owen, and the girls—Eleanor, age two, and Fiona, seven weeks—had attended Marshall's rainy Memorial Day parade. Owen settled a sleeping Fiona into the front seat of Beth's small Toyota pickup. They planned in the next few weeks to buy a larger SUV; their aged Volkswagen Jetta could not comfortably accommodate both the children's car seats. Beth would drive to Colleen's while Fiona napped. Owen, after feeding the cats, would follow with Eleanor.

The longest part of the journey, all freeway, was completed; just ten miles were left to travel on M-59, a two-lane county road. Owen had just left the Interstate, when he saw traffic stopped ahead of him. He slowed to pull around the backup. As he did so, he noticed something down in the culvert. He started to go by, then made out a vehicle—and in the front seat a sleeve the same color as Beth's jacket. He pulled off to one side, made sure Eleanor was safely in her car seat, put one of her favorite CD's in the player, and headed back to where inconceivable horror awaited.

Kay's sister, Mary, received a phone call that afternoon. She couldn't make out the words, only a woman's voice screaming. Mary asked her husband, Tom, to pick up the phone in the other room, in hopes that he could make some sense of the call.

Tom understood just enough of what Kay was screaming. "Beth is dead," he told his wife.

Colleen and Owen tried to keep Kay from her car. But she sped off before anyone could stop her. She had to be with Beth. It was on this wild ride that she had phoned her sister.

The scene was almost as Owen had left it. Fiona had been taken to a nearby hospital, where she would be pronounced dead. Beth's long, thick, chestnut hair spread over her shoulders. Her hands were still on the steering wheel. Kay reached through the broken window and touched her daughter's lifeless head.

A military vehicle returning from a Memorial Day parade had made a sudden turn and gone out of control on the rain-slicked road. It swerved into oncoming traffic, colliding with Beth's pickup. Beth had died instantly. The rescue service would need the ironically named Jaws of Life to extricate her body.

Word spread quickly. Our hearts were breaking for Kay, for her grief, for her loss. Our hearts were breaking for ourselves, for our inability to take this cup from Kay. We wept for Owen, bereft; we wept for Eleanor, unknowingly motherless.

At Ray's funeral, Kay had been flanked by her girls—petite Colleen, a dark-haired Barbie Doll with brains; Beth, the Julia Roberts lookalike with cheekbones many women would kill for; Mary, the tall, striking reservoir of strength.

Now Kay had to bury her beautiful Beth—and Beth's beautiful baby. She had to do this without Ray at her side. She could not break down; she had to be strong for those who were left.

Beth and her baby were buried in the same coffin, Fiona nestled under Beth's arm. Father Ed Prus—the priest Bill and I had come across in the north of Ireland—officiated at the Funeral Mass.

Beth's death shook our extended circle. In days to come, Bill would look thoughtful, and say, "I keep wondering how Fiona would have turned out."

One of Bill's favorite sayings over the years was, "Two minutes after we're dead, we'll know all the answers." I guess now he knows.

In the very heart of [life] there rises a mystic spiritual tone that gives meaning to the whole. It transmutes the dull details into romance.

—OLIVER WENDELL HOLMES, JR.

THE PATTERN OF OUR LIFE continued to repeat itself. Routine was second nature to Bill. Except for occasional public appearances and autographings, he kept the same schedule daily, weekly, monthly, yearly. I, who struggled against scheduling, marveled at his ability to always do the same thing the same way at the same time. He thrived on routine; routine irritated me. But he left me free to be myself, and I had grown accustomed to living with my cadenced husband.

Nonetheless, our lives were slowing down somewhat. Bill still turned out a book a year, but accepted fewer and fewer speaking engagements. There was the occasional trip to Ireland, or to a mystery writers' convention in Chicago or Toronto.

Periodically, we went across the river for Assumption University's Christian Culture Series. Assumption's Basilians were a joy. Father Manny Chircop had invited Bill to participate in the Christian Culture Series, through which we met Father Ulysse Paré, the university president. Evenings spent at Assumption were for me like mornings spent at the Monastery of the Blessed Sacrament: Once there I wanted never to leave.

We felt so at home with the Basilians. I told Bill, "If anything happens to me, you should ask the Basilians to take you in." Later, Bill put Father Chircop in one of his books.

Another joy was visiting my dear friend Lynn, and her husband Gil, at Niagara on the Lake.

Lynn and I had met when Mike was a baby. A friend at Wayne State University's medical research center said to me, "I have a coworker you should meet. I think you'd really like each other."

Just as Father Kienzle had entered my life through a doorway, so too did Lynn. One day, as I was sitting in my friend's office, there appeared in the doorway the most beautiful girl I'd ever seen. She was a cross between Joan Fontaine and Olivia de Havilland. Her smile lit up the room.

Lynn and I hit it off from Day One. She was intelligent, warmhearted, generous, fun-loving—in short, a joy.

In the early days, before Bill met Lynn, he thought my description of her was hyperbole. Nobody could be *that* beautiful. By the time Bill did meet Lynn, many years later, her appearance only hinted at her youthful beauty. Where once she had glowed, now she radiated a mature loveliness, and her joie de vivre more than made up for any fading that the years had inflicted.

One day, going through an old album, Bill came across some photographs of Lynn as she was when I first met her. He was dumbstruck. "She's . . . she's incredibly beautiful," he said.

Like a princess in a fairy tale, Lynn was as good as she was beautiful.

With the advance of years, death continued to intrude. Sadly, usually a funeral was the only time we met with friends of long ago. Modern life somehow keeps us not only too busy to stop and smell the roses but too busy to get together with those we care about. Each time we gathered for a funeral service, someone was sure to say, "We really should get together." All agreed. Then we all went our separate ways until the next funeral.

Some funerals were sorrowful, some a blessing. One of the latter was that of Virginia Sommerfeldt, the "fairy godmother" responsible for Bill's move to the Center for Contemplative Studies. Virginia, a former daily communicant at St. Anselm's, had been widowed young. She was a lovely lady, full of practicality and humor. Father Kienzle had enjoyed her immensely.

With age, Virginia sold her house and moved to a retirement center. Gradually, her health worsened and fewer and fewer were the times she knew her visitors. Both she and her loved ones prayed for God to take her.

When those prayers were finally answered, a service was held at the retirement center. Father Kohler, who had been a resident deacon during Bill's pastorate at St. Anselm's, celebrated the Mass. Bill provided the eulogy. He recalled, as pastor, bending to assist Virginia from her Thunderbird. Whereupon she had informed him, in only half-mock severity, "A gentleman never looks at a lady's legs when she's getting out of a car."

"I'll remember that," Father Kienzle promised.

A Luddite, I finally bowed to technology and bought a computer. This after consulting countless friends throughout the country on the advisability and the various programs. No longer would I type a draft from Bill's manuscript, edit it, retype it, then re-edit and retype it again. I still edited, but now the computer did the scutwork.

Spell-Check I eschewed as next to useless. It could pick up some typos, but basically, an expert eye was still the best at catching errors. Unfortunately, we had lost Ray's proofreading talents, so the typescripts went off not quite as clean as they had been, but still acceptable.

I spent more time gardening, planting over two dozen different roses, as well as numerous daylilies, tulips, daffodils, and other perennials. Bill spent a lot of time on the phone, talking with both active and inactive priest buddies, as well as any number of former parishioners, friends who needed help with various problems, and aspiring writers who were hopeful that Bill could impart to them the magic Open Sesame that would give them entrée to best-sellerdom.

The would-be's didn't seem to realize—although Bill tried in as kindly a way as possible to explain it to them—that it was a combination of talent and luck. First, he would say, you must write an irresistible book. Then you had to be lucky enough to find a publisher who wouldn't turn it down. He would explain the Blockbuster Syndrome, then launch into a litany of books like *The Godfather* and *Jonathan Livingston Seagull*, which had been turned down by shortsighted publishers.

Bill was unfailingly supportive of other authors. He never felt he was in competition. On the contrary, when he gave speeches he mentioned others' work in complimentary terms. If another author—even a comparative unknown—was in the audience, Bill made sure to refer to him or her.

Bill enjoyed meeting other authors. He was particularly charmed by Judith Guest, especially when they compared notes and realized that in addition to their Michigan connection, they had something else in common: The first book that each had written (*Ordinary People* and *The Rosary Murders*) had each been made into a movie starring Donald Sutherland.

On occasion, Bill appeared on panels with other authors. Two whom he always enjoyed were Loren Estleman and William Coughlin. Bill himself was an entertaining speaker, and Estleman and Coughlin were raconteurs extraordinaire. Whenever one or more of these writers addressed a group, the audience more than got its money's worth. Sadly, Bill Coughlin is no longer with us. His wife, Ruth, gave us an account of his last days in her memoir, *Grieving*.

Some authors whose work Bill admired were Pat Conroy, Philip Caputo, Ferrol Sams, and Joanna Trollope. He found Jan Karon's "Mitford" series readable and touching.

He enjoyed the mysteries of Charles Merrill Smith and Donald Westlake, as much for their humor as for their form and content. Westlake is a prolific author, writing under several pseudonyms. (He once told Bill that he had to turn out so many books to keep up with his alimony payments.) Smith, an Anglican clergyman, also authored *How to Become a Bishop Without Being Religious*.

Bearing out the theory that a good book is a good book no matter for what age it is written, Bill also appreciated several books written for young people, including Bob Lytle's *The Mystery of*

Round Tower Light, Chris Crutcher's *Staying Fat for Sarah Byrnes*, Robert O'Brien's *Mrs. Frisby and the Rats of NIMH*, Jerry Spinelli's *Maniac Magee*, and *Amy's Eyes*, by Richard Kennedy.

The Detroit area has had many excellent columnists over the years. Bill felt at home with the writings of Judd Arnett, an Ohio transplant who extolled "Michigan, My Michigan." He admired Jim Fitzgerald's attempts to bring to justice the double- and triple-parking scofflaws in front of the Detroit Club. Sportswriter Joe Falls was another down-to-earth favorite. But when Mike Downey left Detroit for the *Los Angeles Times*, Bill felt his absence keenly. He appreciated Downey's erudition, humor, and class. Sports-reading just wasn't the same for Bill after Downey left.

As for Bill's own work, he once told an interviewer, "Writing a book a year is sort of like being pregnant all the time."

"If I'm in a state of grace, may God keep me there. If I am not, may He put me there."

—St. Joan of Arc

I DON'T KNOW HOW MANY, if any, publishers turned down *The Celestine Prophecy*. It was a phenomenon: one of the most fascinating yet one of the most poorly written books I've ever read. I remember it chiefly because my reading it was a prelude to an unusual event.

I had for some time been studying meditation. I tried to meditate for thirty minutes daily. Sometimes I was more successful than others. I finally decided that in order to successfully meditate I would have to "empty" myself—rid myself of all distracting thoughts—indeed of *all* thoughts . . . in effect, becoming a "channel."

It was difficult. I thought of Bill's stint at the Center for Contemplative Studies. If I recall correctly, one man's meditation is another man's tool. The Western theory seems to be that one meditates in order to free one's mind and thus achieve a higher goal. The Eastern theory is that meditation itself is the goal.

One lovely day, I finished my housework, picked up my copy of *The Celestine Prophecy* and sat by the picture window. I read a short segment of *Prophecy*, then sat quietly, trying to "empty" myself, trying to get rid of anything and everything in order to leave room for God to make himself known to me.

Suddenly, a marvelous ray of light came through the ceiling to my right, expanding in a teepee shape all the way down to the floor. It had a light bluish-gold tinge. As I gazed at it, I was filled with the most incredible, indescribable feeling of total love—love beyond belief, love beyond comprehension, love beyond description, cosmos-encompassing love. I wanted to stay in that love forever—to be part of it forever.

As quickly as the light appeared, it disappeared—taking the fullness of love with it.

I sat dazed, trying to comprehend what had taken place.

Later, I asked Bill—my expert in all things holy—what had happened.

He thought about it for some time. Finally, he said, "You have been given a grace."

"A grace?" Remnants of the pagan farm girl remained.

"God has given you a gift."

I was confused and humbled. "Why me? I'm not a saint. I'm not even holy. I know lots of people much holier than I could ever be. I've done nothing to deserve such a gift." I wasn't being self-deprecating; the things I was saying were what I truly felt.

"It's not for us to know the reason for such a gift. But," he added, "someday, something will happen—something that will make you need this. At that time—when whatever it is does happen—you will be able to look back and take strength and comfort from this."

I tried many times after that to reprise the fullness of the love that light brought me. But I was unsuccessful. I reminded myself that we humans are all too greedy: Why, when given a gift, do we ask for more?

I now realize that my gratitude was insufficient. Had it been sufficient, there would have been no room in me for desire for more.

I think of Eve in the Garden of Eden. Instead of being satisfied with and grateful for what she had—which was everything—she wanted more.

Let's make no mistake about this: The American Dream starts with the neighborhoods.

—HARVEY MILK

IN ANY EVENT, God continued to bless us in His own inimitable way. Another word for blessing is "friends."

Occasionally, out-of-town friends stopped by. Sometimes Bill went off to meet an old friend for lunch. Every so often, when I got my act together, we hosted a dinner party. My culinary skill was nowhere near Kay's, but what I lacked in that direction, I tried to make up for in table decoration.

One of our most pleasuresome gatherings had been some years earlier when Father Prus returned from a sojourn in Recife. He, Kay and Ray, and Bill and I had gotten together for brunch. Hours later, the five of us were still sitting around our dining table chatting away. Kay took a picture of Bill, Ray, and Father Prus—three men who were purely good without being holier than thou. I look at that photo from time to time with much happiness.

But as the years went by and our systems slowed down, we decided that it was time to live more simply so that others could simply live. We would sell our four-bedroom house and move into a small condominium.

I wanted a sense of community and when I read that a new condo complex was planned for downtown Rochester, I knew that was for us. Kay, who had kept up her real estate work, listed our house, and we sat back to wait.

It took longer than we expected, but we weren't overly concerned, as the new condo complex wasn't expected to be ready for some time.

We sold the house to Darlene Najor, a young woman whose family owned a series of local groceries. Darlene was happy with the house and its gardens, and we were happy to turn it over to such a nice person. We would miss our neighbors, the McDonalds, the Seprinos, and the Oldanis, but there would be new neighbors in Rochester.

If you want to make God laugh, tell Him your plans.

The Rochester city council and the contractor couldn't agree on terms. The condo deal fell through. We would shortly be homeless. We rented a two-bedroom apartment at Beacon Hill, in Auburn Hills, not far from Rochester, on the theory that *somebody* would be building some condos in the area, and when that happened, we'd be right there.

We spent a pleasant year at Beacon Hill. The complex was across from Oakland University, and we could enjoy the Detroit Symphony's summer concerts at Meadowbrook. Summer afternoons were spent poolside, where we caught up on some of our reading. Beacon Hill's residents were a veritable United Nations, and I was able to practice my kindergarten-level German on some of the young swimmers.

One of Bill's classmates, Father Ed Mitchell, was pastor of St. Irenaeus, in Rochester Hills, a short distance from us. Bill was happy to attend daily Mass with Father Mitchell on the altar.

The area was home to much wildlife. Early risers could look out their windows and see the deer scampering across the knoll. In the winter, the scene was Christmas-cardlike. The stream that ran along our patio would freeze, deer tracks could be seen in the snow, and the cardinals' wings flashed in the sunlight.

I missed my rosebushes, but was able to plant a couple along the stream. I also found a beautiful, fragrant potted Sharifa rose that bloomed repeatedly throughout the summer. Early in the second summer, I counted fifty buds on it. I watered it daily, and eagerly awaited all those blooms. One morning I awoke to find only one bud left—the other forty-nine had been neatly nipped off by our friendly deer.

Bambi be damned! I sprinkled cayenne pepper liberally over the next series of buds. I also visited a nearby beauty salon and collected a supply of shorn human hair, which I strewed at the base of the roses. It worked. Henceforth the deer dined elsewhere.

The end of our year at Beacon Hill approached with no condo development in sight. We had become increasingly aware that we missed communication with neighbors. Aside from summer visits to the pool, we rarely saw our neighbors, other than perhaps for a "Good morning" or "Good evening." They all either worked, or went to university. We were starting to feel cut off from humanity.

We advertised in the Rochester paper for a rental house on a quiet street, and added, "long term." We got a call from a young man who asked, "What do you mean by 'long term'?"

"Till you bury us," I replied.

"That's just what we're looking for," he said. He and his wife, both of whom were employed, were building a home in northern Michigan, and wanted to rent out their present house for additional income.

We drove into Rochester to look at the house. It was small—but had a good-sized finished basement, a huge garage, and a fair-sized sunny lawn where I could plant roses. And it had a mixture of neighbors—grandparents, working couples, young children, with a variety of pets.

It was a dream come true. It was within walking distance of downtown Rochester, and within a short driving distance of our favorite health food store, the post office, an all-night drugstore, and the university.

Our massage therapist, Jerry Stutz, was located just a block from the post office. When we lived in West Bloomfield, it had taken forty-five minutes to get to Jerry's clinic; now it took two minutes.

Jerry recommended that almost archaic of marvels, a privately owned drugstore and touted us onto an almost hidden German-French bakery that turned out loaves of bread good enough to pass for dessert.

The druggist was Bob Lytle, a throwback to the days of the pharmacist who could be a stand-in for your family doctor. Lytle Pharmacy was one of Rochester's real gems. And wonder of wonders: We learned that Bob wrote books for young people; he had a successful mystery series, and was working on a novel about the history of Rochester for young readers.

I knew I was really "home" when, shortly after we moved in, I looked out the front window to see Bill, who had been raking the lawn, talking with a man from across the street. He too had been raking his lawn, and had ambled across to speak to the new neighbor. There they stood, Bill leaning on his rake, and the neighbor with his rake over his shoulder, the two of them straight out of a Norman Rockwell illustration.

Our next-door neighbors to the north and south were each named Jack. I called them Jack North and Jack South. Jack North was in his eighties. He had emigrated from Canada as a boy, and worked for GM until his retirement. Now he cared tenderly for his terminally ill wife, a lovely woman with much spirit. They were not only grandparents, but great-grandparents. Jack South and his wife were also grandparents. Jack, also a GM retiree, was a compulsive fixer; his creative wife attended weekly arts and crafts classes.

The various neighbors up and down the block also fit the Rockwell mold. I felt I should pinch myself to make sure I wasn't dreaming.

Shortly after we moved in, the annual block party was held. It was a joy. Without living in each other's pockets, these neighbors, many of whom had resided there for years, made up a community. Just before Halloween, the Fire Department came around, selling flares. At 7 P.M. on Halloween, the sirens sounded. Each participating resident—which was everyone who was at home—lit a flare in the driveway, as a sign that each would be providing goodies for the trick-or-treaters. More Norman Rockwell, as the ghosties and ghoulies made their way up and down both sides of the street.

The Santa parade in December boasted that it was one of the largest in Michigan. Throngs lined the sidewalks and overflowed onto Main Street. A popular local TV newsman emceed the proceedings, giving color commentary as each float passed by. I was impressed to see our congressman, Dale Kildee, walk the length of the parade, rather than riding, even though the weather was near freezing. Dale Kildee had been a seminary schoolmate of Bill's, and although he was never ordained, his seminary training did not go to waste: An upright and honest congressman, he has faithfully represented his constituency for many years.

I had brought my potted Sharifa rose with us, and planted it, along with some other roses, along the backyard fence that we shared with Jack South. I installed a collection of perennials, including Russian sage, along the side drive we shared. In a circle in the backyard, I planted pansies. In a circle on the front lawn where the city had cut down a diseased maple, I planted morning glories, zinnias, and a variety of other colorful plants. Passing drivers slowed to enjoy the scene.

We had lived in Rochester about seven months, when we received a letter from our landlord. He was putting the house up for sale, and giving us notice.

I felt uprooted. But what must be must be. As I was so fond of saying to Bill, "God puts us where He wants us." We didn't want to buy the house ourselves. One of the reasons we had sold our own house was because we were tired of being responsible for upkeep and repairs.

After searching unsuccessfully for a similar rental residence in Rochester, we decided to return to West Bloomfield. Our neighbors were saddened, but our longtime friends were pleased; we would be back where visiting us would not require an expedition.

We found a beautiful apartment at Chimney Hill, not far from our former house. I could once more attend Mass at the Monastery and Bill could return to St. Colman's.

We made arrangements to move on September 15.

On September 11, I was in the basement, working on the computer, when Bill arrived home from Mass. He came downstairs and said, "I think you'll want to turn the TV on; two planes just crashed into the World Trade Center." Had he said "a plane" I would have assumed it was an accident. I've never forgotten the image of the plane that crashed into the Empire State Building. But when he said "two planes" I asked, "Terrorists?"

"Yes."

September 11 was Bill's seventy-third birthday. Later that day, he, who rarely used four-letter words, said, "This is a hell of a way to celebrate one's birthday."

Sing along with Mishura

MANY EUROPEANS WHO VISIT THE UNITED STATES are amazed at our garage sales. "Don't you have these at home?" one friend asked a relative visiting from Holland. "Never. We keep things till they wear out."

With each succeeding move we had divested ourselves of additional items. Now we and several of our Rochester neighbors held a monster garage sale. This enabled Bill and me to further pare down our possessions. The new apartment, though good-sized, had no basement, although it did have an attached garage. But by the time we moved in, our belongings fit the new space. We were snug, yet comfortable.

A branch of our favorite health food store was a few hundred yards down the road. Actually, almost everything we needed was again within walking distance: supermarket, post office, cleaners, fast- and slow-food eateries. Yet, since our complex was back in the woods, it was peaceful and quiet. We went for long walks.

As usual, in the wake of our moves, boxes remained to be unpacked. I stacked them on shelves in the garage, where, one by one, I could eventually go through them.

Our luck with neighbors held. Paul and Andrea, the couple upstairs, were friendly without being intrusive.

Once more, our lives fell into the usual pattern, starting with morning Mass. After breakfast, Bill went for a walk, picking up the mail at the nearby post office. Then, as usual, he played the piano—always the same selections, including Tchaikovsky's *Andante Cantabile*, Gershwin's *Rhapsody in Blue*, and "Bess, You is My Woman Now," which was "our song." Often, he would sing it to me as he played it.

Bill's pianistic proficiency had improved since his seminary days. At that earlier time, his playing tended to be more sensational than sensitive. And always it was loud. I joked that it was the German in him that liked loud. He didn't disagree. When he had moved back to Sacred Heart Seminary his LPs of course went with him. Usually, they were played at peak volume. One afternoon, as a recording of "The Battle Hymn of the Republic" boomed away on his stereo, a piece of paper was slipped under Bill's door. When he opened the door, no one was in sight. The note read: "I surrender." It was signed Robert E. Lee.

Years before, I had gotten a duet version of Gershwin's *Rhapsody in Blue*, hoping to play along with Bill. Unfortunately, my talent was as a drop in the ocean compared with his. I left the playing of Gershwin to the expert. I considered Bill's rendition of the *Rhapsody* every bit as good as that of Previn or Bernstein. There were times I was convinced that what I was hearing was a recording.

In the afternoon, Bill did his stretching exercises, then read while on his exercise bike for half an hour. Then a shower, and down to work on another few pages of his next book. Dinner—as always—was at 5:30 P.M. This from the days when the dogs were fed faithfully at 5 P.M.

Our evening routine also remained the same. Our favorite TV shows were *West Wing*, *JAG*, *Law and Order*, and the NFL games. Bill enjoyed *Frasier*, the *District* and *CSI*.

Just before Halloween, Chimney Hill threw a party. I went as a mod Mata Hari, and Bill, in an Astrakhan and his heavy black floor-length clerical capa magna, was a pseudo-Dracula. On Halloween, we again dressed up and drove to Rochester to join our former neighbors in handing out goodies to the trick-or-treaters.

Periodically, death intruded. We would pick up the paper to be confronted with the loss of yet another friend, or one of Bill's erstwhile classmates. It was starting to reach Bill. As the third funeral in ten days loomed, he said, "I can't go—I'm funeraled out."

I didn't argue with him. In spite of Yogi Berra's statement ("If you don't go to other people's funerals, they won't come to yours") I felt Bill had more than paid his dues.

One death in particular rocked us. Bob Laurel died suddenly and unexpectedly after finishing a pickup basketball game.

Once again, memories crowded over Bill. The neighborhood lad who had spent countless hours pounding away on the Kienzle piano; the young man who brought his fiancée to Father Kienzle to arrange for their marriage; the talented musician-performer for whom Father Kienzle had written liner notes for a first album; the entertainer-cum-entrepreneur who had swum with the sharks to bring Father Koesler to the movie screen.

Another chunk of Bill's life was gone.

Late that fall we attended a gathering at the home of Jonathan Swift and Tom St. Charles. Tom had been in the seminary with Bill. Jonathan had been an operatic tenor. Tragically, after appearing internationally and making several successful recordings, Jonathan suffered the loss of his voice when his vocal chords were eaten away by acid reflux. Jonathan had gone on to a successful career as a teacher, as well as a cable television host. One of his shows was an interview series whose motto was "Think globally and act locally." Tom helped produce the show. Over the years, Jonathan had interviewed the famous and the unknown and many in between.

One evening Bill and I were guests on his show. During the intermission, I commented on Jonathan's burr. He told us he had been born in Glasgow and brought to the United States as a young boy.

"We have a dear friend in Glasgow: Menzies Mc Killop," I said. "He's a playwright. We stayed with him when we were in Glasgow." For some inexplicable reason, I added, "He lives at Eight Fergus Court."

Jonathan smiled. "My aunt lived for years at *Six* Fergus Court."

Small world indeed.

Jonathan and Tom threw enjoyable parties. Regulars at such gatherings included the beloved Met performer Ara Berberian and his lovely wife. I was charmed to discover that the great baritone's hobby was collecting old barns. He lived in nearby Southfield on a large acreage that had belonged to his parents. Whenever he found a barn that needed saving, he had it moved to his "farm." At that time, he told us, he had four barns on his property.

Also present—when not appearing in some famous opera house throughout the world—was mezzo-soprano Irina Mishura. Irina, a statuesque redhead, had put her stamp on the role of Dalila, which she had sung with such luminaries as Placido Domingo. Reviewers had run out of superlatives to describe her Carmen. Irina's husband, Jack Morris, a solid, good-humored man, himself a well-known operatic tenor, was content to stand not in his wife's shadow, but in her light.

At the latest autumn gathering, a musician friend of Irina's from Russia was visiting. We gathered around the piano as she played a variety of popular and semiclassical songs. At one point, Irina stopped singing to "conduct" Bill. They were behind me, but I could hear her directing him to "open your mouth w-i-d-e." Then she sang along with him.

As the evening drew to a close, I heard Bill talking to Irina. "Everyone has dreams of glory," he said. "One of mine has always been to sing with a Met star. And now I have. You have given me a beautiful gift. I thank you."

Eat your heart out, Father O'Malley. You may have heard Rise Stevens at the Met, but Bill Kienzle got to sing with Irina Mishura.

O Lord my God, I will give thanks unto thee forever.

—Psalm 30:12

Our Thanksgiving was truly a thankful celebration. We felt that we were entering the best time of our life, that everything had fallen into place—that these would truly be our Golden Years.

After Thanksgiving, we worked on the last changes and corrections for *The Gathering*, the twenty-fourth in the Father Koesler series. Bill seemed satisfied with the final product, and it was with a sense of relief that we sent the emended galleys off to Andrews McMeel on December 19.

Bill had decided that his next book—the last in his current contract—would be a truly different one. It would be a life of Jesus. He had always done a lot of research before writing each book. For this one, he had thrown himself into truly major research. He read books on not only the life of Jesus but the life of St. Paul, who would be one of the major characters in the book. He read books on the Roman life of the times and the Jewish life of the times. He read and reread the New Testament.

If you want to make God laugh, tell Him your plans.

With Christmas approaching, we made plans to host our small annual dinner, which, for the first time, we had skipped the previous year in far Rochester. As always, we were acutely aware that Ray would not be with us. But Kay would be there, and Jim and Irma, and Art and Patti Schaffran. To celebrate the holidays in our new apartment, I bought a large Christmas tree—something we hadn't had since we'd sold our house.

The tree was so heavily adorned that one could barely see the green for the decorations. As a housewarming gift, Dorothy O'Brien had sent us three beautiful heather trees, which guarded the patio doors next to the tree.

We had amassed a huge collection of Christmas tapes, CDs, and LPs, which we started playing the day after Thanksgiving and played every day thereafter. Periodically, in between the favorite carols, Bill put on the full-length version of Handel's *Messiah*. Every so often, he would stop whatever he was doing, cock his head to one side, close his eyes, and slowly shake his head in appreciation of Handel's genius. One of the many joys of Bill was his deep appreciation of music. One day, listening to a Pavarotti recording of *La Bohème*, Bill commented, "Some things are almost too beautiful to bear."

Art and Anne had given us a set of Lenox "Holiday" china. At post-holiday sales over the years, I had picked up complementary Christmas serving pieces. One year, I needed an ovenproof serving piece. I wanted a round platter in the Portmeirion Holly and Ivy pattern. Each Portmeirion pattern was listed by its code. The code for the Holly and Ivy pattern was HIV. It took a while for the clerk to find the platter in the computer: With the advent of AIDS, Portmeirion had decided to change the code to something less intimidating.

I splurged on our Christmas banquet. Irish smoked salmon, tenderloin of beef—and for dessert Büche de Noël. On our second Christmas in Minneapolis, I had made one from scratch. Now over twenty-five years later, taking the wish for the deed, I ordered one from the bakery.

Our dinner was held several days before Christmas. It was a near enchanted evening. The table settings would've made Martha Stewart drool. In the background, on the stereo, the beauty of carols caressed our ears. We clinked wineglasses* in celebration of our long, close friendship. The tree lights twinkled, reflecting in the picture window and the patio doors, and in the mirrored and shimmering ornaments. Like people retelling the ancient Nativity story, Bill and Jim and Art told familiar stories of seminary days. Kay and Irma and Patti and I laughed appreciatively, as we had so many times over the

---

* The clinking of glasses, a Christian custom, is to ward off the devil, who is said to be repelled by bell-like noises.

years. We four had so often voiced our gratitude for the holy and loving men who had chosen us to share their later lives.

As the evening drew to a close, we counted ourselves blessed to be part of such a loving circle. Unspoken, yet strongly present in each of our minds, was the awareness of the absence of Ray, whose trencherman presence at so many previous dinners had given us much fodder for humor. I remembered the Christmas when I'd served Ray a huge slab of standing rib roast. He had looked up at me and said, in mock horror, "Did you give me the whole cow?" But he'd eaten it all, and more. Now he was at the heavenly table.

Health is merely the slowest possible rate at which one can die.

—Unknown

Bill was, the nurse said, the healthiest person who'd ever walked in the door. She told me this on the same day she told me that the doctor was in his office scratching his head over what code to enter on the insurance forms . . . there just wasn't anything wrong with Bill.

Bill was a poster child for how to live a healthy life. He had stopped smoking over twenty years before. Where once he had lived to eat steak and hamburger, he now ate fish and fowl. When he snacked, it was fruit or vegetables. He eschewed dessert in favor of an apple a day. He flossed and brushed after every meal. He occasionally had a glass of wine when dining out. At home, his only alcoholic beverage was a jigger of gin or vodka before bedtime. He drank eight to ten glasses of water daily. He took daily vitamin-mineral supplments that had been prescribed specifically for him. He never drove if he could walk. He did daily stretching and lifting exercises, as well as riding his exercise bike daily. He took a short daily nap. He went to daily Mass, played the piano daily, was happy in his work, loved me, and enjoyed life.

His cholesterol was 160. He had absolutely no history of any heart problem of any kind. His blood pressure and pulse rate were so good that usually, during his annual colonoscopy exam, whichever nurse took his vitals would ask, "Is he an athlete?"

The only problem Bill had was an occasional attack of prostatitis, for which he took Flomax and saw palmetto. Still, he never traveled without a supply of Cipro just in case.

He got complete annual checkups, as well as an annual colonoscopy, and periodic PSA tests.

Over the years, in a series of trial-and-error visits, I myself had come to rely on a variety of health practitioners. Most of them were considered "alternative," rather than allopathic. Bill, the traditionalist, was fairly dubious. He preferred to visit a practitioner with MD after his or her name. Still, he noted how much my alternative practitioners had helped my CFS symptoms. Eventually, he consented to visit my MD, a holistic physician who was a Sikh. When I mentioned to a nun friend that Bill would shortly be seeing a Sikh who wore a turban, she chuckled. "You'd better just have Bill sit there and look at him for the first visit."

Bill and Dr. Khalsa got along just fine, thank you. When Dr. Khalsa retired to check out other spiritual realms, Bill and I continued to rely on his holistic successors, Dr. Bellisario and Dr. Ewald.

Periodically stress would overtake me. At such times, my EKG revealed irregular and/or additional heartbeats. Medical doctors were always concerned. Dr. Khalsa had referred me to an osteopathic cardiologist for a stress test. Dr. Dangovian turned out to be a dream of a doctor. But first we had to get the ground rules straight.

Under his protocol the results of the stress test called for me to have an angiogram. My protocol called for me to protest mightily. We came to an agreement. I would continue with my daily mile-long walks. I would attend Dr. Dangovian's weekly support circle of patients with heart problems. And I would get stress counseling from Kathy Campbell.

Kathy was a gift from God. She worked with me on all the extraneous things that we modern-day Americans allow ourselves to be burdened by.

I passed the next stress test with flying colors.

Another helpful practitioner was our former neighbor, Richard Larned, a chiropractor who had started out to be a cellular biologist. I came to believe that Richard's brain contained more knowledge about the human body than most allopathic practitioners. Bill had to suspend disbelief when it came to Richard's ministrations. Richard took Bill's skepticism in stride.

Along the way, Margaret Cronyn had given us a certificate for massage therapy at the hands of an IHM nun, Sister Marianne Gaynor. Neither of us had ever had massage—other than rubbing each other's back—but we accepted Margaret's kind gift. Bill told Sister Marianne, "The last time a nun laid a hand on me was to punish me in grade school."

Dr. Khalsa had suggested that massage therapy might help my "sluggish lymph system," so when Sister Marianne was unable to be in town on a regular basis, I looked around for another massage therapist. I tried several, then one day did something I would not normally do when looking for a health practitioner: I turned to the Yellow Pages and picked the massage therapist closest to our house.

It was thus that I found myself in the magic hands of Jerry Stutz. Jerry and his wife, Claudia, were excellent massage therapists. Further, Jerry was extremely spiritual. I attended a series of classes he gave on meditation.

Aware of the excellent effect that regular massage therapy had on me, Bill began seeing Jerry. The two of them had many discussions on religion and spirituality. Bill liked Jerry. Jerry liked Bill. Jerry was the one who referred to Bill as "that saint you live with."

From time to time my sister, Judith, a practitioner of Chinese energy healing, practiced long distance healing on me from New Jersey. Amazingly, it seemed effective.

Our friends were interested, but skeptical. We Americans are conditioned from birth to hand our bodies over to the allopathic medical establishment, and our pocketbooks over to the drug man-ufacturers. People in other parts of the world learn to rely more on integrated treatment that combines allopathic and naturopathic health practices.

After so many years of struggling with the effects of CFS, I was game to try just about anything that made sense—and even a few things that didn't.

At one point, when I developed a benign but persistent head tremor, Richard recommended that I see Daniel Reiher, for cranio-sacral work. Although the treatments did not do away with my tremor, the sessions were extremely interesting.

Once, lying on the table with my eyes closed, I "saw" a ball of light so intensely white that there are no words to describe its whiteness. Other times, I smelled roses when there were no roses around. Dan was amused. "Most people smell jasmine," he said. But the most interesting occurrence was when I "saw" a tall man all in white come through the wall next to me and seat himself on the side of my treatment table. He sat there for a short while, smiling, then got up and walked back through the wall. When the session was over, I told Dan what I had seen. He was totally matter-of-fact. "Oh, that was just one of your angels."

"*One?*" I knew we each had a guardian angel; I didn't know we had more than one.

He assured me that was so.

Now it was I who was skeptical. But how many times had I sat in church and listened to a sermon on angels? And how many times had I read about angels in the Bible? And what of that well-known prayer, "Guardian Angel Dear . . ."?

I tracked down a book on the care and handling of one's guardian angels. According to the author, each of us has a guardian angel on each side of us. The author instructed that one speak to one's angels, asking first the one on the right, then the one on the left, its name. What the heck, I thought, I've gone this far . . .

I asked the angel on my right its name. Immediately, in my head I heard "Herschel." I started to laugh. Who ever heard of an angel named Herschel?!

I asked the angel on my left its name. Immediately, in my head I heard "Avenel."

Avenel? I'd never even heard such a name.[*]

Herschel and Avenel—pretty weird names for angels, no? But then, why wouldn't an angel have an unusual name? After all, they *are* unusual beings.

When I mentioned this to Bill, he looked thoughtful, then said, "Hasn't it occurred to you that both names end in 'el'—Hebrew for God?"

Wow!

Jerry, of Jewish ancestry, thought it quite humorous that I had an angel named "Heshie," as he referred to Herschel.

For years, at Dr. Khalsa's suggestion, I had done a three-day juice fast in the spring and the fall, and also fasted one day a week year-round. Bill of course had always observed a Lenten fast. Now he was considering a juice fast for the 2002 Lenten season.

At Dr. Larned's recommendation, I had been seeing Gail Derin, OMD, (doctor of Chinese medicine) quarterly. I felt it was a great help to get "balanced" at each change of season.

My life was replete with alternative practitioners.

But there was one more to go. Another reference of Richard's was Laura Gannan, CCH (Council for Homeopathic Certification). Talk about suspending disbelief! But Laura made a believer out of me—and even out of Bill. The funny thing was that initially, Bill, who liked people, did not care for Laura. "She's a cold person," he said.

What Bill didn't realize is that Laura, like many forceful people, is basically shy. Also, Laura admitted that she was literally afraid of Bill. His presence not infrequently instilled awe in people. In this case, it wasn't awe, but fear: Laura was aware that Bill neither understood nor believed in homeopathy. She knew she was very

---

[*] Some time later, my sister reminded me there is indeed a town in New Jersey called Avenel.

much on trial. So there they were, Bill feeling that Laura was an iceberg, and Laura almost afraid to talk to Bill. Oh, my!

Bill was, as I've said, quite healthy. But there were the pings and pangs of advancing years—especially for one with ancient football injuries.

Bill had developed a strange tingly itch on his thighs. No medical doctor could figure it out. It persisted. He was referred to a dermatologist at Ford Hospital, who prescribed medication. I was not happy when I considered the side effects. I mentioned it to Laura. "He might consider homeopathy," she suggested.

Why not; Bill had tried everything else.

The rapport that eventually developed between Bill and Laura was almost funny in view of their earlier standoffishness. It brought to mind the scene in the film *Father Goose*, where Trevor Howard discovers that, after a period of absolutely loathing each other, Cary Grant and Leslie Caron are going to marry. "What!" exclaims Howard—using the names with which the two had villified each other—"Goody Two-Shoes and the Filthy Beast?"

Live as if you were to die tomorrow.

—MAHATMA GANDHI

ON CHRISTMAS DAY Bill and I hosted his brother-in-law, Art, and Sister Bernadelle for a low-key lunch. We then spent a quiet afternoon, "unlaxing," as Bill put it.

The next afternoon Bill started on the introduction to his life of Jesus. I think it was actually the first of his books that he was looking forward to writing. I remembered during my instruction period when Father Kienzle had lent me a copy of a life of Christ translated from the German. It was a moving account, but the crucifixion segment was extremely explicit. I recalled saying to him when I returned the book, "Wouldn't you know the Germans would write such a bloody description."

December 27, we went to a Christmas party at Kay's. It was a typical Betanzos gathering: friends, relatives, neighbors. The house was a hive of food, conversation, and laughter. Bill, who enjoyed such gatherings immensely, was in his element. He greeted Kay, as he always did—with the line from another of his favorite musical comedies: "Why there's a wench! Come on, and kiss me, Kate"—and, as always, they suited the action to the words. He joked, told stories, and conversed with several of Kay's nieces.

Jan, the daughter of Kay's sister Mary, asked him, "How do you like your new apartment?"

Bill responded that we were so happy at Chimney Hill. But, he added, he recalled all too well how Kay and Ray had been so happy planning their trip up north and an upcoming trip to Europe. And how instead of happiness, the horror of Ray's illness had cut the ground out from under them. "I'm almost afraid to say how happy I am," Bill told Jan. "I don't want to jinx it."

Just before midnight—late for us—we donned our coats and scarves and stood at Kay's front door, saying our good-byes. Bill was still telling stories. Kay stood in the door and watched Bill and me walk arm-in-arm down the sidewalk to our car.

I always felt so guilty when I was with Bill in Kay's presence. I was so aware of her own loss. I often thought that seeing Bill and me together must, in her aloneness, hurt her so much. But Kay was unfailingly gracious and never complained.

Ray had picked a champion in Kay.

God takes people at their peak.

—Sister Mary of the Compassion, OP

It was December 28. I got up to go to Mass. I thought Bill was sleeping as usual. He wasn't. "I'm having some trouble breathing," he said. "Would you rub my chest?"

Off and on for the past week he had mentioned some indiges-tion. It would come and go, so, being the cautious person he was, he had made an appointment for a checkup. He was scheduled to see Dr. Bellisario at 2 P.M. that day.

I started gently massaging his chest, as I asked questions. The pressure had roused him sometime between 4 and 5 A.M. "Why didn't you wake me?" I knew the answer even as I asked the ques-tion: He hadn't wanted to bother me.

Our friend, Dr. Tom Petinga, was head of Emergency Medicine at St. Joseph Mercy Hospital in Pontiac. Bill had met Tom while spending time at Mt. Carmel Hospital's Emergency Room research-ing *Assault with Intent.* Tom had since been a research source for Bill on many of the succeeding books in the Koesler series. "Get up and get dressed," I told Bill. "I'm taking you to St. Joe's."

"No . . . I'll be okay. I'm going to see Dr. Bellisario this afternoon."

I continued massaging. The pressure in Bill's chest moved to his left shoulder. I was getting more and more concerned. "Please let me take you to St. Joe's. I'll call Tom now."

"No, no. It's not necessary. It's only indigestion."

I asked if he felt nauseated. No. Did he feel feverish? No. He wasn't perspiring. There was just this pressure. I could hear rumbles from his abdomen. I gave him some tonic water. He drank some and burped a bit. I continued the massage. After a few minutes he said that the pressure was gone and that it no longer hurt to breathe. He got up and started getting dressed.

Again I pleaded with him to let me take him to the hospital. He shook his head. "I'm seeing Dr. Bellisario in less than five hours. I'm okay now." He reached out and patted my head. "Don't worry. I'm okay," he said again.

And then, as he had every day of our married life, he took me in his arms and said, "I love you all there is and all there ever could be—and more than that tomorrow."

I could feel his chin on the top of my head. Gently, he held me at arm's length and said, "You love me as much as I love you, don't you?" He had never asked this question before.

I shook my head, almost sadly. "No . . . I couldn't—because no one could possibly love as much as you." Why did I always have to tell the truth? Bill used to say, only half-jokingly, "No one ever has to wonder what Javan is thinking."

He hugged me again and said soothingly, "Yes, you do. I know you do."

"No," I repeated, as I hugged him back. "No one could possibly love as much as you do."

I really felt that was true. I had once asked Bill to explain to me what happened when bad people died: Did they receive as much of God's love as the good people who died?

His response was that heaven was heaven—for everyone. The difference, he said, was in each of us. Some people were capable of loving—and receiving love—only to a limited degree. Others were capable of giving and receiving more love. Still others—the saints perhaps—were capable of an almost infinite range of love. Bill compared it to a thimble, a bucket, and a barrel.

Each person would be a receptacle of God's love, and each would be filled with God's love. In each case, the receptacle—whether it was a thimble, a bucket, or a barrel—would be completely filled. Each would receive all of God's love that he or she was capable of receiving. And thus each would be perfectly, totally, and completely happy in God's love.

I knew that as much as I adored Bill, when it came to loving, he far outshone me. Where I was a bucket, he was a barrel. Now, as we embraced, I repeated, "No one could possibly love as much as you do."

He smiled. "You're wrong, you know."

"When was the last time that happened?" I joked.

I had once read that one of the primary duties of each partner in a marriage is to help the other to achieve heaven. Certainly, I felt that Bill had put me on that path; periodically, he assured me that I had done the same for him.

It was too late for Mass, so both of us went ahead with the remainder of our usual routine. Bill turned on the CBC, and read the morning *Free Press* as he ate his breakfast: cold cereal and a banana—just as Father Koesler always did. He took a short walk, played the piano for a while, then went into the den to answer some correspondence. A little before eleven-thirty he came out and asked if I would heat some soup for lunch. After he finished the soup, I asked if he would like some soy pudding. I knew he didn't usually have dessert, but I figured soy pudding would be okay. He finished the pudding and went into the bathroom off his den for his usual postmeal flossing and brushing. It was exactly twelve noon.

I was sitting at my secretary in the living room when I heard a noise as if some heavy object had dropped. I was not concerned; Bill was always dropping things. Actually, both of us tended on occasion to fit the description of "a bull in a china shop"—Bill because of his size; I because I seemed always to be running about without looking where I was going. As a result, my body was usually full of black and blue marks from where I had bumped into something. Bill's black and blue marks were usually on the top or side of his head. This from walking into a closet or cupboard door left open.

When Cardinal Dearden received the red hat, Bill had been dragged kicking and screaming to Rome. In the Holy City, he had accidentally walked into the side of a bus, bloodying his head on the bus mirror.

Ray had once picked up a pair of scissors from under one of our armchairs, and put them on a nearby end table. I explained to him that I had placed the scissors *under* the chair because if they had been left on the table, either Bill or I would've been sure to trip and fall on them and cause a self-inflicted injury.

Now, having heard something drop, it occurred to me that there was nothing in the bathroom heavy enough to make a noise like that.

I went into the den. The bathroom door was closed. "Bill?"

No response.

I called again, a bit louder, "Bill?"

Nothing.

I hesitantly pushed against the door. It wouldn't open. I pushed harder and finally it opened just enough for me to see, reflected in the bathroom mirror, Bill's body sprawled on the floor. His head was back against the tile wall; his stockinged feet against the door. I called 911 and pleaded for them to come quickly. "They're on their way," the dispatcher said. Then, after asking me a couple of questions, he gave me an instant course in CPR.

I was finally able to squeeze through the bathroom door. I knelt alongside Bill's body. His face was gray, his eyes were rolled back in his head, his chest was heaving. The image remains acid-etched in my memory. I started CPR, but there was no response. As the sirens approached, I stopped, and ran outside.

I led the paramedics to Bill. One of the men gently ushered me back into the dining area. "There's not enough room in there," he said.

The den *was* crowded—Bill's desk, my computer desk, several bookcases, two rocking chairs, the television, a lamp table. There was no room for the crew to work in the bathroom. They had to push furniture aside in order to lay Bill's body on the floor of the adjoining den.

While I was answering questions in the living room, the paramedics were trying to get a pulse and start Bill breathing. I was hopeful when my questioner said, "They're intubating him . . . but he's fighting them."

"He's fighting them," I thought. "That's a good sign." Much later, I remembered that Lady, even after being euthanized, had exhibited muscular contractions.

I looked up to see Bill—unmoving, with his chest exposed—being pushed on a gurney through the living room. "Please take him to St. Joe's. Dr. Petinga is a friend—"

"I'm sorry. In a situation like this, we have to take him to the nearest hospital. We're taking him to Providence. Do you want to ride in the ambulance with him?"

I knew I would just be in their way. I also knew I did not want to be stranded at the hospital with no car. It never entered my head that the doctors wouldn't be able to save him. How many years of TV and movies had I watched as ER physicians had performed miracles? I assured the paramedics that I would be all right.

Indeed, my first thought, on seeing Bill sprawled on the bathroom floor, had been, "He's had a stroke. I'm so glad I talked him into taking out that long-term care policy. He's going to need it for all the months of rehab."

"No, I'll follow you."

"Is there someone you can call?"

I assured them again I would be all right. They left, after advising me, "Drive carefully, now."

Call someone.

Who?

Kay lived closer to Providence than anyone I could think of. I dialed the Betanzos number.

Little Mary Sunshine answered. "Mary, Bill's been taken to the hospital. I don't think he's going to make it." I didn't want to believe that, but without lengthy explanations, I wanted Kay to understand the gravity of the situation.

"Mother and I will meet you there."

Had I called two minutes later I would've gotten only the answering machine. The family was getting ready to attend the local appearance of the Radio City Rockettes.

❦

When I pulled up to the ER entrance of Providence, Kay was standing outside. She led me to the doctor. Mary, face tear-stained, sat quietly by.

Bill was dead. There would be no more daily miracle of renewed life, no more love, no more pure goodness, no more joy, no more sharing. God had taken His gift back.

The doctor gently explained that he didn't want me to be shocked when I saw Bill, as the intubation apparatus was still in place. Numbly, I nodded.

Kay and the doctor walked me to the cubicle where Bill's body lay. As in life, he was too tall for the gurney; his feet in his incongruously Christmas-red socks extended over the end. Kay told me later that when the doctor had taken her into the cubicle, her immediate thought was, "They've made a mistake. That's not Bill . . . it's too tall to be Bill." Somehow, she said, never having seen him lying down, she had never realized how very tall he actually was.

It was in that death cubicle that I made my first real mistake. I have regretted it many times. It's possible I will always regret it.

My every instinct was to shriek, and yell, and howl . . . howl as I had howled for Chappie. Only this time howl until there was nothing left to howl with.

That's what I should have done.

But Mother had raised me to be a lady. A lady doesn't make a scene. A lady doesn't make other people feel uncomfortable.

For some reason, the words that Grace Kelly's father had written to his family before his death flew to mind. He didn't want them making a scene at the graveside, he said, because "the true thoroughbred grieves in the heart."

Maybe. But maybe nobody ever gives "the true thoroughbred" lessons in how to deal healthily and realistically with the shock of bereavement.

"Do you want to do an autopsy?" I asked the doctor calmly, as if I had a husband die every day. "Will it help anyone else?"

"We can do one if you like, but it isn't necessary; we know what we'll find."

Some days later, when I looked at the Death Certificate, it read: "Immediate Cause of Death—Arteriosclerotic Cardiovascular Disease." Under "Approximate Interval Between Onset and Death" was written one word: "Years."

PART

9

The price paid for love is pain.

—Priest at funeral of WTC victim

So much of what followed is a blur. Mostly I remember the pain and the horror.

Kay refused to let me drive back to our apartment. She chauffeured me while Mary drove the Betanzos car home.

My heart was an incredibly heavy stone. My throat was filled with a huge, almost breath-stopping black-hole-dense ball of sharp thorns. My mind was numb and at the same time a maelstrom.

Mary. Since losing her father and her sister, she had been visited with repeated fears: Who would be next? Would it be her uncle Jack; Ray's old seminary friend, Tom Litka; Jim Macy; Bill? When Mary was a little girl, Kay had shown her the photo of Bill on the back cover of one of his books. "Do you know who this is?" Kay asked. Mary nodded confidently. "That's the man who lives with Javan." Now, the lightning had struck Bill.

Bill. Images of our life skittered through my mind. The helpful young priest; the editor feeling his way; the leaning post; the man who gave me my faith, who said, "I think I love you," then taught me how to live a life of faith and love—love that would nevermore warm me, hearten me, give me a reason to live. Everything in me was screaming, shrieking, howling—noiselessly.

He had once asked, "Why do you like John Wayne so much?"

"Because," I replied, "a woman who is with John Wayne would always feel totally safe and protected." The way I'd always felt with

Bill. The laughter, the pure goodness, the handsomeness, the masculinity, the sheer joy of his presence; the Irish eyes, smiling, intent, intelligent, but always full of tenderness and love.

Love. "We are so close," he had said, "that we are yin and yang; when one breathes out the other breathes in, when one cries the other tastes the salt." He repeatedly sent me notes that said, "Eternity is not long enough." Now all was lost. Lost. Lost.

Lost. A jagged guillotine had sliced through me, but unmercifully I was still alive.

It hurts. Oh, God, how it hurts! I remembered how, after my hysterectomy, Bill had sat by my hospital bed holding my hand, as I moaned in a haze of pain that morphine could not vanquish. My fingernails had dug into his palm so hard that they left red welts. Afterward, he told me, "For hours, you kept repeating one word: 'Hurt,' 'Hurt,' 'Hurt.'"

While I packed a suitcase, Kay made phone calls.

I looked up to see Jim Macy coming through the door. His arms were outstretched. As Bill's had been countless times. As Jesus' always are. I crept into Jim's arms and wept.

Dear Jim. Jim, whose ancestors had been among the earliest settlers of New England, who at age fourteen had entered Sacred Heart Seminary the same day as Bill. Who had left the priesthood the same day as Bill and Ray. Jim, of whom Bill had said, "He is the one true contemplative among us." Jim, who spent an hour each morning meditating. Jim, who epitomized the Prayer of St. Francis: Who made of himself a channel of peace so that others could be pardoned and consoled, find hope, faith, and understanding, and who gave of himself so that others might be given God's love.

Jim joked that his father had always told him, "Marry above yourself." "And," Jim would add, "I did." Irma, the former Sister Baptista, complemented Jim perfectly. Capable, good-humored, supportive, quietly proud of her husband, and a nurturing mother to their son, Josh—whom Jim referred to as "the child of my dotage."

There was never a time when we were in Jim and Irma's presence that Bill didn't say afterward, "They're such *good* people."

Kay and Jim and Irma took me to the funeral home. The hearse would pick up Bill's body. What other arrangements did I want?

I knew Bill didn't want any fuss. I knew I could not bear up under a wake or funeral parlor visitations. I had always marveled at how Kay had been able to go through that, first with Ray, then with Beth and Fiona. I marveled that *anyone* could go through it. I knew I couldn't.

Bill's body would be cremated. I knew it was what he'd wanted. There would be no wake, no visitation. We would have not a funeral Mass, but a memorial Mass.

Where?

Bill always liked closing circles. It would be so fitting to hold the Mass at Holy Redeemer, the church of his childhood, the church where he had offered his first Mass as a priest. Jim and Irma gently talked me out of that. The logistics would be a problem, they said. To begin with, there was not enough parking.

St. Colman's. Bill had been so happy attending Mass there. Again logistics. It wouldn't be large enough for all the people who would attend. And what about arrangements for a luncheon afterward?

St. Owen's. Bill and I had often attended Mass there while his schoolmate Monsignor Baldwin was pastor. How many times we had dined at the rectory, with Monsignor Baldwin, Monsignor Sherzer, and Monsignor Matyn, who had been Bill and Jim and Ray's professor at Sacred Heart Seminary. One night, Bishop Schoenherr had joined us. Happy memories.

St. Owen's would be large enough to hold the crowd, and Sister Carolyn would arrange for a luncheon at the parish center. Father Cliff Ruskowski, the present pastor, was an old friend. When we first came back from Dallas, Bill and I had attended the performance of a play Cliff had written that was staged at Orchard Lake Seminary. Bill had written about it in *Body Count*.

❦

Father Lou Grandpre, Bill's buddy from his residence days at
Sacred Heart Seminary, now pastor of St. Paul of Tarsus in Clinton
Township, would concelebrate. Lou would have married Bill and
me had he not been scheduled to be out of town at the time.
Instead, Bishop Gumbleton had agreed to perform the ceremony.

I received a phone call from the bishop. He would have offered
the Memorial Mass for Bill, except that this time it was he who had
to be out of town. He would, he said, be flying back from Peru that
day, but if the flight was on time, he would be at St. Owen's for the
post-Mass luncheon.

"With all that's been happening with the airlines these days," I
told him, "I'll be happy if you just get back in one piece."

Some weeks later I was told that the purpose of Bishop
Gumbleton's visit to Peru was to get someone out of prison. I never
asked him if this was so; if it wasn't, knowing Tom Gumbleton, it
easily could have been.

⋐⋚⋑

"What readings do you want?" Jim asked.

I couldn't think. I who hated to ask anyone for help, was now
totally dependent on the kindness of our friends. Was this God's
way of teaching me that we must all accept help? "You knew him,
Jim; would you pick out the readings . . . and the music?" Bill
loathed the modern stuff. "Make it traditional, please."

And then I remembered: the eulogy.

The movie *Broken Arrow* is based on events in the life of Tom
Jeffords, one of the early Pony Express riders. Jimmy Stewart
played Jeffords; Jeff Chandler portrayed Cochise, the great leader
of the Chiricahua Apache, with whom Jeffords was negotiating. In
one scene, Jeffords, having fallen in love with an Apache maiden,
tells Cochise that he wants to marry the girl.

Cochise explains to him, at great length, the obstacles to such a
match. He informs Jeffords that even if all the traditional requisites
are fulfilled, Jeffords himself cannot go to the girl's parents to ask
permission for the marriage; an intercessor must ask on his behalf.

"Will you do it?" Jeffords asks, "Will you be my intercessor?"

Cochise smiles—a prideful, amused, and self-assured smile—
and says simply, "No other could do it."

Jim had, many years before, given the eulogy at Bill's mother's
funeral. He could not possibly have dreamed that someday he
would do the same for Bill himself.

"Would you do it, Jim? Would you give the eulogy?"

Jim nodded, wordlessly.

No other could have done it.

Only months later did it hit me: All the time that I had been in
an agony of grief, and Jim had been a bulwark for me, it had never
once occurred to me—and Jim had given no sign—that he himself
was in deep sorrow over the loss of his dear friend of almost sixty
years.

"O Master, grant that I may never seek so much to be consoled
as to console . . ." Yes, Jim did indeed live the Prayer of St. Francis.

I am weary with my groaning; all the night make I my bed to
swim; I water my couch with my tears. Mine eye is consumed
because of grief . . ."

—Psalm 6:6,7

Bill died at noon. I spent that night at the Betanzos home. I was
sobbing, horribly nauseated, and wanted only to die.

Colleen, Kay's eldest daughter, the Barbie Doll with brains,
drove in from her distant suburban home. A cardiology and ER
nurse, there was little Colleen didn't know about tending those in
need of care. Dr. Petinga had given me a prescription for a tranquilizer that would let me sleep. Colleen administered it, along
with repeated glasses of water. Grief, she explained, was hard on
the kidneys; one had to ingest a lot of water to help the kidneys
handle the toxicity of grief.

Toxicity. Was it that or the shock of losing Bill that was making me so horribly nauseated?

Nauseated. The editor inside me was screaming. Why did people keep saying "nauseous" when what they meant was "nauseated"? Nauseous means "causing nausea," whereas nauseated means "afflicted with nausea." Technically, those who say, "I'm nauseous" are saying, "I cause nausea" or "I cause others to be nauseated." Odd the things that surface in one's mind at such a time.

Whatever, I asked for a basin to keep next to the bed in case my nausea erupted. Colleen gave me a basin. She then took a mattress from another bedroom, laid it on the floor next to my bed, and stretched out on it. She wanted to be there in case I needed anything. All through that night, whenever she realized I was awake, she would give me another tranquilizer and have me down another glass of water. Neither of us got much real sleep that night.

If Jim was St. Francis in action, what can I say of Kay?

She had watched her own husband die by degrees, she had looked on her daughter's body in shock and grief, she had stood by, a Mother of Sorrows, as the coffin containing her daughter and her granddaughter was lowered into the earth.

New trauma awakens and regenerates earlier trauma. Bill's death and my grief had to have opened every related wound in Kay's soul, forcing her to relive the pain of her own losses, lashing her to an agonizing rack of memory. Yet never once did she hesitate, never once did she pull back, never once did she fail to support me in my own grief. Kay and Jim and Irma walked with me every step of my Via Dolorosa.

There were—there are—no words of gratitude sufficient to repay. All I can do is to try to be there for others as Kay and Jim and Irma have been there for me.

At the funeral home, when the final bill was presented and I reached for my checkbook, Jim and Kay simultaneously presented their own charge cards. I was too numb to argue. All I could do was sob.

De mortuis nil nisi bonum [Say nothing but good of the dead].

—LATIN SAYING

WHEN A LOVED ONE DIES, it is natural to idealize him or her. In any case, *Nil nisi bonum* becomes the Eleventh Commandment. This was brought home to me strongly in a pro bono case handled by an attorney I once worked for.

An immigrant woman with teenage daughters had an abusive husband. He beat her, he beat the children, he beat the dog. He threw plates of food through the window, roared, swore, and in general made their life a living hell. And that was when he was sober. When he had been drinking, his wife and daughters feared for their very lives.

My heart ached for the woman. She would come into the office, sit across from me and weep, as she displayed cuts and bruises worthy of a gladiator.

Under the circumstances, the chancery in its kind wisdom was considering her request for separation from bed and board. It was hoped that she would survive till the official permission and documents came through.

One day the woman, replete with her palimpsest of black and blue marks, came in, sat down opposite my desk as usual, and proceeded to sob as if her heart would break. Fearful that perhaps her mate had killed or badly injured one of their daughters, I hesitantly asked her what had happened.

Her reply gave me a never-to-be-forgotten lesson. Her husband had died—of a heart attack. She was crying because she missed him.

Let a few years go by and possibly the death-turned-rosy memories would fade into a more realistic assessment of the departed. That widow might even come to thank her God that He had taken the SOB who had made her life a living hell. Which is probably why the Church used to wait two or three hundred years before canonizing someone. Or why a sports hall of fame lets five years elapse before voting on a retired athlete.

If a horribly abused widow mourns her departed husband, consider then, the pain and sorrow of one who loses a spouse who has been loving, caring, and the epitome of the Judeo-Christian ethic.*

Jim and Irma and Kay accompanied me to the funeral parlor to say a last good-bye to Bill before the cremation. I was taken downstairs to where his body lay in the hall on a gurney. He was dressed informally—sport shirt, sleeveless sweater, chinos. Wound about his fingers was his mother's rosary—the rosary he had carried in the car and took to Mass with him every day. It would go with him now.

As I covered Bill's face with my own rosary of kisses and tears, Jim read from a prayerbook, while Irma and Kay stood by. We then trooped upstairs to dot all the i's and cross all the t's. Could I accompany the hearse that would take his body to the crematorium? There was no point, I was told; there would be nothing to see: The hearse would merely back up to a door and the body would be taken inside.

I could not bear to leave him. I went back downstairs, with Jim and Kay and Irma trailing behind. I think they were hesitant to leave me alone lest I faint. Again I kissed Bill and wept. Again we returned upstairs.

A few minutes later, I again returned to where Bill lay. Again accompanied by our three steadfast friends.

There had to be an end to it. Finally, we left. Again, I put my brain on numb.

---

* Now referred to as the Judeo-Christian-Islamic (or the Abrahamic) ethic.

We returned two days later to pick up Bill's ashes. When the large blue urn was brought in my breath was sucked from me. Guttural inhuman sobs came up like bile at the thought of this magnificent man reduced to nothing more than the space of an urn. Nor did it help to learn that he had *not* been reduced entirely to that space. A small alabaster box held additional "cremains." I was informed that this was not unusual when there were too many ashes to be held by the urn.

In death, he had been too tall for the hospital gurney; his feet had extended over the edge. Now his tall frame had contained more ashes than would fit in an urn. "Dear Bill, thank God for heaven," I thought. "They'll have enough space for you there."

Now there was no one for whom I was the most important person in the world.

I was not lonely—having grown up on a farm, I had always been accustomed to being pretty much by myself. It was not loneliness that assaulted me; rather it was aloneness. It wasn't going to bed by myself that sorrowed me; it was waking by myself. With awakeness came awareness—each morning a renewed awareness of an indescribable loss. A loss so piercing that it repeatedly triggered acute nausea—as if my body needed to vomit up the pain but could not.

Each night I went to bed holding Bill's cardigan in my arms. The sleeves and shoulder were in tatters where the medics had slashed it to gain instant access to his arms and chest. His empty chair mocked me. Each time I opened a closet, the sight of his coats, his jackets, his hats, his boots caused my throat to constrict. The semanier held our pajamas, our underwear—his in the upper drawers, mine in the lower. My eyes glazed with tears each time I took out a handkerchief or lingerie.

The armoire held our sweaters . . . almost a history of our life together. Sweaters from Ireland, Scotland, England, Quebec; from Land's End, Saks, Brooks Brothers, Bonwit's, the Peruvian Connection. Even though we had donated so many of them to charity when we'd moved from Rochester, there was still a good supply. Bill wore clothes so well he could have been a catalog model. Though he complained that he had too many sweaters, like a little girl dressing a favorite doll, I was constantly picking up another one. I hoped that God would forgive me for spending the money on my husband instead of channeling it to those in need.

Ironic that, when interviewers asked why he was so prolific in his writing, one of Bill's responses was, "I write to keep Javan in charities." Bishop Sheen once said, "Never measure your generosity by what you give, but rather by what you have left." Yes, I was a sucker for anyone in need, or any good cause—but I kept reminding myself that I wasn't donating the widow's mite; there was always enough left to buy Bill another sweater.

Vanity of vanities; all is vanity. I had been so vain about my handsome husband; now his haberdashery was suffocating me.

Mary Murray—she whom Bill loved—came to my rescue. Mary sat with me as I went through closets and drawers, packing Bill's clothes in box after box. I couldn't have done it without Mary. Bill's clothes would all go to needy members of the Irish community, in the United States and back in Ireland. Nevermore would I look on Bill's Burberry, his Kandahar boots, or his soft suede jacket. Henceforth any number of brawny Irish lads would be Kienzle-clad.

His cassocks, his beautiful stoles would go to Haiti, many of whose priests were in near rags. His baseball jersey, along with his ball and his mitt, went to Jerry, who had once coached a baseball team.

I kept a few items—the Irish fisherman sweater he had worn to Kay's party the night before his death, the Henry Higgins hat that he and Jim Macy had picked out on a trip to Chicago. And of course, the ragged cardigan he had been wearing when he died. Each time I tried to sew up the slashes, tears blinded me and I had to stop. I phoned Sister Bernadelle at McAuley Center. Could I come and sit with her while I sewed Bill's sweater?

I took with me Bill's Bible—the Bible that he had kept wrapped with the beautiful gold velvet square that Sister Bernadelle had given him so many years before. Like the Rheingold being returned to its owner, the Bible and its protective cover would have a home with Sister Bernadelle.

It was there, in the midst of the peace and solitude of the Sisters of Mercy, that I was able to repair Bill's cardigan. It wasn't a fancy job, but at least the sweater would be wearable.

I recalled Ruth Coughlin's writing about how she'd worn her husband's sweater after his death, and how she had brushed her teeth with his toothbrush. I remembered kidding Bill, "Don't expect me to use your toothbrush after you die." I could not possibly have known how relevant that would be. Bill, having flossed, had been preparing to brush his teeth—the toothpaste lay uncapped on the bathroom counter, his toothbrush on the floor where it had dropped from his lifeless hand. Much later, I picked up the toothbrush and dropped it in the wastebasket.

We had lived at Chimney Hill only three months.

Normally, when a spouse dies, the survivor is advised not to make any decisions, such as moving, for at least a year. But our beautiful apartment had turned into a house of torture for me.

Father Monshau, a Dominican whose book on St. Benedict had been a vade mecum for Bill, offered up a prayer on the spot where Bill had died. Still, horror heaped on horror. Though I kept the door of Bill's bathroom closed, still, each time I went into the den, I saw Bill's body sprawled in his death throes.

I would have to move.

I listed some of the furniture for sale. Bill's exercise bike, his stereo, his desk chair, our king-size bed. What need had I for a king-size bed? It too mocked me. The day the bed left, again I made myself go numb, refusing to allow myself to think of the love it had contained.

But it was the loss of Bill's piano that most devastated me. The piano had accompanied us from Detroit to Minnesota to Kalamazoo to Dallas and back to Michigan. For so many years it had welcomed Bill's hands and at the touch of his fingertips had offered up music from hymns to concertos to love songs.

I could not bear the idea of letting it go. The thought that some stranger would be its "master" racked me. Yet I was moving to a small apartment that would barely hold my basic possessions; I would have had to rent an extra apartment for the piano.

God never closes one door without at least opening a window.

I had asked Lou Morand to help me go through Bill's photo albums and pick out some pictures for the Memorial Mass. I asked Mary Morand to help me take the Christmas decorations down. Each time I had attempted these chores I had been overcome with sobs.

While Mary packed away the decorations, Lou went through the photos. I told them how hard it was for me to even think about selling the piano. That's when God opened the window.

Lou and Mary's granddaughter, Gracie, wanted to take piano lessons. Her mother, Rose, phoned me. Although arrangements had been made to rent a piano for Gracie, they would be interested in buying Bill's piano. It would be like keeping it in the family.

I wept the day the piano was moved out. But Rose would be sending me updates on Gracie's progress. Eventually, I got a note from Gracie herself, telling me how much she was enjoying the piano.

Bill would have been so pleased.

Despite my thirty years of research into the feminine soul, I have not yet been able to answer . . . the great question that has never been answered: What does a woman want?

—SIGMUND FREUD

ACTUALLY, THE QUESTION WAS ANSWERED in a legend. It seems that King Arthur's life hung in the balance. The only means of saving it was to answer a riddle posed by a knight who had the power of life and death over the king. The riddle was: "What is the thing that women desire most?"

The king traveled throughout the kingdom seeking an answer to the riddle. But each woman he questioned had a different answer. One wanted a good-looking husband, one wanted a rich husband, one wanted to be beautiful, one wanted eternal life, and so on.

Time was growing short, when one day the king was accosted by the ugliest old woman he'd ever seen. She was so ugly he didn't even want to talk to her . . . until she said, "Only I know the answer to the riddle . . . the answer that will save your life."

"Tell me," Arthur pleaded.

"I will tell you. But only if you will give me one of your knights as my husband."

King Arthur returned to Camelot totally dejected. He could not imagine anyone, much less one of his knights, deigning to marry the ugly creature.

Sir Gawaine, seeing his king so miserable, asked what the problem was. When Arthur told him, Gawaine, loyal knight that he was, said he would marry the woman.

"But you have no idea how old, how ugly she is," Arthur said.

Gawaine replied that it didn't matter, that it would be a small price to pay for the king's life.

The king, humbled and grateful, returned to the crone and informed her that one of his knights would indeed marry her if she would but give Arthur the answer to the riddle.

"It's simple," she said. "All woman wants is to have her way with man."

And so the king's life was saved. But now Sir Gawaine, true to his word, had to marry the old hag. Noble knight that he was, still he had to use all of his self-control to keep from going back on his word. However, being mannerly, he greeted the hag as if she were a beautiful, highborn lady. They were married and returned to the castle. The townsfolk, and even Gawaine's fellow knights, laughed themselves silly and mocked the couple. Still the knight retained his courtly manner.

But when he had to take his new wife to bed he turned away from her.

When she asked why he was not doing his husbandly duty, Gawaine admitted that he could not overcome his aversion to her age and her ugliness, not to mention the fact that she was lowly born.

"You should not feel thusly," she said. "For with age comes wisdom, and beauty is only skin deep, and rank does not necessarily give quality."

So taken was Gawaine with her reply that he turned to respond. But instead of the ugly crone he had married, there now lay beside him a beautiful young woman.

She laughed at his amazement, and told him that she had been under an evil spell which could be lifted only if a knight of the Round Table married her.

"However," she explained, "the spell is only half broken. I can either be beautiful at night and ugly by day, or I can be beautiful by day and ugly by night. You must choose."

Sir Gawaine pondered for some time. If she were beautiful by day, his fellow knights would no longer mock him. If she were beautiful by night, he would be able to enjoy her charms when they were alone together.

At length he spoke. "I cannot decide. It is for you to choose. And howsoever you decide, that will be my decision too. For you are my wife and I am your husband, and we belong together."

And so it was that the lady was totally released from the evil spell. Because, she told him, the ultimate test was that her husband had to be willing to let her have her way with him.

I thought of this tale often throughout our marriage. We would be getting ready to go out for the evening and I would ask Bill, "Should I wear this dress or that dress?" His response was always, "You look good in everything."

When in high dudgeon I would whip off a Letter to the Editor, I always ran it by Bill for any editorial comment. Sometimes he rolled his eyes heavenward at my umbrage. At which point, not wanting to embarrass him, I would ask, "Would you rather I didn't send it?" His response was always, "You're a person in your own right."

He had no problem with buying a house sight unseen if it was the one I wanted. He ceded possession of the remote control to me.

And—the ultimate test—disliking travel, he accompanied me to Ireland, Scotland, and England without complaint and with graciousness.

Not that it was all one-sided. He didn't care for country and western music. I waited till he was out of the house to play my Hank Williams, Hank Snow, and Eddy Arnold CDs. He liked to go to parties. I didn't, but went along to keep him company. I liked doing things on the spur of the moment; he was not spontaneous. So he scheduled our life and I went along with it. I once said to him, "If you could schedule the rest of your life on a desk calendar, that would be ideal, wouldn't it?" He laughingly agreed that it would.

I tried to make up for the loss of his priesthood; he tried to make up for my less-than-perfect first marriage.

After Bill's death, when I was telling a friend how good Bill had been to me, she said, "You brat, he spoiled you. And I'm going to roll up a newspaper and go in the other room and hit my husband with it."

I didn't blame her; many's the time I told Bill that I wished I could clone him so that other women could have what I had.

A corollary to What does woman want? might well be What does Humanity want? And the answer might well be the same: Humanity wants God to let us have our way with Him.

But one might well reverse the question and ask, What does God want? Would the answer be, God wants to have His way with us?

On the one hand, God gives us free will, which many take to mean that we can do as we wish. But God wants us to educate our consciences so that the conclusion we reach independently is in accord with what He wishes for us.

If God wanted nothing more than for us to know Him and Love Him and be happy with Him in this world and the next, He could very simply have created us with the equivalent of a wind-up key in our brain. Then all He would have to do is wind up the key and watch us be good and love Him. Where is the joy in that? That is the same type of possessiveness that a stalker has for his prey or an abusive man for his wife. He wants the object of his affections to be Stepford-wife-like in her response to him.

Whereas God wants us to love Him of our own free will. So, like the knight, God says, "I will not desert you whatever choice you make." How could we help but love one who loves us so unconditionally? And cannot such largesse on God's part turn each of us, like the ugly hag, into a beautiful object worthy of His love?

God may shake His head over our attempts to know Him, He may laugh over our actions, He may weep over our transgressions—but in any case, He will not roll up a newspaper and hit us over the head with it.

Death is not the worst evil, but rather when we wish to die and cannot.

—UNKNOWN

THE CARDS, NOTES, LETTERS, E-MAIL, the calls of condolence continued to pour in. From all over the United States, from Canada, from the British Isles and Europe, from Australia, even from Africa. The tenor was the same: shock at Bill's unexpected death, reminiscences of his goodness, his excellence as a priest, appreciation of his friendship, of his writings. These communications brought me much needed solace. It was evident that I was not the only one who admired and respected Bill.

Still, each compliment intensified and made more acute my sense of loss. No longer was there anyone for whom I was the most important person in the world. Yet I realized that as much as I missed Bill's presence in my life, still more did I miss his goodness in the world . . . a world that has much need of such goodness.

The nights were black and the days grew blacker. "Write to Bill," friends suggested. I wrote him, through scalding tears that permeated the paper, blobs overwhelming the written words. I finally stopped; all the words did was hammer into me, "He's dead. He's dead." Why couldn't I too die so I could be with him? My letters pleaded with him to come back and get me.

I sat at his desk and watched the snow fall. I thought of Bill, sitting alongside my hospital bed, as my fingers dug into his palm and in a haze of barely morphine-dulled pain, I repeated over and over, "Hurt. Hurt. Hurt." Now, there was no morphine, no Bill, and a wound that would never stop hurting. Maybe if enough snow fell, it would be deep enough for me to crawl into it and let the cold stop my breathing, and deliver me from this pain.

Where was that "grace" that God had—presumably—given me? "Someday you'll need it," Bill had said. Where was it? Where was that cosmic love? I needed it now. Why couldn't I feel it now? I was like a badly wounded animal, trying to crawl away from the horrible pain. But there was no hiding place from the pain. Like a Henry Moore statue; there was a huge hole where my innards should be.

I had read that the worst sin—worse even than murder—is despair. One can repent of murder and be forgiven, but to despair—to lose hope—is ipso facto to lose faith in God—theoretically the unforgivable sin. I've never been certain about this; after all, didn't Jesus himself, in lonely agony on the cross ask, "Father, why have you forsaken me?"

I was in a hell pit of despair. Bill's death had been so horribly sudden, so totally unexpected. There had been no chance to say good-bye. No chance to say I love you. No chance to say I'll see you again. No closure.

I prayed that the upcoming Memorial Mass would give me that closure.

There are only three great puzzles in the world: The puzzle of love, the puzzle of death, and between each of these and part of both of them, the puzzle of God.

—NIALL WILLIAMS
Four Letters of Love

I WAS MET AT ST. OWEN'S BY RICH LASKOS, a friend of Bill's from *Michigan Catholic* days. Rich gently and reverently bore the blue urn containing Bill's ashes into the church. I followed him like a zombie. "Please, Lord," I prayed, "don't let me do anything to embarrass Bill."

The church was teeming with activity. Irma was directing last-minute arrangements. I recalled a description of Ethel Kennedy on the occasion of the death of John F. Kennedy. So motivated and focused was she, someone wrote, that she could have led an army into battle. So it now was with Irma: She could have commanded a galaxy of angels.

Priests were vesting. Mark Radeke, the organist, was tuning up as the members of St. John's Schola Cantorum gathered. Their presence was so fitting: As a seminarian, Bill had been a member of the Schola.

The choir would be joined by Cathy McCotter, St. Owen's young soloist, who had interrupted her mourning for her recently deceased father to contribute her crystal voice to the Mass of a man she knew only by reputation.

A long line had formed to sign the Remembrance Book. I was greeting and being greeted by an almost mind-boggling diversity of mourners—people I knew, people I didn't know, people I recognized, people I hadn't seen in many years. Normally, I wear a hat at Mass. Bill liked me in hats, but today, knowing that a hat would be an impediment, I had not worn one.

I stopped to talk to a priest seated in a back pew reading his prayerbook. It was Monsignor Milewski, the retired chancellor of Orchard Lake Seminary and a long-ago schoolmate of Bill's. He stood. We embraced and suddenly his body was racked with sobs. "I loved him," he said. "I loved him so much."

At that moment, I adored Monsignor Milewski beyond words for his expression of love for Bill. My sobs answered his.

I had received many phone calls, e-mails, and letters from priests, former parishioners, and longtime friends, who, for one reason or another, had to be out of town today. All expressed sorrow that they could not attend, but assured me of their prayers at the time of Bill's Mass. I was grateful, but, in a way, I pitied them that they could not be present. Running through my mind was an excerpt from Henry V's speech to his troops before the Battle of Agincourt. "And gentlemen in England now a-bed/Shall think themselves accurst they were not here . . ."

Those who were present constituted a kaleidoscope of Bill's life. Patronage alumni included Larry Reemmer, Frank Butler in Bill's production of *Annie, Get Your Gun*, and Maria Struck, for whom the young Father Kienzle had been a mentor. Bill had officiated at Maria's wedding—the last wedding of his priesthood.

One of Bill's seminary professors had once told his students, "Make sure you get to know a good doctor and a good lawyer." As far as Bill was concerned, the prof had left out a third very important person: a good auto mechanic. Cass Hershey had fulfilled that need for a succession of Bill's automobiles. Cass, once Father Kienzle's altar boy at St. Anselm's, was there with his young sons. Also present were Cass's brothers and sister Vicki—all of whom had known Father Kienzle since childhood—and their father Lee.

Their mother Marge, St. Anselm's erstwhile outspoken parish council member, had passed on some years back. She and Bill had been great buddies; I knew he was receiving a hearty welcome from Marge in the hereafter.

Thirty priests were present, including our Basilian friends, Father Paré and Father Chircop, some vested, some in clericals, a few in mufti. My heart melted when I saw Bishop Schoenherr, whose spiritual goodness cast a glow over the sanctuary. Also present was Dr. Bart de Merchant, an Anglican priest whom Bill had consulted in writing *The Sacrifice*; and our rabbi friend Dick Weiss

(Rabbi Feldman in *Requiem for Moses*). These men were not in the halest of condition: Bishop Schoenherr was a picture of ascetic fragility; Bart de Merchant, suffering from MS, was in an electric cart, Dick Weiss had heart and spinal problems. Their presence spoke volumes to me.

As did that of Jane Wolford Hughes, weak but smiling encouragement from her wheelchair. Many years before, Jane had dealt with sudden death when her first husband was killed in an auto accident. On hearing of Bill's death, Jane had sent me a note: "Javan, let your friends help you. God acts through other people."

Jim and Mary Grace had driven in from Kalamazoo. Jim had phoned immediately on hearing of Bill's death. God bless Jim; all he had said was, "Bill doesn't need anything; what can we do for you?"

Countless former neighbors and coworkers, as well as so many who had appeared in Bill's books, either as themselves or under assumed names.

Columnist Ginny Stolicker, who had been so kind to Bill over the years, in her reviews and interviews in the *Oakland Press*.

Dr. Martin Herman, Ray's colleague at WSU—and one of the eulogists at Ray's funeral—who had broken his own Sabbath to be here in friendship. How often had we kidded Marty that he attended so many Catholic weddings and funerals that we were going to make him an honorary Catholic.

Jack Kresnak, who had attended Sacred Heart Seminary while Bill was living there as *MC* editor. Jack had started at the *Free Press* as a copy boy during my tenure as TV Listings editor. He was now a respected, award-winning investigative reporter.

Patricia Beck, the longtime *Free Press* photojournalist, whose warm riant photo of Bill had graced the dust jacket of ten of his books.

The Murray clan, except for John, who was in Cleveland and Maureen, who was in Ireland. After Mass, they linked up with the McLaughlin clan (Kay's in-laws) and discovered that they were distant relatives by marriage from back in County Sligo.

Pat Chargot and Bob Ankeny (Pat Lennon and Bob Ankenazy in the Father Koesler series). Only two months earlier, Bill had offered the petitionary prayers at the Funeral Mass for Bob's wife, Gloria, celebrated by Bishop Gumbleton at St. Leo's. Almost thirty-five years before, Father Kienzle had officiated at Gloria and Bob's wedding at St. Mel's.

Sue Papke, Chuck's widow, who, after Bill died, had sent me a huge Teddy bear so I would have something to hold on to.

Bill's cousin Mary Anne and her son, Joe. Mary Anne, the only girl Bill had known in grade school. As a young priest, Bill had officiated at Mary Anne's marriage to her beloved Larry, dead these many years after a long struggle with cancer. After Larry's death, Mary Anne had made a new life for herself as Ann Arbor's "Jazz Lady," authoring several books of poetry on the jazz scene. For years, Mary Anne had kept in touch via weekly phone calls. She would miss Bill as she would a brother.

The St. Anselm contingent included Cy and June Buersmeyer and George and Rosemarie Lubienski. Could he do anything for me, George, a probate attorney, had asked. Yes. I typed a new will and sent it to him. Would he look it over and make sure I hadn't goofed anything up? George and Cy were lectors at St. Anselm's. How often Bill had commented how lucky he was to be pastor of a parish that could claim Roger Rice, Cy Buersmeyer, and George Lubienski as lectors.

Today, Roger would be on the altar as an extraordinary minister. "*If I ever hear God speak, it will be with the voice of Roger Rice.*" I wondered whether Bill, in God's presence, would now be hearing in stereo.

Paul van den Muysenburg, the retired Counsel of the Netherlands—who appeared as himself in one of Bill's books—and his wife Mary Jane, whom I had met so long ago at Hospice of Southeastern Michigan. We had drifted apart over the years. Now, Mary Jane was fighting a debilitating illness, and required much support from her husband. Still they had made the effort to be there and I was grateful.

Kathy Andrews and John McMeel had advised that they would be flying in from Kansas City, along with Donna and Dorothy, Bill's former and present editors. I looked about the church, searching for them, but couldn't locate them. I hoped they had made it.

As it came time for the Mass to begin, I sat down in the first pew, alongside Art, Bill's brother-in-law. Kay, Jim, and Irma filled out the row. In the pew behind me were Art and Patti Schaffran, and Kay's daughters, Mary and Colleen. I looked across the aisle to see Neal Shine, seated with Joe and Mollie Beyer, who had appeared as themselves in *Dead Wrong*. When I had phoned to tell Neal of Bill's death, his response had been a typical Shine oath that spoke volumes more than even a normally articulate Irishman could otherwise express. I stood, and went over to bury my face in his Burberry.

Back in the pew, I knelt to pray. "Dear Bill, we're all here for you. Be happy—" I felt a hand on my shoulder. I looked up to see a girl in overalls and clodhoppers. Tears ran down her face, which was swollen with grief.

Mary Diedrich was in charge of the food supplement department at our health food store in Rochester. A self-professed man-hater, she was extremely brusque with people when she first started in at the store. As a frequent customer, I became friends with Mary. Eventually, she accepted Bill as belonging to Javan. And Bill, given half a chance, came to be one of Mary's favorite people.

Mary had not looked at a newspaper for several days. That morning, the store manager stopped by to offer condolences "at your friend's death."

"My friend? What friend?"

"You know—that author."

Mary was in shock when the manager came back with a newspaper listing the Memorial Mass for eleven that morning. She was beside herself, so upset she felt unable to drive. Further, Mary, a long lapsed Catholic, had no idea where St. Owen's was. She phoned her husband, who was at work in a distant suburb. "Do you know where St. Owen's is?"

"No, but I'll find it," he said. "I'll pick you up—and don't worry: I'll get you there in time."

That's how, just as Mass was about to start, Mary Diedrich came to be standing in the aisle at St. Owen's in her work overalls, crying as if her heart would break.

❧

The processional hymn was "We Walk by Faith."

Father Grandpre asked the priests seated in a cluster to the right of the altar each to stand and introduce himself. Father Bob Morand, ever the joker, turned to the priest at his right and extended his hand as he mouthed, "Hi, I'm Father Morand." Some nine or ten priests—including one from Ohio who had never met Bill, but had admired his work—would concelebrate. And so it began.

There are no words to describe the magnificence of that Mass. The priests, the people, the Mass gave me back my soul. The waves of love that filled St. Owen's wafted me up from my hell pit of despair.

Art Schaffran, Bill's old seminary schoolmate and long-time friend, gave the first reading from Isaiah 25. "He will swallow up death in victory; and the Lord God will wipe away tears from off all faces . . ."

Kay gave the second reading—Romans 8:14–23. "For as many as are led by the Spirit of God, they are the sons of God."

The Gospel was John 17:24–26. "O righteous Father, the world hath not known thee: but I have known thee, and these have known that thou hast sent me. And I have declared unto them thy name, and will declare it: that the love wherewith thou hast loved me may be in them, and I in them."

Father Grandpre's homily described Bill so perfectly. He spoke of their long friendship, chuckling as he recalled attending *The Greatest Story Ever Told* with Bill. When Jesus's side was pierced with the lance, a woman seated in front of them shrieked and sobbed. At which point Bill had commented to Lou Grandpre: "I guess she hasn't read the book."

"Even though Bill took off the collar, he never stopped being a priest," Father Grandpre continued.* He went on to relate how looking out and seeing Bill, towering over nearby members of a congregation, was "like seeing a sunflower in a field of daisies."

He read from Mitch Albom's *Tuesdays with Morrie* ("Are you ready for death?") and concluded with Robert Frost's "The Road Less Traveled": "Two roads diverged in a wood, and I—I took the one less traveled by, and that has made all the difference." That, he said, defined Bill's life.

I felt Art Schaffran's reassuring hand on my shoulder from the pew behind me.

Father Ruskowski, after noting that this was a very special Memorial Mass—it had two homilies and a eulogy—concluded his homily with a reading of a poetic prayer. Even in my numbness, the words registered: "I confess that I am human/of the earth, of the soil,/yet destined to fly and sail the winds. . . . In your grace I am born again/and transformed/and made new . . ."

Irma Macy presented the petitionary prayers.

The voices of the Schola rose like an angelic choir in the traditional "*O Salutaris.*"

As Chris and Mary Murray carried up the offerings, I heard someone ask, "Who are they?" Someone else answered, "I don't know, but Bill must have cared for them very much."

Yes, he did.

So variegated and discrete had Bill's life been that few people from each segment of his life knew those from the other segments. Chris and Mary's son Michael, a major in the Marines, wrote later: "It was remarkable to see how many cross-sections of the community he touched. I know this because I saw people that I knew, yet never realized that they also knew Bill."

---

* This was attested to by the presence of the ranks of priests, who, as Neal Shine wrote, "still considered him their brother."

The events leading up to the Greeting of Peace so moved those present that one friend—not Catholic—told me afterward, "I don't like the Greeting of Peace. I never wanted to take part. But there was so much love in that church that by the time the Greeting of Peace came, I *wanted* it. I *wanted* to touch the people around me— and I wanted them to touch me. I wanted to participate in that love."

So moving was the service that some who were not Catholic felt impelled to accept Communion. For that moment at least, they *believed*. Several who had been estranged from the Church were carried forward by the strains of *Ave Verum* to gratefully receive Communion for the first time in years.

As Jim Macy made his way up to the microphone, I teared up. Dear Jim—Bill's buddy from Day One; the true contemplative, the man of constancy and goodness.

He spoke of Bill's childhood, the influence of his family and his Church; of his youth in the seminary—"He came with solid piety, a never-to-be-questioned desire for the priesthood, academic and athletic skills, a very special gift for lifelong friendship, and behavior just acceptable enough to outweigh his fun-loving and mischievous nature. Bill was a vocation director's dream. No one in the seminary was ever happier or fitted in better."

He spoke of Bill's priesthood and his stint at the *Michigan Catholic:* "Wherever he was assigned, he fitted in. His dedication, his love of what he was doing, great gifts of mind, imagination, and heart brought him the warm affection and adulation of the people he served."

Jim spoke of Bill's Good Friday—"the struggle for his soul over the marriage laws of the Church." How, when told, "Cease and desist; you cannot," Bill had prayed and searched his soul. Then in a line that cried out to be cut in stone, Jim described how Bill's "'I can *not* not' was a *Yes* to his own unique integrity *and to the relationship of a soul with its God that no one else may ever have the boldness to enter or the temerity to judge.*"

He went on to speak of Bill's writing career, of our marriage, and how, "with God, every ending is truly a new beginning."

At one point, just as Bill's voice had broken during his eulogy of Chuck, Jim's voice broke.

When Jim finished, the congregation erupted in applause. "It was," said one man of Jim's description of Bill's struggle, "the first time I ever truly understood why Bill left the priesthood."

Little remained but the Recessional: "How Great Thou Art." This time it was my voice that broke as I tried to join in that musical testament to God's majesty. All around me, the voices of those who had known and loved Bill soared till it seemed that the very roof of the church must melt away to let the sound fly free to heaven.

The intensity of the love that filled St. Owen's moved Irma to say later, "The Holy Spirit was present."

"In all my years," said Sister Bernadelle, now in her eighties, "I have never experienced such a magnificent, such a moving, such a *marvelous* Mass."

I was near mobbed afterward by people who said, "That's the way it's supposed to be." "That's the way it should be." "Why can't it always be like that?"

As I walked up the aisle of the church, I looked up to see, in the doorway, arms outstretched, Jerry Zawideh. How many years had it been since we had seen Jerry and his family? How many years since Bill and I had spent countless Sundays at Kingsley Inn's brunch table after Mass? Jerry and his beautiful wife Hanan now had two children, Farah and Dunya. Dunya, he told me, means "world"; "Farah" means "happiness." "Together," he said, "they're my world of happiness."

A few short months later, I would stand in as eucharistic minister, offering "The Blood of Christ" to Jerry and his family at his father's funeral at St. Owen's.

An old friend—non-Catholic—whom I had not seen in some thirty-five years came up to me after the Mass, and said, insistently, "I have to tell you something." She spoke slowly and deliberately; she wanted me to get the full import of her words. "We came here today expecting to hear a beautiful tribute to Bill. And we got that. What we could not have expected was that this was a magnificent tribute to your Church."

It was the perfect gift. All I could think was, Thank you, God. Thank you, Bill. Thank you, confraternity of priests.*

People were still lined up waiting to sign the Remembrance Book. The line was so long that many gave up and left without signing. In days to come, I would discover that this or that person had been there, but hadn't been able to sign the book. As I made my way to St. Owen's reception center against a sea of faces, I felt a reassuring hand on my arm. It was Dr. Petinga.

I had pleaded with the paramedics to take Bill to St. Joe's so Tom Petinga could care for him. Normally, Oakland County residents can request to be carried to whichever Oakland hospital they prefer—except in cases where the medics feel that the patient's condition requires carriage to the nearest emergency facility. This had been one of those cases.

Tom had talked to the paramedics later. He now assured me that nothing could have been done to save Bill. "Javan, he was dead before he hit the floor. It's the way I want to go. He would have suffered no pain—at most a couple of seconds of dizziness."

Tom and his gorgeous, warmhearted wife, Christine, stayed at my side, giving strength, and making sure I could handle the crowds.

Suddenly, there was Donna Martin, Bill's editor of twenty years. Dear, delightful Donna, to whom Bill—and Father Koesler—owed so much. As we reached the church center, I was greeted by Kathy Andrews. Instantly, my thoughts went back to the loss she had suffered with the death of her beloved Jim, taken so sadly out of due time. Bill and I, as well as John and Susan McMeel, had flown back from Ireland to Kansas City for Jim's funeral. Now Kathy and John were here for Bill.

Dorothy O'Brien, Bill's current editor, was seated at the Andrews McMeel table. Her face was a portrait of vulnerability, her eyes containing such empathetic sorrow that *I* wanted to comfort *her*.

---

* A few days later, I received a note from Bishop Schoenherr, who wrote: "I, and the priests with me . . . like you considered it one of the finest Masses. Bill deserved the best and he got it."

Unfortunately, I was in such a state of shock that some of the things I said that day still haunt me. I would not believe I actually said some of the things I did—except that I remember saying them. In retrospect, they fall under the heading of "I wish I could dig a hole and dive in."

When I looked up to see the forensic pathologist Dr. Spitz (Willie Moellmann in Bill's books) and his regal wife, I said, "Oh, Dr. Spitz, I tried to get you some work—but the hospital said Bill didn't need an autopsy."

Merciful heaven, how could I?!

While I was talking with Donna and Kathy, Irma interrupted to tell me that Bishop Gumbleton had arrived. Obviously, his plane had made it back from Peru in one piece. "You've got to go talk to him," Irma urged. Of course. I was so grateful for the effort he had made to be there. I stood, and in an attempt to excuse myself, said something like, "I know you've come from Kansas City—but Peru trumps Kansas City."

"Peru trumps Kansas City"? How ungracious can one be! So many people commented on the honor that was paid Bill by his publishers. And heaven knows I appreciated the effort they had made to be there. Just as I appreciated what Bishop Gumbleton had gone through to be there.

I could only hope that Kathy, having experienced the shock of losing her own husband, understood that shock can cause one to say and do things that one would never do under normal circumstances, and forgave me my gaucherie. I knew that Bill, in his now infinite wisdom, would have consoled me with one of his favorite reassuring lines: "There's not a jury in the world would convict you."

"Why can't it always be like that?"

I HAD ALWAYS LOVED ATTENDING MASS. But Bill's Memorial Mass was truly the first time that I had felt Church as Family. "That's what a Mass should be," people had said. "That's what a Mass should do." "If only all of them could be that way." "Why can't it always be like that?"

Jim Macy and I talked about that later. What made that particular Mass so moving, so memorable?

Then it came to me: For that to happen, somebody had to die.

Had the Mass been a celebration of something totally happy, it would not have had the same effect. It was a melding of the joy of Bill's life, the sorrow of his death, and the celebration of his going to God.

The more I thought about it, the more I realized that for the first time I truly understood Easter. "Christ died for us." Yes! And one cannot celebrate the joy of Easter without first undergoing the sorrow of Good Friday. They are two sides of the same coin. Bill had frequently noted that for the Anglican Church the main celebration is Christmas—the birth of Christ—whereas for the Roman Catholic Church the main celebration is Easter. "Christ died for us." And Easter is a rising, a victory, a triumph . . . over sorrow, sadness, death . . . even over despair. Christmas gives us joy, yes; but if we think about it, it is not totally unalloyed: We know what is to come—Good Friday.

But with Easter, death has been defeated, the grave has been vanquished, "the dead rise triumphant." And the celebration is total.

Henceforth, Good Friday and Easter would have new and deeper meaning for me.

In the West Virginia mountains, where my mother grew up, there is an old hymn whose exact words I can't recall, but it goes something like, "If you don't bear the cross, you can't wear the crown."

The more I thought about it, the more I realized that every Mass *is* "like that"; we're just not aware of it. *Every* Mass commemorates Jesus, His life, His death, His resurrection. Just as in Bill's case: The love, the sorrow, the glory. If we could but concentrate on that when we're at Mass, maybe we can be more and more aware. So that rather than asking, "Why can't all Masses be like that?" we will come to realize that all Masses *are* like that—if we but open ourselves and let them be.

Bill would say: You knew me; I lived. Know Jesus; He lives. You loved me; love Jesus. Be as close to Jesus as you were to me. Then every Mass will be "the way it's supposed to be."

A saint is the most normal person. In fact, a saint is actually one who has developed his personality to the fullest degree.

—JOHN BUCKLEY
The Gothic, June 1950

Two MONTHS AFTER BILL'S DEATH, I completed my move to a new apartment.

Wendy Lewis and her parents spent two full days helping me pack pictures, antiques, dishes—all the fragile items that I didn't want to consign to the movers' iffy hands.

Moving meant repacking books, clothes, and possessions that I had unpacked only short months before. In addition to the books Bill had written, I also packed a collection of his favorite reading matter—including the books from his seminary days.

Months later, I put those books on the upper shelf in my secretary. Still later, I started going through them. I wanted to feel as close as possible to Bill. I picked up a small black book titled *Manual of Piety for Seminarians.* Bill had kept not only his seminary textbooks, but also the notes he had made in the seminary. His textbooks were stuffed with them. All handwritten, in that neat script that had barely changed over the years. For a graphologist, this lack of change proved that the Bill Kienzle of seminary days, though he may not have been matured in a sociological sense, was already matured in his view of life and in his religious faith.

As I turned the pages of the *Manual of Piety* a handwritten sheet fell out. For me, it encapsulated the life of Bill Kienzle from the time he first set his feet on the path to the priesthood to the faith-filled life that he led through his death.

Meditation 8th Sept.

Adoration:
Christ the perfect man.

Physically	}	always did
Emotionally	}	the perfect
Spiritually	}	thing at the
Intellectually	}	perfect time.

Considerations:
All men want something perf.
Look to the world—all imperf.
Money, friends, love,
honor, stability.

We can find perf. only in
Christ and those who are
trying to be like Christ.

The closer we come to Christ
the happier we are.

Examen.
How close am I to Christ?
Emotionally — Spiritually.

Resolution—
Ask Jesus to take me
and form me in a mold
according to The High Priest.

In reading this sheet, and the many other notes he kept, and from my knowledge of him, it is obvious that he tried to discipline himself from Day One to walk in Jesus's footsteps. He tried always to hold to that discipline. He was not perfect. As Father Grandpre said in his homily, if you said he was saintly, Bill would have responded, "Forget it." He was not a saint—although there are those who tell me that where they started out by praying for Bill after his death, they now pray *to* him. He would have readily professed his faults. But if ever he felt that he had strayed from the path, he quietly found his way back to it, and just as quietly and surely atoned for his lapse. In that respect, he never stopped being that idealistic young seminarian who wanted only "To know Thee more clearly, to love Thee more dearly, to Follow Thee more nearly." Which lines in his *Manual of Piety* predate *Godspell* by many years.

As Karen Rae Mahaffey, the librarian at Sacred Heart Seminary, wrote in a recollection of Bill, "He carried Christ with him in every step he took."

He observed Lent and Easter—the crux of Roman Catholicism—with the greatest reverence.

Over the years, he spoke so often of the Bible, the Apostles, and Jesus, and explained so much that was as water to my sponge of religious ignorance. When he walked with Jesus, he took me along. He gave me a Christ not just to worship but to know. Through Bill, I tried to grow closer to Jesus and through Him to God.

An admiring friend once told him, "Whenever I don't know what to do, I ask myself, "What would Bill do?" Bill replied, "No, no. You should ask yourself instead, 'What would Jesus do?'" This long before the WWJD bracelets were even a gleam in an ad man's eye.

Next to Jesus, the biblical person Bill admired most was David. He felt that David's love for God was worthy of emulation. He found particularly appealing the image of David dancing for joy before the Ark of the Covenant. He believed that David was forgiven much because David loved much.

Bill Kienzle was the most emotionally secure person I've ever known. He was rock solid and not given to second-guessing himself. This undoubtedly was because he never did anything precipitately. He didn't write a word until he had it in his mind. He didn't commit himself until he had it set in his heart. He did not think fast on his feet, nor was he one to hit the ground running. He always wanted to consider all sides of a question before acting or coming to a decision. He never acted without considering the consequences, moral, ethical, or literal. Had he devoted his life to chess he undoubtedly would've been a champion player. Instead, he devoted himself to his Church and his wife. As a priest, he was one of the best; as a husband, I have never seen a better one.

Nonetheless, like all human beings, he had his weaknesses. One that hung over him stemmed from an event that occurred when he was seven.

A ball he was playing with bounced between two parked cars and out into the street. The boy ran in pursuit and was hit by an oncoming car. The impact was so hard that his shoes flew off and he was catapulted through the air, to land like a smashed beanbag. Amazingly, no bones were broken, but he was concussive and totally blind for several days.

Without his realizing the cause, the effect of the concussion and the blindness would affect him to the end of his life.

Anyone who knew Bill knew he was a night owl. He hated to go to bed. It was, he said, "Because I don't want to miss anything."

Even after he went to bed, however, he found it difficult to go to sleep. It was a nascent fear of death, which eventually became almost phobic. Bill's faith was firm and full. But deep phobias are not banished by mere logic, nor, at least in Bill's case, even by faith.

In later years, a night-light grew to be a necessity. If he woke in the darkness, the blackness assailed him and, unable to see, he felt buried alive. So whenever we traveled, a plug-in night-light went with us.

Eventually, Bill mentioned to Laura, our homeopath friend, the details of his childhood experience. Laura felt that homeopathic remedies might help Bill to cope with this traumatic cellular memory. Had she had time to succeed, he undoubtedly could have dispensed with the night-light. But he went home to God before that happened, traveling though the ultimate darkness to the ultimate light.

❧⋆❧

Bill Kienzle was a courtly yet unpretentious soul who wore his body well. He was incredibly self-disciplined, incredibly kind and loving, incredibly patient and good-humored, incredibly easy to live with and—a quality any woman would treasure—he was never indelicate. He didn't use foul language or double entendres, he never left the toilet seat up, he never left his clothes lying around. There were times when the manifestations of my various illnesses were literally stomach-turning. Bill—the boy whose mother and sisters did everything for him, the seminarian who neither washed clothes nor cleaned up after anyone but himself, the priest who joked that nothing was too good for Father, the pastor whose living quarters were managed by a housekeeper—cared for me as a nurse would care for a comatose patient. He scrubbed the bathroom when my illness left it looking like the floor of a zoo cage. He bathed me when I was unable to bathe myself. He supported my head when I couldn't keep my food down.

Yet always he looked at me through the eyes of love, and never made me feel that I was anything but beautiful and desirable. When I read of Mother Teresa for whom each dying body she tended was the body of Christ, I think of Bill caring for my ailing body and I humbly marvel at how God blessed me. At such times, I hear Bill saying, "Put the shoe on the other foot . . ."

And always and ever, I see him looking at me with tenderness, and I hear him saying, "I love you all there is and all there ever could be—and more than that tomorrow."

Epilogue

Time is too slow for those who wait, too swift for those who fear; too long for those who grieve, too short for those who rejoice. But for those who love, time is eternity.

—Henry van Dyke

In May 2000, the Society for the Study of Midwestern Literature presented Bill its Mark Twain Award for Distinguished Contributions to Midwestern Literature.

In May 2002, the society invited me to their annual banquet, which would conclude with a tribute to Bill.

Following is the speech I wrote for that occasion:

I'd like to tell you not about the books Bill Kienzle wrote, but about the book he didn't write.

It was to be a life of Jesus. And yes, it was also to be the twenty-fifth in the Father Koesler series.

I don't blame those of you who may be startled or puzzled. I must tell you that when Bill first told me about this book, I really thought he had lost his marbles. I was convinced of it when he told me it would involve time travel. Ramon Toussaint—whom you may recall as the voodoo practitioner in *Death Wears a Red Hat*—was going to return to Detroit for a visit with his old friend, Father Koesler. Ramon would tell Father Koesler that he had been looking into time travel and had had some success in the field . . . enough so that he planned to go back in time—to the Age of Jesus. Would Father Koesler like to go with him?

Father Koesler would indeed. And so he would become an onlooker to the Greatest Story Ever Told. Except that Father Koesler would be something more than a mere onlooker; he would solve the mystery of who really was responsible for the death of Jesus.

Although it is not unheard-of for mystery buffs to also enjoy science fiction, I felt that this was a radical departure from Father Koesler's norm. Too radical, I feared. It was so unlike Bill, who was always down-to-earth and not the slightest bit fanciful. I felt that his readers would just find it all too unbelievable.

But the more he researched—and he did a lot of that, reading not only many biographies of Jesus, but also biographies of the Apostles, as well as histories of the Jewish and Roman life of the time—the more the idea took hold of him . . . and of me. I had such faith in his ability to make a story come to life. I thought, If anyone can do it, Bill can. And because, as he always said, we were in this together, I pulled information on time travel from the Internet for him to read.

As I've said, Bill was very down-to-earth and even-tempered. Where the average person might enthuse over something or say "I love it," Bill did not throw emotions or words like "love" about loosely or frivolously. Two days before his death, he came to me, eyes aglow with as much enthusiasm as I had ever seen in him. He held out the sheets I had given him to read. I could see there were sentences underlined, and paragraphs demarcated in yellow. "Look at this. Look at this," he repeated. But before I could take the sheets and read them, he started to explain, pacing back and forth, as was his wont when he was deep in thought. Except that now, he was deep in explanation.

"Do you know that the flying machine that Leonardo da Vinci designed was actually capable of flying? It could have flown then, except that there was no engine capable of propelling it. If there had been, da Vinci's flying machine would have flown. Nowadays, we fly all over—to California, to Europe, to the Pacific . . . to the moon. Because we've got an engine capable of propelling a plane."

He stopped pacing. "Time travel is possible. It's possible right now . . . or rather it would be, if there were some sort of propellant. There will be such a propellant in the future, and just as we now travel back and forth in space, in the future we'll be able to travel back and forth in time."

I was amazed. If this had come from my son, who thinks he is going to live forever, and who is convinced that the Internet will save the world, I wouldn't have thought it odd for a moment. But from Bill Kienzle—?!

"If Ray [his dear friend who died some years back, and another very practical, down-to-earth person] had come to you and said, 'Bill, I'm going to travel back in time to Jerusalem,' would you have gone with him?" I asked.

"If there were no You, I'd go . . . in a heartbeat."

We went on to discuss the various ramifications. One of the rules for time travel fiction is that you can't change historical events. You can't stop Lincoln or Kennedy from being shot, or keep the World Trade Center towers standing. And of course, you cannot prevent the Crucifixion.

We discussed Father Koesler's emotions as an onlooker at the Crucifixion. He wouldn't be able to stop the Crucifixion. He would be filled with horror, yet at the same time, he would know it was inevitable. And, as a priest, he would know that his entire faith, his entire religion was grounded on the Crucifixion—and the Resurrection. Father Koesler alone, of all those present, would know that the Crucifixion was not an ignominious end, but a glorious beginning.

Was it only the Apostles' meeting with Jesus after His Resurrection that convinced them of the truth of what He had told them? Or did something a stranger tell them help to convince them . . . a stranger they could not know had come from a time far in the future?

There were so many problems to be solved. How would Father Koesler be attired? In what language would he speak? Or would he, as a time traveler, be invisible to those around him, and incapable of being heard by them?

I could see that not only was Bill champing at the bit to get started on this journey; he had infected me with his enthusiasm. He could do it . . . I knew he could do it . . . and I knew nobody could do it as well as he could.

And so he set to work. Slowly, thoughtfully and with much deliberation—the way he always wrote. At his death, he had completed just three pages of the introduction. The title of the book was to be *King Without a Kingdom*. Like many good writers, Bill believed that the first sentence was so important. The first sentence of the opening chapter of *King Without a Kingdom* was, "He never forgot the day He turned water into wine."

"I'd go in a heartbeat," he had said. And so he did; he dropped like a stone—dead, the doctors said, before he even hit the floor.

Bill is now truly traveling in time—in eternity. We do not have the wherewithal to comprehend eternity any more than da Vinci's machine had a propellant to make it fly. But, as Eckhart Tolle says, eternity is not endless time; it is no time. Yesterday, today, tomorrow, and forever are one.

One of Bill's favorite quotations was from St. Thomas More's farewell letter to his daughter before his execution. So, on Bill's behalf, in the words of St. Thomas More, I pray that all of us "may merrily meet in heaven."